The way to play

**Bantam Books
by the Diagram Group**

RULES OF THE GAME: The Complete Illustrated Encyclopedia
    of all the Sports of the World
THE WAY TO PLAY: The Illustrated Encyclopedia
    of the games of the World
MAN'S BODY: An Owner's Manual

ABOUT THE AUTHORS

The Diagram Group is a team of thirty editors,
writers and illustrators. They have researched
games from North and South America, India,
China, Japan, Korea, Africa, the Middle East,
Europe and Australia. Included in this book
are games spanning a period from ancient
Greece to the present day. The Diagram
Group also created *Rules of the Game: The
Complete Illustrated Encyclopedia of all the
Sports of the World.*

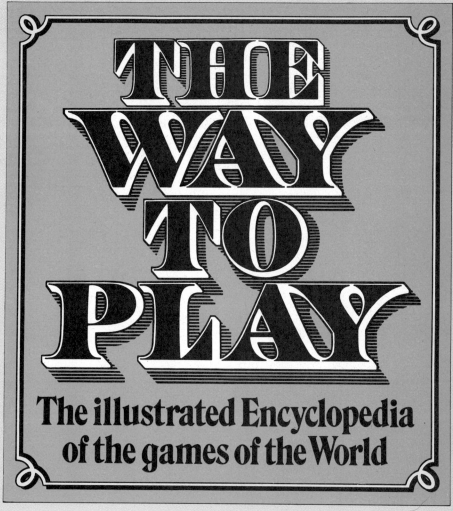

THE WAY TO PLAY

The illustrated Encyclopedia of the games of the World

by the **Diagram Group**

BANTAM BOOKS
TORONTO/NEW YORK/LONDON

THE WAY TO PLAY
*A Bantam Book/published by arrangement
with Paddington Press Ltd.*

PRINTING HISTORY
Paddington Press edition/October 1975
Bantam edition/April 1977

ISBN 0-553-01042-5

Published simultaneously in the United States and Canada

*Bantam Books are published by Bantam Books, Inc. Its trademark,
consisting of the words ''Bantam Books'' and the portrayal of a
bantam, is registered in the United States Patent Office and in other
countries. Marca Registrada. Bantam Books, Inc., 666 Fifth Avenue,
New York, New York 10019.*

PRINTED IN THE UNITED STATES OF AMERICA

0 9 8 7 6 5 4 3 2 1

Foreword

All over the world people play games: from primitive tribesmen to restless executives, and from birthday toddlers to ageing millionaires. Wherever people gather, competition—and love of competition—appear.

Even the lone mind seeks the stimulus of games, and in a sense the opponent is still the same. It is always fickle Fate—or our own limitations!—that we are trying to defeat.

Games rise and fall in popularity, appear and disappear. Inventiveness, and love of novelty, are always modifying the old and devising new. Games have lives, histories, and family trees. Few of us today have heard of the medieval nine men's morris; but millions of hours are spent on bridge, and chess, and Monopoly—and millions of dollars at poker or roulette.

This book covers games that the reader will have seen or heard about—family games and social games, games played for fun, and games played for profit. But it includes, too, many that will be strange: games from foreign countries and ancient times. All are presented through a unique blend of text and illustration. Here the reader can learn not only the secrets of bridge or chemin de fer, but also how to play pachisi or nyout, lasca, or hex, or go. In addition to clearcut, concise rules, the players and equipment each game needs are listed, while the guide on pages 316-317 groups games together according to the number of participants they require. With a little thought, then, it is easy to arrange and even improvise to try an unfamiliar game—whether to make a party go, or to keep a houseful of children quiet!

This book will tempt the reader to relax and experiment. It will let him soon settle those old rules disputes. It will be a friendly guide to those games that "everyone else seems to know." We believe that it is unique—a unique aid to leisure. It is, in fact, the major reference book of how to play the games of the world.

Target games

Solitaire (Patience) card games

Dice games

Table games

Casino and gambling house card games

Word and picture games

Games of chance

Children's party games

Children's card games

REGLEMENT.

De spelers verdeelen zich in twee partijen.
waarvan de eene partij speelt van N°. 1 tot
N°. 63 langs de roode en de andere in om-
gekeerde richting langs de blauwe lijn:
daarna bepaalt men den inzet en
die de hoogste oogen werpt
speelt het eerst. — Die
als eersten worp 5 en
4 gooit gaat on-
middelijk op

op verkeerd

spoor

TRAMW

wissel

Pachisi

Pachisi is thought to have originated several thousand years ago and was the forerunner of many contemporary racing board games. Several older forms of the game are still played in Asia and South America. The game described here is played in the Indian subcontinent and is for two to four players.

Pieces Each player has four shells, stones, or other objects that must be easily identifiable from those of his opponents.

Objective In this race game, each player tries to be the first to get all four of his pieces around the board from the starting point to the finish.

Dice Traditionally, six cowrie shells are used. They are thrown from the hand and the position they adopt indicates the number of squares a piece must be moved, as follows:
two shells with their openings uppermost, two;
three shells, three;
four shells, four;
five shells, five;
six shells, six.

If only one shell falls with its opening uppermost, the player moves forward ten squares.
If all the shells fall with their openings facing down, the player moves forward 25 squares.
If a player throws a 6, 10, or 25 he is allowed another throw.

Board showing route of one player

a Starting square
b Resting squares
c Finish

ASHTA-KASHTE
This is a variant of pachisi and shares its objective and playing procedure. The only differences are as follows.
The board is usually divided into 49 squares.
The middle squares of each outer row are the resting squares, as well as being the starting squares (one for each player).
Pieces are moved in a spiral from their starting square to the finish at the center of the board, as shown.

Dice Four cowrie shells are used to indicate the number of squares to be moved, as follows:
all four shells with their openings uppermost, four squares;
three shells, three;
two shells, two;
one shell, one;
all four shells with their openings facing down, eight squares.

LUDO
Ludo is a very popular modified version of pachisi, with the same objective and basically the same rules.
The board is a square-shaped piece of cardboard, marked out as shown.
The "home base" and starting square for each player (there may be two, three, or four players), the central columns of the cross leading to the finish, and the sections of the finish itself are all colored for easy identification—usually red, green, yellow, and blue. When not traveling around the circuit, the counters are placed on a player's own "home base."
There are no resting squares, unlike in pachisi, but once a counter has reached its own colored column leading to the

Route

1

2

3

Taking move

Play Each player in turn throws the cowrie shells, and moves one of his pieces the number of squares indicated by the shell.

Pieces are moved in a clockwise direction around the board (see illustration).

At the start of the game each player's first piece may enter the race with any throw, but subsequent pieces (or the first piece if it has to repeat the route) may only enter the game if a 6, 10, or 25 is thrown.

A player may have one, two, three, or all of his pieces on the board at any one time.

After the players have each had one turn, they may—if they wish—miss a turn or decline to move a piece after making their throw.

Taking If a piece lands on any square other than a "resting" square already occupied by an opponent's piece, the opponent's piece is obliged to return to the start. It may only re-enter the game with a throw of 6, 10, or 25.

The player who took the opponent's piece is allowed another throw.

Once a piece has reached the central column of its own arm, leading to the finish, it cannot be taken.

Board The traditional Indian board is either woven, or made of cloth with the playing area marked out in embroidery.

The playing area is in the shape of a cross and is divided into small squares, 12 of which are distinctively colored to identify them as "resting" squares (where any number of pieces is safe from capture).

Double pieces If a piece is moved onto a square occupied by another piece belonging to the same player, both pieces may be moved together as a "double piece" on subsequent moves.

A double piece may never be overtaken by other pieces—whether the player's or an opponent's—and can only be taken if an enemy piece of equal strength lands directly on its square.

a Starting squares
b Resting squares
c Finish

End of play The finish can only be reached by a direct throw. If, for example, a piece is seven squares away from the finish and the player throws more than a 7, he is obliged to await his next turn, or move one of his other pieces.

As soon as a piece lands on the finish, the piece is removed from the board.

The winner of the game is the first player to get all four of his pieces to the finish, and the game may be continued to determine the finishing order of the other players.

© DIAGRAM

---

finish, it cannot be followed or taken.

Other equipment Each player has four plastic or cardboard counters—of one of the board's four colors.

One die is used; it may be thrown from the hand or from a small plastic dice cup.

Objective Players race each other in trying to be the first to get all four of their counters to the finish.

Play Each player chooses a set of counters.

The die is thrown to determine the order of play, the person throwing the highest number starting first.

Players take it in turn to throw the die for a 6—the number needed to get a counter from its home base onto its starting square.

Whenever a player gets a 6 he

is allowed another throw, moving one counter the number of squares indicated by the die.

Counters are moved around the circuit in a clockwise direction, as in pachisi.

If a player has more than one counter on the circuit and he has a double throw (a 6 followed by another throw), he may move a different counter for each part of the throw.

Should a player throw two 6s in succession, he is allowed a third throw.

Taking If a counter lands on a square already occupied by an opponent's counter, the opponent's counter must be returned to its home base and can only re-enter the circuit on a throw of 6.

End of play The finish can only be reached by a direct throw.

For example, if a counter is four squares away from the finish and the player throws more than a 4, he must either await his next throw or move one of his other pieces.

The winner is the first player to get all four of his counters to the finish.

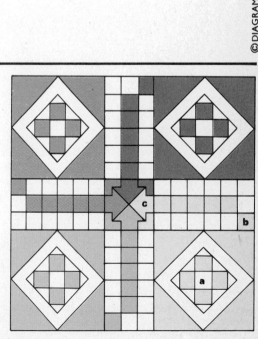

a Home base b Starting square c Finish

Hyena chase

The hyena chase is a race game that originated in North Africa. Any number of players may take part, and it provides an amusing alternative to some of the better-known board games.

Pieces Each player has one counter or other suitable object, different in color or shape from those of his opponents—this counter represents the player's "mother."
One other counter is used to represent the hyena; this counter must also be easily distinguishable.
All the counters are placed in the "village" circle before the start of play.

Board Traditionally, the playing area is marked out on the ground, but it may be drawn on paper or other suitable material.
A spiral circle is marked with a random number of small circles along its length, each circle representing a day's journey.
Two large circles are drawn: one (the "village") next to the start of the spiral; the other (the "well") at the center of the spiral.

Objective Each player tries to be the first to get his mother from the village to the well and back again—entitling him to let loose the hyena on the remaining mothers!

Play Moves are made by each player in turn in accordance with the throw of a die (in the traditional game, pieces of stick are used).
Players must throw a 6 to get their mothers from the village onto the first circle.
Whenever a player throws a 6, he is allowed another throw; if he throws two 6s in succession he is permitted a third throw.
It is permissable for the mothers of two or more players to occupy the same "day."
The well can only be reached by a direct throw. If, for example, a mother is three days' journey from the well, the player cannot move her if he throws more than a 3—he must then await his next turn.

Return journey Once at the well, the mother "washes her clothes" until the player throws a 6—allowing her to start on her return journey to the village.

End play The first player to get his mother back to the village (he does not need a direct throw) wins the "hyena" counter.
He must then throw a 6 to get the hyena from the village onto the first circle; once there the hyena travels along the route to the well at twice the speed of the mothers—moving double the score on the dice (ie if the player throws a 5, the hyena moves forward 10 days).
Once at the well (only reached by a direct throw) the player must again throw a 6 before the hyena can return to the village.
Any mothers that the hyena passes on its way back to the village are "eaten" and removed from the board.
The winning player is, of course, the player who wins the hyena. But the satisfaction of winning is enhanced by the number of mothers that he can eat during the animal's rampage!

Village

Days

Well

Nyout

Nyout is a Korean race game that was probably played over a thousand years ago. It has retained its popularity over the centuries, now being played chiefly for money.

Players Any number of players may take part, although the usual number is four—two players sometimes playing in partnership against the other two.

The board is marked out with colored circles; 20 circles form a ring and enclose a cross of nine other circles, as shown. The central circle and the four circles at the cardinal points are larger than the others. (Traditional boards have marks or symbols in place of circles.)

The pieces are traditionally carved from wood or ivory and are known as "horses." Any other counters or pieces may be used, provided that each player's pieces are easily distinguishable from those of his opponents. Each player has an agreed number of horses—usually two, three, or four.

Dice Koreans play with small flat strips of wood that score a maximum of 5, but a standard die may be used—rethrowing if a 6 shows.

Objective Players race each other to be the first to get their horses around the board.

Play Players throw the die to determine their starting order, the player throwing the highest number starting first. Each player in turn throws the die, advancing one of his horses the appropriate number of circles, and counting the start circle as 1. Players may have more than one of their horses in the ring at any time. (In partnership play, a player may move either his own or his partner's horses.) Horses are moved around the board in a counterclockwise direction, leaving the ring at the "exit" circle.

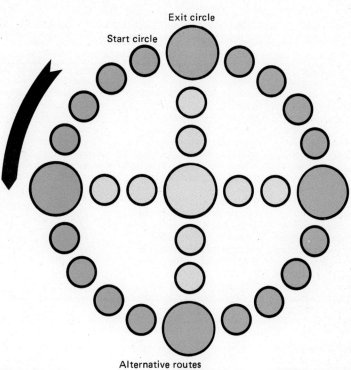

Start circle

Exit circle

Alternative routes
Whenever a horse lands on one of the large circles, it is allowed to take the alternative route along the horizontal and/or vertical arms of the cross.

Routes (**1**) and (**2**) provide a short cut; route (**3**) can be a useful means of evading enemy horses on the circles leading to the exit.

Players need not take the alternative routes if, for strategic purposes, they consider it imprudent to do so.

Taking If a horse lands on a circle occupied by an opponent's horse, the opponent's horse is "taken" and returned to the start. The taker is then allowed another throw.

Double pieces If a horse lands on a circle already occupied by one of his own or his partner's horses, the horses may be moved together as a "double piece" in subsequent moves.

Alternative routes

1

2

3

Game of goose

Reputedly invented in sixteenth-century Italy, the game of goose was a favorite in Europe until the end of the nineteenth century. It was the forerunner of many race board games in which the participants' progress may be either hindered or advanced by landing on certain specially marked squares.

Boards of many different designs were used, but the main feature of all of them was a spiral route divided into 63 numbered spaces—starting at the outside and finishing at the center. The boards were often illustrated by, for example, scenes from history or mythology.

In addition, certain spaces on the route were marked with symbols and printed instructions—sometimes these instructions were shown at the center of the board. One of these symbols, appearing on about every fifth space, was a goose.

By landing on a marked space, the player was instructed to either:
have another throw;
forfeit a turn;

advance a certain number of spaces; or
retreat a certain number of spaces.

Sometimes the instructions would be linked with the theme of the illustrations. For example, on a board with a military theme, the instruction might state that because of an injury received in battle, the player must forfeit a turn.

For contemporary play, the circuit may be drawn on paper or other suitable material. Geese should be drawn on about every fifth space, and other symbols or instructions may be marked at random on the circuit. (See also the section on play.)

Other equipment To mark his position on the circuit, each player needs a colored counter or other object different from his opponents'. One die is used.

The objective is to travel around the circuit as quickly as possible, the first player to land on the finish with an exact throw being the winner.

Play Throwing the die in turn, players move their counters the thrown number of spaces. If a player's counter lands on a goose space, the player may throw again.

By landing on another of the specially marked spaces, the player is instructed to either:
a) miss one or more turns;
b) advance a prescribed number of spaces; or
c) move back a prescribed number of spaces.

18th and 19th century board games

In the 18th and 19th centuries the emphasis of board games was primarily educational. Scores of games were invented, designed not only to while away long winter evenings, but also to impart useful facts or moral teachings. Many of these games are still played in one form or another today.

1

2

Teetotum

Boards were usually colored by hand or stencil and often had protective card or cloth cases. They were usually magnificently illustrated, and their attractiveness has made them popular collectors' items today.

Designs were extremely varied, with numbered circuits or routes in every possible arrangement.

Booklets containing useful information often accompanied the boards; sometimes descriptive passages were printed on the board itself.

Other equipment Dice or teetotums marked with numbers were used.

Players usually had a counter or "marker" made of card, although other objects such as buttons or dried peas were also used to mark the players' positions on the board.

Objective Many of the games were straightforward race games along a numbered

route from start to finish. Other games had hazards or rewards (linked to the theme of the game) that might impede or advance the players' progress.

For example, in a game about geography and travel, the "explorer" might be allowed to advance four numbers on discovering a foreign land.

17

End play The finish can only be reached by an exact throw. Thus a player throwing more than the number required to reach the finish must go back the number of spaces by which he has exceeded the finish. For example, if his counter is on 62 and the player throws a 3, he must move his counter one space forward to the finish, and then back two spaces to space 61.

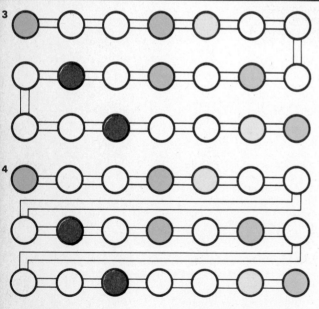

Examples of routes:
1) rambling;
2) spiral;
3) horizontal (backward and forward);
4) horizontal (left to right);
5) branching (choice of paths).

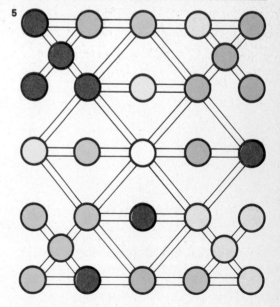

Categories
History Scenes from the past, historical personages, and famous battles were all popular subjects and were accompanied by the relevant dates and descriptive information.
Geography was the theme of many games, being an easy way of enlarging children's knowledge.

Some boards were illustrated with maps of different parts of the globe, and showed characteristic landscapes, animals, or local scenes. During the last century, "grand tours" of Europe or America were much in vogue. This resulted in another type of board design that showed familiar tourist haunts or beauty spots.

Other educational themes included natural history, astronomy, and the arts. Some of these were barely disguised educational exercises, but many were beautifully illustrated and a pleasure to play.
Moral teaching games were especially abundant in the nineteenth century. Scenes from everyday life

were often depicted, with a strong emphasis on the triumph of good over evil.
Amusement Toward the end of the nineteenth century, games designed principally for their participants' amusement became more usual. Well-loved animals or fictional characters were popular subjects, and this type of game is still common today.

©DIAGRAM

Snakes and ladders

Snakes and ladders is a development of earlier games such as the game of goose, and has become a top favorite family game. Like many other race board games its outcome is entirely dependent on chance.

The board is divided into 100 squares.
Snakes and ladders—usually about ten of each—are arranged around the board. Although the positioning of the snakes and ladders may vary from board to board, the snakes' heads are always on a higher number than their tails.
The board is often decorated with scenes of children encountering hazards or having fun.

Other equipment comprises one die, and one differently colored counter for each player.
Objective Players move their counters around the board— hoping not to be "swallowed" down to a lower number by a snake but instead to be given a helping hand up a ladder to a higher number.
The first player to land on the hundredth square wins the game.

Alleyway

Alleyway is a family game popular in Eastern Europe. It is great fun to play, because although its rules are simple, winning is tantalizingly difficult!

Equipment A semi-circle is drawn on a piece of paper or cardboard, and marked with 25 numbered spaces as shown. The thirteenth space or "alleyway" is left open. Each player—of whom there may be any number—has a counter of a different color. One die is used.

Play Each player throws the die and sets his counter on the space with the corresponding number. Players then take turns to throw the die and move their counters the number of spaces indicated by the die.
If at any time a player's counter lands on a space that is already occupied by an opponent's counter, the opponent's counter must be moved back a certain number of spaces, as follows.
a) If the opponent's counter was on any of the spaces from 1–12 or in the alleyway, it must go back to the beginning.
b) Once past the alleyway, however, a counter need only be moved back two spaces— and should that space also be occupied, that counter also must move back the appropriate number of spaces.
c) If the opponent's counter is on space 14 or 15 and has to retreat two spaces (ie to the alleyway or space 12), it has to go right back to the start. If it encounters an "enemy" counter in the alleyway or on space 12, that piece, too, has to go back to the start.

End play If a player's counter lands on space 25, it has to retreat to space 14. Thus the winner is the first player whose throw gets him beyond space 25.

Play Each player in turn moves his counter along the squares in numerical order, in accordance with the number obtained by the throw of the die.

If a player's counter lands on a square bearing the foot of a ladder, the player may move his counter up the ladder to the square at its top—thus "jumping" the intermediate squares.

If a counter lands on the head of a snake, the counter must go down the snake to the square at its tail.

End play The game continues with players throwing the die in turn until one of them reaches the hundredth square with an exact throw.

If a player's throw is higher than the number needed for his counter to land on the last square, he has to count the difference in descending order.

For example, if the counter is on square 97 and the player throws a 5, he must move forward three squares to 100 and back two squares to square 98.

Horseshoe

Horseshoe is a game very like alleyway, its main difference being that it is played for small stakes. Any number of players may take part.

Equipment The layout is drawn onto paper or cardboard and is in the shape of a horseshoe, divided into 30 numbered spaces as shown.

Instead of using counters, players mark their progress along the horseshoe with a stake—such as a candy, coin, or nut.

The only other equipment needed is a die.

Play Each player throws the die and places his stake on the corresponding space.

Players then take turns to advance their stakes along the horseshoe in accordance with the throw of the die.

Every time a player's stake lands on an occupied space, the occupier's stake has to retreat to space 1.

End play If a player's throw is higher than the number needed for his stake to reach space 30, he must move his stake around the horseshoe past space 30 and on to space 1 or beyond. For example, if his stake is on space 28 and the player throws a 5, he must move his stake five spaces to space 3.

He must then continue round the course from that space.

Winner The first player to get an exact throw onto space 30 wins the game and all the stakes.

End play

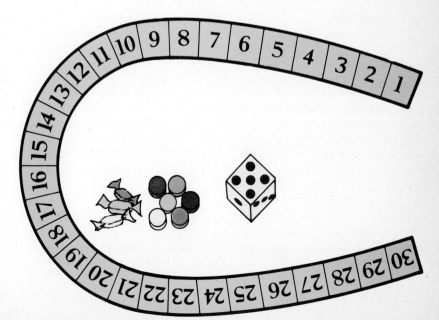

Contemporary board games

Almost every family is familiar with the fun and excitement of a race board game, in which even young children can participate. The outcome of many of the simpler games depends solely on the throw of a die—other games are more sophisticated.

Equipment Boards are usually of stout cardboard, covered with paper and edged with tape or cloth binding. They are printed in bright colors.

Luxury versions, of wood or leather, are sometimes made. The boards are usually sold in a protective cardboard or wooden box, together with printed playing instructions, counters, dice, and any other necessary equipment (such as picture cards, dice, cups, etc).

The objectives of contemporary race board games fall basically into two categories.

1) Straightforward race games—often those designed for children—are those in which players race their opponents along a prescribed route or numbered course in accordance with the throw of a die.

There may or may not be hazards to overcome, or "bonuses" that help the player reach the finish more quickly (the first person to do so being the winner).

2) In more sophisticated games, the winner is usually the first person to achieve a set objective.

As this type of game can often last for many hours, participants sometimes decide to end the game before an absolute winner has been determined. In this case, the winner is the player who is in the most advantageous position when the game is brought to an end.

Although these games require a certain amount of skill and decision making, the inexperienced player can still win by a combination of fortunate dice throws and sheer luck!

Categories As in earlier times, many contemporary race board games combine pleasure with learning. There are many historical or geographical games that differ little from the type of game played a hundred years ago.

Other games deal with current topics such as high finance, space exploration, or spying.

CHILDREN'S GAMES

Many contemporary race board games can be played by adults and children alike. There are others, however, designed specifically for young and even pre-school age children.

These games (invariably straightforward race games) are a useful way of teaching the rudiments of counting and reading, and of encouraging the child to plan or think ahead.

Familiar things like trains, household objects, and animals are popular subjects. Characters from books, films, and fairy tales are also prevalent.

Popular examples are Winnie-the-Pooh, Tom and Jerry, and Pinocchio.

MONOPOLY

Monopoly is perhaps the best-known and most popular board game of its kind. Invented in the United States in the 30s, it was patented by Parker Brothers of America in 1935. The game is now played in many countries on boards showing different cities. Monopoly is a fast-moving game of make-believe property deals and financial bargaining, in which real estate and public utilities are bought and sold; rents, mortgages, and taxes have to be paid; and fines and spells in jail are among the hazards. Between two and eight players may take part, the winner being the last person to evade bankruptcy.

Simple race board games

Sophisticated race board games

a Warfare

b Crime

c Big game hunting

d Space travel

e High finance

f Geography

g Word building

CLUEDO

Cluedo (a registered trademark of John Waddington Limited of Great Britain) is a mystery game in which each player attempts to solve a murder that takes place in a large house. Players move their pieces around the board from room to room. By a process of questioning and deduction, they seek to discover the murderer, the murder weapon, and the scene of the crime.

DIPLOMACY

This compelling game of strategy and political maneuvering needs foresight, shrewdness, diplomacy—and also luck—to win.
Each player takes the role of a different country and is given control of armed forces. By waging land and sea battles and forming—and breaking—alliances with other countries, each player tries to achieve the winning objective of capturing the majority of the bases situated around the board. Diplomacy is patented by Games Research Incorporated.

SCRABBLE

Although Scrabble was not the first "crossword puzzle" game invented, it has rapidly superseded other games of this type since its appearance in the late 1940s and has been adapted for play in many different languages. (Scrabble is patented in the United States of America by Selchow and Righter.) Each player draws tiles printed with a letter of the alphabet and a numerical value. Players form their tiles into words on the board to build a crossword puzzle formation. They score points for the letters used and for making use of specially marked bonus squares. Scrabble requires a good vocabulary and ingenuity in positioning the words—but there is also a degree of luck involved.

Backgammon

Backgammon is an ancient board game developed in the Orient and now played all over the world. It is an excellent game in which the opportunities for strategic play add to the excitement of a race around the board. The fine calculation of odds involved in skilled play has a strong attraction for the player who is prepared to gamble.

Pieces Each player has 15 pieces, similar to those used in checkers. One player has dark pieces (Black) and the other light pieces (White).
The pieces are variously known as "counters," "stones," or "men." In the modern game "men" is the commonly accepted term.
Dice Each player has two dice and a dice cup in which to shake them.
Doubling cube In a game where players agree to bet on the outcome (there is no need to play for anything but fun), a doubling cube is used. This is a large die on which the faces are numbered 2:4:8:16:32:64. (Its significance is explained in the section on gambling.)

Players Only two players compete, but others may participate in the betting when matches are played for money.
Objective According to the numbers thrown on the dice, each player moves his men toward his own inner table. Once all a player's men are located in his own inner table he attempts to remove them—by a process called "bearing off."
The first player to bear off all 15 of his pieces wins the game.
Although the basic objective of the game is simple, the rules and strategies governing a player's moves are much more complex.

The direction of play for each player is always from his opponent's inner table, through his opponent's outer table, through his own outer table, and into his own inner table.
Thus White always moves his men clockwise and Black moves counterclockwise.

Board Backgammon is played on a rectangular board divided into two halves by a "bar." One half of the board is called the "inner table" or "home table," and the other the "outer table."
Along each side of the board are marked 12 triangles, alternately light and dark colored (this coloring has no special significance.)
Each triangle is called a "point." For the purpose of notation, points are numbered 1–12 as shown (**a**). (No numbers actually appear on the board.)
Points 1 (the first points in the inner table) are called "ace points"; points 7 (the first points on the outer table) are called "bar points." No other points are specially designated.
The board is placed between the two players (called Black and White) so that Black has his inner table to his right.
The points on Black's side of the table are known as Black points; those on White's side as White points. In simple notation, points are indicated by their number and the initial B or W.

Start of play Players draw for color and then place their men in their prescribed starting positions (**b**).
White places two men on B1; five men on W6; three men on W8; and five men on B12.
Black places two men on W1; five men on B6; three men on B8; and five men on W12.

a Notation
b Start of play

Having placed their men on their starting positions, each player throws a single die to determine the order of play. The player throwing the higher number has first move. If both players throw the same number they must throw again.

For his first move the opening player moves according to the numbers on both his own and his opponent's dice.

Thereafter, play alternates and each player moves according to the numbers on both his own dice.

Play A player throws both his dice to determine how many points he can move.

For a valid throw the dice must be:

thrown from the cup;

thrown in the player's own half of the board;

thrown so that one face of each die rests wholly on the board;

thrown only when an opponent has completed his turn.

The player then moves according to the numbers thrown on the dice.

Moving men A player attempts to move the number of points shown on each of his die. He may not merely add them together and move the combined total.

The position of the men on the board may affect a player's choice of moves or may even prevent him from moving at all. Provided that none of his men is off the board, a player may move to any point that is:

a) clear of any other men;

b) occupied by one or more of his own men; or

c) occupied by only one of his opponent's men.

When there is only one man on a point, this man is called a "blot."

A player who moves a man to a point on which he already has one man is said to "make" that point, as his opponent cannot then land on it.

(Also see sections on play after a mixed throw and play after a double.)

Moving men

Mixed throw

Double throw

Play after a mixed throw

If the numbers on the two dice are different, the player may make one of four possible moves. For example, a player throwing a 2 and a 6 may move:

a) one man two points, then the same man six points further;

b) one man six points, then the same man two points further;

c) one man two points, and another man six points;

d) one man six points, and another man two points.

At first glance alternatives a) and b) appear to be the same. This is not in fact the case, since the order in which the numbers are taken can affect whether or not a man may be moved (see the section on moving men).

If he can use only the number shown on one of his dice, the other number is disregarded. If he has a choice of two numbers, he must use the higher one.

Play after a double

If a player throws a double, then the number shown on both dice is played four times (or as many times as possible up to four).

Thus if a player throws two 2s he may move:

a) one man four times two points;

b) one man twice two points and another man twice two points;

c) one man twice two points and another two men two points each;

d) four men two points each.

As before, the number shown on the dice is the limit of a move. A player moving one man four times two points must land on open points at the end of each two point move.

Hitting a man

If a player moves a man onto a point on which his opponent has only one man (**a**) he is said to "hit" that man.

The hit man is removed from play and placed on the bar (**b**). A player who has any hit men on the bar must re-enter them before he can move any of his men on the board.

Re-entering men

To re-enter a hit man, a player must throw the number of an open point on his opponent's home table. He may then use the number on his second die to re-enter another man or, if all his men are on the board, to move any of his men the number of points shown on that die.

Bearing off men

Once a player has succeeded in moving all his men into his own inner table, he bears them off by removing them from those points corresponding to the numbers thrown.

For example, if White throws a 4 and a 2 when he has men on both W4 and W2 he may bear off a man from each of these points.

If he throws a 4 and a 2 when he has a man on W4 but not on W2, he may bear off a man from W4 and must then move another man two points down from his highest occupied point.

If he wishes, a player may always move men down the board from his highest point rather than bearing off from the points corresponding to the numbers on the dice.

If both numbers thrown are higher than the player's highest point, the player bears off from his highest point.

If a player's man is hit after he has started bearing off, that man must re-enter and be moved around again to the inner table before bearing off is resumed.

Bearing off continues until one player succeeds in bearing off all his men.

Hitting a man

Fouls and penalties In addition to the rules on throwing the dice, players must observe the following:
a) a player may not change his move after taking his hand from a moved piece;
b) if a player makes an incorrect move, his opponent may insist that the error be corrected provided that he has not made his own following move;
c) a game must be restarted if the board or pieces are found to be incorrectly set up during play.

Scoring The game is won by the player who first bears off all his men. The number of units scored depends on the progress of the loser:
a) if the loser has borne off at least one man and has no men left in the winner's inner table, the winner scores one unit;
b) if the loser has not borne off any men, the winner has made a "gammon" and scores two units;
c) if the loser has not borne off any men and also has a man on the bar or in the winner's inner table, the winner has made a "backgammon" and scores three units.

Gambling Backgammon is often played for an agreed base stake for each game. This stake may be doubled and redoubled during play (in addition to the double payment for a gammon and treble for a backgammon). A doubling cube is often used to show the number of times that the stake has been doubled. (At the start of play it should be placed with the number 64 face uppermost.) Unless players previously agree otherwise, stakes are automatically doubled if the dice match at the first throw of a game. In this case both players then throw again. The number of automatic doubles is usually limited by agreement to one or two per game. There is no limit to the number of voluntary doubles.

Either player has the right to offer the first voluntary double—after which the right alternates between players. A player who wishes to double the stake must offer to do so before throwing the dice when it is his turn to play. His opponent then has the choice of accepting the doubled stake or of forfeiting the game and the stake.

Start of play

PLAKATO
This form of backgammon is widely played in Greek cafes. It is the same as the basic game described here except that:
a) each player positions all his men on his opponent's number 1 point for the start of play;
b) a blot is not hit but is blocked and cannot be moved as long as an opposing man is on the same point;
c) a player must move all his men all 24 points instead of bearing them off when they reach his inner table.

GIOUL
This popular Middle Eastern form of backgammon is played in the same way as the basic game except that:
a) each player positions all his men on his opponent's number 1 point for the start;
b) a blot is not hit but is blocked and cannot be moved while an opposing man is on the same point;
c) when a player throws a double, he attempts to move for the double thrown and then for each subsequent double in turn up to double 6 (for example if he throws double 4 he goes on to move for double 5 and double 6);
d) if a player is unable to use any of his moves from a double, all these moves may be taken by his opponent.

Start of play

DUTCH BACKGAMMON
This is the same as the basic game except that:
a) all the men are placed on the bar for the start of play and players must enter all 15 before moving any man around the board;
b) a player may not hit a blot until he has advanced at least one of his own men to his own inner table.

ACEY DEUCEY
This is an elaboration of Dutch backgammon and is popular in the US Navy. It differs from the basic game in the following ways:
a) men are entered from the bar as in Dutch backgammon;
b) if a player throws a 1 and a 2 (ace-deuce), he moves his men for this throw and then moves his men as if he had thrown any doublet that he chooses;
c) the stake is usually automatically doubled when an ace-deuce is thrown;
d) some players give each man an agreed unit value and the winner collects as many units as the opponent has left on the board.

Este es otro iuego departido en que a'
ueynt un tablero que an a seer enta

Nine men's morris

Nine men's morris, also called mill, morelles, or merels, is one of the oldest games played in Europe and was particularly popular during the Middle Ages. It is a game of strategy for two people in which each player attempts to capture or block his opponent's pieces.

Board The game is played on a specially marked-out board, with three squares one inside the other and with points in the centers of the squares' sides connected by ruled lines. Bought boards are now usually made of wood. In the past, boards have been carved out of stone or, often, cut out of turf.
A perfectly satisfactory board can be quickly drawn on a piece of paper.

Pieces At the start of a game each player has nine "men" (counters, stones, or other appropriate pieces) distinguishable in color from those of his opponent.

Objective By the placing and maneuvering of men on the board, each player attempts to capture all but two of his opponent's pieces or to make it impossible for his opponent to move any piece at his turn.

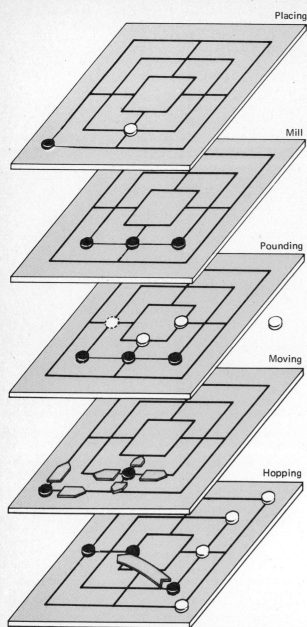

Placing

Mill

Pounding

Moving

Hopping

Play There are usually three stages of play:
1) placing the men on the board;
2) moving the pieces around;
3) "hopping" them.
(The third stage is sometimes disallowed, as it gives one player a distinct advantage over his opponent.)

Placing the pieces The players decide which of them is to start.
Each one, in turn, then places one man of his own color on the board at any point of intersection not already occupied by another piece.
Players aim to get three of their own men into a straight line along one of the lines of the board, so forming a "mill."

Pounding Once a player has formed a mill he is entitled to "pound" his opponent by removing one enemy piece from the board.
A player may not, however, remove an opponent's man that is part of a mill, unless there is no other man available.
Once removed from the board, a piece is dead for the rest of the game.
Players continue their turns (nine turns each) until each of their men has been placed onto the board.

Moving the pieces Still taking alternate turns, players now move their men to try to form new mills and so pound their opponent.
A move consists of moving a man from his existing position on the board to any adjoining vacant point of intersection.
(According to some rules players may take pieces by passing over an enemy piece to a vacant spot beyond it, as in checkers.)

Players may form new mills by opening existing mills. This is achieved by moving a man one place from his position in a mill, and then returning him at the next move to his original position. Mills may be broken and re-made any number of times, and each new mill formation entitles the player to pound his opponent.
Play continues until one of the players is reduced by successive poundings to having only two men on the board; or until one player's pieces have been so blocked by his opponent's men that he is unable to make any move.
Should a player's only remaining pieces form a mill and it is his turn to move, he must do so even if this results in his losing a piece and the game at his opponent's next move.

Hopping is an optional stage of play, and begins when either player has only three men remaining.
The player is now no longer restricted to moving his men along a line to an adjacent point of intersection, but may "hop" to any vacant spot on the board.
This freedom of movement gives him a certain advantage over his opponent, and so restores his chance of winning.

Result A player is defeated when either:
he is reduced to having only two pieces; or
his pieces are blocked by enemy men in such a way as to prevent further moves.
(If hopping has been allowed the game ends when one player has only two pieces remaining.)

THREE MEN'S MORRIS
Three men's morris is a game for two players, each player having four counters of his own color.
The board is marked out as shown.
Players take turns to put one man on a point of intersection, in an attempt to form a mill.
The first player to achieve this is the winner.

SIX MEN'S MORRIS
This game is played in much the same way as nine men's morris.
Players each have six counters and take it in turns to place them, one at a time, on the board (which is marked out as shown).
The objective is to form a mill along one of the sides of either of the squares. If a player succeeds in doing this, he may pound his opponent.
As in nine men's morris, once all the men have been played onto the board, the game continues with players moving their men to form new mills.
When one player only has two men left, he loses the game.

Fox and geese

European fox and geese games originated in Scandinavia in the Middle Ages. Similar games are played in many other parts of the world. In all of them, two unevenly matched forces compete against each other. The smaller force usually comprises one or two pieces and has considerable freedom of movement; the larger force is made up of numerous pieces but has only restricted maneuverability.

Pieces Any suitable pieces such as checkers, counters, or stones may be used (or marbles or pegs if played on a solitaire board).
One of the pieces, representing the fox, must be distinguishable in color from the 15 (or sometimes 17) pieces representing the geese.

Start of play

Moves

Board Fox and geese can be played on several different layouts. The layout in the large illustrations probably gives the players the most even chance of winning. The other layouts give the geese an advantage over the fox.

Start of play The two players decide which of them is to play the fox and which the geese; they change over after each game.
The pieces are put into position on the board—with the geese at the top of the board (as shown) and the fox usually at the center (although it may be placed on any vacant point that the player chooses). Players take alternate turns, with the fox starting first.

The fox may move in any direction along connecting lines, moving one point at each turn (**a**).
It may also "kill" a goose by jumping over it to an adjacent vacant point (**b**); the goose is then removed from the board. The fox may make two or more jumps in one move (killing each goose that it jumps over), provided there is an empty point for it to land on next to each goose that it kills. The fox is obliged to jump if there is no alternative move, even if it puts itself in a vulnerable position by doing so.
Geese may move along connecting lines in any direction except toward the top of the board (**c**). One goose moves one point in a turn.
Geese may not jump over and capture the fox; their aim is to surround the fox so that it cannot move.

Result The fox wins if it:
a) kills so many geese that those remaining are not sufficient in number to trap it; or
b) manages to evade the geese so as to give it a clear path to the top of the board (where the geese cannot chase it).
The geese win if they can immobilize the fox by surrounding it or crowding it into a corner.

Alternative layouts

Chinese rebels

This is a game in the fox and geese family, and is thought to have originated in China. One player (the "general") attempts to evade the rebelling soldiers that have surrounded him. Although the general is heavily outnumbered, he has the advantage of being able to "kill" the soldiers and remove them from the board.

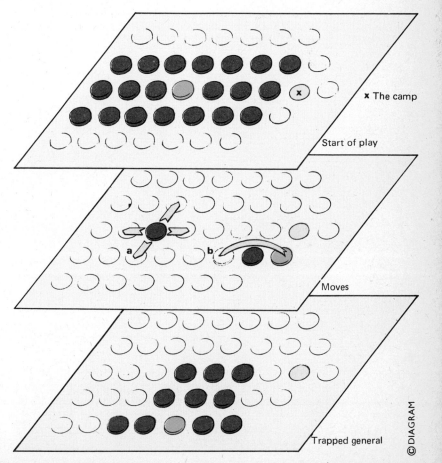

The playing area may be drawn on a sheet of paper. It consists of a rectangle enclosing 39 small circles. One circle is distinctively marked and represents the "camp" (see illustrations).

Pieces Counters or other small objects may be used. One piece represents the general and must be different in appearance from the 20 pieces representing the soldiers.

Start of play The soldiers are positioned around the general, as shown.

Play The players decide which of them is to play the general and which the soldiers.
The general has the opening move, and thereafter the players take alternate turns.
In a turn, a piece may be moved one circle forward, backward, or sideways onto an adjoining vacant circle (**a**). Diagonal moves are not permitted.
The general is allowed to "kill" a soldier by jumping over him from an adjoining circle to an empty circle beyond (**b**). That soldier is then removed from the board. (The general's opening move is always a taking move.)

Result If the general kills, so many soldiers that not enough remain to trap him, or if he manages to return to camp, he wins the game. The soldiers win if they manage to immobilize the general by surrounding him or crowding him into a corner.

Alternative result Once players are familiar with playing tactics, they will find that the general invariably loses the game.
For this reason, two or more games can be played in succession, with players changing roles after each game.
The person playing the soldiers must note how many moves it takes him to trap the general.
At the end of a set number of games, the players compare results, and the winner is the player who trapped the general in fewest moves.

x The camp

Start of play

Moves

Trapped general

© DIAGRAM

Fighting serpents

Fighting serpents is a board game of North American Indian origin. Although the layout and the way in which the pieces are moved bear certain similarities to fox and geese games, fighting serpents is a contest between two forces of equal strength. The player who succeeds in capturing all his opponent's pieces is the winner.

Play After the starting order has been determined, the first player moves one of his pieces along a line to any of the three vacant points. Thereafter, turns alternate between players.

Capturing is compulsory whenever possible and takes precedence if there is a choice of moves.

A piece is captured by jumping over it to an empty point beyond (**a**). A taking move is not permitted if it entails a change of direction (**b**).

Double or multiple captures in one move are permitted; direction may be changed after each enemy piece has been jumped (**c**).

Whenever a piece is captured it is removed from the board.

In a non-taking move, players may move one of their pieces one intersection along a line in any direction.

The game ends as soon as one player has lost all his pieces.

The board is as shown. It has a playing area of three parallel lines, intersected by short lines forming a diamond pattern.

The length of the playing area may vary (the one illustrated here with 49 intersections is of average size) and the ends may be either rounded or straight.

Pieces are placed on all the intersections except three along the middle parallel: the two outermost intersections and the one at the center. Each player has pieces of a different color, positioned at the start of the game as shown.

Traditionally, small black and white stones are used, but the game can also be played with counters or other objects.

The objective is to capture all the opponent's pieces, the first player to achieve this being the winner.

Start of play

Moving

Mancala is the generic name for a group of ancient African and Asian games, in which seeds are moved from cup to cup around a board in an attempt to capture opposing seeds. Names, boards, and rules differ from region to region but the basic principles of play are generally the same. Though traditionally played by primitive tribesmen, the strategy of these games is highly complex and demands a fine mathematical calculation of possible moves and their results.

Mancala boards Mancala games are sometimes played in hollows scooped in the ground. They may equally well be played on a layout drawn on paper.

Traditionally, however, mancala boards are carved from wood—usually from a single large block although hinged boards are not uncommon.

The finest boards are like pieces of sculpture, intricately carved with patterns of symbolic significance. Such boards are often handed down from generation to generation.

Boards can be divided into two basic types according to the number and pattern of their cups. Commonest are two-rank boards. Four-rank boards are largely confined to parts of Southern and East Africa.

Seeds Traditionally mancala games are played with seeds, beans, or small stones. Counters, marbles, or any other small objects may be substituted.

Players Mancala games are for two players.

OWARI

Owari, played in West Africa, is a typical mancala game and demonstrates the basic principles of mancala play.

The board has 12 playing cups, in two rows of six, and two scoring cups.

Players face each other across the board and each is allocated the row of cups nearest to him and also one of the scoring cups.

Seeds 48 seeds are required.

Objective Each player attempts to capture as many seeds as possible.

Start of play Four seeds are placed in each of the 12 playing holes. Order of play is usually decided by lot.

Play Turns alternate. In his turn each player takes all the seeds from a cup on his side of the board and "sows" them one by one in the cups around the board in a clockwise direction—thus if there are four seeds in his cup he sows one of them in each of the next four cups.

If there are 12 or more seeds in a cup, then the movement of the seeds from that cup will be more than one circuit of the board. In this case the emptied cup is missed out when sowing.

If all his opponent's cups are empty a player must, if possible, move a seed into his opponent's half of the board.

Capturing A player makes a capture if he sows a seed into one of his opponent's cups so that this cup then contains two or three seeds. This entitles the sower to take all the seeds from this cup and to place them in his scoring cup. After making any capture, a player is also entitled to capture the seeds in adjacent cups containing two or three seeds.

A player is not, however, allowed to capture all the seeds in his opponent's cups (as this would prevent his opponent moving in his next turn). Instead he must leave intact any one cup that he chooses.

End of game Play ends when a player is unable to make a move or when none of the seeds remaining on the board can be captured.

Result The game is won by the player who captures most seeds.

Start of play

Scoring cup

Moving

Ringo

Ringo is a game of strategy for two people. Invented in Germany, it is played on a circular board and has certain similarities with fox and geese. One player (the "attacker") attempts to capture the central area of the board known as the "fortress," while the other player (the "defender") tries to ward off the attack.

The playing area may be drawn on a sheet of paper. It comprises a large circle divided into eight segments of equal size. One of the segments is distinctively colored and is called the "neutral zone."
The central circle or fortress is also distinctively colored. Six concentric rings spread out beyond it, and the resulting sections are alternately light and dark colored (ie each segment has three light and three dark colored sections).

Pieces Each player has counters (or other suitable objects) distinguishable from his opponent's. The defender has four pieces and the attacker seven.
For the start of play, the defender's pieces are arranged around the fortress (but not in the neutral zone), and the attacker's pieces on the outermost ring.

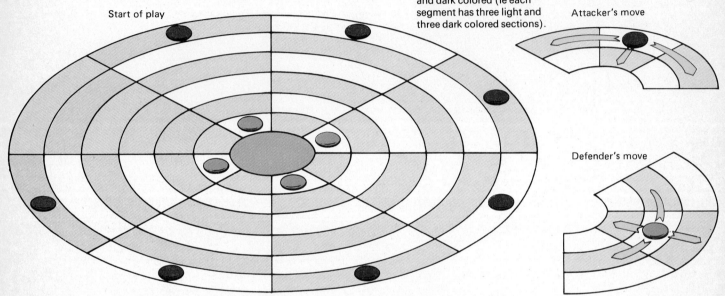

Start of play

Attacker's move

Defender's move

Queen's guard

Queen's guard is an interesting old board game for two players. It can be played with counters on an improvised board. Players attempt to position their pieces in the winning pattern.

The board is in the shape of a hexagon, with 91 small hexagons in alternating dark and light bands.
Pieces There are two sets of pieces. Each set is a distinctive color and consists of one "queen" and six "guards."
Objective The game is won when one player succeeds in positioning his "queen" on the center hexagon and his six guards in the hexagons immediately surrounding it.
Start of play There are two methods of starting play:
a) the pieces are positioned as shown;
b) each player positions his pieces in turn, one at a time, anywhere he likes on the board.

Objective Each player tries to capture or immobilize as many enemy pieces as possible in order to achieve his objective. The attacker's objective is to capture the fortress by getting two of his pieces into it; the defender's objective is to prevent him from doing so.

Play The players decide which of them is to attack and which to defend.
The attacker has the first move, and thereafter players take alternate turns.
The attacker may only move his pieces forward (ie toward the center) or sideways.
The defender—although having fewer pieces—has the advantage of being able to move them in any direction except diagonally. He may not actually enter the fortress, although he is allowed to jump over it when capturing.
When moving sideways (ie into another segment) pieces must remain on the same ring as the one on which they were standing.
Both players may move their pieces into the neutral zone—although the attacker may only have as many pieces in the neutral zone as the defender has on the board. For example, if the defender has only two pieces left on the board, the attacker may only have two pieces within the neutral zone.

Capturing Both players may capture enemy pieces, although there is no compulsion to do so.
A piece is captured by jumping over it from a touching section onto a vacant section beyond it. The captured piece is then removed from the board.
As in ordinary moves, the attacker is restricted to capturing in a forward or sideways direction, while the defender may also capture in a backward direction.
When making a sideways capture, the taking piece and the piece being captured must both be on the same ring.
A player may capture only one piece in a move.
All pieces are safe from capture when within the neutral zone. However, it is permissible for a piece to use the neutral zone as its "take-off" or "landing" area in a capturing move. Although the defender may not actually enter the fortress, he may jump over it in order to capture an enemy piece within it, provided the section directly opposite is vacant (see illustration).

End play The attacker may enter the fortress from any segment (including the neutral zone).
Should a defending piece be positioned on the innermost ring, an attacking piece may jump over it into the fortress (thereby capturing the defending piece).
If the attacker gets one of his pieces into the fortress, it is still prone to capture by a defending piece. Should the attacker succeed in getting two of his pieces into the fortress, however, he wins the game.
The defender wins the game if he either captures all but one of the attacker's pieces, or immobilizes the attacker's pieces so that he is unable to get two pieces into the fortress.

Capturing move

Capture of an attacker in the fortress

Moves Each player moves one piece in a turn.
A piece may only be moved into a vacant hexagon.
A player who touches one of his pieces must move that piece or forfeit his turn.
Except when a piece is trapped between opposing pieces, it may be moved one hexagon sideways or toward the center of the board (**a**).
If a "guard" is trapped between two opposing pieces (**b**), its owner must in his next turn move it to any hexagon in the outside band.
If a "queen" is trapped between two opposing pieces (**c**), its owner must in his next turn move it to any vacant square that his opponent requires.
If more than one piece is trapped, the player must move them back one in each turn. "Guards" may be moved back in any order, but a "queen" must always be moved before a "guard."
Only a "queen" may be placed in the center hexagon. A player forfeits the game if, when the center hexagon is empty, he positions all his six guards in the band immediately surrounding it.

Start of play

Moves

Forfeited game

Won game

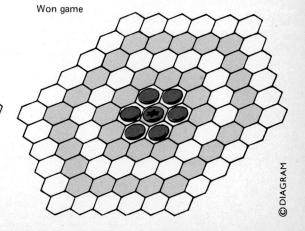

© DIAGRAM

Checkers (Draughts)

Checkers, or draughts as it is called in the United Kingdom, is a board game for two players. It was played in southern Europe in medieval times and appears to have been derived from much older games played in the Middle East. Each player attempts to "take" (capture and remove) his opponent's pieces or to confine them so that they cannot be moved.

Board The game is played on a board made of wood, plastic, or cardboard and 14½–16in square.
It is divided into 64 squares, eight along each side. The squares are alternately a light and a dark color (usually black and white, or sometimes black and red or red and white).
Play is confined to squares of only one color—usually the darker color.

Pieces Each player has a set of 12 pieces—wooden or plastic disks 1¼–1½in in diameter and about ⅜in thick.
One set is usually white, and the other red or black.

Objective A player aims to "take" all his opponent's pieces or to position his own pieces so that his opponent is unable to make any move.

Start of play The players sit facing each other, and the board is positioned so that the players have a playing square at the left of their first row.
Lots are drawn to decide who will have the darker pieces for the first game. Each player has the darker pieces for alternate games.
For the start of play each player positions his pieces on the playing squares in the three rows of the board nearest him.
The player with the darker pieces always makes the first move in a game.

Moving A player may make only one move at a turn.
As play is confined to squares of only one color, all moves are diagonal.
Individual pieces or "men" may only be moved forward (**a**); double pieces or "kings" may be moved either forward or backward (**b**).
A piece may only be moved into a square that is vacant.

Starting position

a

b

Moving

Touch and move Except when he has given notice of his intention to arrange pieces properly in their squares, a player whose turn it is must when possible make his move with the first piece that he touches.
If he first touches an unplayable piece, he is cautioned for a first offense and forfeits the game for a second offense.

Time limit for moves If a player fails to make a move within five minutes, an appointed timekeeper shall call "time." The player must then move within one minute, or forfeit the game through improper delay.
(At master level in some tournaments, players must make a prescribed number of moves within set time limits.)

A non-taking move Except when "taking" an opponent's piece, a player may only move a piece into a touching playing square.

A taking move One of the game's objectives is to "take" (capture and remove) the opposing pieces.

A piece may be taken if it is in a playing square touching the taker's square when there is a vacant square directly beyond it (**1**).

Several pieces can be taken in one move provided that each one has a vacant square beyond it (**2**).

Whenever possible, a player must make a taking move rather than a non-taking move (even if this means that his own piece will in turn be taken).

If a player has a choice of taking moves he may take a smaller instead of a larger number of pieces (**3a**), but if he begins the move enabling him to take the larger number he must continue until he has taken all the pieces possible (**3b**).

Failure to take If a player fails to take a piece when he is able (**4a**), modern tournament play rules state that his opponent should point this out and so force him to take back the wrongly moved piece and make the taking move instead (**4b**).

This ruling has replaced the old "huff or blow" rule, by which a player who failed to make a possible taking move forfeited the piece moved in error.

Crowning When a man reaches the farthest row on the board (known as the "king row" or "crownhead"), it becomes a "king" and is "crowned" by having another piece of its own color placed on it (**5**).

A player's turn always ends when a man is crowned.

A tied game occurs when neither player can remove all his opponent's pieces or prevent him from making a move (**6**).

If one player appears to be in a stronger position, he may be required to force a win within 40 of his own moves or else place himself at a decided advantage over his opponent. If he fails, the game is counted as tied.

1

2

3a

3b

4a

4b

5

6

TOURNAMENT CHECKERS

To reduce the number of tied and repeated games at expert level, a system of restricted openings is applied at major championships and tournaments in the United States and elsewhere.

The first three moves of each game are determined by cards bearing the various openings and subsequent moves. The cards are shuffled and cut, and the top card is turned face up. Opposing players then play two games with the prescribed opening, each player making the first move in one of the games.

LOSING or GIVEAWAY CHECKERS is played under

the same rules as standard British or American checkers. The tactics, however, are very different, as the objective is to be the first player to lose all his pieces.

©DIAGRAM

DIAGONAL CHECKERS is

an interesting variant of the standard game.
It can be played with 12 pieces per player, in which case starting position (**a**) is used, or with nine pieces each if starting position (**b**) is used.

Men are crowned when they have crossed the board to reach the opponent's corner squares (marked K in the diagrams).
Otherwise, rules are the same as for standard checkers.

ITALIAN CHECKERS is

played in the same way as standard British or American checkers except that:
a) the board is positioned with a non-playing square at the left of each player's first row;
b) a player must make a taking move whenever possible—or forfeit the game;
c) a man cannot take a king;

d) if a player has a choice of captures he must take the greater number of pieces;
e) if a player with a king to move has a choice of capturing equal numbers of pieces, he must take the most valuable pieces (ie kings rather than men).

SPANISH CHECKERS is

played in the same way as Italian checkers, except that kings are moved differently.
A player may use his king to take a piece anywhere on a diagonal, provided that there are no pieces between and there is an empty square beyond it. (This is sometimes called the "long move.")
The jump need not end in the

square immediately behind the taken piece, but may continue any distance along the diagonal if there are no intervening pieces (**a**).
The king must make all its jumps before any taken pieces are removed, and these pieces may not be jumped a second time in the same move (**b**).

GERMAN CHECKERS is

played in the same way as Spanish checkers except that:
a) men can make taking moves either forward or backward;
b) a man is only crowned if its move ends on the far row—if it is in a position to make further jumps away from that line it must always take them.

RUSSIAN CHECKERS is

played like German checkers except that:
a) a player with a choice of captures need not take the larger number of pieces;
b) a man is made into a king as soon as it reaches the far row and then jumps as a king for the rest of the move.

CONTINENTAL or POLISH CHECKERS is

played on a board with 100 squares, 10 along each side.
Each player has 20 pieces—positioned on the first four rows for the start of play.
The game is played under the same rules as German checkers.

CANADIAN CHECKERS is another variant of German checkers.
It is played on a board with 144 squares, 12 by 12.
Each player has 30 pieces—positioned on the first five rows for the start of play.

TURKISH CHECKERS may be played on a standard checkerboard, but the traditional Turkish board has squares all the same color.
Each player has 16 pieces—positioned on each player's second and third rows for the start of play (**a**).
Men move as in British or American checkers, but directly forward or sideways and not diagonally (**b**).
Kings move any number of squares directly forward, sideways, or backward.
Multiple captures by kings are made as shown (**c**)—as for Spanish checkers except that moves are not diagonal and pieces are removed as soon as they are jumped (instead of staying on the board to prevent further jumps).

A player must make a capture whenever possible, and must always take the greater number of pieces when he has a choice of captures.
Turkish checkers may be won in the usual ways, and also by a player with a king when his opponent has only a single man remaining on the board.

CHECKERS GO-MOKU is an adaptation of the Japanese game described on page 56.
Play is on all the squares of a standard checkerboard, and the two players have 12 checkers each.
The board is empty at the start of a game, and the players take it in turns to place one checker on any square. After all the checkers have been placed, a player uses his turn to move one checker into any vacant, adjoining square.
If, at any stage of the game, a player succeeds in placing five checkers in a row (horizontally, vertically, or diagonally), he is entitled to remove any one of his opponent's checkers from the board.

The game is won when a player has removed all his opponent's checkers.

CHECKERS FOX AND GEESE Two versions of fox and geese are often played on a standard checkerboard and are particularly popular with children. (Other versions on other boards are described on page 30 .)
In both checkers versions, one player has one dark checker (the "fox") and his opponent has several white checkers (the "geese").
Play is only on the black squares of the board. A player moves only one checker at a turn.
The fox wins the game if it can break through the line of geese. The geese win if they can trap the fox so that it cannot move.

Four geese version
At the start of play, the player with the geese positions them on the four playing squares of his first row; the player with the fox positions it wherever he chooses (**a**).
The geese move diagonally forward like the men in British or American checkers.
The fox moves diagonally forward or backward one square at a time; it is not permitted to jump over the geese, so there is no taking in this version.

Twelve geese version
(sometimes played with a "wolf" and "goats"). At the start of play the geese are positioned on the first three rows, as for British or American checkers; the fox is positioned on one of the corner playing squares on the opposite side of the board.
The geese move like the men and the fox like a king in British or American checkers. (Jumping and taking geese is permitted in this version.)

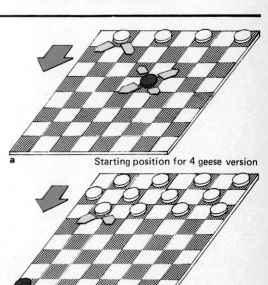

Starting position for 4 geese version

Starting position for 12 geese version

Start

Taking

1

2

3

4

LASCA

This is an interesting game in the checkers family. It is characterized by its unusual method of taking, and by the consequent building up of "columns" of pieces.

The board has 49 squares, seven along each side. The squares are alternately light and dark, and play is only on the light squares.
(A standard checkerboard can be used if the squares along two sides are covered, leaving a light square at each corner.)

Pieces Each player has a set of 11 pieces; one set is usually white and the other red or black.
Each piece is marked on one side—with a sticker, paint, pen, or pencil.

Objective The game is won when one player makes it impossible for his opponent to make any move.

Start of play Each player positions his pieces, with their unmarked sides face up, on the white squares in the three rows of the board nearest him.

Turns alternate, and each player makes only one move in a turn.

A **"soldier"** is a piece with the unmarked side face up. All pieces are soldiers at the start of play.
A soldier moves diagonally forward like a man in British or American checkers.

An **"officer"** is a piece with the marked side face up.
A soldier becomes an officer after it has crossed to the farthest row of the board (like "crowning" in standard checkers).
A player's turn ends whenever a soldier becomes an officer.
An officer moves diagonally backward or forward like a king in American or British checkers.

A **"column"** may be a single piece or a pile of pieces.

A **"guide"** is the top piece of a column. The color of the guide shows to which player that column belongs, and its rank (soldier or officer) determines how the column may be moved.

Taking In Lasca, unlike other checkers games, a piece is not removed from the board when it is taken. Instead, it is added to the bottom of the column that takes it.
If a column contains several pieces, only the guide is taken when another column jumps over it.
In the example illustrated:
1) the red column takes the white guide from the white column;
2) the red column (led by an officer) takes the other white piece and red's turn ends;
3) the other white column (led by a soldier) takes the red guide and white's turn ends (4).
If a taken guide was an officer it retains this rank in the other column.
As in British and American checkers, a player must take a piece whenever possible, but if he has a choice of captures, he need not take the larger number of pieces.

REVERSI

This game of strategy was invented in the late nineteenth century and has recently been revived.
Board Bought boards have 64 playing circles with interconnecting lines. Reversi can also be played on the 64 squares of a standard checkers board.

Pieces 64 pieces are needed. Each piece must have two easily distinguishable faces. Pieces can be improvised by:
a) sticking or drawing symbols (eg stars and circles) on the two faces of 64 checkers; or
b) sticking counters of two different colors (eg red and white) together to make a set of double-faced counters.
Before play starts the players decide which of them will play with which face of the pieces up.

Objective Play ends when there is a piece on every square; the winner is the player who has the most pieces with his face up at the end of the game.

Turns alternate. In his turn each player attempts to place one piece on the board with his color or symbol face up.

First four pieces Each player's first two plays must be in the center four squares of the board. Of the possible starting patterns, (**a**) is generally preferred by expert players.

Starting patterns

a

b

c

d

Taking After the first four pieces are placed, each player attempts to make one move in each turn.
Only taking moves are permitted, and if a player is unable to make a taking move he loses his turn. (Both players are, however, limited to a maximum of 32 plays.)
A taking move is made by positioning a piece so that:
a) it is in a square next to a square containing an opposition piece; and
b) it traps at least one opposition piece in a line in any direction between itself and another of the taker's pieces.
(In the example shown, reds could be positioned in the squares marked R and whites in those marked W).

When a piece is taken it is turned over to show the other player's symbol or color. A piece may be turned over many times during a game as it passes from one player to the other. Pieces are never removed from the board when they are taken.

Multiple takes By positioning a single piece a player may simultaneously take several pieces in more than one line (eg if a red were placed in the square marked T in the situation illustrated). Note that pieces may not be taken if a line is completed only when a piece is turned over.

Taking move

Multiple take

SALTA

This game was invented in about 1900 and takes its name name from *salta*, a Latin word meaning "jump."

Board The game is played on a continental checker board, 10 squares by 10.

Pieces There are two sets of 15 pieces. Each set is of a different color, eg red and white, and has pieces numbered 1 through 15. Sets can easily be made by drawing or sticking numbers on checkers pieces, though original sets have stars on pieces 1 through 5, moons on pieces 6 through 10, and suns on pieces 11 through 15.

Objective The game is won by the first player to move all his pieces onto the corresponding squares originally occupied by his opponent's pieces (eg white 4 onto the square that was occupied by red 4).

Start of play Players position their pieces as shown, with pieces 1 through 5 on the black squares of the first row, 6 through 10 on the second row, and 11 through 15 on the third row.

Starting position

Moves A player may make only one move in a turn. The following moves are permitted:
a) one square diagonally forward or backward, or
b) a jumping move diagonally forward or backward over one piece of either color that has a vacant square beyond it. Multiple jumps are not permitted in this game, and no

jumped piece is removed from the board.
If a player can make a jumping move rather than an ordinary move he must do so—hence the strategic importance of forcing a player to jump his pieces back toward his own starting line.

120-move rule Some players like to play to the 120-move rule.
By this rule, play automatically ends after 120 moves. Each of the players then calculates how many moves he would need to achieve his objective. The winner is the player who is nearest his objective when play ends.

CONQUEST

Conquest is an interesting game that can be played with checkers pieces on an improvised board.

Board The game is played on a checkered board with 81 squares (nine squares by nine).
The central nine squares, called the "fortress," are enclosed within a red line.

Pieces There are two sets of pieces, one for each player. Each set is of a different color and comprises eight ordinary pieces and one specially marked king.

Objective Players attempt to capture the central fortress according to one of the four possible plans of occupation (see illustration).
The plan for a particular game must always be agreed before play starts.

Start of play Players position their pieces as illustrated: in diagonally opposite corners of the board and with the kings surrounded by the ordinary pieces.

Turns alternate, and each player makes only one move at a turn.

Moving The only permitted move for any piece is one square diagonally forward or

backward (so that each piece stays on squares of the same color throughout the game) (**a**).

Exiling If a player traps an opponent's piece between two of his own pieces in a diagonal line (so that all three pieces are on the same color square) (**b**), the player may "exile" the trapped piece to any other square of the same color.

Starting position

Plans of occupation

Halma

Halma, which takes its name from a Greek word for a jump, was invented in England toward the end of the last century. It is a checkers type of game for two, three, or four persons. There are also halma solitaire problems to provide an interesting diversion for one player.

Starting position (a)

Starting position (b)

Moving

Solitaire

Solitaire solution

Board Halma is played on a board with 256 small squares, 16 along each side.
Heavy lines mark off "yards" in the board's corners. Each corner has a yard with 13 squares, and two diagonally opposite corners have an additional heavy line marking off a yard with 19 squares.

Pieces There are four sets of pieces—each of a different color. Two sets have 19 pieces and the other two only 13. The pieces may be:
a) small checkers or counters;
b) wooden or plastic cones;
c) wooden or plastic men resembling small chess pawns.

Forms of play The game may be played:
a) by two players;
b) by three or four players, each playing separately;
c) by four players, each with a partner.

Partnership halma can be played in two ways:
a) pairs are formed by players with pieces in adjacent yards;
b) pairs are formed by players with pieces in yards that are diagonally opposite.
(The second form provides more scope for partners to help each other.)

Objective Each player attempts to move his pieces from his own yard into the yard diagonally opposite. The game is won by the first player or pair to achieve this objective.

Start of play Starting positions vary with the forms of play:
a) when there are two players, each one takes a set of 19 pieces and positions them in the yards with 19 squares;
b) when there are three or four players, each one takes a set of 13 pieces and positions them in the yards with 13 squares.

Turns pass clockwise around the table if there are more than two players. A player may move only one piece in a turn.

Moving Pieces may be moved in any direction—straight or diagonally, forward or backward, to one side or the other.
Two types of move are permitted:
a) a "step"—by which a player moves a piece into an adjoining square;
b) a "hop"—by which a player moves a piece over a piece in an adjoining square into a vacant square directly behind it.
A player may hop over his own or another player's pieces, and all hopped pieces are left on the board.
A player may make several hops in one move, but may not combine steps and hops in a move.
There is no compulsion to make any hop.

HALMA SOLITAIRE
An interesting halma solitaire problem requires the player to place 19 pieces in one of the yards and then in 19 moves position them in a symmetrical figure across the board's diagonal.
This problem can be solved in several hundred ways, and the interest therefore derives from the variety of solutions. A fairly skillful player should be able to find 50 different solutions without too much difficulty.

Chinese checkers

Chinese checkers is a modern game derived from halma. It can be played by two to six persons, playing individually or with partners.

The board is made of metal, plastic, wood, or heavy card. The playing area is a six-pointed star, with holes or indentations to hold the pieces. Each of the star's points is a different color.

The pieces There are six sets of 15 pieces. Each set is the same color as one of the star's points.

The most common types of pieces are:
a) plastic pegs;
b) marbles.

Objective Players attempt to move their pieces into the opposite point. The game is won by the first player or pair to do so.

Start of play For a game between two players, each positions 15 pieces of appropriate colors in opposite points of the star (**a**).
When there are more than two players, each one positions 10 pieces in a point (**b**).
Partners usually take opposite points.

Turns Each player moves one piece in turn.

Moves may be made along any of the lines, ie in six directions.
Moves may be "steps" or "hops." A player may hop over his own or another player's pieces and may make several hops in one move. Steps and hops may not be combined in a single move. There is no compulsion to make a hop. All hopped pieces are left on the board.

Start (**a**)

Start (**b**)

Stepping

Hopping

Brax

Brax was invented in England in the late nineteenth century and can be played by two, three, or four players. Pieces are moved along colored lines on the board, and players attempt to capture all opposing pieces.

Red side

Blue side

"Braxing"

Moving

The board has short red and blue lines making the pattern illustrated. The lines form 64 squares (eight by eight), but all play is on the lines and on the points where the lines meet. There is no play within the squares.
There are numbered starting points along the board's edges.
The pieces are all identical in shape—seven red and seven blue. Each piece has one face plain and the other marked with a star.
Forms of play The basic game is for two players, but there are adaptations for three and four players.
The objective is to remove all enemy pieces from the board by capture.
Start of play Positions of pieces vary with the number of players.

Moving A player may move only one piece in a turn. Pieces are moved along the lines so that they come to rest at a point where two lines meet.
A piece may be moved in any direction, but may not be moved onto a point occupied by a piece belonging to the same side or over a point occupied by any piece of either side.
The distance a piece can be moved depends on the color of the line(s) on which it is moved:
a) a piece moving on a line of the opposing color may move only one space, ie from one point to the point immediately adjacent to it;
b) a piece moving on a line of its own color may move either one or two spaces as

the player wishes.
A piece moving two spaces may change direction in the course of that move (**c**), providing that it remains on a line of its own color and does not return to the point from which it started.
Capture A piece is captured when an opposing piece is moved to its point. A captured piece is immediately removed from the board.
"Braxing" A piece is said to "threaten" an opposing piece when it could capture it in one move—ie when it is one space away, or two spaces if it can reach the opposing piece along a line of its own color.
A player who threatens an opposing piece may call "brax" and so force his opponent to move that piece

immediately. The call must be made immediately after the threatening player has moved one of his own pieces.
If more than one piece is threatened when a player has called "brax," then the opposing player has the choice of which threatened piece to move. The threatening player may not then call "brax" again until after he has moved one of his own pieces.
When "brax" has been called, a threatened piece may move in any direction available to it. It may capture the piece threatening it, if that piece is within reach.
When one player has only one piece and the other player only two pieces left on the board, both players lose the right to brax.

BRAX FOR TWO PLAYERS

Pieces The game for two players is played with all 14 pieces, seven for each player. The pieces may be used with either face up.

Start of play Each player starts with his pieces on the points numbered 1 to 7 on his side of the board.

Play The players decide who will make the first move and then take alternate turns.

Red side

Only blue lines shown

Starting position

BRAX FOR FOUR PLAYERS

In the game for four players, two players act as allies against the other two. No consultation is allowed between allies.

Pieces Six red and six blue pieces are used. In each pair, one player uses three pieces with the star face up and his ally uses three pieces of the same color with the plain face up.

Start Each pair begins with the three plain pieces on points 1,2, and 3, and the three star pieces on points 8,9, and 10.

Play The players decide which pair will have the first move.

Turns are then in the order:
a) first pair, player with the plain pieces;
b) second pair, player with the plain pieces;
c) first pair, player with the star pieces;
d) second pair, player with the star pieces.

Retiring If a player's three pieces are all captured, he retires from the game and the remaining players continue to play in their regular order.

Braxing A player may brax only those opposing pieces that can move immediately after his move, and he can be braxed only by a piece that moves immediately before his move.

BRAX FOR THREE PLAYERS

In the game for three players, two players act as allies against the third. No consultation is allowed between allies.

Pieces The single player has five pieces of one color. The allies use six pieces of the other color: one player uses three pieces with the plain face up and his ally uses three with the star face up.

Start The single player starts with his pieces on points 1,2,3,4, and 5. The alliance player with the plain pieces positions them on points 1,2, and 3, and the player with the stars positions them on points 8,9, and 10.

Play The single player always plays first, followed by the alliance player with the plain pieces and then the alliance player with the starred pieces. At his turn the single player moves two pieces. He may not, however, move the same piece twice in one turn (and so may make only one move when he has only a single piece left on the board).

Retiring If an ally's three pieces are all captured, he retires from the game.

Braxing Because the single player has two moves, he may be braxed by both players. If one of his pieces is braxed he must move that piece before moving any other piece. If two of his pieces are braxed he must move both pieces in his turn, but in any order.

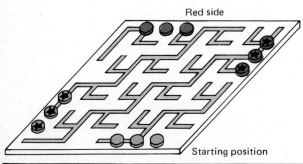

Red side

Starting position

Red side

Starting position

BRAX FOX AND GEESE

This variant of brax makes an interesting game for two players.

Pieces One player uses one piece of one color (the "braxer"), and the other player uses five pieces of the other color (the "enemy").

Start of play The braxer is placed on point 4 on one side of the board. The enemy pieces are placed on points 11,1,4,7, and 12 on the other side of the board.

Objective The player with the enemy pieces attempts to move any one of them across the board onto any one of points 11,1,4,7, or 12. The player with the braxer wins the game if he captures all the enemy pieces before any one of them reaches one of the winning points.

Sequence of play The braxer moves first, and moves again every time an enemy piece has moved. The enemy pieces always move in the sequence: 11,1,4,7, and 12 (the numbers being taken from the pieces' starting points). For convenience, the enemy pieces can all begin the game with the same face up and each one can be reversed each time it is moved.

Moves The braxer moves in the usual way. The enemy can only move forward in a straight line, and must always move as far as the colors of the lines allow, ie two spaces when on their own lines, and one space on lines of the opposing color.

Capture When an enemy piece is captured, the remaining enemy pieces continue to move in their original sequence. The braxer continues to have one turn for every move by an enemy piece.

Braxing Although the enemy pieces can only move in a straight line forward, they threaten all points within their reach in any direction— as in the standard game. The braxer cannot move to, and must move from, any point that they threaten.

When the braxer braxes an enemy piece, the braxed piece must retreat in a straight line as far as the color of the line allows. This does not count as an enemy turn and is followed by a normal move before the braxer's next turn.

Red side

Starting position

Chess

Originating in the East over a thousand years ago, chess has developed into one of the most popular of all games. Although it is a highly complex and sophisticated game, chess can also be enjoyed at a simpler level by inexperienced players. It is a game of strategy for two people, with each piece—from the king to the pawn—representing units in an army.

Objective The objective of each player is to capture his opponent's king.
Unlike the other pieces, the king cannot be removed from the board; it is held to be captured when it has been "checkmated" (see section on check and checkmating).
The player forcing checkmate wins the game—even if the pieces he has left on the board are outnumbered by the opponent's pieces.
A player, seeing the imminent checkmate of his king or recognizing a losing situation, will often resign. The player forcing the resignation wins the game.

Moves Each kind of piece can move a certain distance in one or more directions.
Moves are limited by conditions on the board at the time of play.
A piece may move to any square within its range, provided that:
a) the square is unoccupied by a piece of its own color;
b) if the square is occupied by an opponent's piece, that piece is first "captured" and removed from the board;
c) it does not. with the exception of the knight's move, cross a square that is occupied by a piece of either color.

The board is a large square divided into eight rows of eight squares each.
The squares are alternately dark and light colored (usually black and white).
The board is placed between facing players so that each has a white square at the near righthand corner.
The rows of squares running vertically between facing players are called "files"; those running at right angles to the files are called "ranks."
Rows of squares of the same color that touch only at their corners are called "diagonals."

Pieces At the start of a game 32 pieces are positioned on the board. 16 of these pieces are dark in color, 16 light.
They are called black and white respectively and make up the two sides.
A player's side is made up of six different kinds of pieces.
These are—in descending order of importance: king, queen, rook (castle), bishop, knight, pawn.
Each player has one king and one queen; two rooks, bishops, and knights; and eight pawns.

File

Rank

Diagonal

Start of play

Individual pieces and moves

King

The king is the most important piece on the board, and its capture by checkmate ends the game. It is represented diagrammatically by a crown.
The king can move one square in any direction, provided that this square is not one where he can be taken.
Opposing kings can never stand on touching squares.

Castling The only time that a king may move more than one square is in the "castling" move involving the rook.
A player can make a castling move only once in a game.
The move is made to produce a defensive position around the king and to allow a rook to come into play. It comprises:

1) moving the king two squares to left or right from its original position and toward one of the rooks; then
2) transferring that rook to the square over which the king has just passed.
Castling is permitted only if:
a) neither the king nor the rook involved has moved from its original position;
b) no piece of either color is between the king and the rook involved in the castling move;
c) the square that the king must cross is not under attack by an opponent's piece.

All other pieces have a different attacking value, directly related to the number of squares to which they can move.

King's move

Castling

The queen, represented diagrammatically by a coronet, is the most powerful attacking piece. It can move to any square on the rank, file, or either of the two diagonals on which it is placed.

The rook, sometimes called the castle, is represented diagrammatically by a tower. It can move to any square on the rank or file on which it is placed.

In addition, either one of the rooks in each side may be involved with the king in the castling move.

The bishop, represented diagrammatically by a miter, can move to any square on the diagonal on which it is placed. In each side, therefore, each of the two bishops is restricted to moving on the diagonal of the same color as that on which it was originally placed.

The knight is represented diagrammatically by a horse's head. In a single move it travels two squares in any direction along a rank or file, then one square at right angles to that rank or file.

Thus whenever a knight moves from a black square it must land on a white square—and vice versa.

In moving, a knight may cross a square occupied by any other piece; it is the only piece allowed to do this.

Queen's move

Queen

Rook's move

Rook

Bishop's move

Bishop

Knight's move

Knight

The pawn, represented diagrammatically by a small ball on a collared stem, has the most restricted movements of any piece: it can only move forward.

In its opening move (**a**) a pawn may be moved forward either one or two squares on the file that it occupies. Thereafter, a pawn can only move forward one square at a time, except when capturing. Unlike other pieces, a pawn does not capture in the same way that it moves. Instead of capturing in a forward direction, it does so diagonally —taking a piece that occupies either of the two squares diagonally next to it (**b**).

In addition, a pawn may capture an opposing pawn *"en passant"* (in passing) (**c**).

If the opposing pawn moves forward two squares in its opening move, the square that it crosses is open to attack as though the pawn had only advanced one square.

Thus the capturing pawn may make its usual taking move (ie one square diagonally forward) onto the square just crossed by the opposing pawn —the opposing pawn is then considered "captured" and is removed from the board. (The *en passant* capture must be made immediately the opposing pawn has moved forward two squares.)

Pawn promotion Whenever a pawn reaches the end of the file on which it is moving (ie it reaches the far side of the board) it must—in the same move—be exchanged for a queen, rook, bishop, or knight.

The choice of piece is made by the player promoting the pawn, and is made without taking into account the number and kind of pieces on the board.

Theoretically, therefore, a player could have up to nine queens on the board. The effect of the promoted piece on play is immediate.

Pawn's move

Pawn

Capture "en passant"

Pawn capture

Capture

Meeting check

Starting procedure
Players draw for sides, and position their pieces on the board. The player drawing white makes the first move, and thereafter the players move alternately.

Play
The position of the pieces at the start of play is such that each player can move only a knight or a pawn. After the first move by each player, more pieces can come into play.

In moving their pieces, players are governed not only by the movements laid down for each piece but also by rules that affect how pieces can be handled.

If a player touches a piece that can legitimately be moved, then he must move that piece —unless he has previously warned his opponent that he is adjusting the piece on its square. The usual warning used is "*J'adoube*" (I adjust). Similarly, if a player touches an enemy piece that can be taken, the touched piece must be captured unless the player has given a prior warning.

A move is completed when:
a) a player's hand has left a piece after it has been moved to a vacant square;
b) a player, having captured a piece and placed his attacking piece on the captured square, removes his hand from the piece;
c) in castling, a player's hand has left the rook (once the king has been moved, the castling move must always be completed);
d) in pawn promotion, a player's hand has left the piece that replaces the pawn.

Phases of play
Chess players commonly divide a game into three phases: opening game, middle game, and end game.

These phases are not clear-cut divisions—they simply reflect the strategies and tactics employed.

1) In the opening game, both players position their pieces into what each considers to be an advantageous situation. Castling moves are usually made during this phase.
2) In the middle game, players attempt to capture enemy pieces, thereby reducing the opponent's attacking material.

However, as the main objective is to checkmate the opponent's king, moves or captures should not be made unless they weaken the opponent's defense of his king. The player should also beware of making moves that jeopardize his own position.
3) In the end game, players attempt to checkmate the opponent's king.

If, during this phase, a player has little attacking material, he will attempt—where possible —to promote a pawn to a more powerful piece.

Check and checkmate
Whenever a king is attacked by an opposing piece, the king is said to be "in check."
The check must be met on the following move by either:
a) moving the king one square in any direction onto a square that is not attacked;
b) capturing the piece that is checking the king; or
c) interposing a piece between the king and the attacking piece (if the king is checked by an opponent's knight, it is not possible to intercept the check in this way).
A piece that intercepts a check can—in the same move —give check to the opposing king.

Chess notation
is the method by which moves in a game are recorded.
Two of the systems officially recognized are: the descriptive system and the algebraic system.

Descriptive system
Each piece is represented by its initial letter, but the knight may be represented by either Kt or N.
With the exceptions of the pawns and the king and queen, pieces are further distinguished by the side of the board on which they stand:
pieces to the right of the king take the prefix K;
pieces to the left of the queen take the prefix Q.
Thus the rook to the left of the queen is a queen's rook and is represented as QR.
Each file is represented by the initials of the pieces that occupy the squares at either end.
The eight files (from left to right for white, and inversely for black) are represented as follows:
QR, QKt, QB, Q, K, KB, KKt, KR.

Black

QR1	QKt1	QB1	Q1	K1	KB1	KKt1	KR1
QR2	QKt2	QB2	Q2	K2	KB2	KKt2	KR2
QR3	QKt3	QB3	Q3	K3	KB3	KKt3	KR3
QR4	QKt4	QB4	Q4	K4	KB4	KKt4	KR4
QR5	QKt5	QB5	Q5	K5	KB5	KKt5	KR5
QR6	QKt6	QB6	Q6	K6	KB6	KKt6	KR6
QR7	QKt7	QB7	Q7	K7	KB7	KKt7	KR7
QR8	QKt8	QB8	Q8	K8	KB8	KKt8	KR8

QR8	QKt8	QB8	Q8	K8	KB8	KKt8	KR8
QR7	QKt7	QB7	Q7	K7	KB7	KKt7	KR7
QR6	QKt6	QB6	Q6	K6	KB6	KKt6	KR6
QR5	QKt5	QB5	Q5	K5	KB5	KKt5	KR5
QR4	QKt4	QB4	Q4	K4	KB4	KKt4	KR4
QR3	QKt3	QB3	Q3	K3	KB3	KKt3	KR3
QR2	QKt2	QB2	Q2	K2	KB2	KKt2	KR2
QR1	QKt1	QB1	Q1	K1	KB1	KKt1	KR1

White

KKt – KR3

Each rank is numbered from 1 to 8; both players count from their own ends of the board. Consequently each square has two names: one name as seen from white's side, and one from black's.
For example, QKt3 (white) equals QKt6 (black).
A move is described by the initial letter of the piece moved and the square to which it moved.
For example, the king's knight move to the third square of the king's rook file is represented by KKt–KR3.
If two pieces of the same kind can move to the same square, both the square from which the piece moved and the square it arrived at are given.

For example, KKt (KB4)–KR3 means that the knight on the fourth square of the king's bishop file made the move, although another knight on the board could have reached the same square in the same move.

Other explanatory abbreviations are:
a) O–O or Castles K denotes a castling move involving the KR.
b) O–O–O or Castles Q denotes a castling move involving the QR.
c) x denotes captures.
d) ch or + denotes check.
e) ! denotes well played.
f) ? denotes a bad move.

If the check cannot be met then the king is deemed "in checkmate" or simply "mate." When a checking or checkmating move is made, it is customary for the player making such a move to declare "Check" or "Checkmate" as appropriate.

Winning A player wins if he:
a) checkmates his opponent's king; or
b) forces his opponent to resign.
Checkmate may be made, or a player may resign, at any time during the course of the game.

Drawn game Many games of chess do not end in a victory for either player. A game is deemed drawn in any of the following cases.
a) When the player whose turn it is to move can make no legal move (a situation known as "stalemate").
b) When neither player has sufficient pieces to force checkmate.
c) When a player can check the opponent's king indefinitely but cannot checkmate it (a situation called "perpetual check").
d) When no capture or pawn move has been made by either side during 50 successive moves of each player.
e) When the same position recurs three times, always when it is the same player's turn to move. The right to claim a draw then belongs either to the player who is in a position to play a move leading to such repetition (provided that he declares his intention of making this move); or to the player who must reply to a move by which the repeated position is made.
f) When both players agree to call the game drawn.

Illegal positioning If an illegal move is made during the course of a game, the pieces are set up as they were immediately before the illegal move. If this is impossible, the game is annulled.
If pieces are accidentally displaced and cannot be correctly repositioned or if the initial position of the pieces was incorrect, the game is also annulled.
If the chessboard is found to have been incorrectly placed, the pieces on the board are transferred to a correctly placed board in the same positioning as when the error was discovered and play then continues.

Competition chess is strictly controlled. It differs from the informal game in the following ways.
a) Each player must write down every move made.
b) Each player must make a certain number of moves in a given time (time is kept by a special control clock).
c) If a game is adjourned, the player whose turn it is must write down his move and place it in a sealed envelope, together with his and his opponent's scoresheets. The sealed move is made on the resumption of play.
d) It is forbidden to distract or worry an opponent; ask or receive advice from a third party; use any written or printed notes; or to analyze the game on another chessboard.
e) A designated person must direct the competition. The competition director must ensure that the rules of play are strictly observed—he may impose penalties on any player who infringes these rules.
(These notes on competition chess are an outline only. The official international governing body—the Fédération Internationale des Echecs (FIDE)—lays down the full

Examples of checkmate

rules and interprets any problems arising in the game. Its decision is binding on all affiliated federations.)

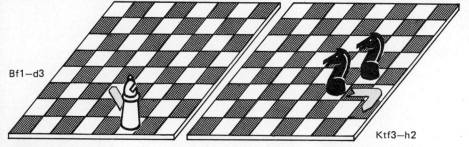

Bf1—d3

Ktf3—h2

Algebraic system
Each piece, with the exception of the pawns, is represented by its initial letter (and the knight by Kt or N). The pawns are not specially indicated.
The eight files (reading from left to right for white) are represented by the letters from a to h.
The eight ranks (counting from white's first rank) are numbered from 1 to 8. Initially, the white pieces stand on ranks 1 and 2, and the black pieces on ranks 7 and 8. Thus each square is represented by the combination of a letter and a number.

A move is described by the initial letter of the piece moved and the square from which it moved, plus the square at which it arrived.
For example, a bishop moving from square f1 to square d3 is represented by Bf1—d3 or in a shortened form by Bd3.
If two pieces of the same kind can move to the same square, both the square from which the piece moved and the square it arrived at are given.
For example, two knights stand on the squares f3 and g4; if the knight on f3 makes the move to h2, the move is written Ktf3—h2 or in the shortened form by Ktf—h2.

The other abbreviations used in the algebraic system are the same as those for the descriptive system, with the following additions:
a) : or x denotes captures;
b) ‡ denotes checkmate.

a8	b8	c8	d8	e8	f8	g8	h8	Black
a7	b7	c7	d7	e7	f7	g7	h7	
a6	b6	c6	d6	e6	f6	g6	h6	
a5	b5	c5	d5	e5	f5	g5	h5	
a4	b4	c4	d4	e4	f4	g4	h4	
a3	b3	c3	d3	e3	f3	g3	h3	
a2	b2	c2	d2	e2	f2	g2	h2	
a1	b1	c1	d1	e1	f1	g1	h1	White

Shogi

Shogi is the Japanese member of the chess family. It is widely popular there and supports professional players. There have been many forms of shogi since its introduction in about the eighth century. A feature peculiar to shogi since the sixteenth century is that captured pieces become members of the capturing side and can be returned to any position on the board.

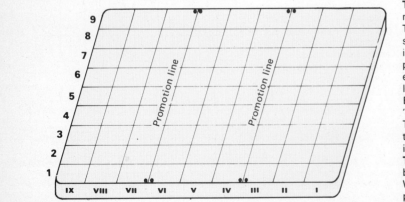

The board is nine squares by nine, giving 81 squares in all. The "squares" are in fact slightly oblong, and the board is placed between the two players so that they are facing each other down its longer length.
Black dots mark the two "promotion lines."
The notation used for referring to squares on the shogi board is shown.

The pieces Each player begins with 20 pieces. Using Western chess names as far as possible and with Western notation in brackets, these pieces are:
a king (K);
a rook (R);
a bishop (B);
two gold generals (G);
two silver generals (S);
two knights (Kt);

two lances (L);
nine pawns (P).
Shogi pieces are all the same shape: they are distinguished only by size and by the Japanese characters written on them.
Shogi pieces are also all the same color—although we have color-coded them for easy recognition in our diagrams. The two players' pieces are distinguished on the board by being pointed toward the opposing player.

The objective is to "checkmate" the enemy king. A king is checkmated when, in the next enemy turn, it could be captured either on its present square or on any square to which it could move.

Pieces and their moves
Pieces are only permitted to move on the board in certain ways. Each piece has a different move:
a) the king can move one square in any direction;
b) the gold general can move one square in any direction except diagonally backward;
c) the silver general can move one square directly forward or one square in any diagonal direction;
d) the pawn can only move one square directly forward (unlike the pawn in chess, the pawn in shogi makes the same move when capturing);
e) the knight can move, in a single turn, one square directly forward and then one square diagonally forward (the square directly forward may be vacant or occupied, but if it is occupied by an enemy piece that piece is not captured);

f) the rook can move an unlimited number of squares in any direction except diagonally;
g) the bishop can move an unlimited number of squares in any diagonal direction;
h) the lance can move an unlimited number of squares but only directly forward.
Pieces that can move an unlimited number of squares (the rook, bishop, and lance) must halt:
if they reach a piece belonging to their own side (in which case they can go no farther than the last vacant square before they reach that piece); or
if they reach an enemy piece (in which case the enemy piece is captured).

Value of pieces Players trying out a game of shogi will probably be helped by a rough guide to the value of the pieces.
As a game ends when a king is checkmated, the king is obviously the most important piece.
The rook is the most powerful piece on the board and its importance increases as the game progresses.
The bishop is almost as powerful as the rook and is most useful in the game opening.
The gold and silver generals are the intermediate pieces, with the gold slightly more useful especially in defense.
The knight and lance are minor pieces, roughly equal in value and of real use only in attack.
Pawns are of very little importance and, unlike in chess, a one pawn advantage is very seldom significant.

Pawn
Lance
Knight
Silver general
Gold general
Bishop
Rook
King

Moves

52

Start of play

Capture

Promotion

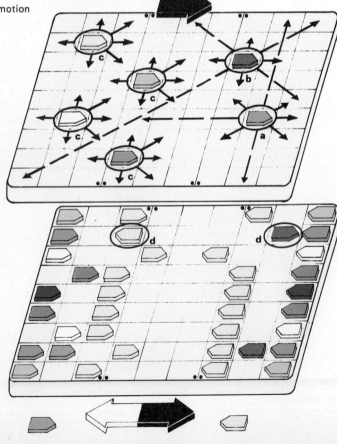

Start of play The pieces are placed on the board as shown. When a game is being described, the players may conveniently be referred to as "black" and "white," even though their pieces are not distinguished by color. Pointers at the side of the board indicate each player's direction of play. Players usually draw lots, and the player drawing black has the first turn.

Play The two players make alternate moves. In a move a player may either:
a) move one of his pieces on the board to a vacant square;
b) capture an enemy piece; or
c) replace a previously captured piece on the board.

Capture A player captures an enemy piece by moving one of his own pieces to the square occupied by that piece. When a player captures a piece it becomes part of his own side, and in any future turn can be returned to the board on any vacant square. (In the capture illustrated it is black's turn to play. He moves by capturing the white pawn with his bishop.)

Promotion When a piece crosses the far "promotion line," its powers of movement may be changed if its player wishes. Promoted pieces move as follows:
a) a rook keeps its original move and adds the power to move one square at a time in any diagonal direction;
b) a bishop keeps its original move and adds the power to move one square at a time in any non-diagonal direction;
c) a silver general, a lance, a knight, and a pawn are all promoted to gold generals. A gold general does not acquire any new powers when it is promoted.
In play, promotion is shown by turning the piece over to expose a different Japanese character underneath.
In diagrams of a game, promotion is shown by drawing a circle around the original piece (**d**).
Once a piece has been promoted, it retains its new powers even if it retreats so that it is no longer beyond the far promotion line.
A piece receives its promotion in the turn in which it crosses the promotion line, or in any subsequent turn, according to

the player's wishes. Its new powers become available to it in the next turn after promotion.
A lance or pawn that reaches the last rank must be promoted; so must a knight that reaches the last two ranks. (Since these pieces cannot be moved backward, promotion is essential if they are to be moved again.)
A promoted piece loses its promotion when captured. For example, if black captures a promoted white pawn, it joins his side as a pawn not as a gold general. (He can, of course, play in such a way that it is again promoted.)

Attacking the king A king is "in check" when it is exposed to capture—ie when it is on a square onto which the opposing player could move one of his pieces in his next turn.

If a player's king is in check he must immediately escape check:
a) by moving the king to a square that is not being attacked;
b) by taking the attacking piece with the king; or
c) by taking the attacking piece with another piece. Whatever he does, however, his turn must not end with his still being in check from any enemy piece.

It is "checkmate" when a player's king is exposed to capture and there is no move that he can make that does not leave it so exposed.

Use of captured pieces A captured piece is removed from the board and becomes the property of the player who made the capture.

In any turn, instead of moving a piece already on the board, a player may place a piece that he has captured on the board on any vacant square. This is called a "drop." The piece is placed so that it points in the same direction as the player's other pieces.

A dropped piece, placed on the board beyond the far promotion line, does not receive promotion as soon as it is placed on the board but must first make a move on the board. Therefore a player must not place a pawn or a lance on the last rank, or a knight on one of the last two ranks, since these pieces would not be able to move again.

There are two restrictions on pawn drops:
a player must not place a pawn on the same file as one of his own unpromoted pawns;
a player cannot checkmate the enemy king by placing a pawn on the square directly in front of the king.

(It is because of the power of the drop as a maneuver that the king in shogi almost always stays in one corner of the board surrounded by a heavy guard.)

Examples of checkmate
a) Basic checkmate: the gold general moves to 9viii and so mates the king. (If the gold general moved to 8viii the king would have been in check but the gold general, unprotected by the bishop, would have been taken in the king's next move.)
b) Checkmate by promoting: the knight moves to 6viii, is promoted, and so mates the king.
c) Checkmate by not promoting: white chooses not to promote his silver general, moves it to 2ix, keeps it unpromoted, and so mates the king. (If the silver general had been promoted to gold general it would have been unable to attack along the reverse diagonal.)
d) Checkmate by promoting and then retreating: the promoted rook returns from beyond the promotion line to 2iv and so mates the king. (The rook needs the additional power given by promotion in order to mate.)
e) Checkmate by forced exchange: white's silver general moves to 9ii, giving check and forcing black's silver general to take it; black's silver general is in turn taken by white's gold general, which, covered by white's lance, then mates black's king.

Checkmate by drop
a) Black takes white's gold general with his bishop, promotes it, and so gives check. White's king must take black's bishop to escape check.
b) Each player now has a captured piece in hand alongside the board: black has the gold general and white the bishop. Black drops the gold general onto 8ii—and so mates white's king.

Examples of checkmate

Checkmate by drop

Go (Wei-ch'i)

Go is thought to be one of the oldest games in existence. It originated in China over 3000 years ago (its Chinese name is wei-ch'i) and was later adopted by Japan and other oriental countries. It is considered one of the greatest games of strategic skill. Two players compete to secure as much of the playing area as possible.

Pieces There are two sets of stones: a set of 181 black stones and a set of 180 white stones (361 in all). Each player has one set.
The stones are disk shaped, about $\frac{7}{8}$in in diameter, and $\frac{1}{8}-\frac{1}{2}$in thick.
The stones may be kept in a lacquered box (go-tsubo) or other container.

Board The traditional Japanese go table (go-ban) is made of wood and is stained yellow. It is about $17\frac{1}{2}$in long, 16in wide, and 4–5in thick, and has four legs roughly 3in high.
The playing area (about $16\frac{1}{2}$in by 15in) is marked out in black lacquer in a grid pattern of 19 parallel lines and 19 lines at right angles to these, forming a total of 361 intersections or points.
The intersections of the fourth, tenth, and sixteenth lines in each direction are marked by dots and are known as handicap points.
The two players kneel opposite each other, at the shorter sides of the table.

Objective By the positioning of his stones on the board, each player aims to surround more unoccupied territory and enemy stones than his opponent.
Order of play Players take alternate turns. The opening move is usually made by the player with the black stones. (Players take it in turn to play black unless there is a known disparity of playing skill—see handicapping section.)
A turn consists of placing a stone on an unoccupied point. Except in the "ko situation," a stone may be placed on any vacant point.
Once in position the stone is not moved again during the game unless it is captured, in which case it is removed from the board.

Handicapping The player taking the first turn is at an advantage.
Black (the opening turn) normally alternates between players. If there is a known disparity of playing skill or if one player wins three consecutive games, the weaker player may be allowed to keep the black stones.
If further handicapping is necessary, the weaker player may place two or more of his stones on the dotted handicap points before the game starts (see the table below), and the opening move then goes to the player with the white stones. Should the stronger player continue to win, the number of handicap stones may be increased.

Table showing positions for handicap stones

Handicap	Positions
2 stones	D4, Q16
3 stones	D4, Q4, Q16
4 stones	D4, D16, Q4, Q16
5 stones	D4, D16, K10, Q4, Q16
6 stones	D4, D10, D16, Q4, Q10, Q16
7 stones	D4, D10, D16, K10, Q4, Q10, Q16
8 stones	D4, D10, D16, K4, K16, Q4, Q10, Q16
9 stones	D4, D10, D16, K4, K10, K16, Q4, Q10, Q16

Playing procedure At the beginning of the game the board is empty except for any handicap stones.

Stones must be placed on the points (line intersections) and not on the squares formed by the lines.

Each player places his stones to form connected groups or chains in such a way as to surround as many vacant points and opponent's stones as possible.

Should all the points adjacent to one or more stones be occupied by stones of the other color, the former stone or group of stones is captured and removed from the board. (Adjacent points are those that are linked directly to a point by a line, and not diagonally.)

It is possible to win a game without capturing any stones, since the objective is territorial gain.

Explanation of diagrams
1) Playing area and standard go notation.
2) Capture of single stones.
3) Capture of groups of stones: a white stone played onto the dotted position would capture the black group attacked.
4a) and **5a**) Black cannot play onto the point marked with a cross, as the stone would be immediately captured (the arrowed point is vacant—white is not completely surrounded).
4b) and **5b**) Black can play onto the dotted point because the play puts the white stones out of contact with any empty point. The white stones are captured and removed. All black stones remain.
6a) and **6b**) A *ko* situation. In (a) a black stone placed on the crossed point captures the white stone; in (b) a white stone replaced on the captured point would recapture the black stone.
6c) A *seki* situation. Neither player can place his stone on the point marked with the cross without losing his formation.

Ko situations A *ko* (threat) situation is one that can be repeated indefinitely.
In *ko* situations the second player may not recapture until he has made at least one move elsewhere on the board. (Forcing play at other parts of the board is therefore important.)
A single *ko* situation may involve many stones. If there are three *ko* situations on a board at any one time, the game is declared drawn.

Seki situations A *seki* (deadlock) situation exists on any part of the board where opposing groups are so placed that neither player can occupy an uncontrolled point without losing his own pieces.
Seki situations are left untouched until the end of the game, and all free points in them are disregarded in scoring.

Dame points are vacant points between territories that cannot be played to with benefit by either side.
Dame points are left untouched until the end of the game, and then disregarded in scoring.

© DIAGRAM

Simplified 9x9 board

1

2

3

4

5

Prohibitions No move may be made that causes repetition of a position formed earlier in the game.

A stone must not remain on the board if it is entirely surrounded by enemy stones. A stone must not be played onto a point that is completely surrounded by stones of another color, unless the move causes the immediate capture of enemy stones.

End of play The game ends when both players agree that there are no further advantages to be gained by either side.

If only one player considers the game to be over, his opponent may continue to make moves until he too is satisfied that no points or stones remain to be secured.

(The first player may continue play, if he wishes, until both players agree that the game is over. But he may not resume play once he has actually missed a turn.)

Scoring An imaginary board, nine lines by nine lines, has been used to illustrate the basic scoring process. (It should be thought of as a simplified complete board, not as a section of a board.)

1) At the end of play all stones left in enemy territory are ruled captured.

2) These captured stones are removed from the board and added to each player's collection of captured enemy stones.

3) Any vacant points in neutral and *seki* situations have stones placed on them to discount them in the scoring. Either player may use his unused stones for this purpose.

4) In order to facilitate counting, black places all the white stones he has captured on vacant points in white's territory and white places all the captured black stones on vacant points in black's territory.

5) The number of vacant points left in each territory is counted.

Result The winner is the player with the larger number of vacant points left in his territory. He scores the difference between his own and his opponent's count. The game is tied if both players have an equal number of points.

GO-MOKU

This is a straightforward game played on a go board. It originated in Japan and is sometimes called go-bang or spoil five.

Players It is a game for two players.

Board A go board is used.

Pieces Each player has a set of 100 stones: one set black and the other white.

Objective Players aim to position five stones so that they form a straight line (horizontally, vertically, or diagonally).

Play The board is empty at the start of the game, and black has the opening move.

The players take it in turns to place a stone on any point (line intersection).

Once a stone has been placed it may not be moved again until the end of the game.

If all the stones are used up before either player has succeeded in forming a "five," the game may either be declared drawn, or the players may take it in turns to move one stone one point in a horizontal or vertical direction until a "five" is formed.

HASAMI SHOGI

Hasami shogi is an interesting Japanese game that can be played on a go board.

Players It is a game for two players.

The board is nine squares by nine. A quarter of a go board is generally used—but note that play is on the squares not the points.

Pieces Each player has a set of 18 stones: one set black and the other white.

The objective is to capture all the opposing stones.

Start of play Each player places his stones on his two home rows.

Play Players take alternate turns. A player may move only one stone in a turn.

Moves All moves must be forward, backward, or to the side. No moves may be diagonal. A stone may:

a) move into an adjacent square;

b) jump over a stone, of either set, into a vacant square beyond it.

Jumped stones are not removed from the board. Double jumps are not permitted.

Capture A stone is captured if an opponent's move traps it between two opposing stones. A stone is not captured if it is flanked diagonally by opposing stones.

A stone is not captured if it moves into a vacant square between two enemy stones.

A stone is captured if an enemy move traps it in a corner of the board.

Hasami shogi: starting position

Moves

Hex

Hex is a game for two players invented by a Dane, Piet Hein. Hex sets are available in some places, but the game can also be played with improvised equipment. Each player tries to form an unbroken line of pieces between his two sides of the board.

The board has a diamond-shaped playing area made up of adjoining hexagons. Two opposite sides of the board belong to black; the other two to white.

The pieces are all identical in shape, and are in two sets of equal number, one colored black and one white. The highest number of pieces that a player can require for a game is 61; usually he will need far fewer.

Objective The game is won by the first player to place his pieces so that they form a line joining his two sides of the board.

The line does not have to be straight, but it must be unbroken. Corner hexagons belong to both players, and either player may use them as hexagons touching his sides of the board.

Play Each player takes one set of pieces.

The first player places one of his pieces on the board, on any hexagon he chooses. Turns then alternate, with each player placing one of his pieces on any unoccupied hexagon.

Pieces may not be moved once they have been placed on the board.

Making a line

Winning position

Solitaire board games

Solitaire board games are an excellent diversion for one person. Board solitaire originated in France, where it is said to have been invented by an imprisoned nobleman. It was introduced into England in the late 1700s and has since spread to other parts of the world.

The objective of some solitaire games is to clear the board of all the pieces; in other games the player tries to position the pieces in a specific pattern.

Equipment Solitaire is played with a special board and a set of pegs or marbles made of ivory, bone, wood, or plastic. The traditional French board is octagonal and has 37 holes to accommodate the same number of pegs.
Traditional English boards are circular and have 33 hollows to hold 33 marbles. A channel running around the edge of the board holds pieces eliminated from the game.
Some solitaire games require all the pieces—others only a certain number of them. The pieces are positioned before the start of play.
(The boards illustrated have been numbered, so that the solutions to the different games can be given.)

Play Pieces are moved in the same manner in all solitaire games.
Each peg or marble is "jumped" over an adjoining piece to an empty hole beyond—the piece that has been jumped over is then removed from the board. Pieces may only be moved horizontally or vertically.

Result A game is considered won only if its objective has been exactly met. For example, the standard game is a success only if the board has been completely cleared of all but one of the pieces.
Although some games can be won by more than one method, a player will usually have to make numerous attempts until he has worked out a winning solution.

English board

French board

Moving

STANDARD SOLITAIRE

The objective of the basic solitaire game is the same whichever type of board is used.

The player tries to clear the board so that at the end of the game only one piece is left—either in the central hole or in some other hole predetermined by the player.

Play starts from the center of the board, after the middle piece has been removed.

It is vital that no pieces are left isolated from the others during play, as they cannot then be cleared.

If the player wishes, the board can be cleared from some other chosen starting point—leaving the center hole filled and removing a piece from elsewhere on the board in order to make a starting space.

Starting position

Starting position

SOLITAIRE VARIANTS

There are numerous variations of board solitaire, particularly for play on a French board. A player may wish to devise a variant of his own—which will require patience, persistence, and plenty of time. Every move of every attempt to make a certain pattern must be noted until an exact solution has been found. The following are a selection of existing solitaire games.

THE CROSS

The cross is played using only nine pieces, positioned as shown.

The object is to remove eight of the nine pieces from the board, leaving only one at the center.

(The cross can be played on either the French or the English board.)

The cross: English start

THE CORSAIR

At the start of the game all the 37 holes of a French board are filled. Any one peg at an angle of the board is then removed (ie 1, 3, 15, 29, 37, 35, 23, or 9).

The objective is to remove all the pieces except one—which should end up in the hole diametrically opposite the starting hole.

For example, if the game were begun at hole 37 the last peg should be in hole 1.

THE OCTAGON

Octagon is a game for play on a French board.

All the holes except those at the angles of the board are filled (ie not 1, 3, 15, 29, 37, 35, 23, and 9).

The player tries to end the game so that only one piece—at the center of the board—remains.

The world: solution

PATTERN FORMING GAMES

Many pattern forming games are designed for play on a French board.

Those illustrated all begin with all 37 pieces in position. The central piece is then removed, and the player tries to end the game by forming the patterns shown.

The apostles: solution

The letter E: solution

The cross: French start

The corsair: start

The octagon: start

Solutions

Standard solitaire (English)	The octagon
5—17	27—37
12—10	31—33
3—11	37—27
18—6	20—33
1—3	22—20
3—11	19—32
30—18	33—31
27—25	30—32
24—26	36—26
13—27	17—30
27—25	26—24
22—24	30—17
31—23	34—21
16—28	21—19
33—31	18—20
31—23	16—18
4—16	8—21
7—9	21—19
10—8	7—20
21—7	11—25
7—9	20—18
24—10	25—11
10—8	11—13
8—22	2—12
22—24	13—11
24—26	10—12
19—17	4—6
16—18	6—19
11—25	
26—24	**The world**
29—17	32—19
	30—32
The cross (French)	17—30
12—2	28—26
26—12	25—27
17—19	14—28
19—6	34—21
21—19	32—34
2—12	4—17
12—26	6—4
32—19	18—5
(English)	13—11
10—4	5—18
24—10	27—13
15—17	7—20
17—5	
19—17	**The letter E**
4—10	32—19
10—24	34—32
29—17	20—33
	29—27
The corsair	33—20
35—37	36—26
26—36	30—32
25—35	26—36
23—25	18—31
34—32	20—18
20—33	7—20
37—27	15—13
7—20	20—7
20—33	22—20
18—31	6—19
35—25	4—6
5—18	18—5
18—31	23—25
29—27	16—17
22—20	9—11
15—13	2—12
16—18	8—6
9—11	12—2
20—7	
7—5	**The apostles**
4—6	32—19
18—5	28—26
1—11	37—27
33—20	35—37
20—18	25—35
18—5	27—25
5—7	24—26
36—26	11—25
30—32	25—27
32—19	16—18
19—6	19—17
2—12	6—19
8—6	4—6
12—2	17—4
3—1	2—12
	8—6
	2—7
	6—8
	22—20
	15—13
	12—14
	27—13
	13—15

© DIAGRAM

Dominoes

Games with dominoes are played in many countries all over the world. They are now particularly popular in Latin America. It is thought that dominoes may have been brought from China to Europe in the fourteenth century. Certainly domino games were played in Italy in the eighteenth century. In most Western games players add matching dominoes to a pattern or "layout" formed in the center of the table.

Suits Dominoes belong to different suits according to the number of spots on each of their halves.
There is a suit for each number, a blank suit, and a doubles suit. "Mixed number" dominoes belong to two number suits or to a number suit and the blank suit. Doubles belong to one number suit and to the doubles suit.

General features of play
Western domino games are characterized by the principle of matching and joining dominoes end to end.
In some games, players add dominoes to either end of a line of dominoes.
More common, are games in which players may build on four ends of a pattern or "layout." In one game, Sebastopol, the layout has up to eight ends.
Doubles in most games are placed across the line of dominoes, and in some rules (eg tiddle-a-wink) a player who, for example, plays a double 6 may immediately play another domino with a 6 at one end.
In some games, players use only the dominoes picked up at the start of play, and must

miss a turn (called "renouncing," "passing," or "knocking") whenever they are unable to add a matching domino to the pattern.
In other games, players must draw a domino from the boneyard whenever they are unable to play a matching domino.

General rules No domino may be withdrawn after it has been added to the layout.
If the wrong domino is accidentally placed face up by a player during his turn, it must be played if it matches an end of the layout.
A player is liable to lose the game if:
a) he fails to play within two minutes;
b) he renounces when he is able to play;
c) he plays a domino that does not match (except that the domino is accepted if the error is not noticed before the next domino is played);
d) he makes a false claim that he has played all his dominoes.

The dominoes are
rectangular tiles made of
wood, ivory, bone, stone, or
plastic, They are sometimes
called ''bones,'' ''stones,'' or
''pieces.'' Typical dimensions
are 1 in by 1$\frac{7}{8}$in by $\frac{3}{8}$in.
Each domino's face is divided
by a central line and each half
is either blank or marked with
indented spots (sometimes
called ''pips'').
Dominoes with the same
number of spots on either side
of the central line are called
''doubles'' or ''doublets.''
A domino is said to be
''heavier'' than another if it
has more spots, or ''lighter'' if
it has less spots. So a double
6 is heavier than a 6:5.
The standard Western domino
set has 28 tiles (with double 6
the heaviest domino). Larger
sets have 55 dominoes
(double 9 the heaviest) or 91
dominoes (double 12 the
heaviest).
Players Some domino games
are for two players only;
others for two or more players
playing singly or as partners.
Partnerships may be decided:
a) by mutual agreement;
b) by draw—in which case
each player draws one domino
and the two players with the
heaviest dominoes form one
pair.
Partners sit opposite each
other at the table.
Playing area Dominoes can
be played on a table or any
other flat surface.

Drawing a hand All the
dominoes are placed face
downward in the center of the
table and are then moved
around by all the players.
(These dominoes in the center
of the table are called the
''boneyard.'')
Each player then selects the
number of dominoes required
for the particular game to be
played—usually seven or five.
Except in the few games in
which players do not look at
their own dominoes—eg
Blind Hughie—players keep
their dominoes:
a) standing on edge on the
table;
b) on a rack;
c) concealed in their hand.

Turns There are several ways
of deciding which player is to
have the first turn.
a) The player who draws the
heaviest domino in a
preliminary draw.
b) One player draws a domino
and his opponent guesses
whether its spots add up to
an odd or an even number.
c) Each player draws his
dominoes for the game and the
first turn goes to the player
with the heaviest double or, if
there are no doubles, to the
player with the heaviest
domino.
In most countries, turns then
pass clockwise around the
table; in Latin America, the
direction of play is
counterclockwise.

End of play Games end:
a) when one player has played
all his dominoes—after which
he calls ''domino!'' or makes
some other recognized signal;
b) when no player can add a
matching domino in games
with no drawing from the
boneyard;
c) in drawing games when no
player can add a matching
domino and only two
dominoes remain in the
boneyard.

Result Most domino games
are played to a set number of
points.
In some games, the player who
first plays all his dominoes
claims one point for each spot
on his opponents' unplayed
dominoes.
If all play is blocked, the
player with fewest spots on
his unplayed dominoes claims
the difference between the
number of spots on his own
and his opponents' unplayed
dominoes. The hand is
replayed if opponents'
dominoes have an equal
number of spots.
In other games—eg Bergen—
players score points for adding
a domino that makes the two
ends of the layout match.

©DIAGRAM

BLOCK DOMINOES

The basic block dominoes game is usually played by two, three, or four players using a standard set of 28 dominoes. (More players can play with larger sets.)

Two players usually play with seven dominoes each, and three or four players with five dominoes each.

The first player begins by laying any of his dominoes in the center of the table.

Turns then pass around the table—with players adding matching dominoes to either end of the line or missing a turn if none of their dominoes matches.

Spots are counted and points scored after one player has played all his dominoes or the game is blocked so that no one can play.

The winner of one hand plays first in the next hand.

A game is usually played to 100 or 200 points.

PARTNERSHIP BLOCK DOMINOES

The partnership form of block dominoes is played by four players with a standard set of 28 dominoes.

Play is the same as for basic block dominoes except that:
a) players sitting opposite each other form a pair;
b) each player draws seven dominoes at the start of the game;
c) the player with the double 6 starts the first hand by laying it on the table;
d) subsequent hands are started by the winner of the previous hand and this player may play any of his dominoes to start;
e) pairs score jointly—as soon as one player has played all his dominoes, he and his partner score the sum of the spots on each of their opponents' unplayed dominoes.
f) in blocked games, the pair with the lowest total of spots on their unplayed dominoes score the difference between their own and their opponents' total of spots on their unplayed dominoes.

LATIN AMERICAN MATCH DOMINOES

This Latin American form of dominoes is played in the same way as partnership block dominoes except that:
a) the player with the double 6 always starts;
b) each hand won counts as one game;
c) a match ends when one pair has won 10 hands;
d) a match win is scored only if the other pair failed to win five hands—otherwise the match is tied.

TIDDLE-A-WINK

This is a form of block dominoes particularly suited to larger groups of people. It is often played with sets of 55 or 91 dominoes.

At the start of each hand the dominoes are shared out equally between the players; any remaining dominoes are left face downward on the table.

Play proceeds as for the basic block game except that:
a) the player with the highest double always starts;
b) any player who plays a double may add another domino if he is able;
c) a player who has played all his dominoes calls "tiddle-a-wink."

(Another version of the game is played by six to nine players with three dominoes each from a set of 28 dominoes. In this version, dominoes are added to only one side of the starting double and bets are made as in domino pool.)

DOMINO POOL

The rules of standard block dominoes apply to domino pool except that, before each hand, players place equal bets in a pool or pot.

The winner of the hand takes all; or if players tie they share the pool between them.

BLIND HUGHIE

Blind Hughie is a block dominoes game of chance. If four or five players are playing with 28 dominoes, each draws five dominoes without looking at them; two or three players each draw seven dominoes. Each player lays his dominoes in a line face downward in front of him.

The first player starts play by taking the domino at the left of his line and laying it face up in the center of the table.

Turns then pass around the table. At his turn each player takes the domino at the left of his line and:
a) if it matches an end of the layout, he plays it;
b) if it doesn't match, he lays it face downward at the right of his line.

Play continues until one player finishes his dominoes or until the game is obviously blocked.

Doubles

Fortress

Sebastopol

DRAW DOMINOES

Draw dominoes is characterized by the drawing of dominoes from the boneyard after the start of play. Players usually start with seven or five dominoes each. Play is as for basic block dominoes except that:
a) a player who is unable or unwilling to add a domino to the layout must draw dominoes from the boneyard until he draws one that he is able or willing to play, or until only two dominoes remain in the boneyard;
b) when only two dominoes remain in the boneyard, a player who cannot play a domino must end or miss a turn;
c) a player who draws or looks at an extra domino, or who turns a domino up so that other players see it, must keep that domino.

DOUBLES

This game, also called Maltese Cross, is played in the same way as basic draw dominoes except that:
a) the player with the heaviest double leads;
b) play is on four ends from the starting double;
c) a player may add a mixed number domino only if the double of the number he is matching has already been played (eg in the hand illustrated, a player could add 2:3 to the double 2 but could not play the same domino as 3:2 on the 5:3).

FORTRESS, SEBASTOPOL, CYPRUS

These are names for two closely related games.
a) The first game, usually called fortress but sometimes called Sebastopol, is a block dominoes game for four people with 28 dominoes. Each player draws seven dominoes and the player with the double 6 starts. Play is on four ends from the double 6, and a domino must be added to each of these ends before play proceeds as for standard block dominoes.
b) The second game, more usually called Sebastopol but sometimes called Cyprus, is a draw dominoes game played with a set of 55 dominoes. Four or five players start with nine dominoes each; more players start with seven or five. Double 9 always starts and if no player has this domino, players should draw one domino in turn until someone draws it. Play is on eight ends from the double 9, and all ends must be opened before a second domino may be added to any end. Players draw one domino from the boneyard whenever they are unable to add a domino to the layout.

ALL FIVES

This game, also called muggins and fives up, is a form of draw dominoes that is particularly popular in the United States. It is an interesting game characterized by its scoring system based on multiples of five.

Using a 28-domino set, two, three, or four players start with five dominoes each.

The first player may lead with any domino—and scores if its ends add up to five (**a**) or 10. The next player scores if the ends of the layout still add up to five or a multiple of five after he has played, (**b**). If he is unable to score, he may play another domino (eg the 1:3, which would make the ends of the layout add up to seven), or may draw one domino from the boneyard.

The first double of the game

(**c**) opens up a third end (in this case there would be no score since $6+6+4=16$). The next domino (**d**) opens up the fourth and final end of the layout (and in this case it scores since $6+6+4+4=20$). Play continues on four ends of the layout until one player finishes all his dominoes or until the game is blocked.

Scoring In one version of the game, a player scores one point for each spot whenever the layout's ends total five or a multiple of five. The winner of a hand also scores points for the spots on his opponents' remaining dominoes. Game is usually 150 or 200 points. More usual, however, is the scoring system in which players score one point when the ends total five, two points for 10, three for 15, and so on.

The winner of the hand scores a fifth of the face value of his opponents' remaining dominoes. In this version, the game is won by the first player to score exactly 61 points. If a player fails to claim his points after playing a domino, the first opponent to call "muggins" (or sometimes "fives") claims those points for himself.

The game is sometimes played by partners—in which case the dominoes left in the losing partner's hand are ignored for scoring purposes.

ALL THREES

All threes, or threes up, is played in the same way as all fives but scoring is based on multiples of three.

FIVES AND THREES

This is played in the same way as all fives, but scoring is based on multiples of both five and three.

A player scores one point for each spot whenever the ends of the layout total five or a multiple of five, or three or a multiple of three.

If a number is a multiple of both five and three, the player scores two points for each spot. The winner also scores for each spot on an opponent's remaining dominoes.

All fives

MATADOR

In this unusual draw game, dominoes are played when they make a specified total with a domino on an end of the layout. There are also wild dominoes called "matadors" that can be played at any turn. There are versions of the game for different sizes of domino sets.

When a 28-domino set is used, added dominoes must make a total of seven and the matadors are the 6:1, 5:2, 4:3 (ie those with ends totaling seven), and the 0:0.

For a 55 set the required total is 10 and the matadors are the 9:1, 8:2, 7:3, 6:4, 5:5, and 0:0. (In the game illustrated, play opened with the double 9. This was followed by the 7:3, a matador, and then by three dominoes making totals of 10.)

For a 92 set the total is 13 and the matadors are the 12:1, 11:2, 10:3, 9:4, 8:5, 7:6, and 0:0.

Players usually start with seven or five dominoes each, depending on the number of players and the size of set. The players with the heaviest double starts. In this game doubles are not placed crossways and the layout has

only two ends.

If a player is unable or unwilling to add a domino, he must draw one domino from the boneyard. When only two dominoes remain in the boneyard, he must play a domino if he is able.

A hand is won by the player who finishes his dominoes or who holds dominoes with the fewest spots if the game is blocked. Points are scored for the spots on an opponent's remaining dominoes, and game is an agreed number of points.

BERGEN

Bergen is a draw dominoes game in which players score points when there are matching dominoes at the ends of the layout.

Using a set of 28 dominoes, two or three players start with six dominoes each and four players with five dominoes each.

The player with the highest double starts. Subsequent play is on two ends only, and a player who is unable or unwilling to add a domino to the layout must draw one domino from the boneyard.

A player scores two points whenever two ends of the layout match (a "double

heading")—as, for example, the 6:2 and the 3:2 in the illustration (ie before the addition of the double 2).

A player scores three points for a "triple heading"—ie when there is a double at one end and a matching domino at the other, as after the addition of the double 2 in the example illustrated.

A player scores two points for winning a hand. If no player finishes his dominoes and the game is blocked, the hand is won by the player holding no doubles, the player with fewest doubles, or the player with fewest spots on his dominoes.

Game is usually 10 or 15 points.

Bergen

Matador

FORTY-TWO

Forty-two, or domino rounce, is an adaptation of a card game for play with dominoes. The object is to score points by winning tricks.

The game is usually played by four players with a set of 28 dominoes. Play is usually with partners. Each player draws seven dominoes at the start of a hand.

Bidding is the first stage of play, and tricks are valued as follows:

a) one point for each trick taken;

b) five additional points for a trick containing the 5:0, 4:1, or 3:2 (ie the dominoes with a total of five spots each);

c) 10 additional points for a trick containing the 5:5 or 6:4 (ie 10 spots each).

The total tricks value is 42 points (and hence the name of the game).

The player holding the 1:0 domino makes the first bid, and the other players bid in turn. Players may make only one bid and no bid may be for less than 30 points or be lower than a preceding bid. A player may pass if he does not wish to bid.

Taking tricks The player or pair with the highest bid then attempts to take tricks worth the value of their bid (or more).

There are eight suits—blanks, the numbers 1 through 6, and doubles. Except when a trump is led, the highest number on a domino determines the suit. The highest bidder plays the first domino and this establishes the trump suit for the hand. If he leads a "mixed number" domino he calls out which number is the trump suit. The other players then play one domino in turn. Except when a trump or a double is played, a trick goes to the player who played the heaviest domino of the correct suit. A double is the strongest domino of its suit, and can be taken only by a trump. As in card games a higher number in the trump suit takes a lower one.

The player who takes a trick always leads for the next trick. (In the examples illustrated:

a) double 3 takes the trick—and scores five extra points because the 3:2 is taken;

b) if 2s are trumps, the 2:1 takes the trick—and scores 10 extra points because the 6:4 is taken.)

Scoring If the bidder and his partner take tricks worth as many or more points than the bid, they score the full value of their tricks plus the number of points bid.

If the bidder and his partner fail in their objective, their opponents score the number of points bid plus the value of the tricks that they have taken.

Value of tricks with 2s as trumps

28 points **a**

14 points **b**

BINGO

This is another game in which dominoes are used like playing cards and players score points for taking tricks.

It is a game for two players with a set of 28 dominoes. Players make a preliminary draw to determine who will lead for the first trick.

At the start of play, each player draws seven dominoes from the boneyard. The leader then establishes trumps for the hand by turning over a domino in the boneyard. This domino is left exposed and its highest number becomes the trump suit for the hand.

The leader for the first trick then plays one domino and his opponent follows him. There is no need for a player to follow suit, except when the game is "closed" or the boneyard is empty.

Taking a trick The double blank, called "bingo," takes any other domino;

If two trumps are played, the higher trump takes the trick;

If one trump is played, the trump takes the trick;

If no trumps are played, the heaviest domino wins the trick;

If no trumps are played and both dominoes have the same total of spots, the leader's domino takes the trick.

As long as any dominoes remain in the boneyard, each player draws a domino after each trick. The winner of a trick always draws first and then leads for the next trick. When only two dominoes remain in the boneyard, the winner of the preceding trick may take the trump domino or the domino that is face down, and the losing player takes the remaining domino.

Value of tricks There is no score just for taking a trick. The value of a trick depends on the dominoes it contains. Only the following dominoes have any points value (with 2s as trumps in the examples illustrated):

a) the double of trumps is worth 28 points;

b) except when blanks are trumps, "bingo" is worth 14 points;

c) other doubles are worth their total number of spots;

d) trumps other than the double are worth their total number of spots;

e) the 6:4 is worth 10 points;

f) the 3:0 is worth 10 points.

10 points **e**

10 points **f**

Value of doubles A player can also claim points for having more than one double in his hand at any time when it is his turn to lead.

To claim these points he should play one double and expose the others.

For two doubles in his hand he calls "double" and claims 20 points;

for three doubles he calls "triples" and claims 40 points;

for four doubles he calls "double doublet" and claims 50 points;

for five doubles he calls "king" and claims 60 points;

for six doubles he calls "emperor" and claims 70 points;

for all seven doubles he calls "invincible" and claims 210 points;

if "bingo" is among his doubles he claims an extra 10 points.

A player is not entitled to these points if he fails to claim them when laying down a double; nor do they count if he fails to take the trick.

Closing If a player with the lead believes that he can bring his score from tricks and doubles to at least 70 points without drawing any further dominoes, he can "close" the game by turning over the trump domino.

After the game is closed neither player may draw any further dominoes and rules for following suit come into force.

Following suit After the game is closed or the boneyard is empty, a player is obliged when possible to follow suit. If a trump is led, he must play another trump.

If a domino that is not a trump is led, he must try and follow its higher number or, failing that, its lowest number. If he can follow neither of these, he may play a trump. Only if he has none of these is he permitted to discard.

Scoring A game is won by the first player to score seven sets or game points.

Sets are scored as follows:

a) one set for every 70 points from tricks or doubles;

b) one set for being the first player to reach 70 points if the other player has at least 30 points;

c) two sets for reaching 70 points after the other player has won a trick but has not scored 30 points;

d) three sets for reaching 70 points before the other player wins a trick;

e) one set for taking the double of trumps with "bingo."

DOMINO CRIBBAGE

This game is an adaptation of playing card cribbage.

The basic domino game is for two players, using a standard set of 28 dominoes.

As in the card game, the score is usually kept on a cribbage board.

Objective The game is won by the first player to score 61 points. Scoring takes place during play and also at the end of a hand.

Play Each player draws six dominoes at the start of play. He then discards two of them, face downward, to form the crib (an extra hand scored by the dealer after the other hands have been scored).

The leader then turns over a domino in the boneyard. This domino is the "starter." It is not used during play but is scored with all hands after play.

Turns alternate. The leader's opponent begins by placing any domino from his hand face upward on the table in front of himself and calling out its total number of spots.

The leader then turns over one of his dominoes and calls out the sum total of spots on both dominoes played so far.

Play proceeds in this way, with each player calling the sum total of spots played, until the "go" rule comes into play.

If, at his turn, a player is unable to play a domino that will bring the count to 31 or below, he must call "go."

The other player must then play as many tiles as he can until he reaches 31 or is unable to play.

Once a count of 31 has been reached, or if no one can play, a new count from 0 is begun. (Pairs etc cannot be carried over into the next count.)

After both players have played all their dominoes, the leader's opponent scores the points in his hand.

The leader then scores the points in his hand and then the points in the crib.

The lead then passes to the other player and another hand is started.

Scoring during play

For turning up a double for starter, one point.

For reaching a count of exactly 15, two points.

For a "pair" (playing a domino with the same total spot count as the last played domino), two points.

For a "triplet" (a third domino with the same total spot count), six points.

For a fourth domino with the same spot count, 12 points.

For a run of three or more dominoes, not necessarily in order (eg dominoes totaling 6,4,5,3), one point for each tile of the run.

For reaching exactly 31, two points.

For being nearest to 31, one point.

For the last tile of the hand, one point.

For reaching 15 with the last tile, three points.

Scoring after play

For a combination totaling 15, two points.

For a double run of three (a three-tile run with a pair to one of them), eight points.

For a double run of four (a run of four with one pair), 10 points.

For a triple run (a triplet with two other dominoes in sequence), 15 points.

For a quadruple run (two pairs and a domino in sequence with both), 16 points.

Scoring during play

Pair, 2 points

15, 2 points

Run, 3 points

31, 2 points

Scoring after play (the "show")

Runs, 6 points

Pair, 2 points

15, 2 points

 "Starter"

Total, 10 points

PICTURE DOMINOES

Dominoes with pictures are very popular with young children and can be easily bought or made.

A typical set contains 28 brightly colored dominoes with combinations of seven different pictures. They are usually made of wood or heavy card.

All the dominoes are shared out among the players, who should keep the pictures hidden from the other players. One player starts by placing one domino face upward on the table. Players then take turns at adding a matching domino. If a player doesn't have a matching domino he misses his turn.

The winner is the first player to add all his dominoes to the row on the table.

© DIAGRAM

Chinese dominoes

Most Chinese domino games are characterized by the collecting of matching pairs. They are played with sets of 32 dominoes divided into two series—the civil and the military. Players can make their own "Chinese set" from two sets of Western dominoes.

The woodpile The dominoes are stacked in a row—called the "woodpile"—at the start of most Chinese domino games.

The banker for the first hand of a game is usually decided by throwing three dice. The total number thrown is counted around the table and the banker is the player sitting where the count stops.

Turns pass around the table in a counterclockwise direction.

Woodpile

K'AP T'AI SHAP

K'ap t'ai shap (collecting tens) was a forerunner of mah jongg, and is popular in Chinese gambling houses in the United States.

Objective The game is won by the first player to complete his hand.

A complete hand consists of:
a) four pairs, each with a total spot count of 10 or a multiple of 10; and
b) any identical pair.

Start of play A long woodpile five dominoes high is built down the center of the table, using several sets. Players join the game by placing equal stakes, and dice are thrown to decide who will have the first turn.

The woodpile is then prepared for play by removing the top domino from the third stack from one end and placing it face down at the other end of the woodpile. The top domino is then taken from each alternate stack up to one less than the number of players, and these are also added in order to the far end of the woodpile.

The first player then takes the end two stacks (with 10 dominoes) and the other players in turn each take two stacks (with nine dominoes).

Turns If the first player does not have a winning hand, he starts play by discarding one domino and placing it face up on the table.

Then each player in his turn:
1) may take any discarded domino to complete his hand or to exchange it for one of his own dominoes; and
2) draws one domino from the end of the woodpile, which he may immediately discard or keep in place of another domino from his hand.

Result The game ends when one player completes his hand. This entitles him to the total staked, less the gambling house commission.

TIU U

Tiu u, or fishing, is a game for two or three players with two sets of Chinese dominoes. Players win points for matching dominoes in their hand with dominoes lying face up in the center of the table.

Pairs The 4:2 and 2:1 (the supreme pair) count as one pair. Other pairs are formed whenever two dominoes have the same total number of spots (regardless of whether they are civil or military dominoes).

Start of play At the start of a hand the dominoes are thoroughly mixed and placed face down in a woodpile four dominoes high.

Four stacks (16 dominoes) are then taken from one end of the woodpile and placed face up on the table.

Each player then draws his own dominoes. If there are three players, each draws two stacks (eight dominoes); if there are only two players, each draws three stacks (12 dominoes).

Turns In this turn, each player first attempts to match a domino in his hand with a domino exposed on the table. If he succeeds, he places the pair face up in front of him. Whether he finds a pair or not, he then draws the top domino from the end of the woodpile where the players first drew their hands.

If the drawn domino matches a domino exposed in the center of the table, he takes the pair and places it face up in front of him. If it doesn't match, he adds the drawn domino to the dominoes exposed in the center of the table.

Scoring When the woodpile is empty, players score points as follows:
a) the total score for dominoes with less than eight spots (small fish) is obtained by counting one point for each red spot and then rounding up the total to 10 or a multiple of 10.

b) dominoes with eight or more spots (big fish) score two points for every spot— red or white.

The player with the highest score then receives from each opponent the number of points by which their scores differ.

The dominoes Chinese dominoes are longer and narrower than Western dominoes—typically 3in by $\frac{7}{8}$in by $\frac{3}{8}$in.
Spots on Chinese dominoes are colored red or white:
all 4s or 1s are red;
double 6 is red and white;
other dominoes have white spots.
There are no blank dominoes in a Chinese set.
The civil series comprises 22 dominoes, forming 11 identical pairs:
all the doubles plus the 6:5, 6:4, 6:1, 5:1, and 3:1.
The military series comprises 10 dominoes. These form five mixed pairs:
the 4:2 and 2:1 (known as the "supreme pair");
the 6:3 and 5:4 (mixed 9s);
the 6:2 and 5:3 (mixed 8s);
the 5:2 and 4:3 (mixed 7s);
the 4:1 and 3:2 (mixed 5s).

Civil series

Military series

TIEN KOW

Tien kow is a game for four players with one set of Chinese dominoes. The object of the game is to score points by winning tricks made up of single dominoes or pairs.
Start of play The dominoes are thoroughly mixed and stacked in a woodpile. The first banker (selected by dice) then deals each player eight dominoes from the woodpile.
Turns The banker plays the first domino for the first trick and the other players follow in turn. After the first trick, the lead goes to the winner of the preceding trick.
At his lead, a player may play either one domino or one or two pairs.
If he leads one domino, the other players must follow with one domino from the same series (discarding if they have no domino from that series).
If he leads one or two pairs, the other players must do likewise.
Taking tricks If one domino is led, the trick goes to the player who plays the heaviest domino from the correct series.
If one pair is led, the trick is taken by the highest ranking pair. If two pairs are led, the trick goes to the player who

Ranking of pairs

plays the highest pair of all—regardless of what pair is played with it.
Ranking of pairs is as follows:
1) the 4:2 and 2:1 (supreme);
2) double 6s (heaven);
3) double 1s (earth);
4) double 4s (man);
5) pair of 3:1s;
6) double 5s;
7) double 3s;
8) double 2s;
9) pair of 6:5s;
10) pair of 6:4s;
11) pair of 6:1s;
12) pair of 5:1s;
13) 6:3 and 5:4 (mixed 9s);
14) 6:2 and 5:3 (mixed 8s);
15) 5:2 and 4:3 (mixed 7s);
16) 4:1 and 3:2 (mixed 5s);
17) double 6 and either of the mixed 9s;
18) double 1 and a mixed 8;
19) double 4 and a mixed 7;
20) 3:1 and a mixed 5.
Scoring Players settle their scores after each hand.
Scoring is as follows:
a) a player with no tricks pays four points to the winner of the last trick (except when the banker for one hand wins the last trick and retains the bank —in which case he pays eight points the first time, 12 points the second, 16 the third, and so on until the bank changes);
b) a player with one, two, or three tricks deducts his number of tricks from four and pays the difference to the winner of the last trick;
c) a player with more than four tricks deducts four from his total and claims the difference from the winner of the last trick;
d) if the banker leads the supreme pair, he claims four

points from each player;
e) if a player leads the supreme pair, he claims four points from the banker and two points from each other player;
f) the banker claims eight points from each player if he leads two of the following pairs: the double 6 and a mixed 9, the double 1 and a mixed 8, the double 4 and a mixed 7, the 3:1 and a mixed 5;
g) a player claims eight points from the banker and four points from each other player if he makes the leads given under (f).

Mah jongg

Mah jongg is a tile game of Chinese origin that reached the West in the 1920s. Its name means "the sparrows." Each of four (or three) players plays for himself. Players collect sets of tiles with the object of completing their hands in a prescribed manner. Scores are settled after each hand, and the winner is the player with the most points when play ends.

Players Mah jongg is best played by four players, but can be played by three. Each player plays for himself.

Deciding the winds Each player is designated the name of a wind—east, south, west, and north.

Winds for the first hand are decided after the players are seated, when each player takes a turn to throw two dice. The player with the highest total throw becomes east. The other players' winds are determined by their position at the table relative to east: west sits opposite east, south sits to east's right and north to east's left (not like a compass). If the player who is east wind does not win the first hand, the winds pass counterclockwise around the table. Thus east becomes north, south becomes east, west becomes south, and north becomes west.

If the player who is east wind wins a hand, the players retain the same winds for the next hand.

The tiles Mah jongg tiles are made of bone, ivory, bamboo, wood, or plastic.

Tile designs vary. Sets sold in the West usually have Arabic numerals in one corner of the suit tiles, and letters denoting the four winds.

A standard set has 144 tiles— 136 playing tiles and eight flower or season tiles.

Suit tiles There are three different suits: circles (or dots), bamboos (or bams), and characters (or craks). Each suit comprises tiles numbered 1 through 9, and there are four of each type of tile.

The 1 bamboo usually shows a symbolic bird. All other tiles have symbols for the suits.

Duration A complete game consists of four rounds, but the game is in no way spoiled if players choose to stop at the end of any hand.

Each round bears the name of a wind: the first is east, the second south, the third west, and the fourth north.

As well as indicating the stage of the game, the "wind of the round" has an effect on scoring.

A round consists of however many hands are taken before the fourth player has lost a hand as east wind.

Building the wall All the tiles are placed face down on the table, and are thoroughly shuffled by the players.

Then, without looking at the tiles' faces, each player builds a wall that is 18 tiles long and two tiles high (with the long sides of the tiles touching and the faces down).

Each player then pushes his wall toward the center of the table until the four walls meet to form a hollow square representing a city wall.

Breaching the wall takes place once the wall is built. There are two stages.

a) East throws two dice to determine which side of the wall is to be breached. If he throws two 1s, he must throw again. Otherwise, he takes the total thrown and, starting with the length of his own wall as one, counts out the total counterclockwise around the table. The breach is to be made in the side of the wall where his count ends.

b) The player whose wall is to be breached now throws the two dice and adds his total to the total previously thrown by east. The new total is used to determine exactly where the breach will be made.

The player counts clockwise along the top of his tiles, beginning at the right-hand corner. If the total is more than 18 he continues along the next wall.

When the count ends, the player takes the two tiles from that stack and places them as shown. These moved tiles are called "loose tiles."

Drawing the hands After the wall is breached east takes the two stacks (four tiles) from the opposite side of the breach to the loose tiles. South then takes the next two stacks, west the next two, and north the next two. The draw continues in this way until each player has 12 tiles. East, south, west, and north then take one more tile in turn, and finally east takes one extra tile from the top of the next stack.

At the end of the initial draw east has 14 tiles and the other players have 13 tiles each.

Flower and season tiles drawn in the initial hand or later in the game must be placed face up in front of the player and replaced by a loose tile. Replacement at the start of the game must be in rotation, with east playing first.

For scoring purposes, each wind has its own season and flower. This is usually shown by numbers on Western mah jongg sets—with east 1, south 2, west 3, and north 4.

Breaching

a

b

Drawing the hands

Dragon tiles There are three different dragons: white, red, and green (left to right in the illustration). As with the suit tiles, there are four of each type of tile.

Wind tiles East, south, west, and north winds are represented. Again there are four of each type of tile.

Flower and season tiles These are eight individually marked tiles.

Racks Each player is provided with a rack to hold his tiles. The player who is east wind takes the different colored rack.

Other equipment includes:
a) two dice;
b) scoring counters (small sticks) or a scoring pad;
c) optional wind indicators—either rotating indicators or separate disks.

Objective Each player aims to complete his hand and go "mah jongg" (sometimes called going "woo").

Starting play East starts play by discarding any one of his 14 tiles.

Discarding tiles When a player discards a tile he must always call out its name, eg red dragon, east wind, 6 bams. Discarded tiles are placed in the center of the table—usually face up in Western countries but face down in China and elsewhere in the East.

Playing order Play passes counterclockwise around the table except when a player interrupts the order to claim a discarded tile.

If more than one player claims a discarded tile, the order of precedence is:
1) a player claiming the tile to go mah jongg;
2) a player claiming the tile to make a *pung* or *kong*;
3) a player claiming the tile to make a *chow*.

If the playing order is interrupted for a claim, intervening players lose their right to any turn they may have missed. Thus if player 1 discards a tile and player 4 claims it, players 2 and 3 lose their turns and player 1 has the next turn unless player 4's discard is claimed by another player.

Playing a turn If no player claims the tile that was last discarded, the player to the right of the last player to discard now takes a tile from the wall.

The new tile is taken from the end of the wall without the loose tiles. The player may conceal the tile's face from his opponents.

If he wishes to keep the new tile, he does so and discards another tile from his rack. Otherwise he discards the new tile.

Claiming tiles Only the tile that was last discarded may be claimed. It may be claimed to complete a *chow, pung,* or *kong,* or to go mah jongg. Claims may be made even after the next player has taken a new tile from the wall—in which case the tile drawn from the wall must be replaced. Claims are not permitted if the next player has already made his discard.

Claiming a chow Only the player sitting to the right of the player who discarded is permitted to claim for a *chow.* The claiming player must already hold in his rack the other two tiles needed for the *chow.*

To claim the discard the player must call "chow," pick up the tile, and then "expose" the complete *chow* by laying it face up in front of him.

The player then ends his turn by discarding a tile from his rack.

Claiming a pung Any player may claim the last discarded tile for a *pung* provided that:
a) he holds in his rack two tiles identical with the tile he is claiming;
b) he has played an intervening turn if he failed to *pung* that same tile on an earlier discard.

To claim the discard he must call "pung," pick up the tile, and "expose" the *pung.* He then ends his turn by discarding a tile from his rack.

Concealed chows or pungs A player who has a *chow* or *pung* in his original hand, or who completes a *chow* or *pung* with a tile drawn from the wall, may keep these tiles "concealed" on his rack.

This gives him greater maneuverability, conceals the state of his hand from his opponents, and doubles the value of a *pung.*

Claiming a kong Any player may claim the last discarded tile for a *kong* if he holds in his rack three tiles identical with the tile he is claiming.

To claim the discard he must call "kong," pick up the tile, and "expose" the complete *kong.*

The player then draws a loose tile before discarding in the usual way.

(A loose tile is always drawn after a *kong* because a complete hand has one extra tile for each *kong* it contains.)

Concealed kong

Mah jongg A complete hand usually consists of four *chows, pungs,* or *kongs,* plus an identical pair.

A chow is a run of three tiles of the same suit, eg 3,4,5 dots (**a**), or 7,8,9 craks. Mixed winds or mixed dragons do not count as *chows.*

A pung is a set of three identical tiles, eg three green dragons (**b**), three 8 bams, or three south winds.

A kong is a set of four identical tiles (**c**).

A pair may be any two identical tiles (**d**).

Special mah jongg hands that do not follow the conventional pattern are accepted by some players as alternative ways of going mah jongg.

These special hands normally score the maximum permitted for any one hand.

Most commonly accepted of these special hands are:
a) "hand of the thirteen odd majors" and
b) "calling nine tiles hand."

Converting an exposed pung into a kong A player may convert an exposed *pung* into a *kong* if he draws the fourth similar piece from the wall. (This is the only time that an exposed set of tiles may be interfered with.)

Players are not permitted to claim discards to convert exposed *pungs* into *kongs*. After a player has converted an exposed *pung* into a *kong*, he ends his turn by drawing a loose tile and then discarding in the usual way.

A concealed kong A kong is "concealed" if:

a) all four tiles are in a player's original hand; or

b) a player with a "concealed" *pung* in his hand draws the fourth similar tile from the wall.

A player with a concealed *kong* may lay it on the table at any time when it is his turn to play.

A concealed *kong* laid on the table is worth double points and is distinguished from an exposed *kong* by turning over the end two tiles. If another player goes mah jongg while a player has a concealed *kong* on his rack, he scores only for a concealed *pung*.

Only after a player has laid a concealed *kong* on the table may he draw the loose tile needed to bring his hand up to the number of tiles required to go mah jongg.

Drawing loose tiles Loose tiles are used to make a player's hand up to the correct number of tiles—after a flower or season tile has been drawn or after a *kong*.

The tile farthest from the breach is used first and then the other loose tile. After both loose tiles have been used they are replaced by the two tiles at that end of the wall—the top tile going farthest from the breach.

Wrong number of tiles A player with the wrong number of tiles in his hand (on his rack and laid out on the table) cannot go mah jongg. Excluding extra tiles in *kongs*, each player should always have 14 tiles after drawing or 13 tiles after discarding.

A player with the wrong number of tiles must draw and discard tiles normally until another player goes mah jongg.

If the player in error had too many tiles, he pays the other players their scores without deducting any score for his own hand.

If he had too few tiles, he deducts the score for his own hand before making payment.

Wrong tile drawn If the wall is breached in the wrong place or if tiles are drawn in the wrong order, the tiles should be reshuffled and the wall rebuilt.

Incorrect combinations If a player exposes an incorrect combination of tiles as a *chow*, *pung*, or *kong*, he must rectify the error before the next player discards or his hand is declared "dead."

A player with a dead hand must pay the other players their scores with no allowance for his own hand.

Last 14 tiles A hand is declared "dead" if no player goes mah jongg before play reaches the last 14 tiles in the wall (including the loose tiles).

There is no scoring and a new hand is played with the same player as east wind.

Calling A player is "calling" (or "fishing") when he requires only one tile to complete his hand.

If two players are calling and both claim the same tile, precedence goes to the player whose turn would have come first.

A standing hand East wind may declare a "standing hand" if he is calling after making his first discard.

Any player may declare a standing hand if he is calling after drawing and discarding for the first time in a hand.

A player who has declared a standing hand must not change any of the 13 tiles then in his hand. At each turn, he draws a tile from the wall in the usual way and then discards it if it is not the tile required to go mah jongg.

A player who completes a standing hand receives a bonus of 100 points.

Snatching a kong A player who is calling may complete his hand by "snatching a kong"—ie claiming a tile drawn from the wall by another player who uses it to convert an exposed *pung* into a *kong*.

Going mah jongg As soon as a player completes his hand, he stops play by calling "mah jongg."

All players then expose their hands for scoring, turning over the middle tile of any *pungs* that were concealed in their hands.

Incorrect mah jongg If a player who has called "mah jongg" completely exposes his hand and then finds he has made an error, he must pay double the points limit to each of the other players.

If his hand is only partially exposed when the error is discovered, he may cancel his call and put the tiles back on his rack.

Hand of the thirteen odd majors comprises a 1 and a 9 of each suit, one of each dragon, one of each wind, and a pair to any of these tiles.

Calling nine tiles hand is made up of tiles from the same suit—three 1s, three 9s, one each of tiles 2 through 8, and any one other tile of the same suit.

Settling the scores After calculating the value of their individual hands, the players settle with each other in the following way.

If east wind goes mah jongg, he receives double the total value of his score from each of the other players.

If another player goes mah jongg, he receives double the value of his score from east wind, and the value of his score from each of the other players.

Each loser also settles with each of the other losers.

When two losers settle (except when one of them is east wind), the player with the lower score pays the difference between his score and the other player's score.

When east wind is a loser, he pays or receives double the difference when settling with another loser.

Scoring Point values vary in different scoring systems, but the system given here shows the typical characteristics. With the exception of certain limit hands (described separately), the points value of each player's hand is calculated from the tables.

Using table A:

points are scored by all players for *pungs* and *kongs* and for each flower and season tile (no points are scored for *chows*);

the player going mah jongg also scores for some pairs.

Scoring a sample hand

Using table B:

the player going mah jongg adds any bonus points.

Using table C:

players double their points as indicated, and again there are additional doubles for the player going mah jongg.

Limit hands Most scoring systems have specified "limit hands," designed to prevent the scoring of an excessive number of points with a single hand.

Limit hands score a fixed number of points—usually 500—regardless of their actual face value. East wind pays or receives double the limit.

Most limit hands may be obtained only by the player going mah jongg. Typical examples are:
a) hand of all winds and dragons;
b) hand of all 1s and 9s;
c) hand of concealed *pungs* and *kongs*;
d) hand of the thirteen odd majors;
e) calling nine tiles hand;
f) an original hand (east wind's hand when play begins);
g) hand completed with east's first discard;
h) east wind's thirteenth consecutive mah jongg.
Other hands score the limit whether or not completed. If the player with these hands fails to go mah jongg, he scores the limit from the other losers.
Examples are:
i) hand with *pungs* or *kongs* of at least three dragons;
j) hand with *pungs* or *kongs* of three winds and a pair of the other wind.

Table A — Tile values

All players	Exposed	Concealed
Any *chow*	0	0
Pung of tiles 2 through 8 of any suit	2	4
Pung of 1 or 9 of any suit	4	8
Pung of winds or dragons	4	8
Kong of tiles 2 through 8 of any suit	8	16
Kong of 1 or 9 of any suit	16	32
Kong of winds or dragons	16	32
Any season or flower	4	
Player going mah jongg		
Pair of any dragon	2	
Pair of player's own wind	2	
Pair of wind of the round	2	

Table B — Bonus scores

Player going mah jongg	
For going mah jongg	20
Winning tile drawn from the wall	2
Winning with only possible tile (ie with all other similar tiles exposed)	2
Winning with the last piece from the wall	10
Winning with a loose tile	10
For having no *chows*	10
For having no scoring value (except flowers or seasons)	10
Completing a standing hand	100

Table C — Doubling

All players	Number of times doubled
Pung or *kong* of any dragon	1
Pung or *kong* of player's own wind	1
Pung or *kong* of the wind of the round	1
Player's own season or flower	1
Four seasons or four flowers	3
Player going mah jongg	
Hand with no *chows*	1
Hand with no scoring tiles except flowers and seasons	1
Hand all one suit except for winds and/or dragons	1
Hand all 1s and 9s except for winds and/or dragons	1
Snatching a *kong* to go mah jongg	1
Hand all one suit	3
Hand all winds and dragons	3
Original hand (east wind's 14 tiles when play begins)	3

Scoring a sample hand

Tile values (see table A and diagram)		*Running total*
Total value of tiles in hand 20 points		20
Bonus scores (see table B)		
For going mahjongg 20 points		40
For having no *chows* 10 points		50
Doubling (see table C)		
Pung of dragons (double once)		100
Hand with no *chows* (double once)		200

Sap tim pun (Ten and a half)

Sap tim pun, or ten and a half, is a gambling game popular among the Chinese in Malaysia. This version is played with mah jongg tiles, but there are obvious similarities to the ten and a half card game known in the Netherlands as "saton pong" (page 222).

Tiles The game is played with one standard set of 144 mah jongg tiles.
The tiles have the following point values:
a) suit tiles count their numerical face value;
b) dragons, flowers, seasons, and winds are each worth $\frac{1}{2}$ point (except that special rules apply if an east wind tile is picked up in the first draw).

Objective Each player tries to get a hand with a point count that is higher than that of the banker—though not in excess of $10\frac{1}{2}$.

Building the walls The tiles are turned face down on the table, shuffled, and then built into four walls. Each wall is 18 tiles long and two tiles high, with the long sides of the tiles touching.

Turns pass clockwise around the players, as in standard mah jongg and Chinese domino games.

First draw and betting
1) the banker for the round declares the maximum stake.
2) Each player in turn draws one tile from the wall, with the player to the banker's right drawing first and the banker drawing last. Each player looks at his tile and then lays it face down in front of him.
3) Players other than the banker place a stake beside their tile and then turn the tile face up.
4) If the banker has drawn an east wind tile, he now turns it over and takes all the stakes on the table. He then discards the east wind tile and replaces it with another tile from the wall.
5) If any other player has drawn an east wind tile, and provided that the banker has not also drawn an east wind, the player receives his stake from the banker, replaces the east wind tile with another tile from the wall, and places a new stake beside it.

Drawing additional tiles
Each player in turn has the opportunity of drawing an additional one or two tiles (to make a maximum of three tiles in his hand).
A player must draw a further tile if his hand with one or two tiles is worth less than 6 points; he has the choice of drawing or standing if his hand is worth 6 points or more.
The drawn tiles are kept concealed unless the player's hand totals more than $10\frac{1}{2}$ points—in which case he throws in his tiles and passes his stake to the banker.

Banker's hand When all the other players have drawn or stood, the banker turns over his first tile and then draws or stands according to the same rules as other players.

Settlement
a) If the banker's hand exceeds $10\frac{1}{2}$ points, he pays the stake of all players still in the game.
b) If his hand totals exactly $10\frac{1}{2}$, he receives all stakes laid.
c) If his hand is less than $10\frac{1}{2}$, he receives the stakes of all players with fewer points and pays all players with more points.

Rotating bank After each round the bank passes one player to the right.

Mah jongg (American)

This modern form of mah jongg, developed and organized by the US National Mah Jongg League, enjoys considerable popularity in North America. It is challenging and rewarding, while also easier to learn and score.

Tiles The modern American game is played with 152 tiles: the 144 tiles of the standard set (but with eight flower and no season tiles), plus eight big jokers (wild tiles with special rules governing their use).
Cards are sometimes used in place of tiles.
Players The basic game is for four players, but is easily adapted for two or three players.
Deciding the winds For the first hand, winds are decided as in the standard game. Thereafter, winds pass counterclockwise around the table after each hand—regardless of whether east wins or loses the hand.
Building the wall is as for the standard game except that each side of the wall has an extra two tiles.
Breaching the wall is as for the standard game, except that there are no loose tiles.
Picking the hands is as for the standard game.

Passing tiles At the start of the American game, players exchange tiles in a series of passes. Tiles are always passed face down. (Big jokers may not be passed.)
The first Charleston is compulsory and comprises three passes:
1) at the first pass each player gives three tiles to the player to his right;
2) at the second pass he gives three tiles to the player opposite;
3) at the third pass he gives three tiles to the player to his left.
(If a player does not have three unwanted tiles for his third pass, he may make a "blind pass" ie take one, two, or three tiles from the pass he is given and, without looking at them, use them in his own pass.)

The second Charleston takes place only if all four players agree. It comprises the following passes:
1) three tiles to the player to the left;
2) three to the player opposite;
3) three to the player to his right.
(A blind pass is permitted at the third pass.)
An optional pass is permitted, if all players agree, after the second Charleston (or after the first if there is no second Charleston).
At an optional pass, one, two, or three tiles are exchanged with the player sitting opposite.
Objective As in the standard game, the players aim to collect a complete mah jongg hand of 14 tiles.

Start of play East starts play by discarding any one of his 14 tiles (except when he has a complete mah jongg hand after the passes).
Discarding tiles When a player discards a tile he must call out its name and place it face up in the center of the table.
A player is not permitted to exchange a discard once he has laid it on the table and named it.
Claiming a discard Any player may claim another player's discard:
a) to complete an "exposure" (a group of like tiles making part of an exposed mah jongg);
b) to go mah jongg (to complete a hand that is either exposed or concealed).

A player claims a discard by calling "take." He may not claim until the discard has been named. Nor may he claim after the player to the discarder's right has drawn a tile from the wall and made his discard.
If several players claim a discard, the tile goes to the player nearest in turn to the discarder (except that a player who wants a tile to go mah jongg has precedence).
A successful claimant picks up the claimed tile and lays his complete exposure (or mah jongg) face up in front of him. After completing an exposure, the claimant discards any one tile from his hand.
The player to the discarder's right has the next turn (unless the new discard is claimed by another player).

Playing a turn Except when a discard is claimed, turns pass counterclockwise around the table.
At his turn a player:
1) picks the end tile from the wall (tiles being picked in a clockwise direction);
2) looks at the picked tile and either immediately discards it or keeps the picked tile and discards any other tile concealed in his hand.
A player is not permitted to "look ahead," ie to pick a tile from the wall before the player to his left has discarded.

Flower tiles In the American game, flower tiles are used in exactly the same way as suit tiles (whereas in the standard game, special rules apply).

Big Jokers Special rules apply to big jokers.
One or more big jokers may be used in place of any tile or tiles in any exposure or when going mah jongg.
If a player holds or picks a tile for which a big joker has been substituted in an exposure, he may, at his turn, exchange this tile for the big joker.
Big jokers may be discarded at any time during play and called the name of the previous discard.
If a big joker has once been exposed in a hand, this hand cannot be counted as a jokerless hand even if the big jokers are later replaced.

Miscalled tiles If a tile is miscalled, a claimant who wants the discard for an exposure must wait until the discarder calls the tile correctly. (In this case there is no penalty for the player who miscalled.)
However, if a player needs only one tile to complete his hand and another player discards a tile and mistakenly gives his discard the name of the tile for which the other player is waiting, the waiting player may claim this tile for mah jongg and the player who made the error must pay four times the value of the claimant's hand.

Wrong number of tiles If players have the wrong number of tiles before the Charleston, the wall must be rebuilt and a new start made. At any other stage in the game, a player's hand is declared "dead" if he has the wrong number of tiles in his hand or in an exposure. A player with a dead hand may not discard or pick, cannot go mah jongg, and pays the winner the same as the other losing players.
If two players have dead hands, the other two players may continue playing.
If three players' hands are declared dead, the game should be replayed.

Going mah jongg As soon as a player completes his hand, he stops all play by calling "mah jongg" and exposing all his tiles.

Mah jongg in error A player should never throw in or expose his hand before the "winner's" hand is verified.
If a player calls mah jongg in error but realizes his mistake before his hand is exposed, or before any other player disturbs his hand, the game continues without penalty.
If a player calls mah jongg in error and exposes his hand, provided that no other player also exposes his hand, the caller's hand is dead and the other players continue.
If a player calls mah jongg in error and one other player throws in his hand, both these players' hands are dead and, when the hand ends, each pays the winner the same as the other loser.
If a player calls mah jongg in error and two other players throw in their hands, whether or not the caller exposes his hand the hand ends, and the caller pays double the value of his miscalled hand to the player whose hand is intact.

Redeeming big jokers If a player who calls mah jongg in error has been playing an exposed hand, any other player may exchange a like tile in his hand for a big joker correctly exposed by the miscaller before his error.
Players may not redeem big jokers when a concealed hand is incorrectly exposed for mah jongg.

Scoring The method of scoring used for the modern American game is extremely straightforward.
Every hand has a set scoring value (called its "limit"), which is listed with the requirements for the hand. According to difficulty, a hand is worth 20, 25, 30, or 35 points.
When a player goes mah jongg after picking his fourteenth tile from the wall, all other players pay him twice the points value of his hand.
When a player goes mah jongg after claiming a discarded tile, the player who made the discard pays him twice his hand's value and the other players pay him the value of the hand.

© DIAGRAM

Typical mah jongg hands

National Mah Jongg League Each year the League sends its members a card showing approximately 50 mah jongg hands for the year's play.
Hands are made up of the following groups of tiles:
a) quints (five flowers or four like tiles and a big joker);
b) *kongs* (four like tiles);
c) *pungs* (three like tiles);

d) pairs (two like tiles).
In every case, all 14 tiles needed for a mah jongg are specified.
Some hands are valid only if they are "concealed." A concealed hand must be built up on the rack from picked tiles, except that the fourteenth tile may be a claimed discard. Other hands, classified as "exposed," may be built up

from picked tiles or from claimed discards.
Specified hands are valid only when jokerless.
The illustrations and table show typical hands from the League's 1974 card.
Further details available from: National Mah Jongg League, Inc, 250 West 57th St, New York, NY 10019, USA.

x Exposed
c Concealed

x 20	1	1	1	9	9	9	7	7	7	7	4	4	4	4
c 25	1	1	2	2	2	3	3	4	4	4	5	5	5	5
c 20	F	F	F	F	1	1	3	3	3	1	1	3	3	3
x 25	9	9	9	9	9	9	9	9	9	9	9	9	2	7

Card games: general rules

The origin of playing cards is a mystery. Chinese playing cards, it seems, grew out of a marriage between divinatory arrows and paper money. Such cards may have reached Europe via the Crusades or the China trade. Alternatively Western playing cards may have had a separate European origin—seeming to have appeared quite suddenly, around 1370, in almost their present form.

THE CARDS

The deck The standard international deck of playing cards consists of 52 cards, divided into four suits of 13 cards each. Many decks also contain two jokers, sometimes used as wild cards.

The suits are named hearts, diamonds, spades, and clubs, and each card of the suit bears the appropriate symbol, as shown. Hearts and diamonds bear red symbols, spades and clubs black symbols.

The cards in any one suit are all of different denominations: nine are numbered from 2 to 10; three are "court" or "face" cards (jack, queen, king); the remaining card is the "ace," which is the "1" but is often the most powerful card of the suit.

The denomination of numbered cards is shown by both numbers and by the appropriate number of suit symbols.

The ace is shown by an "A" and a single large suit symbol. Court cards are shown by stylized drawings and by initial letters, which vary according to the country of origin of the deck. In English language countries these letters are "J" (for jack), "Q" (for queen), and "K" (for king).

The rank of cards is usually either:
2 (low), 3, 4, 5, 6, 7, 8, 9, 10, j, q, k, a (high); or
a (low), 2, 3, 4, 5, 6, 7, 8, 9, 10, j, q, k (high).
In either list, a card beats any card listed before it.
These rankings are referred to in the text as "cards rank normally, ace high," and "cards rank normally, ace low."

A meld is a scoring combination of cards in certain games.
It is usually either:
three or more cards of the same denomination; or
three or more cards in consecutive order of rank and of the same suit.

Trumps In games in which tricks are taken, it is often ruled that certain cards are made trump cards (trumps).
If so, any trump card ranks above any other card.
Usually, all the cards of one suit are chosen as trump cards (trump suit).
But in some games only some cards of one suit are the tump cards; or in other games there are other trump cards in addition to the trump suit.
Within a trump suit, cards rank in the standard order for the game being played.

Choice of trump suit The method depends on the game being played.
Some games use a permanent trump suit, chosen by agreement or convention at the beginning of the game.
But usually a suit has the role of trump suit for only one deal at a time. In this case, the trump suit for a deal is decided in one of the following ways, depending on the game being played:
a) by competitive bidding among the players;
b) by chance, ie turning a certain card face up—the suit revealed becomes trumps;
c) by set order of rotation among the suits.

PREPARING AND DEALING

Choice of partners for partnership play is usually by an initial draw. Each of the four players draws one card from the deck: the two players with the two highest ranking cards form one partnership and the other two players form the second.

Choice of first dealer
a) By high cut. Any agreed player acts as temporary dealer and shuffles the cards. Any other agreed player cuts them.
Each player then cuts the deck, beginning with the player to the temporary dealer's left, going clockwise, and ending with the temporary dealer.
Each cut consists of lifting a section of cards from the top of the face-down deck. The card cut by the player is that at the bottom of this section.
The section is held so all players can see this card. After each cut, the two sections of cards are restacked in their original order, before passing to the next player.
The player cutting the highest denomination card becomes the first dealer. Cards rank normally; ace ranks high or

Shuffling

low according to the game played. Players who cut equal highest cut again until a decision is reached between them.
b) By deal of cards. Any agreed player acts as temporary dealer and shuffles the cards. Any other agreed player cuts them.
The temporary dealer then deals one card face up to each player, including himself, beginning with the player to his left and going clockwise, until the first card of a specified denomination is dealt (eg the first ace). The player receiving this card becomes the first dealer.

Shuffle and cut are often required before every deal.
The dealer shuffles. Any other player also has the right to shuffle, but the dealer has the right to shuffle last.
The procedure of shuffling is not governed by rules—providing that an adequate shuffle is given to the cards in some way. One simple and satisfactory procedure is illustrated.
The player to the dealer's right is offered the cards to cut. If he declines the player to his right is offered the cut, and so on.

If no player wishes to cut, the dealer must cut.
A cut consists of lifting a section of cards from the top of the deck, placing it on the table, and placing the other section on top of it.
Cards remain face down and unexposed throughout.
There must be at least five cards in each section.

The deal Unless otherwise stated, the dealer gives one card at a time to each player, beginning with the player to his left and going clockwise. This rotation is repeated until each player has the required number of cards. The deal must be from the top of a face-down deck.

Deal in packets is a deal in which each player receives more than one card at once. It is required for certain games. On the deal, the dealer gives each player a specified number of cards (eg three cards), before going on to the next player.
Otherwise the deal follows normal procedure.
Sometimes the number of cards specified changes during the deal. For example, in solo whist:
when the dealer goes around the circle of players for the

first, second, and third times, he gives each player three cards each time;
when he goes around the fourth (last) time, he gives each player one card, as in a normal deal.

A widow is a batch of cards dealt separately from the players' hands. Its role varies from game to game.

The stock is, in certain games, the part of the deck which remains undealt after the deal is complete but which becomes available to players in the course of play.

ROTATION OF PLAY

Unless otherwise stated, play begins with the player to the dealer's left, and continues with the other players in clockwise rotation.

Complete deck of cards

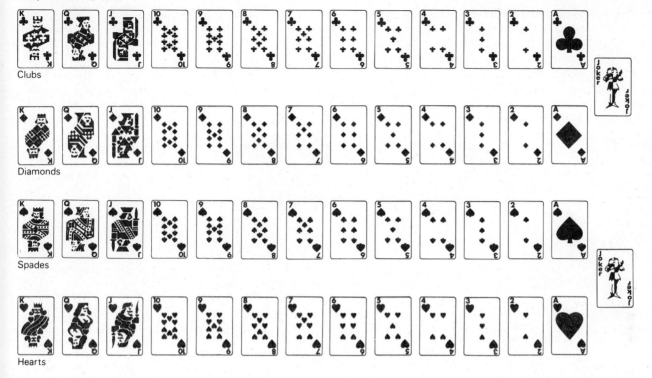

Clubs

Diamonds

Spades

Hearts

TRICKS

A trick signifies, in certain games, one round of cards during play—one card being contributed by each active hand.

It also means the cards themselves when gathered together.

On each trick one player plays first ("has the lead"), and the other players follow in clockwise rotation.

Each player's action consists of taking one card from his hand and placing it face up in the center of the table.

The lead is held, in most games:

on the first trick after a deal— by the player to the dealer's left;

on the remaining tricks of a deal—by the player who won the previous trick.

Choice of cards The lead may play any card he wishes. The other players must "follow suit" if possible, ie each must play a card of the same suit as the lead card if he has one. If a player cannot follow suit, he may play any other card that he has.

A trick is won by the highest ranking card of the suit led— providing that no trump is played.

If one or more trump cards are played, it is won by the highest ranking trump card.

A player may usually only play a trump card if he cannot follow suit.

The player playing the winning card takes the trick: he gathers the cards together, and places them face down on the table, usually near his (or his partner's) position.

Revoking A player who has failed to follow suit when he in fact had a card of the required suit, is said to have "revoked."

Penalties for this vary from game to game.

NOTES ON BETTING

Betting chips When these are required, any counters, matchsticks, or other agreed objects may be used.

An ante is compulsory in certain games. It is a small contribution to the betting pool before a deal.

It is usually required either of all players or of the dealer only.

Odds The recognized forms in which payment odds are stated are:

either "x to y" (eg 30 to 1, 15 to 2)—which signifies that the player's stake is returned in addition to the win payment;

or "x for y" (eg 30 for 1, 15 for 2)—which signifies that the player's stake is returned as part of the win payment.

For example, a player staking 1 chip at 30 to 1 receives 30 chips and his 1 chip stake back. At 30 for 1 he receives 29 chips and his 1 chip stake back.

"30 to 1" can also be written "30–1."

IRREGULARITIES

Rules on irregularities in play vary from one game to another. But the following rules are general.

A misdeal should be declared:

if, during a deal, a card is found face up in the deck;

or if the rules of shuffling, cutting, or dealing are broken.

Imperfect deck If the deck is found to have cards missing, or added, or duplicated, the hand being played is immediately abandoned. However, any scores made so far on that hand are valid.

Lead

Trick

Trumps

Trumping a trick

Whist

Whist evolved in the eighteenth century from an earlier game called triumph. It has since given rise to a whole family of games, including the popular contract bridge and solo whist. The rules are comparatively simple, but a great deal of skill is needed to play really well.

Players Whist is a game for four players, two playing against two as partners. Partnerships are decided by draw (see p 80).
Players sit around a table, with partners facing each other. By convention, players are referred to by the points of the compass, with North and South playing against East and West.

Cards A standard deck of 52 playing cards is used. Cards rank normally, with ace high. The suits are not ranked, except that one suit is designated the trump suit for each hand. A card of the trump suit beats any card from any other suit.

Objective Players aim to win tricks. A trick consists of four cards, one played by each player.

Choice of first dealer is by high cut, with ace ranking low (see p 80).

Shuffle and cut Any player has the right to shuffle, but the dealer has the right to shuffle last. The player to the right of the dealer cuts the cards and passes them to the dealer.

Rank

Deal Beginning with the player to his left and going clockwise, the dealer deals out all but one of the cards, face down and one at a time. The remaining card is placed face up on the table and its suit indicates the trump suit. The dealer adds it to his hand when it is his turn to play.

Misdeal It is a misdeal if:
a) more or fewer than 13 cards are dealt to any player; or
b) any card other than the last one is exposed.
It is not a misdeal if a player is dealt two or more successive cards and the dealer rectifies the error at once.
If there has been a misdeal, players may agree to accept the deal after the error has been rectified.
Any player, however, has the right to demand a new deal until the first trick is completed. After that the deal must stand. If there is to be a redeal, players throw in their cards and the deal passes one player to the left.

Play The player to the dealer's left leads by placing any one of his cards face up in the center of the table.
Each of the other players in turn plays a card to the center of the table.
If a player has a card of the same suit as the card led, he must play this card. This is called "following suit," and failure to do so is penalized (see the section on revoking). If he does not have a card of the suit led he may play any other card.
The trick is won:
a) by the player of the highest trump card, or
b) if no trump cards have been played, by the player of the highest card of the suit led.
The winner of one trick leads to the next. Play continues in this way until all 13 tricks of a hand have been played.
The deal passes to the next player in a clockwise direction. The cards are reshuffled and cut for the new deal.

Revoking is failing to follow suit when able to do so.
A player is not penalized if he corrects his error before the trick is turned over, and the partner of a player who fails to follow suit may caution him by asking if he does not have any cards of the suit led.
Once the trick has been turned over but before play to the next trick has begun, the opposing partnership may challenge and claim a revoke.
Points penalties for revoking vary with the different scoring systems for the game.
A partnership cannot win the game in any hand in which it revokes. If both partnerships revoke in the same hand, all cards are thrown in and a new deal is made.
Calling If a player exposes a card, other than when playing it to a trick, he must leave it face up on the table until one of his opponents "calls" on him to play it to a trick where it will not cause a revoke.
Scoring There are a number of ways of scoring, but the following systems are most common.

In America a seven-point game is usual, with two ways of scoring game points.
1) The first six tricks played are discounted. Thereafter, each trick taken scores one game point.
2) Revoking also provides game points, as the pair that failed to follow suit transfers two of its game points to the other pair.
The first pair to get seven game points scores the difference between seven and the losers' score.
English whist uses a five-point game including the scoring of honors. Games are grouped into rubbers.
There are three ways of scoring game points.
1) Discounting the first six tricks played, one game point is scored for each trick taken.
2) The honors are a,k,q, and j of trumps. A partnership scores four game points if it is dealt all four honors, and three game points if dealt any three. However, if both pairs reach five game points in the same deal, the trick points from that deal take precedence over the honors points. At least one trick must be taken in the last deal before declaring game. After game, the losers' honors

score, if any, is no longer counted in their game points total.

3) There are three alternative rulings concerning the penalties for revoking:
a) the revoking pair loses three game points;
b) the revoking pair transfers three game points to its opponents; or
c) the opponents gain three points.

After each game, additional points are scored by the winners as follows:
a) three points if the opponents had no game points;
b) two points if the opponents had one or two game points; and
c) one point if the opponents had three or four game points.

A rubber is the best of three games.

If the first two games are won by the same pair, a third game is not played.

The winners of two out of three games score two extra points for the rubber. All points are then totaled, and the partnership with the highest score wins.

TERMS USED IN WHIST

Finessing consists of playing the third-best card of a suit when also holding the best—trusting that the opponents do not hold the second best.

Forcing is playing a suit in which another player is void.

Long trumps are the remaining trump or trumps left in a hand after all other trumps in the deck have been played.

Loose card is a card of no value.

Quarte is any four cards of the same suit in sequence.

Quarte major is a sequence of a,k,q,j in the same suit.

Quinte is any five cards of the same suit in sequence.

See-saw occurs when each member of a partnership is trumping a suit, and each plays these suits to the other for that purpose.

Slam is winning every trick.

Tenace consists of holding the cards immediately above and below the opposing side's best in suit, for example ace and queen when the opponents hold the king.

SOLO WHIST

Temporary partnerships are formed in solo whist, but each player scores for himself. Basically play is as for whist, but the game has its own bidding and scoring systems.

Players Solo whist is a game for four players. At the start of each hand each player is on his own.

Cards A standard deck of 52 playing cards is used. Cards rank normally with ace high.

Objective Each player tries to contract and fulfill a bid.

Choice of first dealer is by high cut, with ace low. (See p 80.)

Shuffle and cut are normal (see p 80).

Deal The dealer deals out all the cards, beginning with the player to his left and going clockwise. The cards are dealt three at a time, with a final round of single cards. All but the last card are dealt face down; the last card, dealt to the dealer, is dealt face up and indicates trumps for some bids. Rules for misdeals are the same as for whist.

Bidding Each player in turn, beginning with the player to the dealer's left, may make a bid or pass without making a bid. In certain circumstances players may have a second chance to bid.

The bids are ranked in the following order, with each outbidding the one before.
a) Proposal and acceptance, or "prop and cop," involves a temporary partnership of two players. A call of "I propose" or "Prop" indicates that the player will try to win eight tricks in partnership with any of the others. Play is with the trump suit indicated at the deal. In his turn, a subsequent bidder may call "Accept" or "Cop" to become the partner.
b) "Solo" is a bid to take five tricks playing alone against the other three. Play is with the trump suit indicated at the deal.
c) "Misère" or "nullo" indicates that the player will try to lose every trick, playing with no trump suit.
d) "Abondance" is a bid to take nine tricks, playing with a trump suit nominated by the bidder. He does not announce the trump suit until all remaining players have passed.
e) "Royal abondance" or "abondance in trumps," is a bid to take nine tricks, playing with the trump suit indicated at the deal.

f) "Misère ouverte" or "spread" indicates that a player will try to lose every trick, playing with no trumps and turning his remaining cards face up on the table after the first trick has been taken.
g) "Abondance declarée" is a bid to take 13 tricks, playing with no trump suit.

Second bids may be made in the following cases:
a) by the player to the left of the dealer to accept a proposal;
b) by any player who has been overbid and wishes to make a higher bid;
c) by a proposer who has not been accepted and wishes to amend his proposal to a higher bid.

No bid hands If all players pass, the cards are thrown in and the deal passes to the left.

Play The player to the dealer's left leads first, unless the bid is abondance declarée in which case the bidder leads. The rules for making tricks and trumping are the same as for whist.

It is not always necessary to play a hand right out. For example after a bid of misère the hand ends as soon as the bidder takes a trick.

Revoke A revoke (see p 81) loses or wins three tricks depending on the bid and on which player made the error. A hand is always played out after a revoke, and a bidder who revokes must pay for the three tricks even if he makes his bid without them.

Scoring Chips are usually used for scoring: red ones worth five points each and white ones worth one point. Alternatively a written record may be kept.

Scores are as follows. For a successful proposal and acceptance bid, one partner receives five points from one opponent, and the other partner the same from the other opponent. For an unsuccessful bid, partners pay instead of receive the points. For all other bids, the bidder receives points from each of the other players if successful, or pays each of them if unsuccessful. The number of points varies with the bids:
solo, 10 points;
misère, 15 points;
abondance, 20 points;
royal abondance, 20 points;
misère ouverte, 30 points;
abondance declarée, 40 points.

In addition, for bids other than misère, misère ouverte, or abondance declarée, one extra point changes hands at each payment for each overtrick (trick in excess of the bid) or undertrick (trick fewer than the bid).

THREE-HANDED SOLO

The game can be adapted for three-handed play as follows.

Cards There are two alternative changes:
1) A 40-card deck is used—obtained by stripping the 2s, 3s, and 4s from a standard deck. 39 cards are dealt out and the 40th indicates the trump suit.
2) A 39-card deck is used—obtained by stripping out the whole of one suit. The trump suit is indicated by the last card dealt.

Bids There is no proposal and acceptance bid. Misère overbids abondance and misère ouverte overbids abondance declarée.

Scoring Misère is worth 20 points and abondance 15 points. Misère ouverte is worth 40 points and abondance declarée 30 points.

Rank of cards in three-handed solo

BOSTON

This game developed from whist and is itself an ancestor of the now more popular solo whist. It was very popular at the time of the American Revolution.

Players The game is for four players, each playing for himself.

Cards Two standard decks are used: one in play and the other for determining the "preference" and "color" suits. (If the preference and color suits are determined before the deal the game can be played with only one deck.) Cards rank normally, with ace high.

Chips A large number of chips are required for scoring purposes. (To make settlement simpler, players sometimes use chips of different values.)

Objective Each player tries to contract and fulfill a bid.

Choice of first dealer is by high cut, with ace low.

Pool Before each hand, each player pays 10 chips into a pool.
If the pool exceeds 250 chips, the excess is put aside for the next pool.

Deal The dealer deals out all the playing deck, beginning with the player to his left and going clockwise. The cards are dealt three at a time, with a final round of single cards. If there is a misdeal, the dealer must pay 10 chips into the pool. The deal then passes one player to the left.

Determining preference and color suits After the deal, the second deck is cut by the player sitting opposite the dealer.

The top card of the bottom section is turned face up and denotes the preference suit. The other suit of the same color is called the color suit.

Bidding Each player in turn, beginning with the player to the dealer's left, may make a bid or pass.

The bids are ranked in the following order, with each outbidding the one before:
a) "Boston," ie a bid to win five tricks with one of the plain suits as trumps;
b) six tricks;
c) seven tricks;
d) "little misery," ie a bid to lose 12 tricks, playing with no trumps and after each player has discarded one card face down;
e) eight tricks;
f) nine tricks;
g) "grand misery," ie a bid to lose every trick, playing with no trumps;
h) 10 tricks;
i) 11 tricks;
j) "little spread," ie a bid to lose 12 tricks, playing with no trumps and the hand exposed;
k) 12 tricks;
l) "grand spread," ie a bid to lose every trick, playing with no trumps and the hand exposed;
m) "grand slam," ie a bid to win all 13 tricks.

Trumps There are no trumps for misery and spread bids. For other bids the player chooses his own trump suit, usually stating what it is only when his bid has been accepted.
However, if two or more players wish to make a bid for the same number of tricks, the bids are ranked as follows according to the proposed trump suit: preference suit (high); color suit, plain suits (low).

No bid hands If all players pass, each one throws in his cards and pays 10 chips into the pool. The deal then passes one player to the left.

Play The player to the left of the dealer leads to the first trick. Play is as for whist. A player who revokes loses the hand and must pay 40 chips into the pool.

Settlement If a player fulfills his bid he receives chips from each of the other players and, if his bid was for seven tricks or higher, he also receives the chips in the pool.
If a player fails to fulfill his bid he pays chips to each of the other players and must also double the chips in the pool. For misery and spread bids the bidder pays or receives chips as follows:
20 for little misery;
40 for grand misery;
80 for little spread;
160 for grand spread.
If a player fulfills any other bid he is paid according to table A.
If a player fails to fulfill any other bid he pays according to the number of tricks by which he fails—as given in table B. A player is said to be "put in for" the number of tricks by which he fails.

OH HELL

Also known as blackout, this game has many features in common with whist. It is a game for three or more players, each playing for himself.

Cards A standard deck of 52 cards is used. Aces rank high.

Objective Each player tries to win the exact number of tricks he has bid.

Deal Each game involves a series of deals. Players cut for the first deal (highest card deals) and thereafter the deal passes in a clockwise direction around the table.
In the first deal, each player is dealt one card; in subsequent deals, the number of cards dealt to each player is increased each time by one card.
When the size of the hand can no longer be increased by one card per player, the game is finished.
Thus with four players, the cards will be dealt 13 times, and with five players ten times. At the end of each deal, the dealer turns the top card of the stock face up to denote trumps.
If in the final deal there is no spare card to turn face up, the hand is played without trumps.

Bidding Starting with the dealer, each player in turn bids the number of tricks he expects to win, or "nullo" if he expects to lose every trick.
In the first deal, possible bids are one or nullo; the number of possible bids increases with the size of each hand.

Play is opened by the player to the dealer's left. He leads with any card, and the other players must follow suit; if unable to do so they may trump or discard.
The winner of a trick leads to the next.

Scoring Every player who fulfills his bid exactly scores one point for each trick of his bid and a ten point bonus. There is no standard score for making nullo; sometimes ten points are awarded, sometimes five, or five points plus the number of tricks in the deal.
If a player wins more or fewer tricks than the number he bid, he neither scores nor pays a penalty.

Optional scoring A successful bid of small slam—winning all but one of the tricks in the hand—with a hand of more than five cards earns a 25 point bonus. Similarly, a successful bid of grand slam—winning all the tricks in the hand—earns a 50 point bonus.

Table A

Tricks bid	5	6	7	8	9	10	11	12	13
Payment	10	15	20	25	35	45	65	105	170

Table B

Tricks bid	Numbers put in for													Tricks bid
	1	2	3	4	5	6	7	8	9	10	11	12	13	
	Payment													
5	10	20	30	40	50									5
6	15	25	35	45	55	65								6
7	20	30	40	50	60	70	80							7
8	25	35	45	55	70	85	100	115						8
9	35	45	55	65	80	95	110	125	140					9
10	45	55	70	80	95	110	125	140	155	170				10
11	70	80	95	110	125	140	155	170	185	200	220			11
12	120	130	145	160	180	200	220	240	260	280	300	320		12
13	180	200	220	240	260	280	300	320	340	360	390	420	450	13

The winner is the player with the highest cumulative score after all the deals have been played.

VINT

Another member of the whist family, vint is a game for four players playing in partnerships of two.

Cards A standard deck of cards is used. The cards rank in ascending order from 2 through ace. The suits rank spades (lowest), clubs, diamonds, hearts, and no trumps (highest).

Objective Each partnership aims to make and fulfill a bid by taking tricks.

Deal The entire deck is dealt out, one face-down card at a time to each player. The deal passes clockwise around the table with each round of play.

Bidding Starting with the dealer, each player in turn bids or passes.

Each bid indicates the intention to take six tricks plus the number called, in the suit named or with no trumps. Thus the lowest bid is one spade (ie taking seven tricks with spades as trumps); and the highest is seven no trumps (ie taking thirteen tricks).

A bid is overcalled by a bid of more tricks in the same suit, or the same number of tricks in a higher ranking suit or no trumps.

When a player is overcalled he may call higher when his turn comes round again, even if the only other bidder is his partner.

Play is opened by the player to the left of the highest bidder, and proceeds in a clockwise direction around the table.

Each player must follow suit if able to do so; if he cannot, he either plays a trump or discards.

The winner of a trick leads to the next trick.

Scoring Each partnership records its score on a scorepad or piece of paper divided into two sections by a horizontal line (as in bridge, p 92).

Game points are entered below the line. Each partnership scores for each trick taken—whether or not the bid is fulfilled.

However, the number of tricks bid determines the value of each trick, ranging from ten points per trick for a bid of one, 20 points per trick for a bid of two, and so on up to 70 points per trick for a bid of seven.

The first partnership to score 500 game points wins the game—even if it reaches this score partway through a hand, and regardless of whether or not it won the bidding.

Bonus points are entered above the line. They are scored as follows:
a) winning a game, 1000 points;
b) winning a rubber (two out of three games), 2000 points;
c) "little slam" (12 tricks) made but not bid, 1000 points;
d) little slam bid and made, 6000 points;
e) "grand slam" (13 tricks) made but not bid, 2000 points;
f) grand slam bid and made, 12,000 points.

Honor points are scored above the line and comprise the a, k, q, j, and 10 of trumps and the other aces. In a trump suit, the ace is counted twice, both as an honor and an ace. When playing no trumps, only the four aces are honors.

The partnership holding the most honors scores ten times the trick value for each honor held in trumps, or 25 times the trick value for each honor (ace) held when playing no trumps.

For example, if the final bid is three trumps, each trick is worth 30 points and therefore each honor is worth 300 points ($10 \times 3 = 300$).

If one partnership has a majority of aces and the other a majority of honors, those two majorities are compared, and the partnership that has the bigger majority scores for the difference.

For example, if side A has two honors and one ace, but side B has one honor and three aces, the two honors are deducted from the three aces and side B scores for one honor, worth ten times the trick value.

But if side A has three honors and one ace, and side B has one honor and three aces, neither side scores, as the three honors and the three aces cancel each other out.

If both sides hold two aces:
at no trumps, neither side scores;
at trumps, the side that wins most tricks scores for its honors.

Coronet Any player holding three aces or a sequence of three cards in a plain suit—known as a "coronet"—scores 500 points, entered above the line.

If a player holds the fourth ace, he scores a further 500 points; and each extra card in a sequence also scores a further 500 points.

If the sequence is in the trump suit, or in any suit when no trumps has been declared, coronet is worth double.

Unfulfilled bids If a partnership fails to make its bid, it is penalized for each undertrick by 100 times the value of each trick (entered above the line); but it also scores game points below the line for the number of tricks it took.

For example, if the bidding partnership made a bid of five no trumps (ie 11 tricks) and took only eight tricks (ie it failed by three tricks), scoring would be as follows.
a) $3 \times 50 \times 100 = 15,000$ penalty points;
b) $8 \times 50 = 400$ game points;
c) the opponents score game points in the usual way for the number of tricks they took: $5 \times 50 = 250$ game points.

PREFERENCE

This is a fairly straightforward game usually played for small stakes. Three players take part, each playing for himself.

Cards A standard deck with all the 2s, 3s, 4s, 5s, and 6s removed is used.

The cards are ranked as follows: ace (high), k, q, j, 10, 9, 8, 7 (low).

The suits, in descending order, rank: hearts (known as "preference"), diamonds, clubs, spades.

Objective Each player tries to be the highest bidder and fulfill the contract.

Preliminaries Before the start of play, each player puts an equal agreed number of chips into the pool.

Players must also decide:
a) how much a successful bidder should receive from the pool, depending on the rank of the trump suit; and
b) the payment to be made into the pool by an unsuccessful bidder.

Deal Any player may deal the first hand; thereafter the deal passes clockwise around the table.

The dealer gives ten face-down cards to each player, and also deals two cards face down in the center of the table as the "widow," as follows.

He first deals a packet of three cards to each player, then he deals the widow, then another packet of four cards to each player, and finally a packet of three cards to each player.

Bidding Each player in turn, beginning with the player to the dealer's left, either bids a suit or passes.

By bidding a suit, the player indicates that he intends to win at least six tricks of the possible ten, with the named suit as trumps.

Each player is permitted one bid only, and each bid must be in a higher ranking suit than the previous bid.

If all three players pass in the first round of bidding, there is a second round in which each player can either pass or put chips into the pool. The player putting most chips into the pool then wins the right to name the trump suit; he may also discard any two of his cards and take the widow into his hand.

If a player bids in the first round, the widow is not used.

Play The player to the left of the successful bidder leads to the first trick.

Every other player must follow suit if he can; if he cannot he may play a trump or discard any card.

The highest card in the suit led or the highest trump played takes the trick.

The winner of a trick leads to the next trick, and the game continues until all ten tricks have been taken.

Settlement If the bidder fulfills his bid (takes at least six of the ten tricks) he wins the agreed number of chips from the pool, depending on the rank of the trump suit.

If the bidder fails in his contract, he pays the agreed number of chips into the pool.

Rank of cards in preference

© DIAGRAM

Euchre

Euchre is a derivative of écarté and dates back at least to the 1800s. For a time it was the national game of the United States. It is a game for two to six players depending on the version played; perhaps the most popular form is four-handed euchre.

Tricks bid	♠	♣	♦	♥	No trumps
6	40	60	80	100	120
7	140	160	180	200	220
8	240	260	280	300	320
9	340	360	380	400	420
10	440	460	480	500	520

Rank

Rank of trumps

FOUR-HANDED EUCHRE

Four people play in partnerships of two. Each player sits opposite his partner.

Deck A 32-card deck is used: a standard deck with the 6s, 5s, 4s, 3s, and 2s removed. Ace ranks high, and 7 low.

Trumps The jack of trumps, called the "right bower," ranks as the highest trump. The other jack of the same color, called the "left bower," ranks second.

For example, if diamonds are trumps, the jack of hearts is the left bower.

Thus the trump suit ranks: rb (high), lb, a,k,q,10,9,8,7 (low).

Objective Each partnership tries to win the most tricks.

Deal Players draw for first deal, lowest card dealing. Each player is dealt five face-down cards, in packets of three and two.

The dealer then turns the next card face up to indicate trumps.

The deal passes clockwise around the table.

Nominating trumps Each player, beginning with the player to the dealer's left, has the option of accepting the suit of the face-up card as trumps, or refusing it in the hope of nominating a different suit.

To accept, the dealer's opponents say "I order it up;" the dealer's partner says "I assist;" and the dealer says nothing but indicates his acceptance by discarding one card, and adding the face-up card to his hand.

To refuse, the non-dealers say "I pass," and the dealer puts the face-up card under the stock.

Once one player has accepted, play begins.

If all four players refuse, there is a second round in which each player in turn has the right to nominate the trump suit or pass. Once a player has nominated a suit, play begins. If all the players pass, the hands are thrown in and the

cards are dealt by the next dealer.

Play The player who nominated trumps is called the "maker." Before play begins, he may decide to play the hand without his partner, in which case he says "I play alone."

His partner then lays his hand face down on the table. Although he does not play the hand, he still shares in any stakes.

Rules of play are the same as in whist.

Scoring If the maker and his partner win all five tricks, this constitutes a "march," and scores two points. If the maker is playing alone, he scores four points for a march.

If the maker and his partner win four or three tricks, they score one point; if they win fewer than three tricks they are said to be "euchred," and their opponents score two points.

Game is generally five points, but some players prefer to set a target of seven or ten. Players may use counters to keep the score, but it is customary to use a 3 and a 4 from the unused cards as markers, one card being face up, the other face down, as illustrated:

the 3 exposed with the other card across it signifies one point; 4 exposed with the other card across it is two points; 3 on top of the other card is three points; and 4 on top is four points.

1 point   2 points

3 points   4 points

RAILROAD EUCHRE

In this variation of four-handed euchre, the joker is used as an additional trump, ranking above right bower.

TWO-HANDED EUCHRE

The deck is reduced to 24 cards by discarding the 8s and 7s. Rules are the same as for four-handed euchre, except that there is no need for a declaration to play alone.

THREE-HANDED EUCHRE

In three-handed euchre (also called cutthroat euchre) the maker plays on his own, with the other two players in partnership against him.

The maker scores three points for march; otherwise scoring is the same as in the four-handed game.

CALL-ACE EUCHRE

This is a version for four, five, or six players, each playing for himself.

The rules are the same as for four-handed euchre, with the following differences.

Calling The maker has the right to decide whether to play on his own or with a partner. To choose a partner he says "I call on the ace of . . ." and nominates a suit.

If a player holds the ace named, he plays as the maker's partner, but does not declare his partnership until he plays the ace.

As the ace may in fact not have been dealt, the maker may find he is playing alone!

Scoring A lone maker wins points as follows:
a) march, as many points as there are players;
b) four or three tricks, one point.
A partnership wins points as follows:
a) march, two points for each player if there are three or four players, and three points for each player if there are five or six;
b) four or three tricks, each partner scores one point.
If the maker, with or without partner, is euchred, the other players score two points each.

FIVE HUNDRED

Five hundred is a variant of euchre for three players. It has certain similarities to bridge and whist.

Deck As for euchre, plus a joker (giving 33 cards in all). In the trump suit cards rank, in descending order, as follows: joker, right bower (jack of the trump suit), left bower (other jack of the same color), a,k,q, 10,9,8,7.

In no-trump hands, there are no right and left bowers. The holder of the joker may then nominate it to represent any suit he pleases; the joker automatically ranks as the highest card of that suit and takes any trick to which it is led or played.

Objective Each player aims to make a contract by bidding and to win enough tricks to fulfill it.

Deal Players cut for deal (king ranks high, ace low, and joker lowest); lowest card deals.

Ten face-down cards are dealt to each player, in packets of either three, two, three, two; or three, three, three, one. The remaining packet of three cards constitutes the "widow," and is placed face upward on the table.

The deal passes clockwise around the table.

Bidding Each player in turn makes a bid, starting with the player to the dealer's left. Each player specifies the number of tricks he intends to take and his choice of trumps. The lowest number of tricks that can be bid is six, and the highest ten.

For bidding the calls are ranked: no-trumps (highest), hearts, diamonds, clubs, spades (lowest).

Any player who passes cannot make a further bid in that round of play.

Widow The player who wins the contract adds the three widow cards to his hand and discards face down any three cards of his choice.

Play Rules of play are the same as in whist.

If a player leads the joker in a no-trump hand, he cannot nominate it to a suit in which he has either declared himself void or that he has failed to follow when able.

The winner of a trick leads to the next trick.

Scoring The players opposing the contract play as partners, but each always scores ten points for each trick he makes. The bidder scores points according to the table, provided he has made his contract.

If he fails to score sufficient tricks, he loses the value of the contract.

Bonuses There are no bonuses for overtricks (ie tricks over the number bid).

However, a player who has made a contract of less than eight clubs but has scored "grand slam" (all ten tricks), receives a total of 250 points.

(There is an optional system for when grand slam is scored after a bid of eight clubs or better. In this system, the successful player scores a bonus equal to the contract. For example, a bid of eight diamonds that results in a grand slam is worth 280 points plus a bonus of 280.)

Players losing contracts may well find their scores going into minus figures.

Game is 500 points. If two players reach this total in the same deal, the player who reached 500 first wins.

TWO-HANDED FIVE HUNDRED

This is played in the same way as the three-handed game, except that a third hand, known as a "dead hand," is dealt. It remains face down throughout the game, and adds a degree of uncertainty to the bidding and play.

FOUR-HANDED FIVE HUNDRED

This game is also played like the three-handed game, but facing players act as partners. The deck is increased to 43 cards by adding the 6s, 5s, and two 4s—one of each color.

ECARTE

Ecarté is a card game for two players that first became popular in France in the early 1800s. Its name is the French word for "discarded."

Deck A 32-card deck is used: a standard 52-card deck with the 6s, 5s, 4s, 3s, and 2s removed.

Cards rank: k (high), q, j, a, 10, 9, 8, 7.

Objective Each player tries to take tricks and to score points.

Deal Players cut for deal, highest card dealing first (the cards rank as in play). The dealer gives each player five face-down cards, in packets of either two then three, or three then two. Whichever system is used must be kept throughout the game.

The deal passes clockwise around the table.

Trumps The eleventh card is placed face up beside the stock and indicates trumps.

Exchanging cards The non-dealer may propose an exchange of cards. To do this he says "Cards".

If the dealer accepts, the non-dealer exchanges as many cards as he wishes for cards drawn from the stock. The dealer may then do likewise.

The non-dealer may repeat the proposal, and players go on exchanging cards until the stock is exhausted. But if the dealer refuses at any time, by saying "Play," there is no more exchanging.

If the non-dealer does not wish to exchange at any time, he says "I play."

The dealer cannot propose an exchange.

Play The non-dealer leads first. Players must follow suit if they can, and may trump if they cannot.

A player must always take a trick if he can. The winner of a trick leads to the next trick.

Scoring is as follows:
a) "point" or "the trick" (three tricks won), scores one point;
b) "the vole" (all five tricks won), scores two points;
c) king turned up to indicate trumps, scores one point for the dealer; and
d) king of trumps held in the hand, scores one point if it is declared before the holder plays his first card.

Game is five points.

Penalties If a player has refused to exchange and fails to make at least three tricks (point), his opponent scores an extra point if he makes point.

There is no penalty if the opponent scores vole.

Five hundred

Deal

Player 2

Player 1   Player 3

Widow

Ecarté

Deal

Player 1   Player 2

Trumps   Stock

©DIAGRAM

NAPOLEON

Also called nap, this game is in some ways similar to euchre. Any number of players from two to seven may take part. There are no partnerships.

Deck A standard 52-card deck is used; ace ranks high.

Objective Each player aims to contract a bid and take tricks to fulfill it.

Deal Players cut for deal, highest card dealing first. Each player is dealt five face-down cards, one at a time. The stock is then placed face down on the table. The deal passes in clockwise rotation.

Bidding Beginning with the player to the dealer's left, each player can either pass or bid two, three, four, or "Napoleon" —indicating the number of tricks he intends to win. (Napoleon signifies five tricks.)

Each bid must be higher than the previous bid, and the player with the highest bid becomes the bidder.

There is only one round of bidding.

Trumps The bidder leads to the first trick, and the suit of his opening card denotes trumps.

Play is the same as in whist.

Scoring Napoleon is played for stakes, the usual ones being:

two units for a bid of two; three units for three; four units for four; and ten for Napoleon.

If the bidder wins his contract, each of the other players pays him the stake. If he fails to win his contract, he pays each of the other players the stake. If he fails on a bid of Napoleon, he pays only half the stake.

Optional bids The following optional bids are sometimes used.

a) "Wellington" is a declaration to win all five tricks at double stakes. It cannot be called unless Napoleon has already been called.

b) "Blücher" overcalls Wellington, and is for five tricks at triple stakes.

c) "Misère" or "misery" is a declaration to lose every trick. In the bidding it ranks between three and four, and carries the same stakes as three. There are no trumps in this bid.

PURCHASE NAP

The rules of purchase nap are the same as for Napoleon, except that each player may exchange any number of cards for fresh ones from the stock, on payment of one unit for each card.

The payments are put in a kitty, won by the first player to make a bid of Napoleon.

SEVEN-CARD NAP

In seven-card nap, each player receives seven cards. Play is the same as for Napoleon, but bids of Wellington and Blücher are not permitted.

The order of bids with their stakes are as follows:

three bids, a stake of three; four, stake of four; nap and misère (optional), stake of 10; six, stake of 18; and seven, stake of 24.

Players losing nap, misère, six, or seven pay half stakes.

THREE-CARD LOO

Loo, or lanterloo as it is sometimes called, was once one of the most widely played card games in Europe. It has several variations but is always played for stakes.

Players Three or more people can play, but the best number is about six.

Deck A standard 52-card deck is used. Ace ranks high.

Objective Each player tries to win at least one trick.

Deal Players cut for deal, lowest card dealing.

Each player is dealt three face-down cards, one at a time.

An extra hand known as a "miss" is also dealt, as either the first or the last hand of each deal.

The top card of the remaining cards is turned face up and denotes trumps.

The deal passes clockwise around the table.

Pool In an optional opening deal called a "single," no miss is dealt, and only the dealer puts three counters into a pool. In subsequent deals, or if no single has been played, a miss is dealt and each player contributes three counters to the pool.

The choice Beginning with the player to the dealer's left, each player in turn chooses one of the following:

a) to play with the cards he holds;

b) to throw in his own cards and play with the miss; or

c) to pass.

To indicate their choice, players say "I play," "I take the miss," or "I pass," as appropriate.

If a player passes, he throws in his cards and takes no further part in that deal. If every player passes, the dealer takes the pool.

If only one player decides to play but has not taken the miss, the dealer must play him, using the cards in the miss. If the dealer loses, he does not pay, nor is he paid if he wins.

If only one player decides to play and has taken the miss, the dealer may either play him with standard scoring, or just let him take the pool.

Play The first player to choose to play leads to the first trick, with his highest trump if he has one.

Each player who did not pass plays a card to each trick. If possible, he must:

a) follow suit; and

b) play a higher card of the leading suit than any already played to that trick.

If a player cannot follow suit, he should trump the trick with a higher trump than any already played to that trick; if he cannot do this, he may discard.

The winner of a trick must lead with a trump if possible.

Scoring The winner of each trick takes one third of the pool.

Looing A player who has not won a trick is said to be "looed."

In limited loo, a looed player pays an agreed amount (usually three counters) into the pool.

In unlimited loo, he pays as many counters as there were in the pool at the beginning of the hand.

Penalties A player is also looed if he breaches the rules, including:

a) playing out of turn;

b) looking at the miss without taking it;

c) failing to take a trick when possible; and

d) failing to lead the ace of trumps when holding it.

Variations

a) The trump card is not turned up until a player cannot follow suit.

b) If a player is dealt three trumps, he collects the pool. The hands are thrown in, and the cards are shuffled and dealt for the next round.

FIVE-CARD LOO

This variant is played in the same way as three-card loo, except for the following changes.

Deal Each player receives five cards.

Pool Contributions to the pool are five instead of three counters.

Miss is never dealt.

Exchanges Each player may exchange up to five cards for the same number of cards drawn from the stock. A player who exchanges must then play his hand.

Pam The jack of clubs, called "pam," ranks as the highest trump regardless of suit. If a player leads the ace of trumps and says "Pam be civil," the pam cannot be played to that trick.

Flushes are five cards of the same suit, or four of the same suit plus pam. The holder of a flush exposes it before play and wins the pool. Each of the other players is then looed unless he also holds a flush or flush with pam.

If there is more than one flush, a trump flush wins over one in a plain suit, and if there is a clash between plain suit flushes, the highest card wins. If two or more plain suit flushes are equal, the pool is divided.

Blaze This is an optional winning hand, entirely made up of court cards. The same rules of precedence apply as with flushes, and a blaze outranks a flush.

IRISH LOO

This is played like three-card loo, with the following differences.

a) Miss is not dealt.

b) Exchanging is carried out in the same way as in the five-card game.

c) "Club law:" if clubs are trumps every player must enter the game.

SPOIL FIVE

Spoil five is similar to loo but has an unusual and complex ranking system. It is especially popular in the Republic of Ireland.

Players Two or more people can play, but the game is best played with five or six. Each person plays for himself.

Deck A standard deck of playing cards is used. The cards are ranked, in descending order, as follows.

Spades and clubs
Plain suits (ie non-trump): k,q,j,a,2,3,4,5,6,7,8,9,10.
Trump suits: 5,j,a of hearts, ace of spades or clubs, k,q,2,3, 4,6,7,8,9,10.

Diamonds
Plain suit: k,q,j,10,9,8,7,6,5,4, 3,2,a.
Trump suit: 5,j,a of hearts, a of diamonds, k,q,10,9,8,7,6,4,3, 2.

Hearts
Plain suit: k,q,j,10,9,8,7,6,5,4, 3,2.
Trump suit: 5,j,a,k,q,10,9,8,7, 6,4,3,2.

Note that the ace of hearts is always the third-best trump, regardless of suit; the 5 of the trump suit is highest; and the jack of the trump suit second-highest.

Objective Each player tries to win three tricks and to prevent anyone else from doing so.

Deal Players draw for deal, using standard ranking with ace high and 2 low. Lowest card deals.

Five face-down cards are dealt to each player in packets of two then three, or vice versa. The next card is turned face up to indicate trumps. The deal passes clockwise around the table.

Pool Each player puts an agreed number of counters into the pool. It is won by a player taking three tricks in one hand.

Exchanging If the face-up card denoting the trump suit is an ace, the dealer may exchange it for a card in his hand before the first card is led. This is called "robbing." If a player has been dealt the ace of trumps he may, if he wishes, exchange any card in his hand for the face-up card. If he does not exchange a card, he must announce that he has the ace at his first turn of play —otherwise the ace becomes the lowest-ranking trump for that round, even if it is an ace of hearts.

Play The player to the left of the dealer leads to the first trick and the winner of each trick leads to the next.

Rules of play are the same as for whist, with the following differences.

If a card of a plain suit is led, a player may either trump or follow suit. He may discard another plain suit card only if he can neither follow suit nor trump.

If a card of the trump suit is led, a player must follow suit if he can. He need not play any of the top three trumps if the leading card was a lower trump—holding back a card in this way is called "reneging."

Jinxing A player who wins three tricks may take the pool. and the hand ends. Alternatively, he may call "Jinx," implying that he will try to win the remaining two tricks. Play continues, and if he wins the extra two tricks he takes the pool, plus a sum from each player equal to his original contribution to the pot. If he does not make both tricks he loses the pool and the hand counts as a "spoil."

Spoil is when nobody wins three tricks, or a winner fails to win all five after jinxing. The cards are dealt for a new hand but only the new dealer contributes to the pot. Only when the pot is won do all the players contribute to a new pot.

FORTY-FIVE

In this variant of spoil five only an even number of players can take part, divided into two equal and opposing sides. There is no pool.

Scoring The winning partnership scores as follows:
a) three tricks, 5 points; and
b) five tricks, 10 points; or
alternatively:
a) three tricks, 5 points;
b) four tricks, 15 points;
c) five tricks, 25 points.
Game is 45 points, and the first side to reach it wins.

AUCTION FORTY-FIVE

Auction forty-five is very popular in parts of Canada. Its basic rules are the same as for spoil five, with the following variations.

Players Four or six people play in partnerships of two or three respectively. Each player sits between two players of the opposing side.

Bidding The player to the left of the dealer bids first, followed by each player in turn to his left.

The bids, indicating the number of points each side is contracted to make, are 5,10, 15,20,25, and 30. Each bid must cutbid the previous bid. The dealer has the option of "holding" ie outbidding the previous bid without increasing it.

Each of the other players who bid may then bid again; but the dealer has the option of holding a second time.

Trumps are nominated by the highest bidder.

Discards Each player may exchange as many cards as he likes for cards drawn from the top of the stock.

Play The player to the left of the highest bidder leads first.

Scoring Each trick counts five points, and the highest trump in play scores five extra points to whichever side takes it.

If a side fulfills its contract it scores the number of points bid plus the points scored with its tricks.

If it fails, it loses the number of points bid.

The side that did not make the contract scores all the points it makes in play.

Game is 120 points.

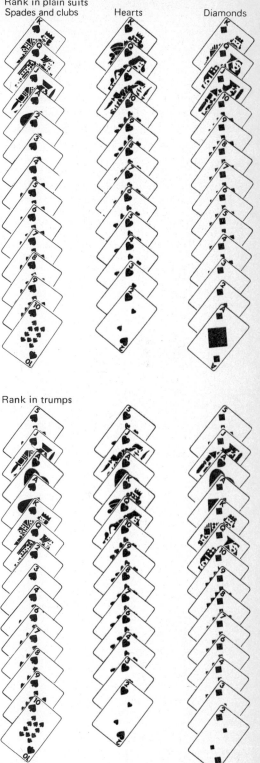

Spoil five
Rank in plain suits
Spades and clubs   Hearts   Diamonds

Rank in trumps

Contract bridge

For very many people, contract bridge is the most fascinating of card games: it is played in houses, clubs, and tournaments throughout the world. Its origins can be traced back some 400 years to the development of whist in England, but it was only in 1896 that the game of bridge itself evolved. In 1925 contract bridge was developed, and within a few years it was by far the most popular form of the game.

GENERAL
Cards A standard deck of 52 cards is used. By convention a second deck, with contrasting backs, is also used, so that while one player deals another can shuffle the alternate deck in readiness for the next deal.
The cards rank: ace (high) through 2 (low). The 2 is commonly called a "deuce," and the 3 a "trey."

Players As in whist, there are four players, each pair forming a partnership. Partners sit opposite each other. One partnership is usually called North-South, the other East-West.
Objective Each partnership aims to win a "rubber," by winning the most points in the best of three games.
A game is won by scoring 100 points, earned by taking tricks that have been contracted for.

Honors

Rank of suits

Rank of cards

Honors are the high-ranking cards in the trump suit, from the ace down through and including the 10. In "no trump" games, the four aces are honors.
Suits For the purpose of bidding the suits are ranked as follows:
spades (highest), hearts, diamonds, clubs (lowest).

The draw At the beginning of a bridge game, one deck is spread out face down on the table, and each player draws one card from the deck.
The two players who draw the highest cards form one partnership; the other two players form the second. The player with the highest card becomes first dealer and chooses his seating position; his partner sits opposite him. If cards of the same denomination appear on the draw, they are ranked according to suit, as for bidding.
Shuffle and cut The player to the left of the dealer shuffles the deck; the player to the dealer's right cuts the deck.
As the cards are being dealt, the alternate deck is shuffled by the dealer's partner.
The deal begins with the player to the dealer's left. The cards are dealt in a clockwise direction, one at a time and face down, until each player including the dealer has 13 cards.

BIDDING
The auction begins once players have had a chance to study their cards. It opens with the dealer and continues in clockwise rotation. Each player, according to his hand, makes a "call," that may be a bid, pass, double, or redouble. If a player passes, he may still make another call at a later stage in the bidding. But when a bid, double, or redouble is followed by three passes in succession, the auction ends. If there are four passes at the opening of bidding, one from each player, the cards are "thrown in" to the center of the table and shuffled. A new hand is then dealt by the next dealer.
A pass indicates that a player does not choose to make any other call at that time in the bidding.

A bid is a statement of a number and a trumps suit, eg "three clubs," or "five no trumps." It offers an undertaking that if that suit is trumps (or if there are "no trumps") the bidding player's partnership will take a certain number of tricks.
Bidding refers to the number of "odd" (ie additional) tricks that a bidder undertakes to make over six tricks.
A bid of "one club," for instance, means that a player thinks that his partnership can make seven tricks in all, if clubs are trumps.
A bid of "four no trumps" offers the undertaking to make ten tricks in all, if no suit is trumps.
Continuing the bidding As the auction continues, each successive bid must be higher than any preceding bid—either by calling a greater number of tricks or by naming a higher ranking suit.
For instance, a bid of "two spades" is higher than two hearts, diamonds, or clubs.
A no trump call ranks above all suits. So, for example, a bid of "two no trumps" is higher than two spades. The next player to bid would have to bid at least "three clubs."

The contract The highest bid of the auction becomes the "contract." The players in the partnership making that bid must, in play, make as many tricks as they have contracted for, or more. Their opponents have only to prevent them from doing this—it does not matter what they themselves have bid.

The first six tricks taken by the contracted bidders are commonly referred to as "making the book."

Slam The maximum number of tricks in any played hand is 13. This gives a maximum bid of "seven," when one side believes it can take all the tricks: the book (of six), plus seven odd tricks.
If a side succeeds in bidding and winning 13 tricks, this is known as a "grand slam." A "small slam" occurs if a side bids and wins a total of 12 tricks.

Doubling If a player says "Double" after any of his opponents' bids, it means that he believes he could prevent them making their bid, if it became the contract.
A bid that has been doubled need not become the contract: it can be overbid in the usual way, by either partnership. If, however, it does become the contract and succeeds, the contracting players' score is doubled. Should the bidders "go down" (ie not make their contract) the side that doubled gets twice the score that it would otherwise have had.

Redoubling If a bid has been doubled, either player of the bidding partnership may say "Redouble." This confirms his confidence in the bid, and —as in doubling— the scoring is affected whether or not the contract is made (see the section on scoring).
A bid that has been redoubled can be overbid in the usual way.

The declarer The player in the contracting side who first made a bid in the trump suit of the contract (spades, hearts, diamonds, clubs, or no trumps), is referred to as the "declarer." He plays both hands of the contracting partnership's game.

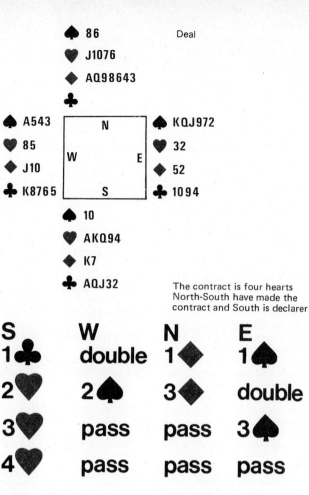

Deal

The contract is four hearts North-South have made the contract and South is declarer

S	**W**	**N**	**E**
1♣	double	1♦	1♠
2♥	2♠	3♦	double
3♥	pass	pass	3♠
4♥	pass	pass	pass

Laying out dummy's hand

PLAY
A trick consists of four cards, one played from each player's hand, in clockwise rotation. The player who must play first is called the "lead."

The lead The opening lead is held by the player to the dealer's left. He plays the first card after the bidding ends. After this, the winner of each trick makes the next lead.
A player may lead any card, and the other three players must follow suit if possible. If a player cannot follow suit, he may play any other card in his hand.

Winning the trick If none of the four cards is a trump, the trick is won by the highest card played in the suit led.
If one or more of the four cards is a trump, the trick is won by the highest trump.

No trump When a "no trump" bid becomes the contract, all suits have equal rank and the highest card in the suit led always wins the trick.

Dummy As soon as the opening lead has been made, declarer's partner lays down his cards face up on the table, sorted out by suit, with trumps to his right.
The exposed cards, and declarer's partner himself, are referred to as "dummy" for that hand.
Only declarer can choose the cards to play for the dummy hand. The dummy partner may not participate in that hand, other than to physically play a specified card at declarer's request.
Plays from dummy must be in correct order of rotation, ie following a card played by the player to declarer's left. Declarer must play a card in dummy that he touches (except when rearranging the cards or touching a card next to the one to be played).

Gathering won tricks is done by either player of the side winning the trick.
The four cards are gathered together and placed face down on the table.
All declarer's and dummy's tricks are placed in front of declarer; all the opponents' tricks are placed in front of one opponent.
The arrangement of gathered tricks must show clearly how many tricks have been won and in which order. Common procedure is to bunch the first six of declarer's tricks into one group, so that it is clear how many odd tricks have been made.

A trick may be inspected by the declarer or by either opponent, until a player of the inspecting side has led or played to the following trick.

SCORING

It is important to master the scoring in contract bridge as it strongly affects the game's strategy.

Both sides should keep score in case of disagreement.

A scoring pad has a central vertical line dividing "we" (one partnership) from "they" (its opponents).

A horizontal line is initially drawn across the scoring pad, and a partnership can score points either "below the line" or "above the line."

Trick points are entered below the line. Only declarer's side can score trick points on a hand, and only if the contract is made. Only the odd tricks contracted for can be scored below the line.

Trick points show each side's progress toward winning the current game.

Premium points are scored above the line, and may be scored by both sides in any hand. They are won for: overtricks; successful doubling or redoubling; bidding and making a slam; having a certain number of honors cards in one hand in the deal; or winning the final game of a rubber.

Undertricks If declarer's side fails to make the contract, the number of tricks it has failed by are known as "undertricks."

These are credited to the opponents' premium points and scored above the line.

Vulnerable A partnership is "vulnerable" if it has won its first game toward the rubber. (It is therefore possible for both partnerships to be vulnerable.)

Winning a game The first side to reach a score of 100 or more, either in one or in several hands, wins the game. A horizontal line is then drawn below the trick scores of both sides.

Trick scores for the next game are entered below this line, both sides beginning again from zero.

Winning the rubber When one side has won two games, the rubber ends.

This side earns 700 premium points if its opponents have won no game, and 500 premium points if its opponents have won one game.

All trick and premium points are then totaled, and the side with the higher total wins the rubber.

The back score indicates an individual player's standing. It is used in any competition in which partners rotate.

After a rubber, the difference between the two sides' final scores is calculated by subtracting the lower from the higher.

This difference is rounded to the nearest 100 (50 and above become 100), and divided by 100. For example, 753 becomes 800, giving 8. Each player of the winning partnership is then given a score of plus 8 and each opponent a score of minus 8. In subsequent rubbers, with different partnerships, the same procedure is followed. The player with the highest plus score at the end is the overall winner.

Contract bridge scoring table

Trick score: scored by declarer below the line

	♣	♦	♥	♠	NT
First trick over six bid and made	20	20	30	30	40
Subsequent tricks bid and made	20	20	30	30	30
Doubling doubles trick score					
Redoubling doubles doubled score					

Premium score: scored by declarer above the line

	Not vulnerable	Vulnerable
Small slam	500	750
Grand slam	1000	1500
Each overtrick undoubled	Trick value	Trick value
Each overtrick doubled	100	200
Each overtrick redoubled	200	400
Making a doubled or redoubled contract	50	50

Rubber, game, and partscore: scored above the line

	Points
For winning rubber, if opponents have won no game	700
For winning rubber, if opponents have won one game	500
For having won one game in an unfinished rubber	300
For having the only partscore in an unfinished rubber	50

Honors: scored by either side above the line

	Points
Four trump honors in one hand	100
Five trump honors in one hand	150
Four aces in one hand, no trump contract	150

Undertricks: scored by opponents above the line

	Undoubled	Doubled	Redoubled
First trick, not vulnerable	50	100	200
Subsequent tricks	50	200	400
First trick, vulnerable	100	200	400
Subsequent tricks	100	300	600

Explanation of scoring diagrams

a) "We" score 70 trick points.

b) "We" score 30 trick points and 150 premium points. "We" win the first game and are now vulnerable.

c) "We" go under by two tricks. "They" score 200 undertrick points.

d) "They" score 60 trick points and 150 premium points.

DUPLICATE CONTRACT BRIDGE

Duplicate contract bridge is very popular among advanced bridge players. It is the only form played in international tournaments. All groups of players are presented, in turn, with the same deal of cards. In this way, the game relies more on skill than on luck of the deal.

Equipment:
1) one table for each deal to be played in the tournament;
2) the same number of duplicate boards or trays;
3) one deck of cards for each board.

Players Competing units may be individuals, pairs, or teams of four or six, depending on the nature of the tournament.
In individual events, partnerships change during the tournament; in team events, partnerships change at half-time; and in pairs matches, the same partnerships are preserved throughout.
A duplicate board is used at each table. Each board has four pockets, an arrow or label indicating North's side, and markers indicating the dealer and the vulnerability or otherwise of partnerships.
Before the tournament the boards are arranged so that a quarter have North-South vulnerable, a quarter East-West vulnerable, a quarter both pairs vulnerable, and a quarter neither pair vulnerable. Within each category, the position of dealer is distributed equally between the pairs.

Basic procedure Each board maintains the same deal of cards throughout the tournament.
The boards and players move from table to table in a specified way.
The tournament ends, according to the system used, either:
when all North-South players have met all East-West players; or
when all players have played with and against all other players.
Deal For the first hand at each board, the designated dealer shuffles and deals the cards in the usual way.
Thereafter, following each hand, this original deal is preserved. Each player's cards are placed in the appropriate board pocket, in readiness for the next set of players.
The auction for any hand takes place in the usual way, commencing with the player indicated as dealer.
If all players pass, there is no redeal.

Play on any hand proceeds as in contract bridge, except that after each trick is completed the cards are not gathered together.
Each player takes back his card, and turns it face down on the table in front of him. He points the card lengthwise toward the partners who won the trick; this allows players to keep track of the number of tricks won by each side.
Scoring a hand No points are given for winning a rubber. If a side bids and makes a contract that gives it a game (100 trick points), it gets 500 premium points if vulnerable, 300 if not.
Additional premium points for making a grand slam are 1500 if vulnerable, 1000 if not; and for a small slam 750 if vulnerable, 500 if not.
If a side bids and makes a contract less than game, it gets 50 premium points.
A score made on one board cannot be carried forward to affect scoring on the next.
Unless cumulative tournament scoring is used, no premium points are given for holding honors in one hand.

Scoring the tournament
a) Match point procedure is always used if the competing units are individuals. It can also be used for pairs.
The comparison is between scores made at the same board, ie success in playing the same deal.
Each score is given two points for each lower score made in the same position on that board, and one point for each exactly equal score.
Each individual in an individual event receives points for the score made by his partnership. The individual or pair with the highest number of match points wins the competition.
b) International match point (imp) scoring is usually used for teams. Each partnership's surplus (or deficit) of points over its opponents is calculated for each hand, and added together at the end to give a team total. This is then converted into match points on the basis of an established scale.
c) Cumulative (total point) scoring is still sometimes used for team competitions.

AUCTION BRIDGE

A forerunner of contract bridge, auction bridge evolved from the game of whist.
Except for the scoring—which greatly affects the strategy of the game—its rules are as for contract bridge.
Major differences The two major differences in scoring are as follows:
1) In auction bridge there is no concept of vulnerability. If one partnership has won a game there is no extra penalty (as in contract bridge) for failure to make a contract.
2) All odd tricks, whether contracted for or not, are scored "below the line." They contribute to winning the game, provided that declarer has succeeded in making the minimum number of tricks named in the contract.

Trick points

	♣	♦	♥	♠	NT
Undoubled	6	7	8	9	10
Doubled	12	14	16	18	20
Redoubled	24	28	32	36	40

Game The first side to score 30 points below the line wins a game. A horizontal line is drawn across the scoring pad, as in contract bridge, to indicate that a game has been completed.
Rubber The first side to win two games out of three wins the rubber and is awarded an additional 250 points.
Honors If either side has three or more honors in the trump suit (or aces at no trumps) then—whether or not that side is declarer—the following scores are given above the line:

three honors or aces, 30 points;
four honours or aces, divided 40 points;
five honors, divided, 50 points;
four honors, one hand, 80 points;
five honors, divided four to one, 90 points;
four aces, one hand 100 points;
five honors, one hand, 100 points.
Bonuses 50 points are given above the line if a doubled contract is bid for and made.
In addition, declarer's side gets 50 points for each trick in excess of the contract.
If declarer succeeds in making a redoubled contract, both the bonuses mentioned above are raised to 100 points each.

Undertricks If declarer's side fails to make its contract, the opponents are given the following points (above the line) for each undertrick:
undoubled contract, 50;
doubled contract, 100;
redoubled contract, 200.
Slams If either side makes a small slam (12 tricks), it receives 50 points above the line—regardless of the bidded contract.
If a grand slam (13 tricks) is won, 100 points are awarded.

Hearts

Penalty cards

Hearts is one of the avoidance games—meaning that it is based on the principle of not taking penalty cards rather than of winning tricks. It evolved in the nineteenth century, since when many interesting variants have appeared.

HEARTS: BASIC GAME

Players Three to seven people can play. There are no partnerships.

Cards A standard deck of 52 playing cards is used.
2s are discarded as follows:
one 2 with three players;
none with four players;
two with five players;
three with seven players.
If possible, the 2 of hearts is not discarded.
The cards rank normally, with ace high. There are no trumps.

Choice of first dealer is by low cut (see p 80).

Deal The dealer deals out all the cards one at a time and face down, beginning with the player to his left and going clockwise.

Play The player to the dealer's left leads to the first trick. Thereafter the winner of one trick leads to the next.
Each player after the lead must follow suit if he can. If he cannot, he may play any card he likes.
A hand ends when all the hearts suit has appeared in play.

Revoking If a player fails to follow suit when he is able to, he may correct his mistake without penalty if he does so before the trick is picked up. Otherwise he scores 13 penalty points and the hand ends. No other players can score penalty points on that hand.

Scoring Each player scores one penalty point for each card of the hearts suit contained in tricks taken by him.

Continuing play After each hand, the deal passes one player to the left.

The winner is the player with the fewest penalty points after an agreed number of hands.
Alternatively, the winner is the player with the fewest penalty points when one player reaches a set number of points (eg 50 points).

SPOT HEARTS

Also called chip hearts, this game is played in the same way as basic hearts except that each heart card counts as many penalty points as its face value. The king counts 13, the queen 12, and the jack 11. (Almost any hearts variant can be scored in this way.)

13 points 12 points 11 points

BLACK LADY HEARTS

In this popular version the queen of spades is an extra penalty card, scoring 13 penalty points. Each heart card counts one penalty point. Sometimes it is ruled that a player must take the first possible opportunity to discard the queen of spades.

13 points

GREEK HEARTS

In this variant the penalties are the same as for black lady hearts, but play and scoring differ in the following ways.

Exchanging Before play begins, each player, after looking at his cards, passes three cards of his choice face down to the player to his right. No player may look at the cards he is receiving until after he has passed on his own cards.

Scoring Each heart is scored as in spot hearts, and the queen of hearts counts 50 penalty points. Except that if one player takes all the penalty cards he does not score at all for this hand and instead all the other players score 150 penalty points each.

50 points

DOMINO HEARTS

The penalty values are as in the basic hearts game, but play varies as follows.

Deal Six cards are dealt to each player, and the remainder are placed face down to form the stock.

Play If a player cannot follow suit he draws cards one at a time from the top of the stock until he can follow suit. Drawn cards of other suits remain in his hand to be played later.
When the stock is exhausted players may discard as in the basic hearts game.
Each player drops out when he has played all his cards. The last player left in scores one penalty point for each heart card left in his hand as well as for those in his tricks.
If a player wins a trick with his last card, the lead passes to the next player to the left.
The winner is the player with the lowest score when one player reaches 31 points.

JOKER HEARTS

In this hearts game, the 2 of hearts is discarded and a joker used.
The joker ranks between the 10 and jack of hearts, and wins any trick in which it is played, regardless of the suit led, unless a higher heart also appears in that trick—in which case the higher heart takes the trick.
A high heart played when the joker is not played is a discard as usual, unless hearts were led.
The joker counts five penalty points.

5 points

HEARTSETTE

In this variant of hearts a widow hand is dealt face down in the center of the table.
The 2 of spades is not used if there are three or four players. The size of the widow depends on the number of players:
with three or four players, three cards;
with five players, two cards;
with six players, four cards.
All other cards are dealt out to the players.
Play and penalties are as in the basic hearts game except that the winner of the first trick adds the widow to it and scores penalty points for any penalty cards it contains.

TWO-HANDED HEARTS

This is an adaptation of the basic game for two players.
It is played like basic hearts except that 13 cards are dealt to each player and the remainder are placed face down to form a stock.
After each trick the winner takes the top card from the stock and the loser takes the next card.
The game continues until all the cards have been played.

BLACK MARIA

This very popular version is also known as Slippery Anne.
Play is as for basic hearts except as follows.

Penalty cards As well as hearts (one point for each card), there are three penalty cards:
the ace of spades, seven points;
the king of spades, 10 points;
the queen of spades (Black Maria), 13 points.

Exchanging occurs before play as in Greek hearts.

Each hand ends when all the penalty cards have been played.

7 points   10 points   13 points

KNAVES

In this game the principles of avoidance games and normal trick-taking games are combined.

Players Knaves is a game for three players.

Cards A standard deck of 52 cards is used.

Objective Each player tries to win tricks without taking any jacks.

Deal and play are as for whist.

Tactics Each player plays for himself, but if one player is winning the other two often act as a temporary partnership to try and reduce his lead.

Scoring At the end of each hand, each player scores one point for each trick he has taken.

If he has taken any jacks, he then subtracts points as follows:
jack of hearts, four points;
jack of diamonds, three;
jack of clubs, two;
jack of spades, one.
A player may have a minus score.

The winner is the first to reach 20 plus points.

POLIGNAC

This is another game in which players try to avoid taking tricks with jacks in them.

Players Four to six can play.

Cards For four players a standard deck without the 2s,3s,4s,5s, and 6s is used. For five or six players the two black 7s are also removed.

Deal and play are as in whist except that there are no trumps.

Scoring At the end of each hand, each player scores penalty points for each jack he has taken, as follows:
one point each for the jacks of hearts, diamonds, and clubs; two points for the jack of spades (polignac).

"General" A player may decide to try and take all the tricks in a hand. This is known as general, and the player must announce his intention before the lead to the first trick.

If he succeeds, all the other players score five penalty points.

If he fails, he scores five penalty points and the jacks score penalty points in the usual way against the players who take them.

The winner is the player with the fewest points after an agreed number of hands.

Grand is a combination of whist, euchre, and hearts (see pages 82, 86, and 94 respectively). Each hand is played like one of these three or a fourth option, depending on the choice of the bidder.

Players Four people play, in partnerships of two.

Deck A standard deck of playing cards is used. The rank of the cards depends on the type of game being played.

Objective Each partnership aims to make a contract and fulfill it.

Deal Players cut for the deal (ace ranks low), and highest card deals. Cards are dealt in a clockwise direction, one at a time and face down, until each player has 13 cards.

Bidding Each player in turn, starting with the player to the left of the dealer, has one chance to either bid or pass. The bids are five and multiples of five, and indicate the number of points the bidder expects to score in that hand if he is the highest bidder.

At the end of bidding the highest bidder names which game (whist, grand, euchre, or hearts) will be played for that round.

If the first three players pass, the dealer must make a bid.

General play Unlike whist, euchre, and hearts, the bidder always leads to the first trick.

Whist

If whist is chosen, the bidder names the trump suit. Play is the same as in whist.

Scoring Each trick more than six counts five points. For example, on a bid of 25 the bidding partnership needs to take 11 tricks to score.

If the bidding partnership makes a grand slam (winning all 13 tricks), it scores for all 13 tricks, making 65 points. No points are scored for honors.

Setbacks If the bidding partnership fails to make its bid, the entire amount of its bid is deducted from its previous score.

In addition, the opposing partnership wins five points for each trick that it takes above six tricks.

Grand

If grand is chosen, play is the same as in whist, except that there are no trumps.

Scoring Each trick more than six scores nine points.

A grand slam also scores 40 points for the first six tricks, making a total of 103 points.

If either partnership makes a grand slam, it wins the game—regardless of its score.

Setbacks are scored in the same way as in the whist option, except that each trick counts nine points.

The opponents also win nine points for each trick they take over six tricks.

Euchre

Euchre can only be chosen on a bid of 25 or less. The bidder names the trump suit. Each player then discards eight cards face down—he may not keep any trumps lower than 8.

Play is the same as in euchre with the following differences. If the bidder calls less than 20 he cannot play alone. If he bid 20, he may choose whether or not to play alone. If he bid 25, he must play alone.

If playing alone, the bidder may exchange any one of his cards for the best card in his partner's hand. The bidder's partner puts his cards face down on the table.

Scoring Points are scored by either partnership as follows:
a) three tricks, 5 points;
b) four tricks, 10 points;
c) five tricks if made in partnership, 20 points;
d) five tricks if made by lone hand, 25 points.

Setbacks If the bidding partnership fails to make its bid, the amount bid plus 20 points is subtracted from its score.

If a lone hand fails to make his bid, he loses twice the amount bid.

Hearts

Hearts can only be selected on a bid of 50 or less.

Play is the same as in hearts.

Scoring If the bidding partnership does not take any tricks containing hearts, it wins 50 points.

Setbacks If the partners do take tricks containing hearts, the amount bid plus one point for each heart taken is subtracted from their score. The opponents are set back one point for each heart they take.

Heart bid option If the first bidder passes when the dealer's partnership has a score of less than 70, it is generally regarded as an indication that he is prepared to play hearts.

If the dealer's side has 70 or more points, the first bidder may determine that hearts are played by leading a heart and saying "Hearts."

Game is 100 points, but the game may finish at the end of a time limit or after a set number of rounds.

Final result The scores at the end of play are used to calculate the final result.

1) The difference between 100 and the lowest score at the end of play stands as a separate score for the side with the highest score at the end of play.

2) The difference between the number of times each side has been setback is multiplied by ten. This stands as a separate score for the side with the fewer setbacks.

3) The result of this final scoring indicates the winner.

For example, if at the end of play side A has a score of 80 with seven setbacks and side B has a score of 60 with five setbacks, then the final result is calculated as follows:

1) $100 - 60 = 40$ (awarded to side A);

2) $(7 - 5) \times 10 = 20$ (awarded to side B);

3) therefore side A wins with a total of 40 against side B's total of 20.

Seven up

Seven up is a card game for two or three players that originated in England in the seventeenth century. Other names by which it is known are all fours, high-low-jack, and old sledge.

4 points

3 points

2 points

1 point

10 points

BASIC SEVEN UP

Deck A standard deck of cards is used. Ace ranks high.

Objective Each player tries to score seven points and so win the game.

Deal Players cut for the deal, highest card dealing. Each player is dealt six face-down cards in packets of three.

The next card is turned face up and denotes trumps, and if it is a jack the dealer scores one point.

The deal passes clockwise around the table.

Trumps If the player to the dealer's left is happy to play with the trump suit shown, he says "Stand" and play begins. Should he prefer to play another trump suit he says "I beg," and the dealer can choose whether or not to change trumps.

If the dealer chooses to keep the same trump suit he says "Take one" to the player, who scores one point. Play then commences.

If the dealer agrees to change the trump suit, he sets aside the face-up card, deals a further three cards to each player, and turns the next card face up to denote trumps. If this card shows a different suit from the first face-up card, play begins with this suit as trumps—and if it is a jack, the dealer scores one point.

Should the face-up card be the same suit again, however, another three cards are dealt to each player and a third card is turned face up. This procedure is repeated until a new trump suit is determined, and the dealer scores one point for each jack that is turned up, provided it is not of the same suit as the suit initially rejected.

If the deck is exhausted before a new trump suit is turned up, the entire deck is shuffled and redealt.

Discarding If the trump suit has been changed, each player discards face down a sufficient number of cards to reduce his hand to six.

Play is the same as in whist.

Scoring At the end of each round the tricks are turned face up for scoring. Points are scored as follows:

a) "high," one point for the player dealt the highest trump;

b) "low," one point for the player dealt the lowest trump;

c) "jack," one point for the player who takes the jack of trumps in a trick;

d) "game," one point for the player who takes the highest total value of cards in tricks. The cards are valued as follows:

four for each ace;
three for each king;
two for each queen;
one for each jack;
ten for each 10.

Game The first player to make seven points wins the game. If more than one player reaches seven points in the same hand, the points are counted in the following order so as to determine the winner: high, low, jack, game.

FOUR-HANDED SEVEN UP

In this version four people play in partnerships of two. Each player sits opposite his partner.

Play is the same as in the basic game, except that the two players to the right of the dealer do not look at their cards until after trumps have been determined.

ALL FIVES

With the exception of the scoring, all fives is just like seven up.

One point is scored for "game," but not for high, low, or jack. Instead, points are scored for taking certain trump cards in tricks, as follows:

four for the ace;
three for the king;
two for the queen;
one for the jack;
ten for the 10; and
five for the 5.

Game is 61 points.

CALIFORNIA JACK

This variant of seven up is sometimes called draw seven or California loo. It is played by two people and differs from seven up in the following ways.

Trumps The first card turned face up denotes trumps. After each trick, first the winner and then the loser of that trick take a card from the top of the stock. The next card of the stock is then turned face up and denotes trumps for the next trick.

When the stock is exhausted, each player's remaining cards are played out using the last trump suit, the winner of each trick leading to the next.

Scoring One point is scored for taking each of the following in tricks: the highest trump, the lowest trump, and the jack of trumps.

The first player to make 10 points wins.

AUCTION PITCH

This is the most popular variation of seven up in the United States, and is also called set back. It is a game for two to seven players.

Deal Players cut for the deal, highest card dealing. Each player is dealt six face-down cards in packets of three.

Bidding Each player in turn, starting with the player to the dealer's left, makes one bid of one, two, three, or four; or passes.

Each bid must be higher than the previous bid—but the dealer may hold the previous bid if it is under four.

Each bid indicates the number of points the bidder intends to make.

A bid of four is called "shoot the moon," "slam," or "smudge."

The highest bidder, or the dealer if he held a previous bid, is called the "pitcher."

All fives

5 points

Play The pitcher leads to the first trick and his card denotes trumps for the deal.

In a trump suit players must follow suit or, if they cannot, discard one card. In a plain (non-trumps) suit, players may either follow suit or play a trump card—if they can do neither, they discard.

The winner of a trick leads to the next.

Scoring Points are scored for high, low, jack, and game as in seven up; each player except the pitcher scores for these as before.

The pitcher only scores if his score is equal to or greater than his bid. If he fails to make his contract, he is set back by the number of points he bid. This means his bid is subtracted from his previous score. If this leaves him with a minus number, he is said to be "in the hole."

Game is usually seven points, but players can decide to play for 10, 11, or 21 points.

If the pitcher ties with another player, the pitcher is the winner.

For ties between other players, points are counted in the order: high, low, jack, and game.

AUCTION PITCH WITH JOKER

A joker is added to the deck for this version of auction pitch. It ranks as the lowest card of the trump suit in play.

If the pitcher leads the joker to the first trick, the trump suit is spades.

The player who takes the joker in a trick scores one point.

"Low" is scored by the player who is dealt the lowest trump card above the joker.

Game is 10 points. If there is a tie, the order for counting points is: high, low, jack, joker, and game.

Auction pitch with joker

1 point

Casino

Casino can be traced back to the fifteenth-century gambling games of France. In the United States, its era of greatest popularity was eclipsed by the gin rummy boom of the 1930s. Although appearing comparatively simple, casino is in fact a game of considerable mathematical skill.

Capturing

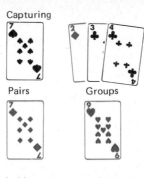

Pairs Groups Court cards

BASIC CASINO

Players The game can be played by two, three, or four players.

A deck of standard playing cards is used.

Court cards have no numerical value; aces count 1; and other cards count their face value.

Objective Each player tries to "capture" certain cards during play and to score the most points.

Deal Players cut for the deal and the lowest card deals. If there are two players, two cards are dealt face down to the non-dealer, then two cards face up to the center of the table, then two cards to the dealer. This procedure is repeated, so that each player has four cards and there are four face-up cards in the center of the table.

If there are three or four players, the dealer deals two cards to each player including himself, two face-up cards to the center of the table, two more cards to each of the players, and then two more cards to the center.

Each time the players have played the cards in their hands, they are each dealt a further four cards in packets of two—no more cards are dealt to the center.

Players take it in turns to deal the whole deck.

Play Beginning with the player to the left of the dealer, players take it in turns to play one card. Each player may "capture," "build," or "trail" with each card.

Capturing Cards are captured in the following ways.

a) **Pairs:** if a face-up card has the same numerical value as a player's card, the player may capture the face-up card. He does this by placing his card face down on the face-up card, and then moving the pair toward him.

For example, a 7 of spades may capture a 7 of diamonds.

If two or more face-up cards match a single card in the player's hand, he may capture them all at the same time.

b) **Groups:** if the combined value of two or more face-up cards is equal to the numerical value of a player's card, the player may capture all the face-up cards involved.

He puts the face-up cards in a pile in front of him and places his own card face down on top of them.

For example, a 9 could capture a 2, 3, and 4 from the center.

If one of a player's cards has the same numerical value as both a single face-up card and a group of face-up cards, he may capture all the cards involved at the same time.

For example, a 9 of spades could capture both a 9 of diamonds and a group of cards (eg a 2, 3, and 4) totaling 9.

c) **Court cards:** if a player holds a court card, he may either capture one matching face-up court card, or alternatively three matching face-up court cards if he holds the fourth.

This means that if, for example, he holds a queen and there are two face-up queens, he can only capture one of them in a turn (but had there been three face-up queens, he could have captured all of them in a turn).

Building may be done in either one of two ways: single or multiple.

Single build: a player may build a card face up onto a central face-up card provided:
a) the combined numerical value of the cards does not exceed ten; and
b) he holds another card that is of equal value to the build he is making, so that in his next turn he would be able to take that build.

For example, if a player holds a 4 and a 7, he may build the 4 onto a face-up 3 (ie 4 + 3 = 7) and say "Building 7."

A build may be increased by either player with a card from his hand, provided that the total of all the cards in the build still does not exceed ten, and that he holds a card equal in value to the build he is making.

For example, if the opponent

holds an ace and an 8, he may build the ace onto an existing build of 7, saying "Building 8."

Multiple build A single build can be changed to a multiple build by duplicating the single-build value with other cards.

For example, a player may add an ace from his hand to a build of 7 in order to make a build of 8 (ie 3 + 4 + 1 = 8), and add to that build another build of 8 (eg 2 + 6) and say "Building 8s."

Once a multiple build has been established, its stated value cannot be altered.

A multiple build is captured by a card equal in value to its stated value (8 in the example above).

Next turn If a player makes or adds to a build, unless his opponent plays to the build immediately, he must in his next turn either:
a) capture it himself (placing the captured build face down in front of him);
b) make a new build; or
c) add to a build.

Trailing If in his turn a player cannot build or capture, he simply places one card from his hand face up on the table.

End of a round When all the cards have been dealt out, the last player to capture cards takes all the remaining face-up cards for scoring.

Scoring Points are scored for capturing certain cards as follows:
a) one point for the 2 of spades ("little casino");
b) two points for the 10 of diamonds ("big casino");
c) one point for each ace;
d) one point for seven or more spades;
e) three points for 27 or more cards.

In addition, one point is scored for capturing all the center face-up cards in any single turn during the course of play; this is known as "making a sweep."

Game Players may either: count each deal as a separate game (the player with most points being the winner); or end the game as soon as one player (the winner) has made a set number of points (usually 21).

ROYAL CASINO

This differs from casino in that the court cards are given numerical values and can be included in builds and captured in tricks like other cards.

A jack numbers 11, a queen 12, and a king 13. Aces may count either one or 14 as the player chooses.

DRAW CASINO

In draw casino only the first 12 cards are dealt. Thereafter, each player draws a card from the stock every time he plays a card.

Otherwise, play is the same as in casino.

SPADE CASINO

Spade casino is played like the basic game, but has additional scoring as follows:
a) jack of spades, two points;
b) 2 of spades, two points as before; and
c) the other spades, one point each.

Game is 61 points.

Pope Joan

Pope Joan is a card game for three or more players that was invented by combining two earlier games, commit and matrimony. Contestants try to play their cards in such a way as to win as many counters as possible.

Cards A standard deck of 52 cards is used, but with the 8 of diamonds removed.
The cards are referred to in the usual way, except for the 9 of diamonds which is called Pope Joan. Aces count low.
Counters At the start of a game, each player should have an equal number of counters.

Bet and deal Players decide upon a dealer.
Each player, including the dealer, then places counters in the different sections of the betting layout. This may be done in one of two ways, either:
a) each player, including the dealer, puts out the same agreed number of counters, dividing them equally between the different sections; or
b) each player, including the dealer, puts four counters in the pope section, two in matrimony, two in intrigue, and one in each of the other sections (**b**).
The dealer then deals one hand to each player including himself, and one extra hand. He deals by giving one card to each player in a clockwise direction, beginning with the player to his left.
The card for the extra hand is dealt just before he deals to himself.
All cards are dealt face down. The deal continues in this way until all the cards but one have been dealt; this card is placed face upward on top of the extra hand.

Betting layout A board or other betting layout is required for the game.
Layouts are usually circular or square (**a**), and are divided into sections labeled ace, jack, intrigue, queen, matrimony, king, Pope Joan, and game. Some traditional Pope Joan boards comprise a circular tray revolving on a central stand. A layout can easily be drawn on a sheet of plain paper or material. Each section should be large enough to hold at least 20 counters.
Objective Each player aims to win as many counters as possible by playing certain cards. Counters are also won by the first contestant to use all his cards.

a Alternative layout

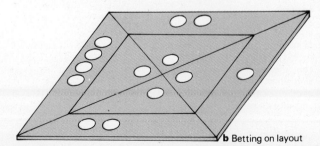

b Betting on layout

The exposed card If the card dealt face upward is Pope Joan (the 9 of diamonds), the dealer wins all the counters in the pope and game sections (**c**). (In an alternative version of play the dealer wins all the counters on the layout.)
The round ends and the player to the dealer's left becomes the new dealer.
If any other card is dealt, its suit determines trumps for that hand.
If the card dealt face upward is an ace or a face card, the dealer wins the counters on the section with the same name.

Play Each player examines his own hand, but no player may look at the extra hand.
The player to the dealer's left begins. He plays any one card from his hand face up onto the middle of the playing area and says its name, eg "3 of hearts."
The player with the 4 of hearts then plays it, followed by the player with the 5, the 6, and so on.
This continues until no player can add to the sequence because either:
a) the sequence has been completed by reaching the king;
b) the next card needed is the 8 of diamonds; or
c) the next card needed is hidden in the extra hand or has already been played.
At this point the cards already played in the sequence are turned face down, and whoever played the last card begins a new sequence by playing any card of his choice.

Claiming counters Anyone who plays the ace, jack, queen, or king of trumps receives all the counters in the section marked with the same name (**d**).
If a player plays the jack and queen of trumps in sequence, he wins all the counters in the intrigue section, as well as those on jack and queen (**e**).
If anyone plays the queen and king of trumps in sequence, he receives all the counters in the matrimony section, as well as those on queen and king (**f**).
A player putting out Pope Joan wins all the counters on that section (**g**).
It should be noted that these cards only win counters when played in the correct way, ie by starting or adding to a sequence. They win nothing if they are still unplayed at the end of a round.

Ending the round The round continues until any one player has played all his cards, when he may take all the counters in the game section. All the other players have to give him one counter for every card still in their hand, with the exception of anyone holding the unplayed Pope Joan, who is exempted from playing for the cards left in his hand.

Unclaimed counters Any counters that are not won in a round remain on the betting layout until won in subsequent rounds.
New counters are added as usual to all sections at the beginning of each round.
Any counters left at the end of a game are distributed by redealing the cards, face up, without an extra hand. The players who receive the ace, jack, and queen of diamonds and the Pope Joan take any remaining counters in those divisions. Any counters in the matrimony section are divided between the holders of the king and queen, and those in the intrigue section between the holders of the queen and jack.

c

Exposed card

Claiming counters

d

Trump suit

e

f

g

Michigan

Calabrasella

Michigan is a popular and fast-moving game usually played for low stakes. It is easy to learn but can also be a challenging game for the experienced player. Other names by which Michigan is known are boodle, Newmarket, Chicago, and Saratoga.

Calabrasella is an interesting and fast-moving card game for three players. Its characteristic features are a stripped deck, unusual ranking of cards, and the absence of a trump suit.

Boodle cards

Players Any number from three to eight can play.
Cards In addition to one standard deck of playing cards, an ace, king, queen and jack—each in a different suit—from a second deck of cards are used. These four cards are called "boodle" cards and are placed face up in the center of the table.
Cards rank normally, with ace high.
Chips Each player is given a supply of betting chips or counters.
Objective Each player tries to play certain cards, thereby collecting chips, and to be the first to get rid of all his cards.
Ante Before each hand is dealt, every player must ante by putting one chip on each of the four boodle cards.
Deal Players cut for the deal, highest card dealing.
The dealer gives one face-down card at a time to each player and to an extra hand (widow) to the dealer's left. Each player must have the same number of cards. Any card or cards left over at the end of the deal are placed face down on the table.
Auction Before the start of play the dealer has the right to exchange his hand for the widow. If he does so, he discards his hand face down.
If the dealer chooses not to take the widow, the other players may bid for it. The highest bidder pays the dealer in chips, discards his hand face down, and takes the widow.
If no player wants the widow, it is left face down without being seen by any player.
Play begins with the player to the dealer's left. He places his lowest card in any suit face up in front of him.
The player with the next card higher in that suit (ie either the same or another player) plays it face up. This continues with cards played in sequence until either the ace is reached or nobody has the next card in the sequence.

Usually, players announce the rank and suit of cards as they play them.
Each player forms a pile of face-up cards in front of him. Once a card is covered, it cannot be inspected.
Stopped play At the end of a sequence play is said to be "stopped." The last person to have played a card starts a new sequence with his lowest card in any other suit. If he cannot do this, the next player to his left able to lead with another suit does so.
If none of the other players can lead another suit, the first player may lead with his lowest card in the same suit as the previous sequence.
Boodle winnings Whenever a player lays down a card that matches one of the four boodle cards, he wins all the chips on that card.
If no player claims the chips on a boodle card during a hand, the chips remain on the card and carry over to the next deal. Before each hand, each player antes one chip on each boodle card.
Play ends as soon as one player has got rid of all his cards. Every other player must then pay him one chip for each card still in his hand.
Penalty If a player fails to play a card in a sequence when able to, he must pay one chip to each of the other players. If by failing to play a card he prevented another player from winning boodle chips, he must make up the loss to the dispossessed player with his own chips. The chips on the boodle card remain and are carried over to the next deal.
The winner of a game is either:
a) the first person to win an agreed number of chips; or
b) the player with the most chips at the end of a set number of deals or a time limit.

Cards A standard deck of playing cards with the 8s, 9s, and 10s removed is used.
The cards rank: 3 (high), 2,a, k,q,j,7,6,5,4 (low).
Players: three
Objective Each player tries to take certain tricks.
Deal Players cut for the deal and lowest card deals.
The dealer gives each player 12 face-down cards in packets of four.
The four remaining cards are placed face down in a pile in the center of the table as the widow (extra hand).
Bidding Starting with the player to the left of the dealer, each player in turn may choose either to play or pass.
The first player to choose to play is opposed by the other two players in partnership for that round.
If none of the three players wishes to play, the hand is thrown in and the cards are redealt.
Widow The player who decided to play may discard, face down, up to four of his cards and replace them with cards from the widow, turned face up. The discarded cards, if any, and any remaining widow cards are then placed face down in a pile. These four cards will go to the winner of the last trick.
Play The player to the left of the dealer leads to the first trick with any card he likes. In turn, each of the other players must follow suit if possible, or discard if not.
The winner of each trick leads to the next.
Scoring Players score for taking certain cards in tricks as follows:
a) aces, three points each;
b) 3s,2s,ks,qs, and js, one point each.
The player who takes the last trick scores an extra three points, and also scores for the four spare (widow or discard) cards.
Thus the maximum possible score is 35 points.
Each side totals its score, and the difference between them is the final score for that hand.

Rank

Payoff If the single player wins, each of the opponents pays him the final score in counters or points.
If he loses, he pays each opponent the final score.
If one side scored the maximum of 35 points, the payoff is 70 points or counters.
Game is 100 points. Alternatively, play can continue until one player has lost all his counters.

Bezique

Bezique is a card game that originated in France, and is based on games played over 350 years ago. It became particularly popular in the mid-nineteenth century. The standard game is for two players, but there are variants for three or more players. The popular American game of pinochle is derived from bezique.

STANDARD (TWO-HANDED) BEZIQUE

The deck comprises a double piquet deck, or two standard 52-card decks from which the 2s, 3s, 4s, 5s, and 6s have been removed—making a total of 64 cards in play.
The cards rank: a (high), 10, k, q, j, 9, 8, 7.
The objective of the game is to make winning melds or declarations, and to take tricks containing certain scoring cards known as *brisques.*

Deal Players cut for deal. The dealer gives eight cards to each player, dealing three, two, and three cards at a time. The next (the seventeenth) card is placed face up on the table and indicates the trump suit for that hand. If this card is a 7, the dealer scores 10 points.
The remaining cards are turned face down in a pile, forming the "stock."

Play is in two stages.
The first stage lasts as long as there are cards in the stock. The non-dealer leads first; thereafter the winner of each trick leads to the next one. After each trick the winner may make any declaration, and then both players draw cards from the stock to replenish their hands, the winner of the trick drawing first.
The winner of the last trick takes the last stock card, and the loser takes the exposed trump card.
During this stage the players are not obliged to follow suit.
A trick is taken by the higher card of the suit led or by a trump card.
If cards of equal value are played, the card that led takes the trick.

The second stage begins when the stock is exhausted. The players must follow suit for these last eight tricks, except they may trump if they cannot follow suit. A player must win a trick if he is able to. The winner of the last trick scores 10 points.

Rank

© DIAGRAM

Standard bezique

Trumps	20 points	40 points	40 points	40 points	60 points	80 points	100 points	250 points	500 points
	a	b	c	d	e	f	g	h	i

Three-handed bezique

1500 points

Declarations may be made after winning a trick.

The cards of each meld must be laid face up in front of the player, but they may be played to tricks as if they were still in the hand.

The possible declarations are as follows:

a) common marriage: king and queen of the same suit, except trumps, 20 points;

b) royal marriage: king and queen of the trump suit, 40 points;

c) bezique: queen of spades and jack of diamonds, 40 points (when spades or diamonds are trumps, some players prefer to make "bezique" the queen of clubs and jack of hearts);

d) any four jacks, 40 points;

e) any four queens, 60 points;

f) any four kings, 80 points;

g) any four aces, 100 points;

h) sequence: a,10,k,q,j of the trump suit only, 250 points;

i) double bezique: both queens of spades and both jacks of diamonds, 500 points; exchanging the 7 of trumps for the face-up card, 10 points (the holder of the other 7 of trumps scores 10 points when he plays it, which does not count as a declaration).

A player may make only one declaration after winning a trick. But if his exposed cards show a second possible declaration, he can announce that he will declare it when he next takes a trick.

No card may form part of a second similar declaration. For example, a queen of spades in "four queens" cannot form part of a second

declaration of "four queens," but she can form part of a "bezique," "double bezique," "royal marriage," or "sequence."

The cards used to form a "bezique" can be used again to form part of a "double bezique," but neither card can be used with a fresh partner for a second "bezique."

Brisques are every ace and every 10 taken in tricks, and they count 10 points each. The *brisques* are counted up by each player examining his tricks at the end of the game.

Game is either 1000 or 2000 points up.

Penalties If a player draws out of turn, his opponent scores 10 points.

If a player holds more than eight cards, his opponent scores 100 points, provided he himself has the right number of cards.

A player who plays to the next trick without having drawn a card during the first stage forfeits 10 points to his opponent.

A player who revokes (fails to follow suit although able to) during the last eight tricks, or fails to take a trick if he is able to do so forfeits all eight tricks to his opponent.

Scoring is most easily done using special bezique markers; but it can also be done with pencil and paper, counters, or with a cribbage board (each hole on the board counting as 10).

THREE-HANDED BEZIQUE

Three-handed bezique is the same as ordinary bezique, except that 96 cards are used. Each player plays for himself. Triple bezique scores 1500 points.

RUBICON BEZIQUE

Rubicon bezique is a popular variation of bezique for two players. It is similar to standard bezique, with the following differences.

The deck consists of 128 cards, or four piquet decks.

The deal consists of nine cards to each player, dealt either singly or in threes.

Trumps are established by the first sequence or marriage declared by either player. No stock cards are turned up, and the 7 of trumps has no value.

Play is the same as for standard bezique, except that the last trick counts 50 points.

Declarations are as in standard bezique, with the following additions.

a) *Carte blanche*: worth 50 points, and scored if either player is dealt a hand not containing a court card. The hand must be displayed.

If, after drawing a further card, the player's hand still does not contain a court card, *carte blanche* may be scored again, and this continues until a court card is drawn.

Once a player has held a court card, *carte blanche* cannot be scored.

b) Ordinary sequence/back

door: a sequence not of the trump suit, 150 points;

c) triple bezique: three queens of spades and three jacks of diamonds, 1500 points;

d) quadruple bezique: four queens of spades and four jacks of diamonds, 4500 points.

Cards may be reused to form the same combinations. For example, if "four queens" are declared and one queen is played, a fifth queen may be laid down to form "four queens" again. Two marriages of the same suit may be rearranged to form two more marriages.

Brisques are only counted if there is a tied score, or to save a player from being "rubiconed," ie failing to reach 1000 points.

If one player chooses to count *brisques*, the other player's *brisques* are also scored.

Game is a single deal. The player with the higher score wins 500 points plus the difference between his and the loser's score.

If the loser is rubiconed, the winner gets 1000 points, plus the sum of his and the loser's scores, plus 320 points for all *brisques*. (This applies even if the winner himself has scored fewer than 1000 points.)

If the loser fails to score 100 points, the winner scores an extra 100 points.

Any fractions of 100 points may be ignored in scoring, except if the players' scores are very close.

Rubicon bezique

Trumps	50 points	150 points	1500 points	4500 points
	a	b	c	d

Six-deck bezique

Trumps

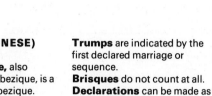
400 points **a**

600 points **b**

800 points **c**

900 points **d**

1000 points **e**

Carte blanche
250 points

SIX-DECK (CHINESE) BEZIQUE

Six-deck bezique, also known as Chinese bezique, is a variant of rubicon bezique. The rules are the same as for rubicon bezique, with the following changes.
The deck comprises 192 cards, or six piquet decks shuffled together.
The deal consists of 12 cards to each player, dealt singly or in threes.

Trumps are indicated by the first declared marriage or sequence.
Brisques do not count at all.
Declarations can be made as in rubicon bezique, reusing cards in similar scoring combinations.
In Chinese bezique, *carte blanche* is worth 250 points, as is winning the last trick.
Declarations in addition to those in rubicon bezique are, in the trump suit only:

a) four jacks, 400 points;
b) four queens, 600 points;
c) four kings, 800 points;
d) four 10s, 900 points;
e) four aces, 1000 points.
Bezique varies according to which suit is trumps, as follows:
hearts, queen of hearts and jack of clubs;
diamonds, queen of diamonds and jack of spades;
clubs, queen of clubs and jack of hearts;

spades, queen of spades and jack of diamonds.
Game is a single deal. Scores are calculated as for rubicon bezique, except that:
the winner gets a game bonus of 1000 points instead of 500; and
the rubicon point is 3000 instead of 1000.

EIGHT-DECK BEZIQUE

Eight-deck bezique is played like six-deck bezique, with the following variations.
The deck consists of 256 cards, or eight piquet decks.
The deal is 15 cards to each player.

Declarations are the same, with the following changes and additions:
bezique, 50 points;
quintuple bezique, 9000 points.

In the trump suit only:
a) five jacks, 800 points;
b) five queens, 1200 points;
c) five kings, 1600 points;
d) five 10s, 1800 points;
e) five aces, 2000 points.
A player is rubiconed if he fails to score 5000 points.

Eight-deck bezique

Trumps

800 points **a**

1200 points **b**

1600 points **c**

1800 points **d**

2000 points **e**

50 points

Quintuple bezique
9000 points

FOUR-HANDED BEZIQUE

Four-handed bezique is similar to rubicon bezique, but the game is played with 192 cards. The players play in partnership, two against two.
The deal is nine cards to each player; the player on the dealer's left leads to the first trick.

Declarations may be made by any player after winning a trick; alternatively he may allow his partner to make the declaration.
A player may use both his own cards and any of his partner's declared cards to make a declaration.
Scoring is as in rubicon bezique, with the following variations and additions:

a) *double carte blanche*: both players in a partnership being dealt a hand without a court card, 500 points;
b) any four jacks, 400 points;
c) any four queens, 600 points;
d) any four kings, 800 points;
e) any four 10s, 900 points;
f) any four aces, 1000 points;
g) quintuple bezique, 13,500 points;
h) sextuple bezique, 40,500 points.

Double carte blanche
500 points **a**

Four-handed bezique

Trumps

400 points **b**

600 points **c**

800 points **d**

900 points **e**

1000 points **f**

13,500 points **g**

40,500 points **h**

© DIAGRAM

Piquet

Piquet is a card game for two players that allows great opportunities for skill. It has been known, under various names, since the middle of the fifteenth century. The present French name and terminology were adopted in English during the reign of Charles I of England, as a compliment to his French wife, Henrietta Maria.

Rank of cards

Players The game is for two.
Objective Each player aims to score points, both with certain combinations of cards in his hand and by playing for tricks.
Cards A deck of 32 playing cards is used, commonly called a piquet deck. This is a standard 52 card deck from which all the 2s, 3s, 4s, 5s, and 6s have been removed. Usually two decks are used alternately, one being shuffled in readiness for the next hand while the other is being dealt into play.
The cards rank normally, from 7 low to ace high.
Choice of first dealer is by low cut (see p 80). The first dealer also has choice of seats.
Shuffle is normal. (See p 80).
Cut is by the non-dealer. There need be only two cards in each section. Otherwise the cut is normal (see p 80).
The deal is in packets of two cards, face down. The dealer gives two cards to his opponent, then two to himself, until each has 12 cards.
The remaining eight cards form the stock, which is placed face down in the center of the table. The stock is divided so that the upper five cards rest at an angle to the lower three.
Discards The dealer has the chance to discard first. Under American rules, he need not discard; under English rules, he must discard at least one card. In either case, the most cards he can discard is five.
If he is discarding, he places the discards face down beside him, and draws an equal number from the stock. (Players must draw cards in the order in which they are stacked in the stock.)
Even if the dealer does not draw, or does not draw all five, he may look at the cards that he could have drawn, and then replace them without showing them to his opponent.
Then the non-dealer discards at least one card and at most as many cards as remain in the stock.
He places his discards face

down beside him and draws an equal number of stock cards, beginning with any left by the dealer.
The non-dealer may look at any cards in the stock that remain undrawn. But in this case the dealer may turn these cards face up for himself to see also.
(Sometimes it is ruled that the dealer may do this only after leading to the first trick.)
A player may inspect his own discards during play.
Scoring Points are scored in two ways. Some points are scored by "declaration," which occurs immediately after discarding and before play. Other points are scored during play.
Declarations Each player declares certain combinations of cards held in his hand, and scores points if his declaration ranks higher than his opponent's.
A player does not have to declare a potentially winning combination if he prefers not to—but he cannot then score points for it. This is called "sinking."
A player may include any card in more than one combination.
Scoring combinations
Point The player with the most cards of one suit scores one point for each card he holds in that suit.
If both players have long suits of the same length, the better point is the one with the higher face value. (Face value is calculated by counting the ace as 11, court cards as 10 each, and other cards as their numerical face value.) If the players still tie, neither scores.
A player can only score for one point—even if he has more than one suit longer than his opponent's longest.
Sequences The player with the most cards in rank order in one suit scores as follows:
tierce (three cards), three points;
quart (four cards), four points;
quint (five cards), 15 points;
sextet or sixième (six cards), 16 points;
septet or septième (seven

cards), 17 points;
octet or huitième (eight cards), 18 points.
The holder of the highest sequence can also score for any other sequences he holds. If players tie for longest sequence, the sequence with the higher top card wins. If both sequences have the same top card, neither scores for any sequences.
Meld The player with the highest ranking meld, of three or four cards of a kind, scores as follows:
trio or "three" (three cards of the same denomination), three points;
quatorze or "fourteen" (four cards of the same denomination), 14 points.
But only aces, kings, queens, jacks, or 10s may be declared for melds (and sometimes it is ruled that 10s only count if a quatorze is held).
If both players have sets of equal length, the one with the higher ranking cards wins. The winner also scores for any other melds he holds.
Announcing the declarations is by a formal dialogue, designed to reveal no more information than necessary.
The non-dealer makes the first declaration in each category of combination, and takes them in the order point, sequence, meld.
Declaring a point Non-dealer says: "A point of ——," stating whatever number of cards he holds in his longest suit.
Dealer replies:
"Good," if he concedes the point;
"Not good," if he holds a longer suit—stating its length;
"How many?" if he holds a suit of equal length.
If the reply is "How many?" the non-dealer must then declare the face value of his point. The dealer then replies "Good," "Not good" (stating the face value of his point), or "Equal" (in which case no one scores).
Whoever has won the point then states the length of his point again (adding the face value if that also had to be declared), and announces his score.
Declaring a sequence Non-dealer says: "A sequence of —— " (or "A tierce," etc), stating the number of cards in his longest sequence.
The procedure then follows as in declaring a point—except that when the dealer holds a

sequence of equal length his reply is "How high?" The non-dealer then declares the top card of his sequence, and the dealer states "Good," "Not good," or "Equal."
Declaring a meld Non-dealer says "A three (or fourteen) of ——," naming the denomination. (Alternatively he can use the words "trio" or "quatorze.") The dealer cannot hold a meld of the same length and denomination, and so his only possible replies are "Good" or "Not good."
A sample declaration
Non-dealer: "A point of five."
Dealer: "Good."
Non-dealer: "A point of five. I score five." Then he names his best sequence: "A sequence of four" (or "A quart").
Dealer: "How high?"
Non-dealer: "Queen."
Dealer: "Not good. Ace. Also a tierce. I score seven."
Non-dealer (naming his best meld): "Three kings" (or "A trio of kings").
Dealer: "Not good. Fourteen queens (or "quatorze of queens"). I score 14. I start with 21."
Non-dealer (playing the lead to the first trick and automatically adding one point to his score—see below): "I start with six."
English style declaration
In this, the dealer only names his combinations after the non-dealer has led to the first trick. For example:
Non-dealer: "A point of five."
Dealer: "Good."
Non-dealer: "A point of five. I score five. A quart."
Dealer: "How high?"
Non-dealer: "Queen."
Dealer: "Not good."
Non-dealer: "A trio of kings."
Dealer: "Not good."
Non-dealer (playing first card): "I start with six."
Dealer: "A quart to the ace. Also a tierce. Seven. And a quatorze of queens: 14. I start with 21."
Showing combinations
Sometimes it is ruled that all winning combinations must be shown before they score. More usually, winning combinations are shown only at the opponent's request. A combination that is shown is replaced in the holder's hand as soon as the opponent has seen it.
Play The non-dealer leads to the first trick. Each player must follow suit to a lead if he can. If not he may discard any card. The winner of a trick leads to the next.

Scoring during play A player scores for tricks; also players may score additional points in various ways.
Scoring for tricks Each player scores as follows:
a) one point for leading to a trick;
b) one point for taking a trick that his opponent led to;
c) one point for taking the last trick; and
d) 10 points for taking the majority of the tricks (seven or more).
Each time a player scores he announces his total score so far.
Variation Sometimes it is played that:
a) a player scores for leading to a trick only if the card led is higher than a 9;
b) a player scores for winning a trick only if the winning card is higher than a 9.
Additional scoring Points may also be scored in the following ways.
a) Carte blanche is a hand devoid of court cards, and scores 10 points. It must be claimed by a player immediately before he discards after the deal. (Under English rules, it must be claimed before either player discards.)
b) Pique is scored by the non-dealer if he scores 30 points before the dealer scores anything. It scores 30 bonus points.
c) Repique is scored by either player if he scores 30 points on declaration, ie before the lead to the first trick. It is worth 60 bonus points.
d) Capot is scored by either player if he captures all 12 tricks in play. It is worth 40 bonus points, but the 10 standard points for taking a majority of tricks are not scored.
A game is known as a partie. It consists usually of six deals, though some players prefer to have a partie of four deals, with scores for the first and fourth deals counting double. The turn to deal alternates between the two players.
Scoring the partie
a) The scores for the individual deals are added together to give a total for each player. The procedure then depends on whether these totals exceed the "rubicon" of 100 points.
b) If both players have 100 or more points, the player with the higher total wins by the difference between the two totals plus 100 points bonus for the partie.
For example, if the dealer has totaled 120 and the non-

dealer 108, the dealer wins and scores 112 points (120−108+100).
c) If either or both players have less than 100 points, the player with the lower total is said to be "rubiconed." The player with the higher total wins by the sum of the totals plus 100 points bonus.
For example:
if the scores are 125 and 92, the player with 125 wins and scores 317 (125+92+100);
if the scores are 98 and 92, the player with 98 wins and scores 290 (98+92+100).
Piquet au cent has different final scoring. Deals continue until one player totals 100 points or more. At the end of that deal, the player with the higher total scores the difference between his own and his opponent's totals—or double that difference if his opponent's total was below 50.

AUCTION PIQUET
This variation puts more emphasis on the play of the hands.
Bidding takes place before the discard. The non-dealer bids or passes first.
If both pass, the cards are dealt again by the same player. Once a bid has been made, bidding continues until one player passes.
The minimum bid is seven. A bid may be either "plus" (winning the stated number of tricks) or "minus" (losing that number). Plus and minus bids rank equally: to continue the bidding a player must bid a greater number of tricks.
The final bid is the "contract" as in contract bridge.
Other rules are as for basic piquet, with the following exceptions.
Discards Players need not discard at all.
Declarations may be made in any order.
Sinking is not allowed on minus contracts.
Pique is scored after 29 points in plus contracts and 21 points in minus ones.
Repique is scored after 30 points in plus contracts and 21 points in minus ones.
Scoring for tricks Each player scores one point for each trick that he takes (whoever led to that trick). Players do not score for leading to a trick or for taking the last trick.

Scoring the contract If the contracted player exceeds his contract, he scores 10 points for every trick won (on plus contracts) or lost (on minus contracts) in excess of his contract.
If he fails to make his contract, every trick by which he fell short scores 10 points for his opponent.
Doubling and redoubling are allowed, as in bridge, but affect only the scores for overtricks or undertricks.
Scoring the partie Rubicon is 150 points, and bonus for the partie is also 150 points.

IMPERIAL
This game is a form of piquet, but there is a trump suit and the cards rank differently.
Players: two.
Cards A 32-card piquet deck is used—a standard deck with the 2s,3s,4s,5s, and 6s removed.
Cards rank k (high), q,j,a,10, 9,8,7 (low).
"Honors" are the k,q,j,a, and 7 of trumps.
Chips are used for scoring: 12 white chips and eight red. One red chip is worth six white.
At the beginning of the game all chips are placed together in a central pool.
Shuffle and cut is as in piquet.
The deal is as in piquet, but in packets of three.
When both players have 12 cards each, the 25th card is placed face up in the center of the table. The suit of this card becomes trumps for the hand. The undealt part of the deck is placed to one side, out of use for the remainder of the hand. There is no discarding or drawing in play.
Scoring procedure
1) Whenever a player scores, he takes the appropriate chip from the pool.
2) Whenever a player has collected six white chips, he immediately exchanges them for one red chip from the pool.
3) Whenever a player gains a red chip in any way, his opponent must put back into the pool any white chips that he holds. (His red chips are safe.)
Scoring before play occurs in the following order:
1) the dealer scores one white chip if the turned up (25th) card is an honor card;
2) either player scores one red chip if he has been dealt carte blanche, ie a hand containing no king, queen, or jack;
3) players declare and score as

in piquet for each combination that they hold;
4) players declare and score for any sequence or meld using the turned up card.
Declaring is as in piquet, except that:
a) players must show any winning combinations;
b) when players declare equally good combinations, the non-dealer wins.
Point is called exactly as in piquet. The player with the better point scores one white chip.
Sequences may be of three or four cards but may contain only kings, queens, jacks, and aces. A four-card sequence beats a three-card sequence. Three-card sequences rank according to the top card. The winner scores one red chip.
Melds Only fours of kings, queens, jacks, aces, and 7s are counted—ranking in that order, with king high. Threes do not count. The winner scores one red chip.
Combinations using the turned up card
1) Players declare any sequence that includes the turned up card. The higher ranking sequence wins one red chip.
2) A player declares if he has a meld of four using the turned up card. If so, he wins one red chip.
Play is as for piquet, except that the second player to each trick must take it if he can. (This includes trumping if he cannot follow suit.)
Cards are not collected in tricks. Each player puts the cards he has played face up in front of him, and is free to examine them at any time.
Scoring during play
1) A player taking the jack of trumps by leading the king or queen wins one red chip.
2) A player taking the ace also wins one red chip.
3) A player takes one white chip for each trump honor contained in tricks that he wins.
Scoring after play If one player takes more tricks in a hand than his opponent, he wins one white chip for every trick in excess of his opponent's total.
Thus if a player wins all 12 tricks—referred to as "capot" —he wins two red chips.
The winner is the first player to win five red chips. Hands continue until one player does this, with the deal alternating between players.
If a player gains five red chips in the middle of a hand, the hand is abandoned at once.

Imperial

Rank of cards

Honors

Chips

©DIAGRAM

Rank of cards

PINOCHLE

This game is derived from bezique and is widely played in North America. Its name is also spelled pinocle and sometimes penuchle.

Players The basic game is for two players.

Cards A 48-card deck is used: made from two standard decks excluding all the 2s, 3s, 4s, 5s, 6s, 7s, and 8s. Cards rank a (high), 10, k, q, j, 9 (low).

Objective Each player aims to take tricks containing certain cards, and to make melds.

Choice of first dealer is by high cut. Thereafter the deal alternates.

Shuffle and cut are normal (see p 80), except that the non-dealer must cut.

Deal The dealer gives 12 cards to each player in packets of three or four.

The thirteenth card is then turned face up on the table, and its suit becomes trumps for that hand.

The rest of the deck, the "stock," is then placed face down on the table, half covering the trump card.

First stage of play This lasts as long as there are any cards in the stock.

The non-dealer leads to the first trick. Thereafter the winner of one trick leads to the next.

In this stage, players may play any card to a trick. This includes playing a trump when holding a card of a plain suit led. Each trick is won by the highest trump, or, if no trumps appear, by the highest card of the suit led. If two cards of the same denomination and suit appear, the one played first wins.

The winner of a trick places it face down in front of him. After each trick, the winner may make one meld (see the section on melding). Then, whether or not a meld has been made, the winner draws the top card from the stock and the loser draws the next card. The winner then leads to the next trick.

Drawing after tricks continues until all the stock and the exposed trump card have been drawn. (It is often ruled that the player who draws the last face-down card must also expose it.)

Melding After each trick in the first stage, the winner of the trick may claim one meld.

A meld is claimed by placing the cards involved face up on the table, and stating the score. A player can only score for one meld in a turn — even if the cards he exposes for that meld

have also given him another scoring combination.

Each card melded can also be used later to form another meld of a different class (see the section on melds) or one of a higher score in the same class. However, each new meld formed in this way requires a new turn and the addition of at least one card from the player's hand.

Any card that a player uses in a meld may still be played to a later trick, but once a card has been played to a trick it cannot then be used in further melds.

Melds There are three classes of meld. Points are scored as follows when the melds are put on the table.

Class A:
"sequence" (or "flush") — a, 10, k, q, j of trumps — 150 points;
"royal marriage" — k and q of trumps — 40 points;
"marriage" — k and q of any plain suit — 20 points.

Class B:
"pinochle" — q of spades and j of diamonds — 40 points;

Class C:
four aces, 100 points;
four kings, 80 points;
four queens, 60 points;
four jacks, 40 points.
(Note that all "fours" must contain one card of each suit.)

The second stage of play, or "play out," begins with each player taking back into his hand any cards that he has melded. The players then play for the remaining 12 tricks to use up the cards in their hands. The winner of the last trick in the first stage leads to the first trick in the second.

In this stage a player must follow suit if he can, and may only trump if he cannot.

If a trump is led, the following player must play a higher trump if he can.

(Usually it is made a general rule for this stage that a following player must win any trick he can.)

Tricks are won as in the first stage, and the winner of one trick leads to the next. No melds are made in this stage.

The "dix" is the name given to the 9 of trumps.

If the card turned up to decide trumps is a 9, the dealer scores 10 points immediately.

If a player holds a dix during the first stage of play, he can declare it and win 10 points by placing it face up on the table after winning a trick. (Most players rule that a meld can also be made in the same turn.)

If the first dix to appear is one declared by a player, it is not

left face up in front of him but is exchanged for the exposed trump card at the bottom of the stock pile. The player takes that trump card into his hand and puts the dix in its place.

Scoring of tricks Points for cards taken in tricks are scored at the end of each hand. Cards are scored as follows:
a) each ace, 11 points;
b) each 10, 10 points;
c) each king, four points;
d) each queen, three points;
e) each jack, two points.
The winner of the last trick in the second stage scores a further 10 points.

Points for tricks are rounded to multiples of 10 (only 7, 8, or 9 being rounded up) before being added to the player's total score.

Game is usually 1000 points. If both players reach 1000 or more after the same hand, play continues until one player reaches 1250. If the same happens again, play continues to 1500, etc.

AUCTION PINOCHLE

In this version, players bid on how many points they expect to score. Chips are collected by successful players.

Players Three people play. Usually the game is played at tables of four, with the dealer taking no active part.

Cards The deck and rank of cards are as in basic pinochle.

Deal 15 cards are dealt to each player in five packets of three. After each player has been dealt one packet, a widow of three cards is dealt face down.

Bidding Each player in turn, starting with the player to the dealer's left, may make a bid as to the number of points he expects to score.

Bidding must start at an agreed minimum (usually 300) and must rise 10 points at a time.

A player must bid or pass. If he passes, he may not bid again in that hand. Bidding ends when two players have passed. The other player is then the "bidder," and his highest bid is his contract.

The other two players together try to prevent him making his contract.

Melding The bidder takes up the widow cards, shows them to the other players, and then adds them to his hand.

He then names the trump suit and lays down his melds. No other player is allowed to make melds at any time.

Melds and their scores are as in basic pinochle, except that the dix counts as a Class A meld scoring 10 points, and is

scored only if the bidder places it on the table with his other melds.

Starting play The bidder begins by discarding three cards face down from those still in his hand. He then picks up his meld cards and leads to the first trick.

He may change his mind about his melds, discards, or trumps at any time before he actually leads to the first trick. But if he discards a meld card that he has scored for, he forfeits the game unless he corrects the mistake before leading to the first trick.

Tricks are won as in basic pinochle. Each player must follow suit if he can; and, if trumps are led, must try to win the trick if he can.

If a player cannot follow suit he must trump rather than discard. This still applies after a trick has been trumped, but he need not trump higher if he does not wish to.

The winner of each trick leads to the next.

Scoring of tricks may be as in basic pinochle.

Alternatives are:
a) 10 points for each ace or 10, and 5 points for each king or queen; or
b) 10 points for each ace, 10, or king.

Whatever the points system, the bidder scores for any scoring cards contained in the three cards he discards, and there is a bonus of 10 points to the bidder if he wins the last trick.

Game Each hand is a complete game. If the bidder makes or exceeds his contract, he wins chips from each player. Typical amounts are:
a) 300-340 bid, three chips;
b) 350-390 bid, five chips;
c) 400-440 bid, 10 chips;
d) 450-490 bid, 15 chips;
e) 500-540 bid, 20 chips;
f) 550-590 bid, 25 chips;
g) 600 or more, 30 chips.
These amounts are doubled if spades are trumps.

A kitty usually features in auction pinochle. The following are typical rules.
1) Each player must put three chips into the kitty before play begins.
2) If all players pass on a deal, all pay three chips into the kitty.
3) If a bidder makes, or fails on, a contract of 350 or more, he collects from, or pays to, the kitty, as well as each other player. Amounts are the same as for settlements between players.

KALABRIASZ

This excellent game is also known as klaberjass, clab, and clobber. It is essentially the same as the French game, belote.

Players The basic game is for two players.

Cards Play is with a standard deck of cards from which the 2s, 3s, 4s, 5s, and 6s have been removed.

The cards rank as follows:
a) in the trump suit, j (high), 9, a, 10, k, q, 8, 7 (low);
b) in plain suits, a (high), 10, k, q, j, 9, 8, 7 (low).

Objective Players aim to meld sequences and to take certain scoring cards in tricks.

Choice of dealer for the first hand is by high cut, with ace low.

First deal The dealer gives each player six cards face down in packets of three. He then places the next card face up in the center of the table, and places the rest of the deck — the stock — face down in a pile beside it.

Determining trumps Players make bids to determine the trump suit.

1) The non-dealer opens with a bid of "Accept," "Schmeiss," or "Pass."

If he bids to accept, the suit of the central face-up card becomes trumps for the hand.

A bid of schmeiss is a proposal for a new deal. The dealer then has the opportunity of agreeing to a new deal or of accepting the suit of the central face-up card as the trump suit.

If the non-dealer says "Pass," the dealer has a turn at bidding.

2) The dealer may now either: accept the suit of the central face-up card as trumps; bid Schmeiss, in which case the non-dealer must agree to the new deal or accept the suit of the face-up card as trumps; or pass, in which case there is a second round of bidding.

3) If both players pass in the first round of bidding, the non-dealer may then either: nominate any trump suit that he wishes, in which case play will be with this suit as trumps; or pass, in which case the dealer may nominate a trump suit or pass.

If both players pass in the second round of bidding, the cards are thrown in and a new first deal made.

The player who actually determines the trump suit is called the "maker."

Second deal Once the trump suit has been established, each player is dealt a further three cards, one at a time and face down.

The dealer then takes the bottom card of the stock and places it face up on top of the stock.

If the suit of the central face-up card was accepted as trumps, a player holding the 7 of that suit may exchange it for the central face-up card if he wishes. The 7 of trumps is known as the "dix."

Declaring sequences usually takes place before play begins, but may be after the non-dealer has led to the first trick. By their declarations players establish which of them holds the highest sequence.

Sequences All cards in a sequence must be consecutive and of the same suit. There are two kinds of sequence:
a) a sequence of three cards, worth 20 points; and
b) a sequence of four or more cards, worth 50 points.

For sequences cards rank in the order a (high), k, q, j, 10, 9, 8, 7 (low).

Sequences of equal value are ranked according to their highest card. Note that a sequence of four cards beats a longer sequence provided that the four-card sequence is headed by the highest card.

If sequences are of equal value and are headed by cards of the same rank, a sequence in the trump suit is higher.

If equal sequences headed by cards of the same rank are both in plain suits, some versions of the game rule that the non-dealer's sequence is higher while others rule that the sequences are equal and neither player may score.

Declaration procedure The non-dealer begins by announcing "Sequence of 50" if he has a sequence of four or more cards, or "Sequence of 20" if he has a three-card sequence.

The dealer then replies "Good" if he cannot beat it, "Not good" if he can beat it, or "how high?" if he has a sequence with the same points value.

If the dealer replies "How high?" the non-dealer states the rank of the card that heads his sequence, and then the non-dealer replies "Good" if he cannot beat it, or "Not good" if he can.

Scoring of sequences Only the player with the highest sequence scores any points at this stage of the game.

He scores for his highest sequence after first showing it to his opponent.

He also scores for any other sequences that he is prepared to show.

Play Non-dealer leads to the first trick.

Players must follow suit if they are able, and if they cannot follow suit must play a trump if they have one. If a trump is led the opposing player must take the trick if he can.

The winner of a trick places it face down in front of him and leads to the next trick.

Bella is an additional meld comprising the king and queen of trumps.

It is worth 20 points to any player who holds it, and is scored automatically when the holder plays the second of the two cards.

Scoring during play Players score points as follows for cards taken in tricks;
a) "jasz" (jack of trumps), 20 points;
b) "menel" (9 of trumps), 14 points;
c) each ace, 11 points;
d) each 10, 10 points;
e) each king, four points;
f) each queen, three points;
g) each jack but jasz, two points.

The player who takes the last trick scores a further 10 points.

The final score for each hand is calculated as follows.

a) If the player who determined the trump suit (the maker) has a points total higher than his opponent, each player scores his own total.

b) if the opposing player has a higher total, he scores both his own points total and that of the maker. This is called "going bate."

c) If the players have an equal number of points, the maker scores no points and his opponent scores his own points total. The maker's opponent is said to have gone "half bate."

Game is usually 500 points. If both players reach the agreed game total in the same hand, the one who has most points is the winner

THREE-HANDED KALABRIASZ

In the three-handed game turns pass clockwise around the table. The maker must score more than both his opponents together, or go bate. Players score their own sequences and points won in play, but opponents share the maker's points if he goes bate.

PARTNERSHIP KALABRIASZ

This differs from the basic game as follows.

All but the last card are dealt out so that the dealer has seven cards and the other players eight cards.

The last card becomes the central face-up card. Before play, the player with the dix exchanges it for the face-up card, and the dealer takes the dix to complete his hand.

After one player has established the highest sequence, his partner may also score for any sequences. Partners keep their tricks together and score as a side.

Kalabriasz

Rank of trumps

Trumps

Rank of plain suits

Scoring cards

a   b   c   d   e   f   g   Trumps

Skat

Skat developed in Germany in the early 1800s and its rules were codified at a congress in 1896. It has since flourished on both sides of the Atlantic, being one of the most skillful of all card games. The simplified variant described here — Rauber Skat — is gradually replacing the original game.

Rank of cards with trumps

Trump suit

Plain suits

Rank in no trumps

Players Three to five people can play, but only three play on any one deal.

With four players, the dealer sits out. With five, the dealer and the third player to his left sit out: the first, second, and fourth play.

The first player to the dealer's left is called "forehand," the next "middlehand," and the last player with cards "endhand."

Cards Skat is played with a standard deck from which all the 2s, 3s, 4s, 5s, and 6s have been removed.

Rank of cards Most contracts require trumps.

The highest trumps are always the four jacks, which rank in the order clubs (high), spades, hearts, diamonds (low).

In addition there may also be a trump suit. If so, the rest of that suit rank below the lowest jack, in the order a (high), 10, k, q, 9, 8, 7 (low). When play is with trumps, cards in plain suits also rank a (high), 10, k, q, 9, 8, 7 (low). When there are no trumps, all suits rank a (high), k, q, j, 10, 9, 8, 7 (low).

Objective Each player tries to win the right to choose the game that will be played, and then successfully to complete that game.

Choice of first dealer is by high cut (see p 80). Thereafter the deal passes one player to the left after each game.

Deal A packet of three cards is dealt to each active player. Then a "skat" of two face-down cards is set aside. A packet of four is next dealt to each active player, and finally a further packet of three. This gives three hands of ten cards each, and two cards in the skat.

Bidding The player who makes the highest bid wins the right to name the game. He then tries to fulfill his bid and the other two players try to prevent him. A bid states only the number of game points that the player believes he can make if he wins the right to choose the game.

The lowest permitted bid is 18; the highest practicable bid is about 100.

Bidding follows the deal. Middlehand bids first, or passes.

If middlehand bids, forehand must reply. He must state either "Pass" or "Hold." "Hold" means that he makes the same bid as middleman. By bidding hold, he retains the right to name the game, because a player cannot lose this to a player to his left unless that player has bid higher.

This continues with forehand holding bids and middlehand raising bids until either player passes.

Then endhand must either raise the bid or pass; and if he bids, the survivor of the first pair replies by passing or holding. This continues as between the first pair, until one bidder gives in.

If both middlehand and endhand pass without bidding, forehand may make a bid or may pass. Once a player has passed, he may not make a bid. The player who survives in the bidding will now be referred to as the "bidder."

The skat The bidder begins by deciding whether or not to pick up the two cards that form the skat.

If he picks up the skat, he must then discard any two cards from his hand. These discards will eventually count toward his final score.

If he does not pick up, this is referred to as "handplay." The skat is then set aside for the duration of play, the fate of the skat depends on the game that has been played.

If the bidder chooses to pick up the skat, this limits his choice of game for the hand (since for certain games it is ruled that the skat may not be picked up).

The games The bidder then chooses which game will be played in that hand. His choice is between "suits," "grand," "simple null," "open null," and "reject."
(A bidder who has picked up the skat is not permitted to choose simple null, open null, or reject.)
To fulfill his bid, he must not only successfully complete the game he chooses (for example, by making sufficient trick points if that is required), but must also score sufficient "game" points to equal or exceed his bid.

Suits The bidder names a suit. All the cards in that suit become trumps, together with the jacks.
The bidder's aim is to make at least 61 trick points by taking tricks containing scoring cards.

Grand Only the four jacks are trumps. The bidder's aim is as in suits.

Simple null There are no trumps. The bidder aims to lose every trick.

Open null As in simple null, but the bidder must play with all his cards exposed. He lays them face up on the table before the opening lead.

Reject This game may be chosen by forehand, and he may choose it only if middlehand and endhand have both passed without a bid. He does not make a numerical bid, but simply states "Reject."
Only the four jacks are trumps. Each player tries to take fewer trick points than any other player.

Open If the bidder has opted for handplay, and names suits or grand, he may increase the value of his game by declaring "Open."
The bidder must then play with all his cards exposed, laying them face up on the table before the opening lead.

Schneider and schwarz If the bidder has named suits or grand, he may before the opening lead, declare:
a) schneider, ie he aims to win at least 91 trick points; or
b) schwarz, ie he aims to take every trick.
He need not declare either — in which case his goal remains 61 trick points.

Play Forehand leads to the first trick. Thereafter the winner of one trick leads to the next.
Other players must follow suit if possible. If unable to follow suit they may trump (if there are trumps in the game) or they may discard.
The highest trump played, or the highest card of the suit led if no trumps appear, wins the trick.

Scoring of trick points Cards taken in tricks score as follows:
a) each ace, 11 points;
b) each 10, 10 points;
c) each king, four points;
d) each queen, three points;
e) each jack, two trick points.

Scoring the skat After the last trick has been taken, the skat is allocated as follows:
a) at suits or grand, to the bidder (if he took the skat before play, he is given the cards he discarded);
b) at reject, to the winner of the last trick;
c) at null, to no one — the skat is discarded.
Whoever receives the skat (or discards) counts trick points for any scoring cards it contains.

Making the game Except at reject (see separate section), the bidder makes the game if he achieves that game's object (ie 61 trick points, 91 trick points, all tricks, or no tricks).
He must, however, then consider if he has made the number of game points that he bid.

Making the bid Except at reject, a bid is made if the bidder's game score equals or exceeds the number of game points stated in his bid. Game points are scored as follows.
a) At null games, the game value is fixed: 23 game points for making simple null, and 24 for making open null. Provided that the player's bid was not higher than this, he makes his bid.
b) At suits or grand, the game value has to be calculated — by multiplying a base game value by a number of multipliers. The player does not know how many multipliers he will qualify for until after play ends. The player makes his bid if the total game value (base x all multipliers) equals or exceeds his bid.

Trumps

Holding matadors

Base values for the games are:
a) diamonds, nine game points;
b) hearts, 10 game points;
c) spades, 11 game points;
d) clubs, 12 game points;
e) grand, 20 game points.

The multipliers are as follows:
a) automatic multiplier for having made game, one;
b) for holding "matadors" (see separate section) the multiplier varies but is at least one;
c) for choosing handplay, one;
d) for making schneider or schwarz (see separate section), the multiplier varies but is at least one.
The player adds all his multipliers together. The total will be between two and 14. He then multiplies the base value for his game by this total.

Matadors The jack of clubs and all other trumps in unbroken sequence in the bidder's hand (including the skat, whether or not it is used in play) are called matadors. When the bidder holds the jack of clubs, his hand is said to be "with" a number of matadors. When he does not hold the jack of clubs, his hand is said to be "without" a number of matadors.
The multiplier is the number of matadors that the bidder is with or without (it does not matter which).
Two examples are shown.
a) Spades are trumps, the player is with three matadors (the missing jack of diamonds breaks the sequence before the ace of spades). The multiplier is three.
b) Hearts are trumps, the player is without two matadors (the top two trumps are missing). The multiplier is two.

Multipliers for schneider and schwarz The bidder may only count one of the following multipliers:
a) schneider made but not predicted, one;
b) schwarz made but not predicted, two;
c) schneider predicted and made, three;
d) schneider predicted and schwarz made, four;
e) schwarz predicted and made, five.

Scoring is as follows. (Except see the separate section for reject.) Only the bidder scores.
If he has made his bid, he scores the total of his game points (which may be higher than his bid).
If he has not made his bid:
a) at suits or grand, he loses the amount of his bid at handplay — or twice that amount if he took the skat;
b) at null, he loses the absolute game value.

Reject There is no bidder and no bid. Normally the player who makes the fewest trick points scores 10. But:
a) if he takes no tricks, he scores 20;
b) if two players tie for fewest trick points, the one who did not take the last trick receives the score of 10;
c) if one player takes all tricks, he loses 30 and the others score nothing;
d) if all players tie with 40 trick points, forehand alone scores 10 for naming the game.

Winning The scores are recorded on a piece of paper and totaled at the end of a session.
The winner is the player with the highest score.
Often, an average score is worked out — players above the average then collect money accordingly, while players whose score is below average must make the payments.

Rummy

One of the most popular games in the United States, rummy is a straightforward card game for two to six players. Among its many variations, gin rummy—which can be traced back to the gambling casinos and saloons of nineteenth-century America—is the best liked and the most played.

Melds

BASIC RUMMY

Cards A standard deck of 52 cards is used.
In play, the cards rank normally with ace low.
For scoring, the jack, queen, and king are each worth 10 points; all other cards are worth their face value.
Players Two to six may play. There are no partnerships.
Objective Each player attempts to be the first to go out through having "melded" all his cards.
Cards are melded in either groups or sequences.
A group is three or four cards of the same rank (eg 4 of hearts, 4 of spades, and 4 of clubs).
A sequence is three or more cards of the same suit falling in numerical order (eg 9,10, and jack of diamonds).
Starting the game The player with the lowest cut or draw shuffles the cards, with the player to his right cutting the deck.
The cards are dealt in a clockwise direction. The number of cards dealt varies according to the number of players:
two players, 10 cards each;
three to four players, seven cards each;
five to six players, six cards each.
After the deal, the remaining cards are turned face down to form the stock. The top card from the stock is turned face up beside it to start the discard pile (this card is called the upcard).

Play Players take their turns in a clockwise direction, beginning with the player to the dealer's left.
The player starts his turn by drawing the top card from either the stock or the discard pile. He may then meld a group or a sequence face up on the table.
He may also "lay off" (add) as many cards as possible to any matched sets already melded on the table, whether the original melds were his own or an opponent's.
He ends his turn by rejecting one card from his hand and placing it face up on the discard pile. If he began his turn by drawing a card from the discard pile, he is not permitted to end the turn by discarding that same card.
If the stock is used up before any player goes out, the discard pile is turned face down (unshuffled) to form a new stock.
Going out A player goes out—and wins the hand—if he succeeds in getting rid of all his cards, with or without a final discard.
Going rummy A player "goes rummy" if he goes out by melding all his cards in one turn without having previously melded or laid off any cards.
Scoring If a player goes out, the numerical value of all the cards then left in his opponents' hands is totaled to give the winner's score for the round. This score is doubled if the player went rummy.
Continuing play The deal passes to the next player to the left if there are more than two players. If there are two players, the winner of one round deals the next.
Game The first player to reach a previously agreed total wins the game.

GIN RUMMY

Cards Two standard decks of 52 cards are used. While one player deals, the other shuffles the second deck ready for the next deal.
The cards rank normally, with ace low. They are valued as for basic rummy.
Players Basic gin rummy is for two players. It can be adapted for any larger even number by dividing players into two equal sides, and holding separate but simultaneous games between pairs of players.
Objective As in rummy each player tries to meld his cards in groups or sequences. Unlike basic rummy, however, it is possible for a player to win a hand without melding all his cards.
Choice of first dealer The player cutting the higher card has the choice of seat, deck of cards, and whether he wants first deal.
Shuffle and cut are normal (see p 80).
Deal The dealer deals 10 face-down cards to each player, beginning with his opponent and dealing one card at a time.
The twenty-first card is then turned face up and becomes the first card on the discard pile (the upcard).
The remaining cards are placed face down on the table alongside the upcard to form the stock.
Start of play The non-dealer decides whether or not he wants the upcard.
If he decides not to take it, the dealer has the option of taking it. If the dealer does not want it, then the non-dealer must draw the top stock card. Whichever player takes a card must then discard one.
Turn of play In subsequent turns a player takes the top card from either the discard pile or the stock, and then discards.
Players do not lay melds on the table until one player ends the hand by "going gin" or "knocking."
Going gin A player goes gin if he can meld all 10 of his cards in matched sets. He declares this when it is his turn, and lays all his cards face up on the table.
His opponent may then lay down his own melds, but he may not lay off any cards onto the winner's melds.

Knocking is an alternative way of going out. It may be done if the unmatched cards—deadwood—in a player's hand add up to 10 points or less. A player can knock only when it is his turn. He draws a card in the usual way, knocks on the table, and discards one card face down. He then lays out all his remaining cards face up on the table, grouping them into melds and unmatched cards.
His opponent must then, without drawing, lay his cards on the table. Cards should be grouped into melds and unmatched cards, but the player also has the opportunity of laying off cards onto the knocker's melds.
Each player's deadwood cards are then totaled, and the totals compared.
Scoring a hand
1) If a player goes gin he gets a 25 point bonus in addition to the value of his opponent's deadwood.
2) If a player knocks and his deadwood count is less than his opponent's, the knocker wins the hand and his score is the difference between the two counts.
3) If a player knocks and his opponent's deadwood count is lower than or the same as his own, the opponent has "undercut" the knocker and wins the hand. For this he scores a 25 point bonus as well as any difference between the deadwood counts.
"No game" The last two cards in the stock may not be drawn. If the player who draws the fiftieth card is unable to go gin or knock, the hand is a tie and no points are scored. The same dealer deals for the next hand.
Box (or line) A running total is kept of each player's score. When a player wins a hand, a horizontal line called a box (or line) is drawn under his score.
Game score The first player to score 100 or more points ends the game and has 100 points added to his score.
If his opponent has failed to win a hand, the winner then doubles his score (including the 100 point bonus).
Finally, for every hand a player has won—as shown by the boxes in his running score—he receives an additional 25 point bonus.

CANASTA

Canasta is a partnership game of the rummy family. Originating in Uruguay, it reached the United States in 1949. Here, in the early 1950s, it became one of the biggest fads in the history of card playing.

Cards Two standard decks of 52 cards and four jokers are used, shuffled together. The cards are not ranked. There are 12 wild cards: the four jokers and all eight deuces (2s).

Wild cards can be given any denomination that the holder wishes.

Players In the standard game there are four players divided into two partnerships.

The objective is to be the first side to score 5000 points over a series of hands. Points are mainly scored by making melds.

A meld is a set of at least three cards of the same denomination. They can be all natural cards, or a mixture of natural and wild cards. But whatever the size of the meld, there must be at least two natural cards and not more than three wild cards. Melds score according to the cards they contain (see table A).

Cutting for partners Each player cuts a card from the deck, and the two who cut the highest cards play against the other two.

For this purpose, cards rank normally (ace high) and suits rank spades (high), hearts, diamonds, clubs (low). Players cutting a joker or exactly equal cards cut again. The player cutting highest becomes first dealer and has choice of seats.

Shuffle and cut are normal (see p 80).

The deal begins with the player to the dealer's left. The cards are dealt one at a time and face down in a clockwise direction until each player including the dealer has 11 cards.

The remaining cards are then placed face down on the table as the stock. The top card of the stock is turned face up alongside to start the discard pile.

Play starts with the player to the dealer's left.

In a normal turn a player first takes the top card of the stock. He then makes any melds that he can, or adds to those that he or his partner have already laid out on the table.

Finally he discards by placing one card from his hand face up on the discard pile.

The initial meld of a partnership after each deal must total at least a certain number of points—how many depends on their score so far (see table B).

Once either partner has made this first meld, both partners can make new melds of any value and can add to melds that they have already laid out on the table.

A player may add to either his own or his partner's melds.

A canasta is a meld of seven cards.

A natural canasta consists of seven cards of the same rank and has a bonus value of 500 points on top of the card score.

A mixed canasta has natural cards and one to three wild cards, and has a bonus value of 300 points.

Once a canasta is completed, the cards are gathered into a pile. A natural canasta has a red card placed on top for identification, and a mixed canasta a black card.

Further cards may be added to a canasta. But a mixed canasta may not receive a fourth wild card and a natural canasta loses its value if a wild card is added.

Taking the discard pile In place of taking the top card from the stock, a player may in his turn take the upcard from the discard pile—but only if he has in his hand at least two natural cards of the same denomination.

He must lay the appropriate hand cards face up on the table and meld the upcard with them.

He then also takes all the remainder of the discard pile, and immediately uses as many cards as possible by adding to existing melds or laying out new ones. Any cards that he cannot use become part of his hand.

The player ends his turn by discarding one card to start a new discard pile.

Provided it is not "frozen," a player may also take the discard pile:

a) if he can meld the upcard with one card of the same denomination and one wild card; or

b) if the upcard matches an existing meld of his partnership.

Frozen discard pile The discard pile is frozen as follows.

1) It is frozen for a partnership that has not made its initial meld.

2) It is frozen for a player if a black 3 is the upcard. In this case it is no longer frozen after the player has drawn from the stock and discarded.

3) It is frozen for all players if the discard pile contains a red 3 or a wild card. In this case further discards are placed crosswise on top of the freezing card. The discard pile remains frozen until one player unfreezes it by melding the upcard or wild card with two natural cards from his hand.

Red 3s are bonus cards counting 100 points each. They cannot be melded.

If a player draws a red 3 from the stock, he must lay it face up on the table and draw another card from the stock.

If he is dealt a red 3 he must lay it face up on the table and draw a card from the stock in addition to his regular draw.

If a red 3 is taken as part of the discard pile, it must be laid face up on the table without any extra card being drawn from the stock.

If a partnership holds all four red 3s, these cards count 200 points each (800 points in all). All red 3 points count against a partnership if it has not made an initial meld when play ends.

Black 3s may only be melded when a player is going out. They can never be melded with wild cards. Their main use is as "stop cards" to freeze the discard pile.

Going out occurs when a player is able to meld all his cards, providing that when he has gone out his side has made at least one canasta. A player can go out without discarding if he wishes.

Concealed going out occurs when a player melds all his cards when he has not previously melded any cards. Note that he must meld a canasta unless his partner has already melded one.

Permission is usually asked to go out, in the form of "May I go out partner?" A yes or no answer is required and is binding.

This procedure is generally used as a warning to a partner to meld as many cards as possible, so that the requesting player can go out in his next turn.

Table A

Card	Points for each card in meld
Joker	50
Deuce (2)	20
Ace	20
8, 9, 10, j, q, k	10
4, 5, 6, 7	5
Black 3	5
Red 3	see text

Table B

Accumulated score of partnership	Value required for initial meld
Minus	15
0-1495	50
1500-2995	90
3000 or more	120

Table C

	Points
Natural canasta	500
Mixed canasta	300
Going out	100
Concealed going out	100 extra
Red 3s	see text

Scoring Each partnership receives the total of all bonus points earned in the hand (see table C), plus the total point value of all melded cards, less the value of any cards remaining in the hands of either player in the partnership at the end of play.

(Note that the low bonuses for going out make the completion of high-scoring melds more significant than being first to go out.)

If one partnership has failed to meld at all, the value of any red 3s it has laid down count against it.

It is possible for a partnership to make a minus score on a hand.

Hands continue until one side has made a total of 5000 points and wins the game. For each successive hand the deal passes clockwise.

Variant rules The following variations on the standard rules are widely accepted.

1) Even if the discard pile is not frozen, a player may not take the upcard to add it to a completed canasta of his own side.

2) When taking the upcard from the discard pile to make a new meld, a player must always have a natural pair to match it (ie not a matching card and a wild card).

Wild cards

Melds

Natural

Mixed

A canasta

Cribbage

Cribbage is reputed to have been invented by Sir John Suckling, an English poet and courtier who lived in the early 1600s. Six-card cribbage for two players is the most popular form of the game today, but there are also five- and seven-card forms as well as adaptations for three and four players.

Pair, 2 points
Pair royal, 6 points
Double pair royal, 12 points
Sequence, 4 points
Flush, 4 points
Fifteen, 2 points

Specimen hand worth 24 points
The "start"
Four fifteens, 8 points
Four sequences, 12 points
Pair, 2 points
Pair, 2 points

Cards All forms of cribbage are played with a single standard deck of 52 cards.
Card values Court cards count 10 each, and all other cards count their face value.

Cribbage board The score can be kept with pencil and paper, but it is easier to use a special cribbage board. Most cribbage boards are made of wood and measure about 10in by 3in.
There are four rows of 30 holes, two rows for each player, and additional game holes at one or both ends of the board.
Each player has two pegs, usually red or black for one player and white for the other. When there are four game holes, the players usually put their pegs in them for the start of play.
A player marks his score by moving his pegs first along his outer row and then back along his inner row of holes.
Both pegs are used to score in the following way:

a) a player marks his first score by moving one peg that number of holes from the start;
b) his second score is marked by placing his second peg that number of holes beyond his first peg;
c) his third score is marked by placing his first peg that number of holes beyond his second peg;
d) scoring continues in this way until a player's forward peg has passed all the scoring holes to end in one of the game holes.

SIX-CARD CRIBBAGE
Players The basic game is for two players.
Objective The game is won by the first player to score 121 points, ie to go "twice around the board."
The deal Players cut for deal. The player with the lower cut (with ace low) deals first, and then the deal alternates between players.
The deal is six cards, one at a time, to each player. The remaining cards are placed face down to one side.
The crib is an extra hand scored by the dealer.
It is formed by each of the players discarding two cards and placing them, face down, to the dealer's right. Each player is thus left with a hand of four cards.
The cut After the discards the non-dealer cuts the deck, and the dealer turns up the top card of the remaining stack.
This card is placed face up on the stack for the rest of the game. It is known as the "start" or "starter."
If the start is a jack, the dealer scores "two for his heels."

Scoring Points are scored both during the playing of a hand and when the hands are shown after play.

Combinations of cards score as follows.

a) A pair, two cards of the same rank, scores two points.

b) A pair royal, three cards of the same rank, scores six points (two points for each of the possible pairs to be made).

c) A double pair royal, four cards of the same rank, scores 12 points.

d) A sequence or run is a series of cards in face order (ace low) and scores one point for each card. The cards do not have to be of the same suit.

e) A flush is four or five cards of the same suit and scores one point for each card. If a flush is also a run, points are scored for both features.

f) Fifteen is any combination of cards with a face value totaling that number. It scores two points.

Play begins with the non-dealer. He places a card face upward in front of him and calls out its face value as he does so. Court cards are called as 10.

The dealer then places one of his cards face upward in front of himself and calls out its value.

Whenever a pair, pair royal, double pair royal, sequence, or fifteen (but not a flush) is formed during play, the player putting down the card that forms it scores the appropriate points.

If the non-dealer lays down a 5 and the dealer follows it with another 5, the dealer would say "ten for a pair" and score two points. If a third 5 is played, the non-dealer would say "fifteen for eight," the eight points being made up of a fifteen and a pair royal.

A sequence of cards scores regardless of the order in which it is played. Thus if cards are played in the order ace, 2, 5, 4, 3, the player putting out the 3 can count a run of five cards. Should the second player be able to add a 6 he can score a run of six cards, and so on.

When the count during play reaches 31, the cards are turned face down and the player whose card brought the total to 31 scores two points. If a player at his turn is unable to play a card that is within the limit of 31, he says "go." His opponent then plays any of his cards that are low enough to be within the limit. If they make 31 he scores two points; if less than 31 he scores one point and also says "go." Play then resumes with the remaining cards in hand, and proceeds until all the cards are played or another 31 limit is reached.

The player who plays the last card of a hand scores "one for last."

The show After all the cards have been played, each player picks up his own cards from in front of him.

The non-dealer shows and scores his hand first, which gives him an advantage if he is very near reaching 121.

The start is taken into the reckoning as part of each hand.

A card may be ranked for scoring in any number of different combinations. Thus two 10s and two 5s would give a score of eight points for fifteens plus four points for pairs—giving a total of 12 points. The combination 4,4,5,6,6 scores eight points for fifteens, four points for pairs, and 12 points for sequences—giving a total of 24 points (see illustration).

If a player holds a jack of the same suit as the start, he scores "one for his nob."

A flush of four cards in hand scores four points. If the start is of the same suit the player scores five points, but a flush of four cards including the start scores nothing.

After the non-dealer has declared his score, the dealer shows and scores his own hand. After which, he shows and also scores for the crib.

The crib is scored in the same way as the hands, except that the only flush allowed is a five-card one.

Muggins If a player overlooks a score, whether in his hand or in play, his opponent may call "muggins" and claim the overlooked score for himself. (Some players prefer not to employ this rule.)

Lurch If a player reaches 121 before his opponent is halfway around the board, he scores a lurch and counts two games instead of one.

Errors If an error in dealing is noticed during the deal, there should be a redeal.

If an error in dealing is found after play has started, the non-dealer scores two points and the error is rectified either by a redeal or by drawing additional cards from the stock.

If after "go" is called a player fails to play his additional cards, he may not subsequently play those cards and his opponent scores two points. Errors in counting during play are not penalized.

FIVE-CARD CRIBBAGE

This is an earlier form of the game than six-card cribbage. Except as specified, the rules are the same as for the six-card game.

Objective Game is 61 points.

The deal is five cards to each player.

The crib consists of two cards from each player.

Play Non-dealer pegs three points before play begins, to compensate for not having the crib.

Hands are not played out after 31 is reached or "go" is called. Hands are shown and scored; then there is a new deal.

SEVEN-CARD CRIBBAGE

This version is played in the same way as six-card cribbage, except that: game is 181 points; the deal is seven cards to each player (of which two go to the crib).

THREE-HANDED CRIBBAGE

The game is adapted for three-handed play in the following ways.

Game is 61 points.

The deal is five cards to each player and one to the crib. Each player then gives one card to the crib.

Play begins with the player to the left of the dealer, and passes to the left.

The player who leads also has the first show.

FOUR-HANDED CRIBBAGE

This is a partnership form of the game.

Partners sit opposite each other, and play begins with the player to the dealer's left.

Game is 121 points.

The deal is usually five cards to each player (of which one goes to the crib).

Tarot card games

The exact origins of tarot cards are not known, but it is probable that they have been used since medieval times both as a means of foretelling the future and for playing card games. Many different tarot games are played today, often using a mixed deck of tarot and standard playing cards.

Trump cards

AUSTRIAN TAROCK
This is a popular 54-card tarot game played in many parts of Europe. It is played with a mixed deck of numbered tarot cards and standard playing cards.
Players It is a game for three people (**a**), but can be adapted for four players.
The player to the left of the dealer is called forehand, the next middlehand, and the dealer himself, endhand.
(If four players take part (**b**), the dealer does not receive cards, but he may share in the payments for that hand. The third player is then called endhand.)

Forehand

a

(Dealer) Endhand   Middlehand

Forehand   **b**   Middlehand

Dealer   Endhand

The deck comprises:
a) 32 cards divided equally into four suits—hearts, diamonds, spades, and clubs. Four of the eight cards in each suit are court cards: king, queen, knight, and jack.
Cards in the red suits rank: k (high),q,kt,j,a,2,3,4 (low).
Cards in the black suits rank: k (high),q,kt,j,10,9,8,7 (low).
b) 22 trump cards numbered XXII (high) through I (low). Number XXII is called the joker or "skus;" number XXI "mond;" and number I "pagat."
The trump cards are sometimes illustrated as well as bearing a number.

The objective is to make a winning bid and to score points in melds and tricks.
Deal The dealer gives eight face-down cards at a time to each player, including himself. He then deals a face-down "widow" (see p 80) of six cards to the center of the table, before dealing a further batch of eight cards to each player.
(Should any player not have received a trump card, he must immediately show his cards, and a redeal takes place after the cards have been thoroughly shuffled.)

Suit cards

Bidding is in a clockwise direction, beginning with forehand. Players may either bid or pass. If all the players pass, the deal moves one player to the left without a score.

There are two permissable bids: a threesome (worth 50 points) and a solo (worth 100 points). The solo bid overcalls the threesome, so that if forehand opens with a solo bid, there can be no further bidding.

Threesome When the winning bid is threesome, the bidder takes up the top three cards of the widow. If these are not to his liking, he puts them face up on the table and takes the remaining three cards of the widow.

He may either incorporate these three cards into his hand (in which case the game counts double); or he may reject them face up and take up the exposed first three cards of the widow (in which case the game counts triple).

Whichever cards he chooses, he then discards any three cards, except kings, from his hand. His discards are put face down on the table but if they include a trump this must be declared.

At the end of play, the discards belong to the winning bidder and the rejected cards of the widow to his two opponents (see the section on trick scores).

After choosing his widow cards, the bidder must choose to play either:

a) game—in which case he must try to win 36 or more points in play; or

b) consolation—in which case he must try to win 35 or fewer points.

Solo When solo is the winning bid, the widow remains unexposed. At the end of play it goes to the bidder's opponents, who, in both solo and threesome, play in partnership against him.

Melds are declared after the bidding and the discarding, if any.

Possible melds are:
a) joker, mond, and pagat;
b) four kings.
Each meld scores 50 in threesome and 100 in solo. (see scoring).

Melds

5 points

5 points

5 points

5 points

4 points

3 points

3 points

Play After the bidding, forehand leads with any card he likes. The other players must either follow suit or, if this is impossible, trump.

If a player can neither follow suit nor trump he may play any card he likes.

The highest trump, or the highest card of the suit led if there are no trumps, takes the trick. The winner of each trick leads to the next trick.

Points in play depend on the combination of "point" cards and "nulls" in each trick. Point cards and their point values are as follows:

a) joker (XXII), mond (XXI), pagat (I), and kings, five points each;
b) queens, four points each; and
c) knights and jacks, three points each.

Nulls are the other 35 cards and have no point values.

Each trick counts points as follows:
a) one point for three nulls;
b) the value of the point card for one point card and two nulls;
c) the sum of the point cards minus one, for two point cards and one null; and

d) the sum of the point cards minus two, for three point cards.

The bidder also scores for his discards, if any, and the opponents for the widow. The bidder fulfills his bid if either:

he chose solo or game and makes 36 or more trick points; or he chose consolation and makes 35 or fewer trick points.

Scoring At solo or game a successful bidder scores double the number of trick points he made over 35, plus 50 for threesome and 100 for solo.

If he played consolation, his score would be double the difference between 35 and his actual trick points, plus 50 for threesome.

For example, if he took 24 trick points, his score would be $(35-24) \times 2 + 50 = 72$.

If the bidder fails to make his bid, each of his opponents scores the value of the bid plus twice the number of points the opponent has scored over 35.

Each player then scores for any melds he has made.

Pagat Any player who wins the last trick with the pagat receives a bonus of 50 in threesome, and 100 in solo.

Before play opens the bidder may declare "Ultimo," signifying his intention of taking the last trick with the pagat.

If he does so and succeeds, he gains a bonus of twice the value of the game.

If he fails, he loses that same amount. If he has to play the pagat earlier in the game and loses it, he may score 5 points for it if he takes the last trick. He does not score if he played the pagat unnecessarily.

If the bidder declares ultimo, an opponent may declare "Contra-ultimo," signifying that he intends to win the bidder's pagat.

If he does so and succeeds, each opponent wins a bonus of 200 in threesome, and 400 in solo.

If he fails, the same bonus goes to the bidder.

Trick scores

1 point

5 points

7 points

9 points

©DIAGRAM

Batons

Cups

Swords

Coins

| I | II | III | IV | V | VI | VII | VIII | IX | X |

The fool

The juggler

The high priestess

The empress

The emperor

The pope

The lovers

The chariot

Strength

The hermit

The wheel of fortune

TAROCCO

Tarocco is a tarot game played with the traditional 78-card tarot deck that is also used for fortune telling.

Players The game is for three players. Play is in a counterclockwise direction: the player to the dealer's right is called forehand, the second player middlehand, and the dealer endhand.

The deck comprises:
a) 22 cards that function as a trump suit;
b) 56 cards in four suits of 14 cards each: batons, cups, swords, and coins.
The trump cards rank from XXI (high) to I (low). (The fool, when ranked, ranks below the I.)
The suit cards rank k(high), q,kt(knight),j,10,etc.

The trump cards are:
the fool (the only one of the 22 cards that is not numbered), the juggler (I), the high priestess (II), the empress (III), the emperor (IV), the pope (V), the lovers (VI), the chariot (VII), strength (VIII), the hermit (IX), the wheel of fortune (X), justice (XI), the hanging man (XII), death (XIII), temperance (XIV), the devil (XV), the tower (XVI), the star (XVII), the moon (XVIII), the sun (XIX), the day of judgment (XX), and the world (XXI).
The world, the juggler, and the fool are called "honor" cards.

The objective is to score the maximum number of points by taking certain cards in tricks.

Deal Players draw cards for the right to deal; lowest card deals first. The deal passes one player to the right for each new hand.
Each player is dealt 24 cards, one at a time and face down. The remaining six cards are added to the dealer's hand.

Buying cards takes place as soon as the deck has been dealt.
It is an optional procedure and has many variations, but usually a player wanting a particular card may announce this and buy it from the player who holds it (assuming he is willing to part with it) by "paying" ten points ie ten points are deducted from the buyer's score and added to the seller's score.

Justice

The hanging man

Death

Temperance

The devil

The tower

The star

The moon

The sun

The day of judgment

The world

Play The dealer discards face down any six cards except honors and kings.
He then leads to the first trick by putting out face up any card of his choice. Play then proceeds in a counterclockwise direction.
If the lead is in batons, cups, swords, or coins the players must play a card of the same suit but of any value. If he cannot follow suit, he must play a trump card; if this is not possible he may play a card of any suit.
If the lead is a trump card, a player must follow with another trump card—usually a rule is applied that it should also be of a higher value; if this is not possible he may play a card of any suit.
The winner of a trick leads to the next trick.

The fool A player holding the fool may, during any trick except the last, show it instead of playing a card. The trick is then contested between his two opponents only, and the fool is placed with any tricks the player may have taken.
In the last trick, the fool counts as the lowest ranking trump card and is played normally.
The juggler If a player wins the last trick with a juggler, he scores ten points. If he plays the juggler to the last trick and loses, he forfeits ten points.

Scoring in tricks If accompanied by a low-value card (ace through 10) certain cards score as follows:
a) the world (XXI), the juggler (I), the fool, five points each;
b) kings, five points each;
c) queens, four points each;
d) knights, two points each.
The dealer also scores as above for his discards.

Bonus points A player with 15 trumps in his hand must declare them before play begins, and earns a bonus of ten points.
A player who wins all tricks receives a bonus of 20 points.
The winner is the player with the highest score at the end of three hands.
Each loser pays the difference between his and the winner's score, according to a points or money scale agreed on by the players before the game.

© DIAGRAM

Japanese flower card games

Japanese flower cards—or "hanafuda" cards— grew from the meeting between Western playing cards and ancient Japanese painted seashell games. Once a cult in court life, hanafuda games spread to the geisha houses and then throughout Japanese society. Cards can be bought in Western countries.

The cards Hanafuda cards are only $2\frac{1}{8}$in high by $1\frac{1}{4}$in wide. They are much thicker than Western playing cards. Because of this the Japanese play onto cushions, on which the cards slide less easily. The deck consists of 48 cards. These are divided into 12 suits of four cards each.

Each suit represents one of the 12 months of the year. Each card shows a tree or plant, usually one that the Japanese associate with that card's month. Many of the cards show other objects as well. Most decks also have an additional blank card, which can be used to replace a lost or damaged card.

Card values Each hanafuda card has a point value. These values range from one through 20 points, and there is a distribution within each suit. The standard distribution is one 10 point card, one 5 point card, and two 1 point cards. There are, however, several suits with other distributions.
Usually, in each suit:
a) the low scoring cards show only a stylized plant;
b) the intermediate card also shows a "tanzaku"—a piece of paper traditionally used for writing poetry;
c) the high scoring card shows an animal or object in addition to the plant.

January: pine

| 20 points Pine with crane | 5 points Red lettered tanzaku | 1 point Plain pine | 1 point Plain pine |

February: plum

| 10 points Plum with nightingale | 5 points Red lettered tanzaku | 1 point Plain plum | 1 point Plain plum |

March: cherry

| 20 points Cherry with curtain | 5 points Red lettered tanzaku | 1 point Plain cherry | 1 point Plain cherry |

April: wisteria

| 10 points Wisteria with cuckoo | 5 points Plain red tanzaku | 1 point Plain wisteria | 1 point Plain wisteria |

May: iris

| 10 points Iris with bridge | 5 points Plain red tanzaku | 1 point Plain iris | 1 point Plain iris |

June: peony

   |

| 10 points Peony with butterfly | 5 points Blue tanzaku | 1 point Plain peony | 1 point Plain peony |

© DIAGRAM

July: clover

| 10 points Clover with wild boar | 5 points Plain red tanzaku | 1 point Plain clover | 1 point Plain clover |

August: pampas

| 20 points Pampas with full moon | 10 points Pampas with geese | 1 point Plain pampas | 1 point Plain pampas |

September: chrysanthemum

| 10 points Chrysanthemum with wine cup | 5 points Blue tanzaku | 1 point Plain chrysanthemum | 1 point Plain chrysanthemum |

October: maple

| 10 points Maple with deer | 5 points Blue tanzaku | 1 point Plain maple | 1 point Plain maple |

November: rain (also called willow)

| 20 points Rain with poet | 10 points Rain with swallow | 5 points Plain red tanzaku | 1 point Rain and lightning |

December: paulownia

| 20 points Paulownia with phoenix | 1 point Plain paulownia | 1 point Plain paulownia | 1 point Plain paulownia |

Matching flowers : turn of play
a

b

c

GENERAL RULES
Many hanafuda card games share the same general playing arrangements.

Series of games A complete series consists of 12 hands.

The objective is to make the highest total score.

Players Two to seven players may take part in a game, but only two or three can actually play in any hand. (Two-play is not very satisfactory in many hanafuda games.) If there are four to seven players, some must drop out from each hand (see the section on dropping out).

Seating order for all players is decided before the series begins.

Any player deals a single card face up to each player, and the player who receives the card representing the earliest month of the year becomes dealer for the first hand. This player sits where he chooses.

The other players take the other seats in counterclockwise rotation, beginning with the player with the next earliest month, who sits to the dealer's right.

If two or more players hold cards of the same month, they are dealt further cards until the tie is settled.

These relative seating positions hold good for the series—even though in each hand only three players will be active.

Shuffle and cut Counting the dealer as first player and going counterclockwise, the third player shuffles and the second player cuts.

Because of the thickness and stiffness of hanafuda cards, shuffling consists of multiple rapid cuts.

Normal rotation of play begins with the player to the dealer's right and goes counterclockwise.

Deal for up to five players
1) The dealer gives each player four cards together, face down, in normal rotation, finishing with himself.
2) He next deals three cards face up into the center of the playing area.
3) He then gives each player three more cards together, face down, in normal rotation, finishing with himself.
4) He finally deals three more cards face up into the center of the playing area—these cards complete the "board."
5) The remainder of the deck is placed face down in the center of the playing area. These cards form the stock, from which players draw cards during the course of play. Any mistake is judged a misdeal, after which the cards are reshuffled, recut, and redealt.

Players may not look at their cards until the deal is completed.

Dealer's hand exchange can be called by any player before anyone has looked at his cards. The player who calls then exchanges his cards for those in front of the dealer. Any number of such exchanges is permitted.

Dropping out Each player examines his cards to see whether he wishes to play the hand.

The dealer is the first person to state whether he is playing or dropping out.

Then the other players state their intention in normal rotation. As soon as three persons have declared to play, the others drop out unless any of them feels that he has a particularly good hand. In the latter case, a player may pay a number of points to the dealer and play in his place.

When a player drops out, he places his cards face down on top of the stock.

It is sometimes ruled that at least three players must stay in a hand, in which case the last players to declare have no choice if they are needed to make up the number.

Otherwise it is ruled that if every player but one drops out, that player immediately claims a number of points from each other player and then the hand ends.

When the dealer drops out, the role passes for that hand to the first player in normal rotation who has stayed in.

Deal with six players The deal uses up the entire deck—there is no stock until one of the players discards his hand.

Deal with seven players The blank card is included in the deck for the deal.

The dealer does not deal any board cards into the center, but gives seven cards to each player in the usual way. This uses up the entire deck.

The player receiving the blank card as one of his cards is obliged to drop out. The blank card is put out of play and his remaining six cards become the board cards.

There is no stock until the first player who voluntarily drops out has discarded his hand.

Bonus combinations at "matching flowers"

Name	Number of cards	Point score	Cards needed
Straight paulownia	4	10	All cards of paulownia suit
Straight wisteria	4	10	All cards of wisteria suit
Grass tanzaku	3	20	Wisteria, iris, clover tanzaku cards
Boar-deer-butterfly	3	20	Clover-and-boar, maple-and-deer, peony-and-butterfly
Crane-phoenix-moon	3	20	Pine-and-crane, paulownia-and-phoenix, pampas-and-full moon
Three bright	3	30	Pine-and-crane, plum-and-nightingale, cherry-and-curtain
Six tanzaku	6	30	Any six tanzaku cards, except the rain tanzaku
The views	2 or 3	20 for 2 40 for 3	Pampas-and-full moon, chrysanthemum-and-wine cup, cherry-and-curtain cards
Blue tanzaku	3	40	Peony, chrysanthemum, maple tanzaku cards
Red lettered tanzaku	3	40	Pine, plum, cherry tanzaku cards
Seven tanzaku	7	40	Any seven tanzaku cards, except the rain tanzaku
Four bright	4	60	Pine-and-crane, cherry-and-curtain, pampas-and-full moon, paulownia-and-phoenix cards
Five bright	5	100	"Four bright" and rain-and-poet card
Straight rain	4	10*	All cards of rain suit

*But also all bonus points of all other players for that hand are lost

Bonus score combinations (examples)

The views

Boar–deer–butterfly

MATCHING FLOWERS
This is a good family game for young and old. Because it is simple, it is also known as fool flowers. It does, however, make a good introduction to hanafuda play since it illustrates the basic procedures.

The objective A player aims to take cards from the board by matching them with cards from the same suit in his hand. Points are scored according to the point values of the cards matched; and bonus points are scored if the player builds up certain sets among his matched cards.

Play Going to the right from the dealer, play begins with the first player who has stayed in the hand. It continues in normal rotation.

Turn of play
To begin his turn a player examines his cards to see if he has a card of the same month as any of the cards on the board (**a**).
If he has, he exposes the relevant card from his hand and takes the appropriate card from the board. The two cards are placed together face up in front of the player (**b**).
If he is unable to match any card in the board. he must discard any one card from his hand and place it face up as one of the board cards.
In either case, the player then draws one card from the top of the stock and exposes it.
If the drawn card matches the suit of any one of the board cards, the player may take this card and place it and the drawn card face up together in front of him.
If the drawn card does not match any board card it is added to the board (**c**).
The player's turn now ends: a player is only permitted to match from his hand once and to make one draw in any one turn.

No board cards If there are no board cards at any time, a player must discard to the board and then draw.
The drawn card can take the discard as usual if they are of the same suit.

No stock If the stock is exhausted play still continues if players have unmatched cards.
In each turn a player must match a card in the board; or, if he cannot match, he must discard any card from his hand to the board.

Three of a kind If three cards of the same suit appear in the board at the beginning of play, then the player who receives the remaining card of that suit may take all three. It does not matter whether he receives the other card in the original deal or by drawing. If the three board cards are not claimed immediately, they are stacked together until a player claims them.

Tactics of play include, of course, trying to prevent other players from scoring points and bonuses as well as trying to score points for oneself.

A hand ends when players have no unmatched hand cards remaining.
One player may continue to play even after all the others have finished.

Scoring A player's score for a hand is made up of basic points and bonus points.
1) Basic points: each player receives the points total of the cards that he has matched.
2) Bonus points are scored for combinations formed from any of a player's matched cards. One card may be reckoned in any number of combinations. Standard combinations are shown in the table.

Continuing play The series continues with the next hand. The player with the highest points total from a hand becomes the dealer for the next hand.

"Low man out" Any player who is dealt a very poor hand can request a hand of low man out. He then tries to make as few points as possible—but he must always make a match if he can.
If, at the end of the hand, he has fewer than 20 points, then the winner of the hand loses all his points for that hand. Other players score normally.

Result The winner is the player who makes the highest total score over the series.

5

Marbles

Games with marbles have been popular for thousands of years and are played in countries all over the world. The names and rules of marbles games vary tremendously from place to place, but the basic objective of any marbles game is to test how accurately a player can aim his marbles.

Marbles are small, hard balls made from stone, wood, baked clay, plastic, glass, or steel. They are usually about ½in in diameter.
A marble actually being used by a player is sometimes called a "taw."

Shooting In some games players throw or drop their marbles. Usually, however, marbles must be rolled along the ground.
Maximum accuracy and distance can be obtained by shooting the marble as illustrated—a method sometimes called "knuckling down."
The knuckle of the forefinger is placed on the ground, the marble is balanced on the forefinger, the thumb is put behind the forefinger—and then released to shoot the marble.

Shooting

Claiming marbles is a feature of many marbles games.
In some games a player may keep an opponent's marble if his own marble hits it.
Other games are played for points—with the difference in players' scores at the end of the game being settled by the payment of an agreed number of marbles for an agreed number of points.

Spanning

CAPTURE
This is a simple marbles game for two players.
Player A shoots his marble and then player B attempts to hit it with his marble.
If player B hits A's marble, he may keep it.
If player B's marble misses A's marble, B's marble stays where it is and A attempts to hit it with a shot from where his marble lay after his first shot. If A hits B's marble he keeps it, otherwise turns alternate until one player takes the other's marble.

SPANNERS
Spanners, or hit and span, is a variation of capture.
As in capture, a player who hits his opponent's marble may keep it. But in this game, a player may choose to attempt a "span" if his marble is near enough to his opponent's. He does so by placing his thumb on his own marble and a finger on his opponent's marble, and then flicking them together.
In one version of the game a successful span entitles him to take his opponent's marble as if he had hit it with his shot, but an unsuccessful span means that he loses his own marble.
In another version a player gains one point for a successful span—after which both players pick up their marbles and the player who did not win the point shoots first in the next play. (An unsuccessful span is ignored in this version.)

SPANGY
Spangy is a game for five players.
A square is marked on the floor, and each player places one marble in the square to make the pattern illustrated.
Each player then plays in turn, always shooting his taw from the same point about 10yd from the square.
A player may claim any marble that he knocks out of the square, and if his taw stops within a "span" of any other marble he may also claim that marble if he makes a successful span (see spanners).
Each player picks up his taw at the end of his turn.

Spangy

RING TAW

Ring taw is a game for any small number of players.

Two circles are drawn on the ground—an inner circle about 1ft in diameter and an outer circle about 7ft in diameter.

At the start of the game each player puts one or two marbles in the inner circle.

Each player then shoots in turn from any point outside the outer circle.

If a player knocks one or more marbles from the inner circle, he wins them and is entitled to another shot. This shot is taken from where his "taw" (the marble he last shot with) came to rest.

If a player fails to knock any marble from the inner circle, his turn ends and he must leave his taw where it stopped. Succeeding players may shoot at any marble within either of the circles—taws as well as the marbles originally placed in the inner circle.

Whenever a taw is hit its owner must pay one marble to the player who hit it.

After his first turn, each player shoots his taw from where it came to rest at the end of his previous turn.

The game ends when all marbles have been cleared from the inner circle.

INCREASE POUND

In this variation of ring taw the inner circle is known as the "pound" and the outer ring as the "bar."

Play is exactly the same as for ring taw except that:

there is no extra shot for hitting a marble out of the pound;

a player whose taw stops in the pound must lift his taw and pay a marble into the pound;

a player whose taw is struck by the taw of another player must pay that player one marble plus all the marbles that he has won up to this stage of the game.

FORTIFICATIONS

This is another variation of ring taw, for which players draw four circles one inside the other.

At the start of the game each player places three marbles in the innermost circle or "fort" (**a**); two marbles in the next ring out (**b**); and one in the next (**c**). The outermost ring is left empty.

Each player plays in turn. With his first shot, made from any point outside the outer circle, each player attempts to knock a target marble from ring (**c**). If he succeeds, he keeps the target marble and leaves his taw in the target marble's place. If he fails, he pays one marble into ring (**c**) and drops out of the game.

If a player's taw hits an opponent's taw at any stage of the game, the opponent's taw remains in its new position until its owner uses it for his next turn. When requested, a taw may be temporarily lifted to allow a player a clear shot at a target marble.

For all turns after the first, each player still in the game plays his taw from where it lies or from any point on the outside circle. As in his first turn, he claims any target marble that he hits and, unless he is entitled to an extra shot, leaves his taw in the target marble's place.

As long as any target marbles remain in ring (**c**), players must attack that ring and are allowed only one shot in a turn. A miss at this stage of the game, however, does not compel players to drop out. Once ring (**c**) is cleared of target marbles, players must attack ring (**b**). Play then proceeds exactly as for ring (**c**), except that a player who hits one target marble in ring (**b**) is allowed a second shot. Once ring (**b**) is cleared of target marbles, players may attack ring (**a**). This time the only difference in procedure is that a player is entitled to a third shot if his first two shots both claim a target marble.

Ring taw

Fortifications

BOUNCE EYE

Bounce eye

In this game for two or more players, each player places one or more marbles in a central cluster in a circle about 1 ft in diameter.

The first player then stands over the ring and drops a marble onto the cluster. He may claim any marbles that roll out of the circle, but if no marbles roll out of the circle must add one marble to the cluster.

Players then drop a marble in turn until all the marbles in the central cluster have been claimed.

WALL MARBLES

In this variation of capture several players shoot or throw their marbles against a wall.

The first player sends a marble against the wall and leaves it where it stops.

Each of the other players then follows in turn, and:

a) leaves his marble where it stops if it fails to hit another marble as it rebounds from the wall; or

b) claims all the marbles on the ground if his rebounding marble hits any other.

If no player has hit another marble when all the players have had a turn, play continues in the same way but with each player delivering his marble from where it stopped in the first round.

Wall marbles

DIE SHOT

In die shot, or die marble, players shoot their marbles at a target comprising a die balanced on a marble that has been filed down to make it more stable.

Each player becomes "die-keeper" for one round, while the other players make one shot in each turn.

Before making a shot, each player must pay the die-keeper one marble.

If a player knocks the die off the marble, the die-keeper must pay him the number of marbles shown on the uppermost face of the die.

HUNDREDS

This game for two players is usually played outdoors but can easily be adapted to indoor play. Outdoors, players shoot marbles into a shallow hole; indoors, a drawn circle can be used.

At the start of the game each player shoots one marble toward the ring.

If both players' marbles stop in the ring, both players shoot again.

When only one player's marble stops in the ring, he scores 10 points and then continues shooting and scoring until he misses or scores 100 points.

If he misses, his opponent shoots and scores until he misses.

The game is won by the first player to reach 100 points.

THREE HOLES

This game can also be played indoors with drawn rings instead of holes.

Three rings, about 3in in diameter and 5ft apart, are marked on the floor.

The game is won by the player who "kills" (puts out) all his opponents or is first to shoot a marble into each ring in the correct order.

Each player plays in turn, and gains an extra shot if his marble stops in the correct ring or hits another player's marble. At the end of his turn a player must leave his marble where it lies.

Only after a player has scored the first ring may he "kill" another player by hitting his marble. Before he scores the first ring, however, he may move another player's marble by hitting it.

When a player is "killed" he must pay his hitter the marble that was hit plus any marbles won in the game.

ARCHBOARD

In archboard, or bridge board, players attempt to shoot their marbles through arches cut out of a narrow piece of card or board.

Each player is keeper of the arches for one round of the game, while the other players shoot one marble in each turn. Before making a shot, each player pays the keeper one marble.

When his marble passes completely through an arch a player receives from the banker the number of marbles shown above that arch. (Usually numbers are higher toward the outside of the bridge.)

If a player's marble misses the bridge completely, he must pay another marble to the keeper.

PICKING PLUMS

Picking plums is a game for any small number of players. Each player places one or two marbles in a row—with room for two marbles to pass through the gaps.

Each player then shoots in turn and may keep any "plums" knocked from the line.

A player is entitled to an extra shot whenever he picks a plum; all shots are made from the original position and not from where the marble lies after the previous shot.

DOBBLERS

This game is played in the same way as picking plums except that:

a player's taw stays where it lies at the end of a turn;

subsequent turns are played from where the taw lies;

a player whose taw is hit by another player's taw must add one marble to the row.

ONE STEP

One step is another game in which the target is a row of marbles made up by the players.

It is played in the same way as dobblers except that:

a player's first shot is made by taking one step and then throwing his taw from an upright position;

subsequent shots are made from an upright position but with no step forward;

a successful shot entitles a player to an extra shot from where his taw lies.

Die shot

Hundreds

Three holes

Archboard

Picking plums

One step

Conkers

Conkers is a popular game with British children. Two players each have a "conker" threaded on a knotted string. Players take alternate hits at their opponent's conker and the game is won when one player destroys the other's conker.

The conkers The game is usually played with nuts from the horsechestnut tree, but is sometimes played with hazelnuts (often called "cobnuts").

When preparing their conkers, players make a hole through the center with a sharp instrument such as a meat skewer, or a compass or a pair of geometry dividers. Many players then harden their conkers by soaking them in vinegar or salt and water and/or baking them for about half an hour. Excellent conkers are obtained by storing them in the dark for a year.

When the conker is ready, a strong piece of string or a bootlace is threaded through the hole and knotted at one end. The string should be long enough for about 9in to hang down after it is wrapped once or twice around the hand.

The game Players take alternate hits at their opponent's conker.

The player whose conker is to be hit first, holds his conker as shown (**a**)—with the string wrapped around his hand. He must adjust the height of his hand to suit his opponent, and must then keep his conker perfectly still for the hit.

The striker takes his conker in one hand and holds the opposite end of his string in the other hand (**b**). For the strike, he first draws the conker back and then releases it in a fast swinging motion in the direction of his opponent's conker (**c**).

If the striker misses his opponent's conker he is allowed a maximum of two further attempts to make a hit. If the players' strings tangle, the first player to call "strings" can claim an extra shot.

Play continues until one of the conkers is destroyed—ie until no part of it remains on the string.

Scoring Conkers are usually described according to the number of victories won with them—eg a "oner," "fiver," "seventy-fiver."

A conker adds one to its title each time it destroys a conker that has never won a game. A conker that defeats a conker with previous wins claims one for defeating it plus all the defeated conker's wins—so a "fiver" that defeats another "fiver" becomes an "elevener."

CONQUERORS

This is a similar game to conkers and seems to have been very popular in the eighteenth and nineteenth centuries.

Two players press empty snail shells tip to tip until one of them breaks.

Scoring is the same as for conkers.

SOLDIERS

This game is now usually played with lollipop, or ice cream, sticks.

One player holds his stick with both hands, one at each end. The other holds his stick in one hand and gives his opponent's stick a sharp blow. Turns at striking alternate as in conkers, and the game continues until one of the sticks breaks. Scoring is as for conkers.

The game used to be played with stalks from the ribwort plantain—the winner being the first player to knock the head off his opponent's stalk.

Coin throwing games

Money has been changing hands in games of chance and skill since time immemorial. In another, much smaller group of games it is the coins themselves that play the principal role.

BROTHER JONATHAN

This coin throwing game originated in North America in the eighteenth century.

It is a game for two or more players, playing for themselves or in teams.

The board may be marked on the ground, or drawn on a large sheet of paper laid on the floor. It is a rectangle divided into sections, with a scoring value marked in each one.

Note that the larger sections bear the lower scores whereas the smaller sections contain higher numbers.

Play Each player takes it in turn to pitch a coin from a previously designated spot onto the board.

If a coin touches any of the dividing lines it does not count towards the player's score.

The winner may be decided in one of two ways:

a) the first player or team to score an agreed total; or

b) the player or team with the highest score after an agreed number of throws.

WALL JONATHAN

This game is played in the same way as Brother Jonathan except that players must throw their coins against a wall in such a way that they rebound onto the board.

CRACK LOO

In this game, players score points by throwing coins onto numbered cracks on a wood floor (or onto lines drawn on a large sheet of paper).

Otherwise play is the same as for Brother Jonathan.

COVER IT

Cover it is a game for two or more players.

The first player throws a coin against a wall and leaves it where it comes to rest on the ground.

Then each player in turn throws a coin against the wall. If his coin is touching another coin when it comes to rest, he picks up both coins. If it is not touching another coin, he leaves his coin on the ground. (This game is also played with playing cards or other small cards.)

HITTING THE MUMMY

This is a variation of cover it in which the first coin thrown is designated the "mummy" and players aim only to cover this one coin.

A player whose coin is not touching the mummy after being thrown against the wall, must leave his coin where it lies.

A player whose coin is touching the mummy, is entitled to pick up all coins on the ground except the mummy. If he mistakenly picks up the mummy, he must pay one coin to each of the other players.

PENNIES ON THE PLATE

A metal plate or lid is placed on the ground.

At his turn a player throws an agreed number of coins at the plate. The coins must be thrown one at a time from an agreed distance of several feet. The player who gets the most coins to stay on the plate wins the game. (It is usually quite easy to hit the plate, but much more difficult to ensure that a coin falls in such a way that it does not immediately bounce or roll off it.)

TOSSING A COIN

Tossing a coin is a widely known method of deciding the order of play for many different games between two players or teams.

The coin is tossed by a player or non-player, who:
a) flicks the coin into the air by releasing his thumb from between his clenched fingers;
b) catches the coin in his other hand;
c) quickly turns this hand over to lay the coin on the back of his tossing hand.

If a non-player makes the toss, he asks one of the players to "call." If a player makes the toss, his opponent should call. A player calls either "heads" or "tails" in an attempt to forecast which side of the coin will be face up after the toss. He should make his call while the coin is in the air.

A player who "wins the toss" (ie makes a correct forecast) generally has the right to choose the order of play for the game.

HEADS OR TAILS

Heads or tails is an adaptation of tossing a coin to make a game for any number of players.

Each player tosses a coin in turn, and all players, including the thrower, guess whether it will fall with the head or tail up.

The winner is either:
a) the first player to make an agreed number of correct guesses; or
b) the player with the most correct guesses after an agreed number of throws.

CATCH

The skills of juggling and coordination play an important part in the game of catch.

For the first round, each player:
a) balances one coin on his elbow;
b) drops his hand and tries to catch his coin as it falls.

For the second round, players balance and attempt to catch two coins together, and the number of coins is then increased by one for each further round.

Any player who fails to catch the required number of coins for a round is eliminated from any further rounds, and the winner is the last player left in the game.

Tossing

SPINNING A COIN

This game is played in the same way as heads or tails, except that the coins are spun instead of tossed.

(Probably the easiest method of spinning a coin is to hold it on its edge on a smooth, hard surface and then spin it between the thumb of one hand and the forefinger of the other, as shown.)

Spinning

Catching

HOLE IN ONE

For this game players need a coin and a plastic tumbler or similar receptacle.

The tumbler is placed on its side on the floor and the players take it in turn to try rolling a coin into it.

The winner is the player who gets the coin into the tumbler most times, out of an agreed number of shots.

ROLL A GOAL

This game is played in the same way as hole in one, except that players attempt to roll a coin between two "goalposts" made from folded paper, books, or other objects.

COIN ARCHBOARD

This is a coin version of marbles archboard (p 126). Players attempt to roll coins through arches in a board and, when successful, score the number of points indicated above the arch.

PENNY ROLL

This game is popular at fairgrounds in many parts of the world. It can easily be played at home with improvised equipment.

Players roll coins down a metal and wood chute onto a board divided into numbered squares.

If a player's coin stops completely within a square, he receives a sum of money in accordance with that square's number.

Fivestones and Jacks

Fivestones and jacks are two almost identical games derived from knucklebones, a primitive form of dice played with the knucklebones of sheep. Knucklebones probably originated in Asia Minor, and later became popular in ancient Greece and Rome. Today, fivestones and jacks are played in many countries. In both these games, players in a crouching position throw small objects in the air and catch them in various ways in a usually increasingly difficult series of throws.

FIVESTONES
The game of fivestones (sometimes called chuckstones or jacks) is played with five small rounded stones or with five small plastic cubes of different colors.

The objective is to complete a series of throws in an agreed sequence, each throw to be successfully completed before the next is attempted.

Players The game can be enjoyed by a player on his own —or two or more players may attempt to be first to complete an agreed sequence of throws.

Turns If there are two or more players, the usual practice is to play in turn.
First turn may be decided by a preliminary throw, by the toss of a coin, or by agreement. A player's turn ends when he fails to accomplish any part of a particular throw, and his next turn begins with another attempt at the failed throw.

Throws There are many hundreds of variations of the game, but those given here are among the most widely known.

Basic throw

a   b   c   d   e

Basic throw For the basic throw, sometimes called the "jockey," the player must:
a) put the five stones in the open palm of one hand;
b) toss the stones up in the air;
c) while the stones are in the air, turn his hand over and catch the stones on the back of his hand;
d) toss the stones from the back of his hand;
e) turn his hand over and catch the stones in the palm of his hand.

Ones The player attempts the basic throw. If he catches all the stones, he goes on to twos. If he fails to catch any stones his turn ends.
If he catches one or more stones, he must:
leave any stones on the ground where they lie;
transfer to his other hand all but one of the stones he has caught;
throw the single stone in the air;
pick up one stone from the ground with his throwing hand;
catch the thrown stone with the same hand.
The player must repeat the procedure for picking up individual stones until all have been retrieved.

Twos The player scatters the the stones on the ground, taking care that they do not land too far apart.
He then selects one stone, throws it up in the air, and must pick up two other stones from the ground with his throwing hand before catching the thrown stone with that same hand.
When he has done this, he transfers the two stones to his other hand, tosses up the third stone, and must pick up the remaining two stones from the ground.

Threes is like twos, except that the player must pick up one stone followed by three, or three stones followed by one.

Fours In fours, all four stones are picked up at one time.

Pecks The player attempts the basic throw. If he succeeds in catching all five stones, he goes on to bushels. If he fails to catch any stones his turn ends.
If he catches one or more stones, he must:
keep the caught stones in his throwing hand;
push one stone out between his forefinger and thumb and then:
toss the pushed out stone into the air (**a**);
pick up one stone from the ground with his throwing hand (**b**);
catch the thrown stone with his throwing hand (**c**);
repeat this procedure until all stones are picked up.

Bushels If the player succeeds with a basic throw, he goes on to claws. If he fails to catch any stones his turn ends.
If he catches one or more stones, he must:
throw all the caught stones in the air;
pick up one stone from the ground with his throwing hand;
catch the thrown stones;
repeat this until all stones on the ground are picked up.

Claws The fivestones are tossed from the palm onto the back of the hand—as in the basic throw.
If all five are caught, the player attempts to complete the basic throw and if successful may go on to ones under the arch.
If none is caught on the back of the hand, the player's turn ends.
If one or more are caught on the back of the hand, the player:
leaves the caught stones on the back of his hand;
picks up the stones on the ground between the outstretched fingers of his throwing hand, with only one stone between any two fingers or between finger and thumb;
tosses the stones from the back of his hand and catches them in his palm;
maneuvers the stones from between his fingers into his palm.

Pecks

Under the arch

Ones under the arch The player first scatters the stones on the ground and makes an arch near them with the thumb and forefinger of his non-throwing hand.
He then selects one stone and throws it up in the air (**a**). While the stone is in the air, he knocks the other stones through the arch (**b**), and then catches the thrown stone (**c**). When all four stones have been knocked through the arch, the player throws the fifth stone in the air and before catching it must pick up the other four stones.
Twos under the arch is similar to ones under the arch, except that the stones must be knocked through the arch in two pairs.

Threes under the arch is similar except that the stones are knocked through as a three and a one or a one and a three.
Fours under the arch requires all four stones to be knocked through together.
Horse in the stable The stones are scattered on the ground and the non-throwing hand is placed near them, with the fingers and thumb spread out, the fingertips touching the ground, and the palm raised. The gaps between the fingers and thumb are the "stables."
One stone is then thrown into the air (**a**), and before catching it the player must knock a stone into or toward one of the stables (**b**). No more than one stone may be knocked into any one stable.

The player continues throwing, knocking, and catching in this way until all four stables are filled.
He then moves his non-throwing hand away from the four stones, tosses the throwing stone and before catching it must pick up the four stones from the ground.

Horse in the stable

©DIAGRAM

Toad in the hole The stones are first scattered on the ground. A "hole" is then made by laying the thumb of the non-throwing hand straight along the ground and curling the fingers around so that the tip of the forefinger touches the tip of the thumb.
One stone is then thrown into the air, and before catching it the player must pick up one of the other stones, a "toad," and drop it into the hole.
This is repeated until four toads are in the hole. The player then moves his non-throwing hand, tosses up the single stone and before catching it must pick up all four toads.

Over the line The non-throwing hand is placed with the palm on the ground, and four stones are scattered on the ground to its outer side. The player then throws the fifth stone in the air, and before catching it must transfer one of the other stones to the other side of his non-throwing hand. This is repeated until all four stones on the ground have been transferred. (It is advisable to place the transferred stones as close together as possible.)
The player then throws up the fifth stone and before catching it must pick up the other four stones in his throwing hand.

Over the jump is similar to over the line, except that the non-throwing hand is placed on edge to make a jump or wall —so making the transference of stones more difficult.
Threading the needle is also similar, but the stones have to be dropped one at a time through a circle formed by the thumb and forefinger of the non-throwing hand held about 8in above the ground.

Over the jump

Snake in the grass The player sets out four stones in a straight line, with a gap of several inches from one stone to the next.
He then throws the fifth stone in the air, and before catching it, must pick up one of the end stones, use it to trace part of the pattern illustrated, and lay the picked up stone down at the point of the pattern reached.

A player is allowed any number of throws to complete his tracing, but his turn ends if he drops the throwing stone, fails to touch the stone he is using for tracing, or touches any other stone.

Building a tower can only be played with fivestones that are cubes.
The player first scatters four of his stones. He then throws the other stone and before catching it moves one of the stones on the ground away from the others.
At his second throw he places a second stone on top of the first, at his third throw he places a third stone on top of the other two, and at his fourth throw he completes the tower.
Demolishing a tower is the obvious sequel to building a tower. At each throw, the player must remove a single stone from the tower.

Snake in the grass

Building a tower

Backward ones After first scattering four stones on the ground, the player throws the fifth stone in the air and catches it on the back of his throwing hand.
He then tosses the fifth stone into the air from the back of his hand and before catching it in the normal way must pick up one stone from the ground.
The player then throws the two held stones in the same manner and picks up a third stone. The three held stones are used for the next throw, and four stones for the throw to pick up the fifth stone.

Backward twos is similar to backward ones, except that the player must pick up two stones at his first throw and then the remaining two.
Backward threes is similar except that three and then one or one and then three stones must be picked up.
Backward fours requires the player to pick up all four stones at one time.

JACKS
Jacks or jackstones are small, six-legged, metal objects. They are usually bought in sets of five or six.
As well as the jacks, a player needs a small rubber ball. This is thrown in the air and then must be caught after agreed moves have been made with the jacks.
Most fivestone games can be adapted for play with jacks.

Jacks and ball

Spellicans

Spellicans and jackstraws are two similar games that test a player's skill at removing straws or small sticks from a pile, one at a time and without disturbing any of its neighbors. They are games for any number of players.

SPELLICANS

This game, sometimes called spillikins, originated in China and is played with a set of about 30 thin strips of ivory, wood, or plastic.

These strips, called spellicans, have carved heads representing animals, people, etc. There is also a carved hook for moving the strips.

Start of play The order of play is determined by the throw of a die or some other means.

The last person in the playing order then takes all the spellicans in one hand and drops them on to the table or floor. He must not interfere with any spellican after it has left his hand.

Play At his turn, each player takes the carved hook and attempts to remove a spellican from the pile without disturbing any of the others. Once a player has started moving a particular spellican he is not permitted to transfer his attack to a different spellican.

If he successfully removes a spellican from the pile, he keeps it and tries to remove another spellican from the pile. A player's turn continues until he disturbs a spellican other than the one that he is attacking.

Play continues in this way until all the spellicans have been taken.

Scoring Each spellican has a points value, and a game is won by the player with the highest score.

Spellicans that are generally fairly easy to move have a low value, and more elaborate and difficult to move spellicans have a correspondingly higher value.

JACKSTRAWS

This variant of spellicans is also variously known as jerkstraws, juggling sticks, pick-up sticks, and pick-a-stick.

It is played with about 50 wood or plastic sticks or straws. These are about 6in long, rounded, and with pointed ends, and colored according to their points value.

Play The rules are the same as for spellicans except that players remove the sticks with their fingers or, in some versions of the game, may use a stick of a specified color after they have drawn one from the pile.

MAGNETIC JACKSTRAWS

This is a modern form of jackstraws in which the straws are made of metal and must be removed from the pile by means of a small horseshoe magnet.

Rolling a stick with fingers

Raising a stick by pressing its end

Using one stick to move another

Tiddlywinks

Tiddlywinks is a game for any small number of players. In the standard game, each player attempts to put small disks or "winks" into a cup by shooting them with a larger disk called a "shooter." Various tiddlywinks games based on sports such as tennis and golf can be bought or easily improvised.

Playing area The game is played on the floor or on a table.
Any shape of table may be used but a square or round one is best for more than two players. The table should be covered with a thick cloth or piece of felt.

Equipment For the standard tiddlywinks game players need "winks," "shooters," and a target cup.
Winks and shooters must be slightly pliable and are usually made of bone or plastic. Winks are usually about $\frac{5}{8}$ in and shooters about 1 in in diameter. Each player's winks and shooter should be a different color.
Cups are made of plastic, wood, or glass and are usually $1\frac{1}{2}$ in across and 1–2 in high.

Players The standard game is usually played by two, three, or four players with four winks each.

Start of play The cup is placed in the center of the table, and each player places his winks in a line in front of him.

Turns Order of play is often decided by a preliminary shot —the first shot of the game going to the player who gets his wink nearest the cup.
Play is then usually clockwise around the table.
Each player shoots one wink in a turn plus one extra shot each time he gets a wink into the cup.

Scoring Tiddlywinks may be scored in two ways:
a) players count the number of games they win;
b) players score one point for each wink in the cup when each game ends.

Objective The game is won by the first player to get all his tiddlywinks in the cup.

Out of play Any wink that is partly covered by another is out of play. A player whose wink is covered by an opponent's wink must either wait until the opponent moves his wink or attempt to remove the opponent's wink by hitting it with one of his own winks. Any wink that stops against the side of the cup is out of play until it is knocked level on to the table by another wink. A wink that is shot off the table does not go out of play. It must be replaced on the table at the point where it went off.

Partners Tiddlywinks can be played by partners in the same way as the standard singles game except that:
players pair up with the player sitting opposite;
partners play alternately and may play either their own or their partner's winks.

Shooting A player shoots a wink by stroking and pressing the edge of his shooter against the edge of the wink and so making the wink jump into the air.
A wink is shot from where it lies after the player's previous turn.

FORFEIT GAME

An interesting variation of the standard game is played by drawing six concentric circles around the cup.
Play is the same as for the standard game except that any wink that lands in one of the circles is forfeited and immediately removed from the table.

Forfeit

TARGET GAMES

Variations on the standard tiddlywinks game can be played by using numbered targets.
Typical layouts are:
a) a target with concentric circles each worth a set number of points;
b) a raised target with numbered scoring areas.
Target tiddlywinks games are played in the same way as the standard game except that: players score a set number of points for landing their winks on different parts of the target (a wink touching two scoring areas always scores the lower number);
a wink may not be shot again once it has landed on any part of the target, but may be knocked by another wink.

Target

TIDDLYWINKS TENNIS

The lines of a tennis court should be marked on the floor or the tiddlywinks cloth. (Dimensions for the court should be varied to suit the skill of the players and the height of the net.)
An improvised net can be made with folded paper or card, or with a row of books. Players shoot a wink back and forth over the net—gaining points whenever their opponent fails to get the wink over the net or shoots it so that it goes outside the limits of the court.

Rules for service can be modified to suit the skill of the players—eg extra shots allowed to get the wink over the net or no restrictions on where in the opponent's court the wink must land.
A match is scored in games and sets as in ordinary tennis.

© DIAGRAM

Tennis

TIDDLYWINKS GOLF

Tiddlywinks golf sets, with tiddlywinks, greens, obstacles, and holes, are produced by various toy manufacturers.
The game can also be played on an easily improvised course. Nine "holes" should be positioned at intervals around the course. Holes can be egg cups, napkin rings, or just circles drawn on the tiddlywinks cloth.
The course is then made more interesting by the addition of obstacles—such as rumpled or corrugated paper under the cloth to make rough ground, upturned books to make bunkers, and box or jar lids for water obstacles.

The game can be scored by "stroke" or by "hole" as in real golf. In the first, each player counts the number of shots he takes to complete the course. In the second, players score one for each hole won and a half for each hole tied.

Golf

Ball games

Although ball games are usually associated with outdoor play, there are many enjoyable games that can be played indoors. A table tennis ball is recommended for minimum damage!

Cup and ball

Containers

CUP AND BALL

Cup and ball is a game for one person that was first played several hundred years ago. It was especially popular among children in the late nineteenth century and can still be bought today.

The cup and ball are made of wood and joined by a length of string. Sometimes the cup is replaced by a wooden spike and the ball has a hole bored through its center.

The player holds the cup around its base and stretches out his arm so that the ball hangs toward the ground. He then swings his arm and tries to catch the ball in the cup—with a little practice this can be done almost every time.

The version with a spike is more difficult to accomplish, as the ball has to be impaled on the spike.

JAM JARS

This is a game needing only a few table tennis balls and some jam jars for equipment. Five or six jam jars are placed close together on the floor or on a table.

Players stand a few feet away and take it in turns to throw a set number of table tennis balls (usually two or three) in an attempt to get them into the jars.

As table tennis balls are extremely bouncy, this task is more difficult than it might at first seem!

The player who manages to get the most balls into the jam jars after each round of play is the winner. (Any number of rounds may be played.)

IN THE BOWL

In the bowl is a game very like jam jars.

A deep bowl or bucket is placed on the floor.

Each player in turn tries to throw a table tennis ball so that it lands (and remains!) in the bowl.

If the player is successful he may throw again.

At the end of a set time, the player with the most successful throws wins the game.

CONTAINERS

This game is played in the same way as in the bowl, except that players try to get a ball into one of several containers—each with a points value depending on its size.

The player with most points wins the game.

Blow football

Holey board game

BLOW FOOTBALL

Blow football is a game played at a table by two players or by two teams of two or three.
Each person blows through a drinking straw at a table tennis ball, and tries to get the ball into the opposing goal.
The player or team that scores the most goals after a given time wins the game.
Equipment Blow football is best played at a long table, although it can also be played on the floor.
A goal must be marked at each end of the table—using pencils or other suitable objects.
It is a good idea to make a wall around the edges of the table to help keep the ball in play. (Strips of wood or cardboard can be used.)
Each player is given a drinking straw, and the only other equipment needed is a table tennis ball.
Play The table tennis ball is placed in the middle of the table. At a given signal, the players start to blow through their straws in an attempt to get the ball into the opponents' goal—while at the same time defending their own goal from attack.
Whenever a goal is scored (ie the ball passes between the "goalposts"), the ball is repositioned at the center of the table and the game is restarted.
If the ball is blown off the table, the opposing side places the ball on the table at the spot where it came off and then takes a "free" blow before the other side may continue blowing.

HOLEY BOARD GAME

This is a target game in which players score points by throwing a table tennis ball through a "holey board."
The holey board can be made quite easily out of stiff cardboard. A random number of holes is cut out, each one a different size. (The smallest hole should be just big enough for a table tennis ball to pass through it.) A scoring value is written above each hole—the bigger the hole, the lower the value.
The board is propped up between two chairs—books can be used to keep it in position. Players stand as far away from the board as possible and take turns to throw the ball.
Each time a player gets the ball through a hole, he scores the number of points written above the hole. (The smaller the hole, the more difficult it is to get the ball through it!)
The player with the highest score after a set number of throws is the winner.
Once players have become quite skilled, they can try throwing the ball so that it bounces on the floor before going through a hole.

THROUGH THE TUNNEL

Through the tunnel is very like the archboard game (see the section on marble games). Playing procedure is exactly the same, but table tennis balls are used instead of marbles, and the arches through which they are rolled are correspondingly bigger.

Darts

A traditional English "pub" game, darts now has enthusiasts in many different countries. Players throw darts at a circular target divided into different scoring areas. Games are played by individuals, pairs, or teams. In the standard game, players aim to reduce a starting score exactly to zero. Other games provide a great variety of objectives designed to test the players' skill.

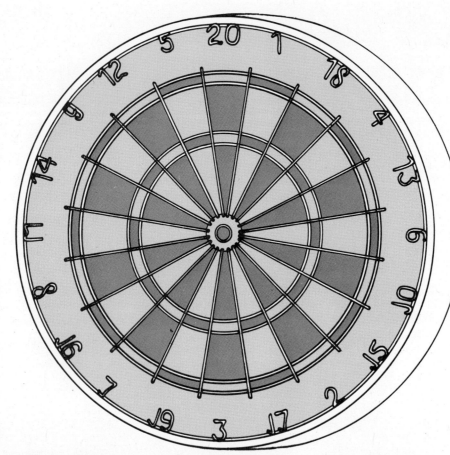

Standard dartboard Most dartboards are made of cork, bristle, or elm, with the divisions and sector numbers marked by wires.
The standard tournament board is 18in in diameter and has twenty sectors, an outer "doubles" ring, an inner "trebles" ring, and an inner and outer "bull" in the center. Adjacent sectors are differentiated by color.
Darts Each player has a set of three darts.
Designs vary, but most darts are about 6in long. All darts have:
a sharp point, usually made of steel;
a barrel, with finger grips, made of metal (usually brass), of plastic weighted with metal, or of wood;
a tail, "flighted" with feathers, plastic, or paper.

Yorkshire

Narrow five

Target

Irish black

Unusual dartboards
Examples of unusual dartboards are:
a) the Yorkshire board, with a single bull, diamonds between the numbers 14 and 9 and 4 and 13, and no trebles ring;
b) the Irish black, again with a single bull and no trebles ring;

c) the narrow five board from London's East End, with three 20s, three 15s, three 10s, and three 5s; and
d) the target board, with circles increasing in value toward the center.

Games using different boards Any game played on the standard tournament board can be played on the Yorkshire board or the Irish black—the only difference being that there are no trebles and no outer bull.
The narrow five board—now very rare—is used for a game in which players seek to be first to reach a set target score.
The target board—a very early type—is used for a game in which players throw three darts in a turn and aim to be the first to throw 1000 points.

STANDARD TOURNAMENT GAME

Players Games are played by individuals, pairs, or teams of any fixed number of players.

Starting Each player, or one member of each pair or team, must get a dart in the doubles ring to begin scoring.
The starting double is scored, as are darts thrown after but not before it in the same turn.

Turns In singles games, each opponent throws in turn. In pairs and team games, the different sides throw in turn, with members of each side playing in the order established at the start of the game.
The first turn goes to the player, pair, or team that wins the toss of a coin or gets a dart nearest the bull in a preliminary throw.

Scored throws A throw is invalid if the player is not behind the toe-line when throwing.
Only those darts sticking in the board at the end of a player's turn are scored. Thus darts are not scored if they rebound, stick in another dart, fall from the board, or are knocked out before the player ends his turn. Re-throws are not permitted. (Also note starting and finishing procedures.)

Scoring Scored throws are deducted from a starting total —usually 301, 501, or 1001. Darts in the inner bull score 50, and in the outer bull 25. Darts in a sector score according to the sector number—unless they are within the outer (doubles) ring, when they score double the sector number, or the inner (trebles) ring, when they score three times the sector number.

Finishing The game ends with a double bringing the score exactly to zero.
If the scores in a player's turn take him past zero, or to one, he goes back to the score before that turn and forfeits any darts remaining in that turn.

The scoreboard is a slate or blackboard, usually positioned to one side of the dartboard. Each side's score is recorded in chalk.

"Chalking" Traditionally in English pubs, a person who wishes to play on the dartboard when other players are using it, must offer to "chalk" (keep the score) for these players. Chalking entitles him to play the winner of the game then in progress.

Playing area The dartboard is hung on a wall, with the center 5ft 8in from the ground. Toe lines may be marked on a mat or on the floor, at distances of 8ft, 8ft 6in, and 9ft from the dartboard.

8ft
8ft 6in
9ft

© DIAGRAM

AROUND THE CLOCK

This is a singles game for any number of players. Each player throws three darts in a turn.
After a starting double, each player must throw one dart into each of the sectors, in order, from 1 to 20. Darts in the doubles or trebles rings of the correct sector are usually allowed.
The winner is the first player to finish.
As a variation, players may be awarded an extra turn for scoring with the last dart of a turn.

SHANGHAI

Shanghai is another "around the clock" game for any number of players with three darts each.
In his first turn, each player throws all his darts at sector number 1. Singles, doubles, and trebles all score their value.
In his second turn, each player throws all his darts at sector number 2 (even if he made no score in his first turn).
Play proceeds in this manner right "around the clock," and the winner is usually the player with the highest total score.
In a popular variation of this game, a player may win by going "Shanghai," ie by scoring in one turn a single, double, and treble of the required number.

SCRAM

Scram is a game for two players throwing three darts in each turn.
The player with the first turn is the "stopper," and any sector he hits with a dart is closed to his opponent.
The second player is known as the "scorer," and he aims to score as many points as possible before all the sectors are closed.
When all the sectors are closed, the two players change roles.
The winner is the player who scores most when playing scorer.

CLOSING

This is a game for two players, each with three darts.
Each player aims to make as high a score as possible while seeking to prevent his opponent from making a high score.
As soon as one of the players has scored three times from any one sector, that sector is "closed" and no further score may be made from it by either player.
Doubles and trebles score their value, and count as two and three scores respectively.
The winner is the player with the highest score when the last sector is closed.

	A	B
20	xxx	x
19		
18	x	xx
17	xx	
16	xx	x
15		x
14		
13		
12		xxx
11		
10		
	144	123

Closing

KILLER

Killer is probably best with four to eight players, but can be played by either more or less. In his first turn, each player throws one dart with the hand that he normally does not use for playing darts. This throw decides a player's own sector for the rest of the game. Unless a very large number of people are playing, it is usual for a

First turn

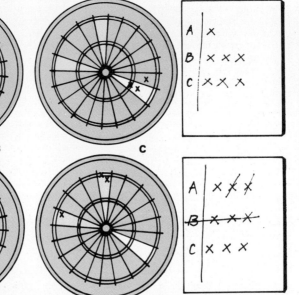

Second turn

Third turn

player to throw again if a sector has already been given to another player.

In every other turn, each player throws three darts with his usual hand.

The game has several versions, but in all cases the winner is the player left in the game when all other players have lost all their "lives."

First version In one version of the game, all players begin with no lives and a player's first objective is to acquire three lives by throwing three darts into his own sector (two lives for a double and three for a treble).

Once a player has three lives he becomes a "killer" and starts throwing darts at other players' sectors (in the

example illustrated, players B and C become killers after their second turns and player A after the first throw of his third turn.

If a killer throws a dart into the sector of a player with three or two lives, that player loses one life (or two for a double or three for a treble).

If a killer throws a dart into the sector of a player with one or no lives, that player is out (player B after C's third turn in the example illustrated).

A killer who loses a life loses his right to kill until he makes up his lost life by throwing another dart into his own sector.

Second version All players start with an agreed number of lives—usually three or five. To start killing, a player has to throw a double of his own number. Kills are made by throwing doubles and trebles of other players' numbers— one kill for a double and two kills for a treble. Lost lives cannot be won back again.

HALVE IT

Halve it is a game for any number of players, each throwing three darts in a turn. Before play begins, players select a series of objectives and chalk them up on the scoreboard. A typical series would be: 20, 19, 18, any double, 17, 16, 15, any treble, 14, 13, 12, double, treble, 11, 10, bull.

In his first turn, each player aims for 20 and scores for each dart in that sector (doubles and trebles count their value). Players then take turns to make their way through the list of objectives, scoring for each dart in the correct sector or halving their total score (rounding down) whenever none of their darts scores. There are no minus scores, and

a player whose score is reduced to zero stays at zero until he throws a dart that scores.

FIVES

Fives can be played by two players or sides using a standard dartboard.

The winner is the first player to reach an agreed number of points, usually 50.

Each player throws three darts in a turn. He scores only if the sum of his three darts can be divided by five—in which case he scores the result of this division.

A player who throws a dart out of the scoring area when he has a total divisible by five, scores no points for that turn.

DARTS FOOTBALL

This is a game for two players, each throwing three darts in a turn.

A dart in the inner bull "gains control of the ball." This player can then start scoring

"goals"—one for each double. He continues scoring until his opponent "takes the ball away" by scoring an inner bull. The first player to score ten goals wins the game.

DARTS CRICKET

Darts cricket is a game for two teams of equal size.

The team that wins the toss of a coin decides whether to "bat" or to "bowl."

Turns alternate between teams, and each player throws one dart in a turn.

When "batting," a team aims to score as many "runs" as possible; when "bowling," to "take wickets" by scoring inner bulls.

The teams change roles after five wickets are taken.

The team with the highest batting score wins the game.

DARTS BASEBALL

This is a darts game for two players, each representing a baseball team.

There are nine innings, and each player has a turn at "bat" in each inning. A player's turn consists of three throws.

In the first inning players throw darts at sector 1, in the second inning at sector 2, through to sector 9 in the ninth inning. Extra innings are played if there is a tie.

A single "run" is scored by getting a dart into the correct sector for the inning (with two runs for a double and three for a treble). Getting a bull at any stage of the game is a "grand slam home run" and scores four runs.

DARTS SHOVE HA'PENNY

This game for two players or pairs is based on the rules of an old English board game (p 180).

Each player throws three darts in a turn, and the objective is to score three times in each of the sectors numbered 1 through 9.

The scores may be made in any order, and doubles count as two scores and trebles as three.

If a player scores more than three times in any one sector, the extra scores are given to the opposition. The score that wins the game, however, must always be actually thrown by the winner.

The game is won by the first side to finish.

Ring target games

Several good games can be played with small rings and different types of target. Best known of these games is ringboard, or hoopla as it is sometimes called, but ring the bull and ringolette are enjoyable alternatives.

RINGBOARD/HOOPLA
Ringboard, or hoopla, has for generations been a popular indoor target game.
Boards of different shapes and sizes are generally easy to buy—or may be made by the do-it-yourself enthusiast from plywood, hardboard, or chipboard.
Most bought boards are diamond- or shield-shaped, about 18in high, and decorated with brightly colored patterns or illustrations.
Screwed into the boards are a number of hooks—usually between 12 and 16. A figure below each hook indicates the number of points scored whenever a player throws a ring onto the hook.
The back of a ringboard has a thin rope loop for hanging the board on a wall or door.
Rings At least six rings should be provided.
Bought rings are usually made of rubber, and are about 3in in diameter. They are similar to those used on jars of homemade preserves—which could easily be substituted.
Other ideas for improvised rings are large curtain rings, or rings made from string or heavy card.
Play The players throw as individuals, or may form into teams.
At his turn, each player stands an agreed distance from the ringboard and throws six rings.
Scoring At the end of his turn, a player scores the designated number of points for each ring on a hook.
The game is won by the player or team with most points after an agreed number of throws.

RING THE BULL
This game is a variation of ringboard and was played in England during the reign of Queen Victoria. It is an amusing game and calls for more agility and control than first meets the eye.
The board can be made by: painting a bull's head on a piece of plywood, hardboard, or chipboard;
attaching a rod, about 18in long, to the board above the bull's head;
screwing hooks into the board, one in the nose and one in each horn;
tying a piece of string, about 30in long, to a ring and then fastening the other end of the string to the rod.
Play Each player in turn makes an agreed number of attempts to throw the ring onto the hook on the bull's nose.
A player scores one point each time he succeeds. There is no score for throwing a ring onto the hooks on the bull's horns.
The winner is the player with most points. (A re-throw may be held if a game is drawn.)

RINGOLETTE
Ringolette is another target game played with rings.
Equipment Victorian ringolette sets usually contained 10 or 12 small skittles and a similar number of wooden rings. A figure on each skittle indicated its points value.
The game can easily be played with improvised materials—rings like the ones used for ringboard, and bottles instead of skittles.
Play The game is for two players or teams.
At his turn each player stands an agreed distance from the targets and throws all the rings, attempting to get each one over a different target.
For a target with one ring over it at the end of his turn, a player scores that target's points value.
If any target has more than one ring over it, the player's opponent is awarded the points value of that skittle for each extra ring.
The game is won by the player or team scoring most points.

6

Solitaire (Patience) card games

Solitaire and patience are general names for any card game for one player. The exact origin of such games is obscure, but they have probably existed for centuries and several hundred different games exist today. Although the outcome of many of the games depends mainly on the luck of the shuffle, others involve real skill and judgment.

GENERAL PROCEDURE

Cards Solitaire games can be played with a standard 52-card deck, or with two decks shuffled together.

Some games are played with a "stripped" deck, from which certain cards have been discarded prior to play.

Special solitaire cards, smaller than ordinary playing cards, may be used; these are especially useful when playing in a confined space.

Certain games allow for the inclusion of a joker.

Ace, unless otherwise specified, ranks low.

Objective The object of many solitaire games is to build up sequences of cards in their suits onto base cards known as "foundations."

A second group of solitaires involves the pairing up of certain cards.

Other solitaires have a quite different objective, such as rebuilding the deck into a single pile, or discarding all the cards in the deck.

If a solitaire game is successful, ie the game's objective is exactly achieved, it is said to "come out" or to "go through."

If a game is "blocked," however, this means that the cards are such that the game cannot possibly be won.

Layout At the start of most solitaire games, cards are laid out in a prescribed formation that varies from game to game. This formation or "tableau," together with any other cards dealt out at the beginning of play, forms the "layout."

Foundation cards are the first cards of certain piles onto which sequences of cards are built (the objective of many solitaire games).

In some games they form part of the layout and are set out at the beginning of the game. More often, they are not included in the layout, but are put out as they come into play.

They are usually cards of a specified rank—often aces. With rare exceptions (such as in King Albert) a card cannot be removed once it has been placed on a foundation.

Spaces (sometimes called vacancies) are gaps in the layout into which cards may legitimately be played, or places from which cards have been removed and which may or may not be reoccupied, depending on the rules of the game.

Reserve In some games the layout includes one or more cards that may be brought into play as appropriate. This "reserve" of cards may not, however, be built onto— unlike the cards in the tableau.

The stock comprises those cards that remain after the layout has been dealt.

The stock is invariably kept face down, and may be brought into play in different ways according to the rules for particular games.

Waste pile or heap Cards from the stock that cannot immediately be played onto the layout are sometimes placed face up in one or more waste piles, to be brought back into the game as appropriate.

The discard pile is made up of any cards that have been set aside during the course of play and that are not brought back into the game.

The objective of some solitaire games is to discard all or most of the deck.

Available cards Any card that can, in accordance with the rules, be played onto the tableau, foundations, or spaces is termed "available." Sometimes the removal of a card "releases" the card next to it, for example when the top card of a waste pile is removed and makes the next card in the pile available for play.

Exposed cards A card is usually only available for play if it is fully exposed, ie if no other card covers it either wholly or partially.

Building

a   b   c   d   e   f

Building is the term used for placing a card onto the tableau, foundations, or a space in its correct sequence. This may be done numerically, by suit, or by color.

a) Cards may be "built down" numerically (eg a 7 is built onto an 8, a 6 onto the 7, etc).

b) Cards may be "built up" numerically (eg a 3 is built onto a 2, a 4 onto the 3, etc).

c) Sometimes the numerical sequence may be continuous or "round the corner" (eg 3, 2,a,k,q), or in twos (eg 7,9,j,k, 2,4, etc).

d) A card may only be built onto another card of the same suit (eg all hearts). Or, in other games, a card may only be built onto a card of a suit other than its own.

e) A card may only be built onto a card of the same color (eg all red cards).

f) A card may only be built onto a card of the other color (eg red, black, red, black).

Solitaire (one - deck games)

KLONDIKE

Klondike probably owes its great popularity to its combination of judgment, luck, attractive layout, and fast-moving tempo—all ingredients of a good solitaire game.
(In the United Kingdom this game is sometimes called Canfield. The game known as Canfield in the United States is described on p 151 .)

Layout Deal a row of seven cards, with only the first card face up. Add another row of six cards, with the first card face up on the second card of the first row, and the others face down. Deal five more rows in the same way, each row having one card fewer than the row beneath it and with only its first card face up.

Objective The four aces are the foundation cards, and they are set out above the tableau as they become available. The object is to build up the four suits on their respective aces in correct ascending order.

Play The hand is played one card at a time and once only. Cards that are not immediately playable are put face up in a waste heap, the top card of which is always available. Cards are built up in their correct suits on the foundations, or added to the columns of the tableau in descending, alternate-color order (regardless of suit). The top (fully exposed) card of each tableau column is always available for play onto a foundation or another column.
By removing an exposed card, the face-down card beneath it is turned up and becomes available.
Sequences in the tableau may be transferred from one column to another, but only as a complete unit.
Spaces created in the tableau can only be filled by kings. These may be taken (together with any cards built onto them) either from the stock or from anywhere in the tableau.

Klondike

Foundations

Tableau

King Albert

Reserve

Tableau

Eight away

Foundations

Tableau

Reserve

KING ALBERT

Layout Forty-five cards are dealt face up in rows from left to right, to form a tableau of nine columns.
The first column has one card, the second column two, and so on—the last column comprising nine cards.
The cards in each column should overlap so that all are visible.
The remaining seven cards, known as the "Belgian reserve," may either be held in the hand or fanned out next to the tableau.

The objective is to free the four aces (the foundations), which are placed above the tableau as they come into play. Cards are built onto them in ascending suit sequence, from ace through king.

Play All cards in the reserve are available, as are the exposed cards of the tableau.
Only one card may be moved at a time, either onto a foundation pile or in descending, alternate-color sequence on the columns of the tableau.
If an entire column becomes vacant, the space may be filled by any available card.
If the player wishes, he may transfer cards from the foundations to the tableau, provided that they fit into the correct numerical and color sequence.

EIGHT AWAY (EIGHT OFF)

Layout Deal 48 cards face up in eight columns of six cards each. The cards in each column should overlap so that all are visible.
Deal the remaining four cards face up in a row below the tableau to form the start of the reserve.

Objective The player's aim is to free the aces (which are moved as they become available to form a row above the tableau), and to build on them suit sequences, ace through king.

Play The exposed cards in the tableau (those at the bottoms of the eight columns) and all the reserve cards are available for play:
They can be moved to the foundations, built in descending suit sequence on other exposed cards, or moved to the reserve—which, however, must never contain more than eight cards.
Only one card may be moved at a time. Any space that occurs in the tableau can be filled only by an available king.

FLOWER GARDEN

Layout Deal 36 cards into six fans or "beds" of six cards each. These are collectively called the "garden" (ie the tableau).
The remaining 16 cards or the "bouquet" may be held in the hand or spread out on the table.

The objective is to free the aces, which are set out below the garden as they become available, and to build onto them suit sequences in ascending order, ace through king.

Play The exposed cards of each bed and all the bouquet cards are available for play. They may be played onto a foundation, or added to a bed in downward numerical sequence, regardless of suit. A sequence may be transferred from one bed to another, provided that the correct numerical order is preserved. If a space is created by the

removal of an entire bed, it may be filled by any available card, or by a sequence from another bed.

Flower garden

Tableau

LA BELLE LUCIE

Layout The deck is dealt out into 17 fans of three cards each and one single card.
Objective The aces are the foundation cards, and they are set out in a row above the tableau as they come into play. Cards are built onto the foundations in ascending suit sequence, from ace through king.

Play The end card of each fan and the single card are available for play. One card at a time may be moved onto a foundation, or built onto another fan in downward suit sequence.
Cards may always safely be built onto the foundations, but any building down on the fans should be carefully considered, as any cards to the

left of the built-down cards will consequently be immobilized.
Any spaces caused by the removal of a fan are left unfilled.
Redealing Two redeals are permitted.
When no further play is possible, all cards other than those on the foundation piles are gathered up, thoroughly

shuffled, and redealt into fans of three cards (any one or two remaining cards forming a separate fan).
After the second redeal, the player may pick out and play one card from any fan of his choice.

La belle Lucie

BRISTOL

Layout Deal 24 cards, face up, in eight fans each of three cards. Any kings that turn up in the deal are placed at the bottom of their respective fans. Next to this tableau, deal three more cards face up in a row to form the start of the waste heaps or reserve.

Objective The foundation cards are the aces, which are set out in a row above the tableau as they occur in play. The aim is to build four ascending sequences, ace through king, regardless of suit or color.

Play The top cards of the fans and the three waste heaps are available for play, but only one card may be moved at a time—either to a foundation or in descending sequence, regardless of suit or color, onto the exposed card of another fan.
The stock is dealt three cards at a time, one card to each of the three waste heaps.

Spaces in the waste heaps are filled only in the deal. Spaces in the tableau (caused by the removal of an entire fan) remain unfilled. Only one deal is permitted.

Bristol

Waste heaps

BELEAGUERED CASTLE

Beleaguered castle is also known by the names of sham battle and laying siege.

Layout Set out the four aces in a column as foundation cards and deal out the rest of the deck face up to form wings of six overlapping cards to the left and right of each ace.

The objective is to build up each suit in ascending numerical order, from ace through king, on its correct foundation card.

Play Only the fully exposed cards at the ends of the rows in each wing are available for play (one card only being moved at a time).

Playing onto the tableau In beleaguered castle it is essential to plan several moves in advance, rather than to play cards onto the tableau as soon as they become available. Otherwise, key cards can quickly become inaccessible and block further play. Spaces—created by the removal of an entire row—are also important to the progress of the game, and may be filled by transferring any exposed card.

Playing onto the foundations Eligible cards can, of course, be placed on the appropriate foundation card as soon as they come into play.

As far as possible, the build-up onto the four foundations should be fairly even.

Beleaguered castle

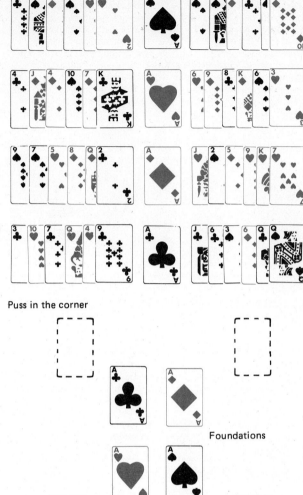

PUSS IN THE CORNER

Layout Puss in the corner has one of the most straightforward layouts of the single-deck solitaires.

The four aces are put face up in a square, and during the course of play four waste heaps are established at its corners.

The object of the game is to build up ascending sequences, ace through king, according to color but irrespective of suit.

Play Cards are played from the stock one at a time, either onto the aces (the foundation cards) or— if ineligible—onto one of the four waste heaps. The top cards of the waste heaps are always available for play.

The player can choose onto which of the four waste heaps he wishes to put a card.

It is wise to reserve one heap for court cards, and if possible low-value cards should not be buried under higher-ranking ones.

Redeal When the stock is exhausted, the cards in the waste heaps are collected in any order and redealt once without shuffling.

Puss in the corner

Foundations

Waste heaps

CALCULATION

Calculation is an aptly named game, for it involves a considerable amount of thinking ahead. (It is sometimes called broken intervals.)

Layout Set out in a row any ace, 2, 3, and 4 as the foundation cards.

The objective is to build up the rest of the deck on these base cards regardless of suit or color, but strictly in accordance with the following order:

On the ace: 2, 3, 4, 5, 6, 7, 8, 9, 10, j, q, k.
On the 2: 4, 6, 8, 10, q, a, 3, 5, 7, 9, j, k.
On the 3: 6, 9, q, 2, 5, 8, j, a, 4, 7, 10, k.
On the 4: 8, q, 3, 7, j, 2, 6, 10, a, 5, 9, k.

Play Cards are turned up one at a time and either built onto the appropriate base card or placed on one of four waste heaps immediately beside these.

Only the top card on each waste heap is available and cards cannot be moved from one waste heap to another. Any space in the waste heaps is filled with the top card of the stock.

Much of the skill of the game lies in playing the cards to the various waste heaps in such a way that they are later readily available for transfer to the foundations.

For example, it is best to keep kings in one waste heap or, if they come out early, at the bottom of waste heaps. Cards of the same rank should be dispersed between the waste heaps rather than concentrated in any single heap.

Whenever possible, cards should be played to the waste heaps in the reverse order to their build-up on the foundations.

Calculation

Foundations

Waste heaps

BISLEY

Layout Set out the four aces at the beginning of the top row of the tableau. Deal nine cards to the right of the aces; then deal the rest of the deck to complete a layout of four rows of 13 cards each. In the course of play, as they become available, the four kings are put out in a row above their aces (king of hearts above ace of hearts, etc).

Objective The aces and kings are foundation cards, and the aim is to complete entire suits, by building up in suit sequence on the aces and building down in suit sequence on the kings. When the two sequences meet they are put together (it does not matter at which point they meet).

Play The bottom card of each column of the tableau is available for play, either onto a foundation or onto the bottom card of another column.
Building onto the bottom cards of the columns is in ascending or descending suit sequence as the player wishes, and he may at any time reverse the order.

Spaces created in the tableau are not filled.
It is evidently important to free the kings as soon as possible, and to use every opportunity of building onto the foundations.

Bisley

Foundations

Tableau

FRIDAY THE THIRTEENTH

Layout Set out in a row from left to right any jack, queen, king, and ace—regardless of suit. Leave enough space to the right of them for a further nine cards to be added to the row.

The objective is to establish a total of 13 foundation cards —the jack, queen, king, and ace and then any 2 through 10 as they come up in play—onto which the remaining cards (the stock) are built up four to a pile in ascending numerical order, regardless of suit or color.

Play Work through the stock, turning one card at a time face upward and building it onto one of the foundations (eg a queen onto the jack), or putting it out as the next foundation card. The foundations must be set out in their correct order, for example a 3 cannot be laid out before the 2 has been established.
If a card cannot be played immediately, it is put face up on a waste heap.
Where there is a choice, it is usually better to establish a new base card rather than to build onto an existing pile.
For example, if the first card turned up were a 2, it would be wiser to use it as the next base card rather than building it onto the ace.

The waste heap Any exposed card on the waste heap is available for play.
When the stock is exhausted, the waste heap is turned over and may be replayed once without shuffling.

Friday the thirteenth

Foundations

SCORPION

The unwary player may be caught out by the scorpion's "sting" at the tail end of the game—since delay in exposing the hidden cards may prevent the solitaire going through!

Layout Deal three rows of seven cards each—the first four cards in each row face down and the remainder face up.

Below these deal four more rows of seven cards each, all face up. This makes a total of 49 cards in the tableau, and the three cards left over are put face down as the reserve.

Objective The four kings are the foundations onto which the cards are built in descending suit sequence (king through ace).

The kings are not removed to separate foundation piles, but are built onto within the tableau.

Play Cards are built on the exposed cards of the layout (ie the bottom card of each column) in correct descending order and suit.

If, as in the example illustrated, the 6 of hearts is exposed, the 5 of hearts may be moved onto it. It may be taken from anywhere within the layout, but all the cards laid on top of it must also be moved.

Nothing may be built onto an ace.

Face-down cards As each face-down card is reached (by the removal of the card or cards on top of it) it is turned face up.

The sooner the hidden cards are uncovered, the better the player's chances of getting the solitaire through. It is therefore advisable to plan moves that will clear the face-down cards as rapidly as possible.

Spaces and reserve If an entire column is cleared away the space may be filled by a king (together with any cards laid on top of it).

A space need not be filled as soon as it occurs.

When no further moves are possible, the three reserve cards are turned up and added to the layout, one to the foot of each of the three left-hand columns.

Not all spaces need to be filled before using the reserve cards. It often helps to see the reserve before filling a space, and this may be done provided that all other moves have been exhausted.

Scorpion

Tableau

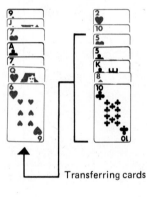

Transferring cards

Reserve

FLORENTINE

Layout Deal five cards face up to form a cross. Deal a sixth card face up at the top left-hand corner. The rank of this card denotes the foundations; the other three cards of that rank being placed at the other corners as they come into play.

The objective is to build up ascending suit sequences on the four foundation cards. Aces follow kings.

Play Cards from the stock are dealt one at a time. They can be played on the foundations if eligible, or packed in downward sequences regardless of suit on the four outer cards of the cross. The center card of the cross is at all times kept clear.

If one of the outer cards is transferred to a foundation card or packed on another outer card, the vacancy thus created is filled by a card from the waste heap, or by the center card of the cross (which is then replaced by a card from the waste heap).

The waste heap can be turned over and replayed once without shuffling.

Florentine

Foundations

Tableau

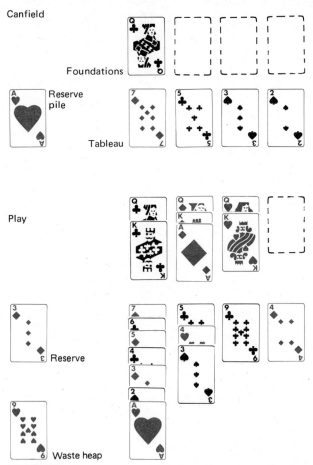

Canfield

Foundations

Reserve pile

Tableau

Play

Reserve

Waste heap

CANFIELD

Named for the nineteenth-century American gambler and art collector Richard A. Canfield, this game is one of the most popular single-deck games. It is known in the United Kingdom as "demon."

Layout Deal out a reserve pile of 13 cards face down, then turn the pile over to expose one card. Deal four more face-up cards to the right of the reserve to form the tableau. Above the first card of the tableau place the next card face up; this is the first of the four foundation cards and its rank determines the other three cards (which are laid out as they come into play). Should one of the tableau cards have the same rank as the foundation, move it up into position and deal another card into the space left in the tableau.

The object of the game is to build up the four suits on the foundation cards.

The cards rank continuously, ie if the foundation cards are kings, the next cards in the sequences must be aces.

Play The stock is turned over three cards at a time, only the exposed card of each three being in play (although cards below it can be played as they become available).

If there are only one or two cards at the end of the stock, they are dealt singly.

Cards are built up by suit on the foundations, and in descending alternate-color sequence in any suit on the columns of the tableau. Provided the correct color and numerical sequences are maintained, an entire column of the tableau can be transferred to another column.

Spaces in the tableau are filled immediately from the reserve. If the reserve is exhausted, the player may fill the space from the top of the waste heap, but he need not do so immediately.

Redeal The stock may be redealt, without shuffling, as many times as necessary until the game either blocks or is won.

PYRAMID

In its opening stages this pairing solitaire game appears deceptively easy, and the player may think he is well on the way to winning. He will need a lot of lucky card combinations, however, for the solitaire to go through!

Layout Twenty-eight cards are dealt face up in seven rows to form a pyramid.

Each card is overlapped by two other cards in the row below, except for the cards in the bottom row, which are fully exposed.

Only the fully exposed cards are available for play (ie at the start of the game the seven cards in the bottom row). When two cards are discarded during the course of play, the card they were overlapping becomes exposed and available for play.

The objective is to pair off the entire deck.

Play Any two available cards that together total 13 (regardless of color or suit) are paired off and placed in a waste heap.

The kings are worth 13 and may be discarded singly. Queens are worth 12, jacks 11, and aces one.

For example, a 10 can be paired with a 3, a jack with a 2, or a 4 with a 9.

Cards in the stock are turned up one by one onto a waste heap, of which the top card is always available.

A pair may be made up of: two tableau cards; one tableau card and one card from the stock; or two stock cards (the top card from the waste pile plus the next stock card turned up).

Redeal When the stock has been dealt once and no further pairing is possible, the waste pile may be redealt without shuffling.

Some players permit two redeals; others prefer not to allow any redeal.

MONTE CARLO

Monte Carlo, also called weddings or double and quits, is a straightforward pairing game.

Layout Twenty cards are dealt out into four rows of five cards each. (Some players may prefer to deal out 25 cards in five rows of five cards each.)

Objective At the end of a successful game the player will have dealt out the entire deck and paired up all the cards, leaving an empty layout.

Play Any two cards of the same rank that touch each other top or bottom, side to side, or corner to corner, are discarded.

The spaces thus made are filled by closing up the remaining cards of the layout from right to left, moving up cards from row to row as necessary, but preserving their order as originally laid out.

Extra cards are added from the stock to complete the layout, and the process is repeated until further pairing is impossible, or until the solitaire goes through.

Pyramid

Tableau

Waste heap

CLOCK

Although the chances of winning this solitaire are slight, it is fun to play and very fast-moving.

Clock gets its name from its layout, which is in the form of a clock dial. Other names by which it is known are sun dial, travelers, hidden cards, or four of a kind.

Layout The deck is dealt face down into 13 piles of four cards each. The cards may be dealt singly or in fours.

The piles are arranged to represent a clock dial, one pile corresponding to each hour. The thirteenth pile is placed in the center.

Objective By rearranging the cards, the player hopes to end up with thirteen piles of like-numbered cards in their correct "time" position: the four aces at one o'clock, the four 2s at two o'clock, and so on around the dial.

The jacks represent 11 o'clock, and the queens twelve o'clock. The four kings make up the thirteenth, central pile.

Play The player takes the card at the top of the central pile and places it face up at the bottom of the pile of the same number or "time."

For example, if the card is a 7, it is put face up underneath the seven o'clock pile.

The player then takes the top card of the seven o'clock pile and puts it under its matching pile.

In this way the player works his way from pile to pile, always removing the top card of the pile under which he has just put its matching card.

If the player turns up a card that happens to be on its correct pile (eg a 3 is turned up from the three o'clock pile), it is still placed at the bottom of the pile in the usual way, and the next face-down card is taken from the top of the pile.

Clock

The outcome depends on the order in which the kings are turned up. If the fourth king is turned up before all the other cards are face up, then the game is blocked.

This means in effect that the game can only be won if the last card to be turned up is the fourth king. As the chance of this happening is very small, the king may be exchanged for any one face-down card in the layout. Only one exchange is allowed, and if the fourth king is again turned up before the other cards are in their correct piles, then the game is lost.

MAZE

Although maze is not one of the better known solitaire games, it is particularly satisfying and requires time and ingenuity to succeed.

Layout The entire deck is dealt face up into two rows of eight cards and four rows of nine cards.

The four kings are then discarded, leaving a total of six spaces.

Objective By rearranging the cards one at a time, the player aims to get the four suits into their correct ascending sequence, ace through queen —one suit following the next. (The order of the suits is immaterial.)

The cards must run from left to right and from the end of one row to the beginning of the next. During play the top row is counted as following on from the bottom row.

In the final sequence, the first card must be an ace and the last card a queen.

For example, in a successful game the order might be: ace of hearts through queen of hearts, ace of spades through queen of spades, ace of clubs through queen of clubs, ace of diamonds through queen of diamonds.

Play A card may be moved into any one of the six spaces provided it is in the same suit as the card to the left or the right side of the space and that it is either:

lower than the card to the right of the space, or higher than the card to the left of the space.

(For example, a 2 of diamonds may be moved into a space that either has an ace of diamonds to its left or a 3 of diamonds to its right.)

Whenever there is a space to the right of a queen, it may be filled with any of the four aces (even if there is no matching 2 on the right of the space).

Maze

LEAPFROG

Layout Deal out 20 cards face up into four rows of five cards each.

The objective is to deal out all the remaining cards onto the table, and to end with as many spaces as possible in the layout.

Play Moves in leapfrog are very like the "taking" moves in a game of checkers.

A card in the layout may be "leapfrogged" over an adjoining card (either horizontally, vertically, or diagonally), provided that the card onto which it lands is of the same suit or rank.

A card so played now becomes the top and identifying card of a pile, and in any subsequent leapfrogging the whole pile is moved.

A move is not limited to a

single leapfrog: a succession of leapfrogs is sometimes possible.

Any card leapfrogged by another card is removed to a waste heap.

Empty spaces are filled by cards dealt from the hand whenever the player wishes. (It is better to fill the gaps as soon as they occur, in order to provide a wider choice of moves.)

POKER SOLITAIRE

Poker solitaire is a very challenging single-deck game that needs a mixture of luck, judgment, and practice to score well. It is a useful game for familiarizing the beginner with the scoring combinations used in regular poker.

Layout The tableau for poker solitaire comprises five rows of five face-up cards each.

Play The cards are dealt out one by one from a thoroughly shuffled deck. Each card may be placed anywhere within the limits of the tableau.

Once in position a card may not be moved; its placing on the tableau is therefore of great importance.

Objective Each row and each column of the tableau is the equivalent of a poker hand (ie there is a total of 10 hands). The player tries to place the cards of each "hand" to give the highest possible scoring poker combinations.

Scoring The American and British scoring systems are as follows:

Ace can rank either high or low, but may not form part of a "round the corner" sequence (ie king, ace, 2 is not allowed).

A score of about 150 (American) or 50 (British) is considered good, and a score of about 200 (American) or 60 (British) excellent.

Alternative rules

1) In order to improve his chance of a good score, the player may include a joker in the deal.

He can either:

substitute the joker for one of the 25 cards before dealing them; or

play all 25 cards in the usual way, exchanging the joker for any one card of his choice before totaling the score.

2) Another simplification of the game involves dealing out all 25 cards at the start of play in random order, and then rearranging them at will to form the best possible hands.

3) If the player wishes to make the game more taxing, he may only place a card onto the tableau if it touches a previously played card either horizontally, vertically, or diagonally (rather than placing it anywhere within the confines of the tableau).

ACCORDION

Accordion, also called Tower of Babel, idle year, or Methuselah, is one of the most difficult single-deck games to get out. It is unusual in that there is no formal layout at the start of the game: the cards are merely dealt in a single row.

Objective The player aims to rebuild the deck into a single pile.

Play The cards are dealt out face up in a row, as many at a time as space allows.

Any card may be moved onto the card immediately to the left, or onto the third card to the left, provided it is of the same suit or has the same rank. A pile of two or more cards, identified by its top card, can be similarly moved.

If a card matches both its neighbor and the card three to the left, the player may choose either move, taking into account the various possibilities.

Poker solitaire, with American scores

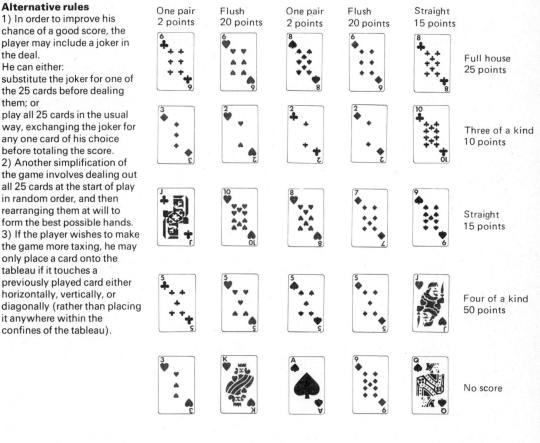

One pair 2 points	Flush 20 points	One pair 2 points	Flush 20 points	Straight 15 points
				Full house 25 points
				Three of a kind 10 points
				Straight 15 points
				Four of a kind 50 points
				No score

Scoring table

Combination	American	British	Definition
Royal flush	100	30	A, k, q, j, 10 of one suit
Straight flush	75	30	Sequence of five cards in one suit
Four of a kind	50	16	Four cards of the same rank with one odd card
Full house	25	10	Three cards of one rank and two of another
Flush	20	5	Any five cards of the same suit
Straight	15	12	Five cards in sequence regardless of suit
Three of a kind	10	6	Three cards of the same rank with two odd cards
Two pairs	5	3	Two pairs with one odd card
One pair	2	1	One pair with three odd cards

Solitaire (two-deck games)

NAPOLEON AT ST HELENA

Although Napoleon was recorded as having played solitaire while in exile on St Helena, it is most unlikely that he invented or even played the many solitaires attributed to him today. The game described here is among the most interesting of this group. Its other names are forty thieves and big forty.

Layout Deal out forty cards into four overlapping rows of ten cards each. The bottom card in each column is available for play.

The objective is to build up suit sequences through to the kings on the eight aces, which are set out in a row above the tableau as they come into play.

Play The stock is turned over one card at a time and is either played onto the foundations, or built onto the tableau in downward suit sequence. If unplayable, cards are placed on a waste heap, of which the top card is always available. Available tableau cards may similarly be played one at a time onto the foundations or onto another column of the tableau.

Spaces If an entire column of the tableau is cleared away, the resulting space may be filled by any one available card from elsewhere in the tableau or from the top of the waste heap.

The player should choose this card carefully, as it may give him the opportunity of releasing useful cards.

Napoleon at St Helena

Foundations

Tableau

Waste heap

MISS MILLIGAN

Objective With the eight aces as the foundations, the player aims to build up the cards into ascending suit sequences.

Play Deal out eight cards face up in a row. If any of these is an ace, set it out above the row as a foundation. Also move any cards that can be built up on the ace in correct suit sequence, or arranged in descending alternate-color sequence on other cards in the row.

Now deal out another row of eight cards, overlapping cards already in position or filling in any spaces as appropriate. Once again, study the layout to see which cards may be built onto the foundations or transferred to other columns. (Several cards may be transferred together, provided they are in correct sequence.) If at this stage a space occurs, it may only be filled by a king (plus any cards built onto it). Continue in this way until the entire stock has been dealt—always completing all possible moves before dealing out the next batch of cards.

Weaving When no cards remain in the stock, the player may lift up any one available card or build from the tableau, and set it aside as a reserve. Each of these reserve cards is available, and the player tries to rebuild them onto the tableau or foundations. If he fails in rebuilding the reserve, the game is lost. If he succeeds, however, he may repeat the "weaving" process until the solitaire goes through or is blocked.

Miss Milligan

Foundations

a) First row of eight cards is dealt

b) Player moves cards where appropriate

CRAZY QUILT

Crazy quilt is an unusual and interesting solitaire that gets its name from its layout of interwoven cards. It is also known as Indian carpet or Japanese rug.

Layout Take an ace and a king of each suit and set them out face up in a row. These are the eight foundations.

Above them, deal out a reserve or "quilt" of eight rows of eight face-up cards each, laying the cards vertically and horizontally in turn.

Any card in the quilt that has one or both of its narrow sides free is available for play. For example, at the start of play the four projecting cards at each side of the quilt are available.

Objective The aim is to build ascending suit sequences on the aces, and descending suit sequences on the kings.

Play Study the reserve to see if any available cards can be built onto the foundations. The removal of a reserve card releases one or more other reserve cards for play.

Spaces in the reserve remain unfilled.

Then turn up the stock one card at a time, putting the card in a waste heap if it cannot be played to a foundation. (The top card of the waste heap is always available.)

In order to release a useful card in the quilt, an available card may be played from the quilt to the top of the waste heap in either ascending or descending suit sequence. The stock may be redealt once.

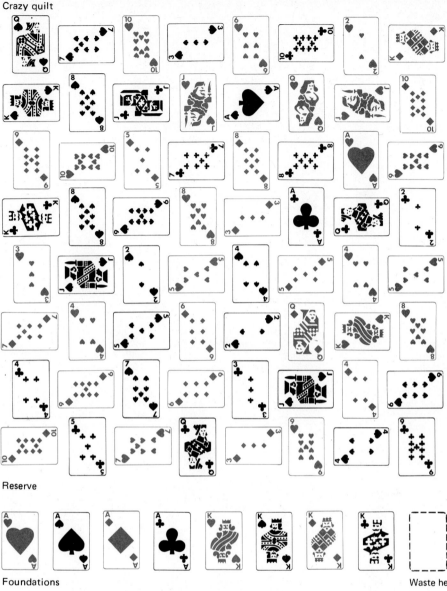

Crazy quilt

Reserve

Foundations   Waste heap

FROG (TOAD IN THE HOLE)

Layout Deal a reserve pile of 13 cards face up. If any of these cards are aces, set them out to the right of the reserve as foundations.

If no aces are turned up, take one ace of any suit from the stock to begin the foundation row.

The other aces are added to the row as they turn up in play, to complete the foundation of all eight aces.

The objective is to build on the aces ascending sequences from ace to king, regardless of suit or color.

Play Cards are turned up from the stock one at a time and played either onto the foundations or onto any one of five waste heaps.

The waste heaps are set out below the foundations, and cards may be added to them in any order the player chooses.

The top card of the reserve and the top cards of the waste heaps are available at all times for playing onto the foundations.

If a space occurs in the waste heaps it is filled from the stock; if the reserve is exhausted it is not replaced.

It is sound strategy to keep one waste heap for high-value cards such as kings and queens, and—if at all possible—to add cards to the waste heaps in descending numerical order so as to avoid burying low-ranking cards.

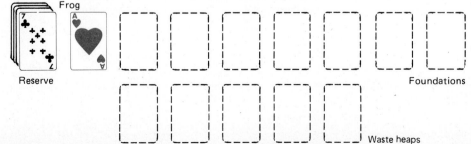

Frog

Reserve   Foundations

Waste heaps

Royal cotillion

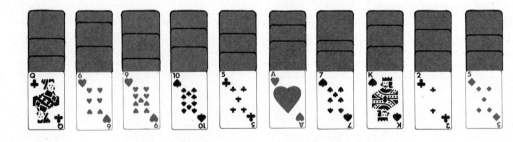

ROYAL COTILLION

Layout Set out face up in two columns an ace and a 2 of each suit.

To the left of the ace column, deal 12 cards face up in three rows of four cards each.

To the right of the 2 column, deal 16 cards face up in four rows of four cards each. (Some players prefer to establish the two central columns by putting out the aces and 2s as they come into play.)

The objective is to build suit sequences in the following order:

on the aces, 3, 5, 7, 9, j, k, 2, 4, 6, 8, 10, q;

on the 2s, 4, 6, 8, 10, q, a, 3, 5, 7, 9, j, k.

Play Only the bottom card of each column in the left wing of cards is available for play onto a foundation card, and the space made by such a move is not filled.

All the cards in the right wing are available, however, and spaces that occur must be filled immediately, with the top card of either the waste heap or the stock.

The stock is played one card at a time. Any card that cannot be built on a foundation or is not required for filling a space, is put on the waste heap, of which the top card is always available.

There is no redeal.

Spider

SPIDER

There are numerous versions of spider; the one described here is reputed to have been the favorite solitaire of President Franklin D. Roosevelt.

Layout Deal out a tableau of four overlapping rows, each row having ten cards. Deal the first three rows face down and the fourth row face up.

Objective Cards are built onto the eight kings in descending suit sequence. Instead of setting out the kings in separate piles as they come into play, they are built onto within the tableau. Only when a sequence is complete (ie king through ace in any one suit) is it discarded from the tableau.

If the solitaire comes out, all eight completed sequences will have been discarded.

Play The face-up cards in the bottom row are all available, and may be built on any other available card in descending numerical sequence, irrespective of suit or color. When a card is moved to another column, the player must also transfer all the cards built onto it.

Nothing may be built onto an ace, which ranks low and can only follow a two.

When a face-down card is reached, it is turned face up and becomes available for play.

A space in the tableau may be filled by any available card or build.

Stock When there are no more moves to be made in the tableau and all the spaces have been filled, ten cards are dealt face up from the stock—one to the bottom of each column. Play continues in the same way, a fresh batch of ten cards being dealt from the stock each time all possible moves in the tableau have been completed.

(The last deal will be of only four cards, one to be dealt to the bottom of the first four columns.)

WINDMILL (PROPELLER)

Layout Place any king face up at the center of the playing area. Then deal out a reserve (called the "sails") of eight face-up cards: two above the king, two below it, and two to either side.

The objective is to build:
a) a descending sequence of 52 cards on the central king, regardless of suit or color and with kings following aces;
b) ascending sequences, ace through king and regardless of suit and color, on the first four aces that come up in play.

Play Cards are turned up from the stock one at a time and if unplayable are put on a waste heap. The stock is only dealt once.

The first four aces to appear are put as foundation cards in the four angles of the sails. Cards are played to the foundations from either the stock, the sails, or from the top of the waste heap (which is always available for play). The top card of any ace foundation may be transferred to the central king foundation (building on the central pile is of prime importance if the game is to go through).

Spaces A space in the layout must be filled by the top card of either the stock or the waste heap, but it need not be filled as soon as it occurs.

This means that a space can be "saved" for a useful card—and by using his judgment in the way he fills spaces, the player can greatly increase his chances of winning.

Alternative rule Some players prefer the central foundation card to be an ace and the other four foundations to be kings.

Should he choose this alternative, the player must build an ascending sequence on the central ace and descending sequences on the four kings.

Windmill

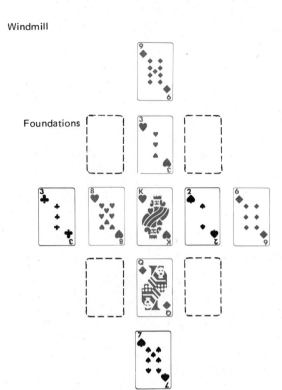

Foundations

BRAID (PLAIT)

Braid or plait is a straight-forward solitaire that gets its name from its particularly attractive layout.

Layout Twenty cards are dealt face up in the form of a braid: the cards are laid out diagonally, and alternately pointing to right and left—each card partially covering the card beneath it (as illustrated).

Columns of six face-up cards are dealt to either side of the braid; the braid and the columns together form the reserve.

The next (33rd) card is placed to the right of the reserve. It determines the rank of the other seven foundations, which are set out as they become available to make two rows of four cards.

Objective The player tries to build ascending "round the corner" suit sequences on the eight foundations (ace following king and preceding 2).

Play The bottom (fully exposed) card of the braid and all the cards in the two columns are available for play onto the foundations.

The stock is dealt one card at a time, and if the card is unplayable it is placed on a waste heap.

Any number of redeals is permitted, until the game either becomes blocked or goes through.

A space in the columns must be filled as soon as it occurs. If the top or bottom card of a column has been removed, the vacancy may be filled by the available card of the braid, or from the top of the waste heap (which is always available). If the vacancy is anywhere else in the column, it may only be filled from the stock.

Braid

Foundations

Waste heap

Reserve

Double solitaires

Although solitaire card games are really just for one person they can be played by two or more players in competition—either racing each other or comparing scores. In addition, there are "double solitaires" intended specifically for two players. Two of these are Russian bank and spite and malice.

RUSSIAN BANK

This popular game, also known as crapette, requires a great deal of concentration. Moves are made according to a strict procedure that, if broken, may result in the player forfeiting his turn.

Cards Two standard decks are used. Each player should have his own deck with a distinctive back in order to avoid confusion.
Cards rank: k(high),q,j,10,9,8, 7,6,5,4,3,2,a.

The objective A player's objective is to build all or as many as possible of the cards in his deck onto the foundations, the tableau, or his opponent's reserve or discard piles.

Preliminaries Each player draws a card from one of the decks: the player drawing the lower card will play first. Players then shuffle and cut their opponent's deck.

Layout To establish his reserve, each player counts out 12 cards from his deck and places them face down in a pile to his right.
Both players then deal out a column of four face-up cards above their reserve; these eight cards form the tableau and are for common use.
The remaining cards in each deck are placed face down in a pile in front of each player and form his stock.

Foundations The eight aces are the foundations. They are laid out between the two columns of the tableau as they come into play. Cards are built onto the foundations in ascending suit sequence.
Building cards onto the foundations is also called building to the "center."
Once a card has been built onto a foundation, it may not be removed.

Play The player who drew the lower card plays first; thereafter players take alternate turns.
Cards must be moved according to a set procedure, as follows.
1) Both players must start their opening turns by playing any available tableau cards to the center. They must then turn up the top card of their reserve and—if possible— play that to the center. If it cannot be played to the center, it may be played elsewhere on the layout.
2) In subsequent turns, players may turn over the top card of their reserve prior to making a play.
3) Building onto the foundations always takes precedence over building elsewhere on the layout. Also, if there is a choice of cards for building onto the center, cards from the reserve must always be used before cards from the tableau or stock.
4) If no more cards can be built onto the foundations, the player may build onto the tableau in descending alternate-color sequence. He may use the top card from another tableau pile, the reserve, or the stock—there is

no order of precedence. (Players should take every opportunity of rearranging tableau cards, so as to free blocked cards for play to the center.)
Cards in the tableau piles should be built in overlapping rows, so that all the cards are visible.
5) A space in the tableau may be filled by the top card of another tableau pile, the reserve, or, once the reserve is exhausted, from the stock. (Spaces need not be filled as soon as they occur.)
6) If no cards can be built to the center and the top reserve card cannot be built onto the tableau, the player may turn up the top card in his stock. If this card can be played directly to the center or the tableau, the next card in the stock may be turned up, and so on until an unplayable stock card is turned up. As soon as this happens, the player must move the unplayable card face up onto a waste pile to his left. His turn then ends.
7) Cards in the waste pile cannot be played. If the player's stock is exhausted, he may, however, take the waste pile and turn it face down and unshuffled to form a new stock.

SPITE AND MALICE

Cards Two standard decks and four jokers are used. The decks should be distinctively backed. Ace ranks low; jokers are wild.

The objective A player aims to get rid of all the cards on his payoff pile.

Preliminaries One of the decks is shuffled—without its jokers—and divided into two separate "payoff" piles of 26 cards, one for each player. The top card of each pile is turned face up and the player with the highest card will play first.
If by chance the two cards have the same value, the procedure is repeated.
The player with the lower card shuffles the second deck, including the four jokers. He then gives himself and his opponent five cards, dealing them one at a time and face down.
The remaining cards form the stock and are placed face down in a pile in the middle of the table.

Play The player who had the higher card has the opening turn; thereafter play is alternate.

1) Aces must be played to the center of the table as soon as they become available; they are the base cards of "center stacks" (equivalent to foundation piles).

Available 2s must be built on the aces whenever possible. Cards are built on the center stacks in ascending sequence regardless of suit; a card from the payoff pile, the hand, or a side stack (see paragraph 3) may be used.

Whenever a center stack has been built up through to the king, it is shuffled together with the stock at the next break in play.

2) The top card of the payoff pile may be played only to the center stacks. Whenever this happens, the player may turn up the next card in the payoff pile, and so on, until an unplayable card is turned up.

3) Each player may build up to four "side stacks" using only cards from his hand. A side stack may be started with a card of any value, and is built on regardless of suit either in descending sequence or with a card of the same

value (eg a 7 on a 7). Only one build onto a side stack may be made in any one turn.

4) Jokers may take the place of any card except an ace.

End of turn A player may make any number of legal plays to the center stacks, but his turn ends as soon as he plays a card from his hand to a side stack.

A player may also finish his turn by saying "End" if he cannot, or wishes not to, make further moves.

Stock At the start of their second and subsequent turns, players take as many cards from the stock as they need to replenish their hand (ie anything up to five cards).

Result The winner is the first player to have exhausted his payoff pile. Should neither player be able to make any further moves but still have cards left in his payoff pile, the game is considered drawn.

Spite and malice

Payoff pile

Player B

Side stacks

Center stacks

Stock

Side stacks

Player A

Payoff pile

Loading Once all available cards have been played to the center, the player has the option of "loading" cards onto his opponent's reserve or waste piles in up or down suit sequence.

The player may use cards from the tableau, or from his own reserve and stock.

Should the opponent's top reserve card be face down, the player may ask him at any time to turn it face up.

If an opponent has used up his reserve or waste pile (ie toward the end of the game) a player cannot off-load cards onto the resultant spaces.

Stops If a player thinks that his opponent has made an error in procedure, he may call "Stop," and play must immediately be halted.

If the error is proved, the wrongly moved card is returned to its former position and the offending player forfeits the rest of that turn. Should an error not be noticed until after further moves have been made, the offender is allowed to continue without penalty.

Result The game is won by the first person who succeeds in discarding his entire deck, ie all the cards in his reserve, stock, and waste pile.

He scores 30 points for winning, plus two points for each card left in his opponent's reserve and one point for each card left in his opponent's stock and waste pile.

If neither player succeeds in winning outright, the game is considered a draw.

Alternatively, players can evaluate their remaining cards (using the system described above); the player with fewest points then scores the difference between his points total and that of his opponent.

Russian bank

Player B

Reserve   Stock   Waste pile

Tableau

Waste pile   Stock   Reserve

Player A

Dice

Casting objects to see how they will fall has universally fascinated man. Modern-looking dice from 1500BC have been found in the tombs of Egypt; and in ancient India one prince wagered his kingdom and his wife at dice, and lost. Nero played happily for the equivalent of $15,000 a throw; and once, King Henry VIII of England staked—and lost—the bells of old St Paul's church.

A standard modern die is a regular cube, with the six sides numbered with dots from 1 through 6. Any two opposing sides add up to 7.

The evolution of dice

Casting must have begun with common objects such as stones and shells. The Indian game of pachisi is still played with six cowrie shells, scored by which way up they fall.

Later the anklebones of sheep were used as four-sided dice. These led to the cubic dice of the ancient Etruscans.

In Asia divination sticks led to the "long dice" still used in some Eastern games. These have from two to six sides and are rolled rather than tumbled. Another Eastern type is the "teetotum" or spinning die.

Unusual dice of ancient and medieval times include many-sided dice, and dice marked on small carved figures of animals or men.

If you don't have dice:

a) dot a sugar cube with ink;
b) scratch lines on a pencil's six sides, and roll it;
c) make a "spinning die" from a pencil and card;
d) divide a sheet of paper into six numbered areas, and throw any object to see where it falls.

A mis-spotted die

Odds With one true die, each face has an equal chance of landing face up. With two dice thrown together, some scores are more likely than others because there are more ways in which they can be made.

Cheating includes weighted, distorted, and mis-spotted dice; tampered edges; false throws; and sleight of hand.

Ways of throwing different numbers, with two dice

2   3   4   5   6   7   8   9   10   11   12

Family dice games

These are family games—ways of passing a happy hour, some games for the young and some for both young and old.

Shut the box

FIFTY

This game, for two or more players, is one of the simplest dice games. It requires two dice, and the winner is the first player to score 50 points. Each player in turn rolls the two dice, but scores only when identical numbers are thrown (two 1s, two 2s, and so on). All these doubles, except two 6s and two 3s, score five points. A double 6 scores 25 points; and a double 3 wipes out the player's total score and he has to start again.

ROUND THE CLOCK

This is a game for three or four players, using two dice.
Objective Players try to throw 1 through 12 in correct sequence. The winner is the first player to complete the full sequence.
Play Each player throws in turn, rolling the dice once only.
From 1 through 6, he can score on either of the two dice, or on both of them. For example, if he threw a 1 and a 3, but wanted only a 1, this die alone would count, and at his next throw he would try for a 2. But if he wanted a 4, he would count both dice (1+3= 4).
A player can also count both dice as separate scores, if he can use both of them. For example, if he needs 1 and throws a 1 and a 2, he can count both 1 and 2.
From 7 through 12, however, the combined spot values of both dice will obviously be needed.

SHUT THE BOX

This game, for two or more players, has long been popular in northern France.
Equipment:
1) two dice;
2) a board or sheet of paper with nine boxes numbered 1 to 9;
3) nine counters used to cover the numbers during the course of the game—in some parts of the world, specially made trays with sliding covers for the numbers are available.
Objective Players aim to cover as many of the numbers as possible, in accordance with the throws of the dice. High-numbered boxes should be covered first, since it is the player with the lowest score who wins.
Play begins after a preliminary round has decided the first shooter (usually the player with the highest score). Each player in turn throws the two dice. He then adds the spot values of the two dice and decides which box numbers he will cover.
For example, a throw totaling 10 would allow him to cover 5 and 5, 6 and 4, 7 and 3, 8 and 2, or 9 and 1.
Once the player has covered his chosen numbers, he throws again and makes a further choice. But he cannot make use of numbers he has already covered—he must use up his entire score with uncovered numbers.
When a player has covered the three highest numbers (7, 8, and 9), he is allowed to throw with only one die whenever he wishes. He continues throwing until he can no longer find combinations in his latest throw to match the numbers still uncovered. His turn is now complete and the uncovered numbers remaining are totaled and constitute his score.
All numbers on the board are once more exposed. The next player takes the dice and has his turn, and so on.

HEARTS

Hearts, or hearts due, is a game for two or more players.
Equipment Six dice are used. Special dice marked with the letters H,E,A,R,T,S instead of numbers are sometimes used, but the game is now more commonly played with ordinary dice.
The objective is simply to score more than your opponents over an agreed series of rounds, or a single round, or to be the first to reach an agreed total.
Play begins after a preliminary round has decided the first shooter (usually the player with the highest score).
Each player in turn rolls the six dice once and calculates his score according to the following ratings:
1 (H)=5 points;
1,2 (HE)= 10 points;
1,2,3 (HEA)= 15 points;
1,2,3,4 (HEAR)= 20 points;
1,2,3,4,5 (HEART)= 25 points;
1,2,3,4,5,6 (HEARTS)= 35 points.
If a double (two dice of the same spot value) or a treble appears in the throw, only one of the letters or numbers counts. But if three 1s (or Hs) appear, the player's whole score is wiped out and he has to start again.

BEETLE

This is a lively game for two or more players—more than six tend to slow down the game.
Equipment:
1) one die, either an ordinary one or a special "beetle die" marked B (body), H (head), L (legs), E (eyes), F (feelers), and T (tail);
2) a simple drawing of a beetle as a guide, showing its various parts and (when an ordinary die is used) their corresponding numbers;
3) a pencil and a piece of paper for each player.
Objective Each player, by throwing the die, tries to complete his drawing of the beetle. The first to do so scores 13 points and is the winner. The 13 points represent one for each part of the beetle (body, head, tail, two feelers, two eyes, and six legs).
Play Each player throws the die once only in each round. Each player must begin by throwing a B (or a 1); this permits him to draw the body. When this has been drawn, he can throw for other parts of the beetle which can be joined to the body.
An H or a 2 must be thrown to link the head to the body before the feelers (F or 5) and eyes (E or 4) can be added. Each eye or feeler requires its own throw.
A throw of L or 3 permits the player to add three legs to one side of the body. A further throw of L or 3 is necessary for the other three legs. Sometimes it is agreed that a player may continue to throw in his turn for as long as he throws parts of the body he can use.
Continuing play When a series of games is played, each player counts one point for every part of the beetle he has been able to draw and cumulative scores are carried forward from round to round. The winner is the player with the highest score at the end of the series, or the first to reach a previously agreed total score.

Beetle

© DIAGRAM

Drop dead

Running total   0

    0

    0

    3

    7

    7

DROP DEAD

This is an exciting game for any number of players.
Equipment:
1) five dice;
2) a sheet of paper on which to record players' scores.
Objective Players aim to make the highest total score.
Play Each player in turn rolls the five dice several times. His score for each throw is the total of the numbers in that throw. However, any throw containing a 2 or a 5 scores nothing. Any dice showing those numbers must be removed from succeeding throws by that player.
For example, if a player threw 2,4,6,3,4 on his first throw, the die showing 2 would count zero, and on his second throw he would roll only four dice. Eventually he may be reduced to only one die. When this shows a 2 or a 5, he is said to have "dropped dead" and is out of the game.
It is possible, of course, for a sudden demise to result from the very first throw, eg 5,5,5,2,2; and equally possible to survive profitably for a long time with only one die!
The game can also be played with each player having several throws, exactly as above, but throwing only one die in a turn and passing it to the player to his left after each throw.
This makes the game more exciting, but after each player's throw a careful note must be made of his score so far and how many dice (if any) he has left.

CHICAGO

Chicago, also called rotation, is a game for any number of players. Two dice are used. The game is based on the 11 possible combinations of the two dice—2,3,4,5,6,7,8,9,10, 11 and 12—and so consists of 11 rounds.
The objective is to score each of these combinations in turn. The player with the highest score is the winner.
Play Each player in turn rolls the dice once in each round. During the first round, he will try to make a total of 2, during the second, a total of 3, and so on up to 12.
Each time he is successful, that number of points is added to his score.
For example, if he is shooting for 5 and throws a total of 5, he gains five points. If he fails to make the desired number, he scores nothing on that throw.

GOING TO BOSTON

Also known as Newmarket or Yankee grab, this game is ideal for three or four players, although more can play.
Equipment: three dice.
Play Each player in turn rolls the three dice together. After the first roll, he leaves the die showing the highest number on the table, then rolls the other two again. Of these, the die with the highest number is also left on the table and the remaining die is rolled again. This completes the player's throw and the total of his three dice is his score.
When all players have thrown, the player with the highest score wins the round. Ties are settled by further rolling.
A game usually consists of an agreed number of rounds: the player who wins the most games is the winner.
Alternatively, each player can contribute counters to a pool that is won at the end of each game.

MULTIPLICATION

This game is played like going to Boston, but with one important difference.
When each player has completed his turn, his score is the sum of the spot values of the first two dice rolled, multiplied by that of the third.
For example, if his first throw is 5, his second throw 4, and his final throw 6, his score will be 54: $(5+4) \times 6$.

PIG

This simple game, for any number of players, requires only one die. The winner is the first player to reach a previously agreed high score (usually 100).
Order of play is determined by a preliminary round. Each player throws the die once and the player with the lowest score becomes first shooter. The next-lowest scoring player shoots second, and so on. The order of play is important because the first and last shooters have natural advantages (see below).
Play begins with the first shooter. Like the other players, he may roll the die as many times as he wishes. He totals his score throw by throw until he elects to end his turn. He passes the die to the next player, memorizing his score so far.
But if he throws a 1, he loses the entire score he has made on that turn, and the die passes to the next player. Play passes from player to player until someone reaches the agreed total.
Given a little luck, the first shooter is the player most likely to win. But his advantage can be counteracted by allowing other players to continue until they have had the same number of turns. The player with the highest score is then the winner.
The last shooter still has the advantage of knowing the scores made by all his opponents. Provided he does not roll a 1, he can continue throwing until he has beaten all those scores.
The fairest way of playing the game is to organize it as a series, with each player in turn becoming first shooter.

Player 1   Player 2   Player 3

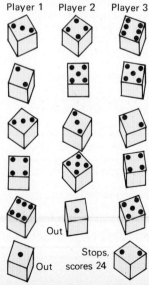

Pig   Out   Stops, scores 24

CENTENNIAL

Also known as martinetti or Ohio, this is a game for two to eight players.
Equipment:
1) three dice;
2) a long board or piece of paper marked with a row of boxes numbered 1 to 12;
3) a distinctive counter or other object for each player.
Objective Each player tries to be the first to move his counter, in accordance with throws of the dice, from 1 to 12 and back again.
Play begins after a preliminary round has determined the first "shooter" (thrower)— usually the player rolling the highest score.
Each player in turn throws the three dice once. His throw must contain a 1 before he can put his counter in the box so numbered. After his throw, the dice are passed to the next player and so on.
Once a player has thrown a 1, he must try for 2. He can make 2 by throwing either a 2 or two 1s.
He continues to move his counter in this way from box to box.
Some throws may enable him to move through more than one box on a single throw. For example, a throw of 1,2,3 would not only take him through the first three boxes, but on through the fourth $(1+3=4)$, to the fifth $(2+3=5)$ and finally the sixth $(1+2+3=6)$.
Other players' throws must be watched constantly. If a player throws a number he needs but overlooks and does not use, that number may be claimed by any other player. He must do this as soon as the dice are passed, however, and must be able to use it at once.

EVEREST

This game is like centennial but has a different layout and scoring system.
Equipment Each player has a sheet of paper showing two columns, each divided into 12 boxes. In one column the boxes are numbered from 1 to 12 in ascending order. In the other they are numbered from 1 to 12 in descending order.
Objective Each player tries to be the first to score all 24 numbers. The numbers do not have to be scored consecutively as in centennial, but as desired and in either column.
Scoring Each die in a throw can be counted only once.

Centennial

Everest

BASEBALL

As a dice game for two players, baseball can be played in several different ways. Of the three described below, the most popular is probably the two-dice game.

Equipment:
1) one, two, or three dice, according to the type of game being played;
2) the one-die and two-dice games require at least three counters for each player to represent his men;
3) a sheet of paper with a simple diagram of a baseball diamond drawn on it;
4) another piece of paper for recording scores.

The objective is to score the highest total number of runs in the nine innings per player that constitute the game.

If the two players have equal scores after the usual nine innings, an extra-inning game is played.

(Note that in baseball, each player's turn at bat is called a "half-inning.")

One-die baseball

The players throw the die to decide who shall "bat" first (ie shoot the die first).

Each player in turn then throws a half-inning. A half-inning is ended when a player has thrown three "outs" (see below).

Value of the throws At the start of the game, or whenever all bases are empty, a throw of 1,2 or 3 permits the player to put a man (counter) on whichever of those three bases he has thrown. A player may have only one man on a base at a time.

If he throws 1, 2, or 3 again, this permits him to move the man around the diamond by the number of bases thrown, and to place another man on the base that bears the number thrown.

For example, if he has a man on 1, and throws a 2, the man advances to base 3 (1+2) and a new man is entered on base 2.

Each time a man reaches the home (fourth) base or "home plate," a run is scored.

A single throw may give a score of more than one run if it results in more than one man reaching home base. (The rule against more than one man on a base does not apply to the fourth base.)

For example, if a player with men on bases 2 and 3 throws a 2, both men advance to home base and two runs are scored. At the same time a new man is entered on base 2.

A throw of 4 counts as a home run and advances all men on the bases to home base. The score is thus the home run plus one run for each man brought home.

Outs Throws of 5 or 6 are "outs."

A throw of 5 is as though there had been a hit and a throw-in, so that men on the bases may also be out, as follows.

a) If the shooter has only one man on the bases, he is out;
b) if he has men on all bases, the man on base 1 is out;
c) if he has men on bases 1 and 2, the man on base 2 is out;
d) if he has men on bases 1 and 3, the man on base 1 is out;
e) if he has men on bases 2 and 3, both are safe.

Men on the bases who are not out remain where they are.

A throw of 6 is also an out, but it is as if the batter were out without striking the ball; men on bases are safe, and remain where they are.

Note that three outs end a half-inning. The other player then throws his half-inning to complete the inning.

Two-dice baseball is similar to the one-die game, but the dice scores count as follows.

Any 12 or 2 is a home run.

Any 4 or 10 is a "one," any 11 a "two," any 3 a "three." With these, all men already on bases advance the appropriate number of bases, and a new man is entered on the appropriate base.

Any 6 or 9 is an out, and the men on bases do not move.

Any 8 is an out, except for double 4s (4+4), which is a "walk." On a walk, a new man is entered on first base and other basemen advance only if they are forced on by him.

Any 5 is an out, but any basemen advance one base each ("sacrifice").

Any 7 is an out, and if there are any basemen one of them is also out. When there is more than one baseman, it is the one nearest home base; the others do not move.

Three-dice baseball is the simplest and perhaps least satisfying version of baseball dice.

Each player throws the dice in turn, scoring one run for every 1 that is rolled.

When he fails to throw a 1, a player's half-inning is ended and his opponent takes over.

The game consists of the usual nine innings, with extra innings to decide any tie.

BASKETBALL

As a dice game, basketball is usually played by two players, but more can take part, each player representing a team. As in the real game, the winner is the team (ie player) making the highest score in the game or series of games.

Equipment Basketball may be played with only two dice or with as many as 10. Many players use eight dice as there are then enough to ensure a rapid game and realistic scores.

Play A game consists of four quarters. In each quarter each player in turn rolls the eight dice once, their total being his score for that quarter.

If the game is played with only two dice, each player rolls the dice four times to determine his score for that quarter.

The player with the highest score for the four quarters wins the game.

If the game, or agreed series of games, ends in a tie, this is resolved by playing extra quarters until the outright winner is established.

One-die baseball

Moves   Outs

a

b

c

d

e

©DIAGRAM

Cheerio combinations

Ones

Twos

Threes

Fours

Fives

Sixes

Little straight

Big straight

Full house

Big hand

Cheerio

CHEERIO
This game can be played by any number of players up to a maximum of 12. The greater the number of players, the slower the pace of the game.

Equipment:
1) five dice;
2) a dice cup;
3) a sheet of paper showing the various combinations and a scoring column for each player.

Objective Each player tries to score the maximum possible for each of the 11 scoring combinations (see below). The player with the highest total score wins the game.

Games are often played as a series, the player who wins the most games in the series being the overall winner. Alternatively, the scores in each game can be carried forward to the next game until a player has reached a previously agreed cumulative total. If two or more players exceed the total, the player with the highest score wins. Ties are settled by an extra game.

The combinations are given here in ascending order, but that order need not be followed in play. Each player may choose the combinations for which he is rolling (see the section on rolling).

Cheerio score sheet

	Pauline	Ruth	Susan	Kathy
1's	3		0	0
2's		8	4	
3's	3	9		
4's	16			12
5's		20		
6's				24
Little straight				
Big straight			25	
Full house	22		16	
Big hand				30
Cheevio		50		

Ones Scores one point for each die showing one spot. Maximum possible: five.

Twos Scores two points for each two-spot die. Possible scores: 2,4,6,8,10.

Threes Scores three points for each three-spot die. Possible scores: 3,6,9,12,15.

Fours Scores four points for each four-spot die. Possible scores: 4,8,12,16,20.

Fives Scores five points for each five-spot die. Possible scores: 5,10,15,20,25.

Sixes Scores six points for each six-spot die. Possible scores: 6,12,18,24,30.

Little straight A show of 1,2,3,4,5 scores 20 points.

Big straight A show of 2,3,4,5,6 scores 25 points.

Full house Three of a kind plus two of a kind scores according to the numbers shown on the dice.
For example, a "full house" comprising 1,1,1,2,2 would score seven points; 2,2,2,1,1 would score eight points, and so on to a maximum of 28 points (6,6,6,5,5).

Big hand The total spot value of the dice. Maximum score: 30 points (6,6,6,6,6).

Cheerio Five of a kind in any value, 1 through 6. Always scores 50 points.

Rolling Each player in turn rolls all five dice. Having rolled the dice once, he may pick up all or any of them and roll once more in an attempt to improve his score.
He does not have to declare his combination until he has finished rolling. This gives him considerable freedom of choice. For example, if he has rolled 6,6,2,3,3 he might call sixes (score 12). But if he wanted to keep sixes for a later turn, when he might roll more than two of them, he could call twos (score 2), or threes (score 6), or even ones (zero) depending on the combinations he has still to roll.
All combinations, except big hand, may rate zero. However, once a player has scored a combination, he cannot score it again in that game.
For example, 6,6,6,5,5, a full house normally scoring 28 points, could not rate this score if the player had rolled a full house in a previous turn and counted it as such. It could only be counted as sixes (score 18) or fives (score 10).
If the player had also previously rolled sixes and fives, it would rank zero and be recorded against some other combination.

GENERAL
General is a major gambling game in Puerto Rico. It has many similarities with cheerio and can be played as a family game.
Five dice are used. The combinations and the players' names are recorded on a sheet of paper. The combinations are as follows:

The numbers 1 through 6 score their spot values.

Straight Either 1,2,3,4,5 or 2,3,4,5,6, scores 25 points if made on the first throw, but only 20 points if made on the second or third throw (see the section on rolling). Only one straight is scored.

Full house Scores 35 points on first throw, but only 30 points on the second or third throw.

Four of a kind Scores 45 points on first throw, but only 40 points on the second or third throw.

Five of a kind If made on the first throw, it ranks as the "big general" and immediately wins the game. Made on the second or third throw, it is a "small general" and scores 60 points.

Aces wild "Aces" (1s) may be counted as 2 or as 6, if one or both of these are needed to complete a straight—but not as any other number or for any other purpose.

Order of play is determined by a preliminary round in which each player rolls the dice once. The player with the lowest spot score shoots first, the player with the next lowest score second, and so on.

Players Any number may play, either singly or in partnership. Partnerships are usually determined by the scores made in the preliminary round, the two highest scorers being paired, the two lowest, and so on.

Rolling A game normally consists of 10 turns ("frames") per player, but of course ends immediately if any player rolls a big general.
Each player may roll the dice once, twice, or three times during each frame.
If, on his first throw, he fails to make an obvious scoring combination like a straight or a full house, he may pick up all or any of the dice for his second roll. But the value of any combination he now rolls is diminished, and a big general now becomes a small general.
After his second roll he may again, if he wishes, pick up all or any of the dice for a third roll.

After the third roll, he must state which combination he has scored. His score is determined according to the combinations he still needs, exactly as in cheerio and subject to the same rules.
If the game runs its full course of ten frames, the player with the highest score wins.

Payment When general is played as a gambling game, the winner receives from each of the other players the difference between his own and that player's point score. The monetary value per point is settled before the game.

DOUBLE CAMEROON
This game is similar to general but has important differences. It is played with ten dice.
After a player has rolled them for the third time in each turn, he divides them into two groups of five, and then allots the score of each group to one of the ten combinations in the game. So in the course of a game, each player has five turns.

The combinations are:

Numbers 1 through 6 Score their spot values.

Full house Scores its spot value.

Little cameroon (1,2,3,4,5) scores 21 points.

Big cameroon (2,3,4,5,6) scores 30 points.

Five of a kind Scores 50 points.
(Unlike in "general," a score does not decrease if the combination is made on a second or third throw.)

Private betting games

These are the games for playing on a bar counter, or at a friend's over beer and cheese. They can be played for high stakes or for low, or just for counters or matchsticks for fun.

POKER DICE

This game, for two or more players, is often played in bars to decide such simple questions as who shall pay for the next round of drinks. As a gambling game, it is played for a "pot" (pool) to which each player contributes at the start of each round.

Equipment Five dice are used, and these are normally special poker dice marked with a,k,q,j,10,9 (instead of the numbers 1 through 6). The game may also be played with standard dice, with 1 ranking highest, then 6,5,4,3,2; or alternatively as in Indian dice.

Objective Players aim to make the best possible poker "hand" in not more than two rolls of the dice (or three rolls of the dice in the old form of the game).

Rank of hands is as follows: five of a kind (highest rank); four of a kind; straight (an unbroken sequence, either a,k,q,j,10 or k,q,j,10,9); full house (three of a kind and one pair); three of a kind; two pairs; one pair; no pair (the lowest rank—five unmatched values not in sequence).

Hands of the same rank need not tie. They compare as follows.
1) Five of a kind: five aces rank higher than five kings, and so on.
2) Four of a kind: as for five of a kind.
3) Full house: the threes decide, with a,a,a,j,j ranking higher than k,k,k,q,q, and so on.
4) Straight: a,k,q,j,10 beats k,q,j,10,9.
5) Three of a kind: three aces rank higher than three kings, and so on.
6) Two pairs: the highest pair wins.
7) One pair: the higher pair wins.
8) No pair: the highest die wins.
The odd dice in any combination are used by some schools as tiebreakers. For example, a,a,q,q,j (two pairs) would rank above a,a,q,q,9.

It is more common, however, for the odd dice to be disregarded, and if two or more players make equal-ranking hands they must roll again.

Order of play is decided by a preliminary round in which each player throws a single die.

The highest scorer throws first in the first round. The second highest scorer sits to his left, and so on. Play goes clockwise and each round is commenced by a different player in turn.

Play Each player rolls in turn. He may accept the hand produced by his first throw; or, if he wishes, he may pick up one or more of the dice and roll them again in an attempt to improve his hand. Some schools limit to three the number of dice he may pick up. The outcome of his second throw completes his hand and the dice are passed to the next player.

The highest hand in the round wins. Alternatively, the lowest hand pays for the drinks! If there are only two players, the best two out of three rounds, or the best three out of five, win.

Aces wild Poker dice may be played with aces "wild," ie they may rank normally or count as any other value the player wishes. For example, a throw of q,q,q,q,a could rank as five queens; a throw of a,a,a,a,j could rank as five jacks; or a throw of k,q,j,a,9 could rank as a straight.

INDIAN DICE

Indian dice, a favorite bar game in the United States, is very similar to poker dice. It is played with five ordinary dice, with 6 ranking highest and 1s ("aces") wild. Any number of players may take part.

Objective Players aim to make the highest poker hand. The hands rank as in poker dice except that straights do not count.

Play begins after a preliminary round to decide the order of play. The highest scorer becomes first shooter, the second highest scorer sits to his left, and so on.

The player who shoots first may have up to three throws to establish his hand. He may "stand" on his first throw, or pick up all or any of the dice for a second throw. He may then stand on that throw or pick up the dice again for a third and final throw.

No subsequent player in the round or "leg" may make more throws than the first player.

A game usually consists of two legs, with the winners of each leg playing off if stakes are involved, or the lowest scoring players playing off if no stakes have been placed.

If there are only two players, the victor is the one who wins two out of three legs.

Indian dice

Poker die faces

Five of a kind

Four of a kind

Full house

Three of a kind

Two pairs

Pair

No pair

Thirty six

Player 1

30 points

Player 2

33 points

31 points

Player 3

THIRTY-SIX

This is a game for any number of players, using only one die.

Order of play is determined by a preliminary round in which each player throws a single die. The lowest scorer becomes first shooter, the next-lowest second shooter, and so on.

Each player puts an agreed stake in the pot.

Objective Players aim to score a total of 36 points. Any player scoring more than 36, however, is eliminated from the game.

The winner is the player with the score nearest 36 points and he takes the pot.

Play Each player in turn rolls the dice once, totaling his score round by round. As he nears 36 he may choose to stand on his score, especially if it is 33 or more.

In the event of a tie, the pot is divided.

ACES

This is a game for any number of players. It is usually played for a pot and the winner is the player throwing the last ace (1) with the last die.

Equipment Each player requires five dice and a throwing cup.

Order of play is determined by a preliminary round in which each player tries to throw the highest poker hand. Numbers rank: 1 (high), 6,5,4, 3,2, (low).

The player with the highest ranking hand becomes first shooter. The other players then sit in clockwise order in accordance with the hands they have thrown.

Ties are resolved by further throws.

Play The first shooter throws his dice and transfers to the center of the table any 1s that come up. Any 2s in his throw are passed to the player to his left, and any 5s to the player to his right.

He continues throwing until he fails to make any of these numbers on a throw, or until he has disposed of all his dice. Although he may have no dice left, he is still in the game, since he may later receive dice from the players to his left and right.

Play continues in a clockwise direction around the table until all the dice except one have been transferred to the center.

The winner (or loser) is the player who throws the last ace with that die.

PAR

Par can be played with any number of players, but is best played with six or seven.

Equipment:
1) five dice;
2) chips (or counters) representing the betting unit.

Objective Each player tries to achieve a total score of 24 or more by throwing the dice.

Order of play is established by a preliminary round in which the highest scoring player becomes the first shooter. The second highest scorer throws next, and so on.

Play The first shooter rolls all five dice. He may "stand" on that throw if it makes 24 or more, but may throw four of the dice again if he desires. He may continue throwing to try to improve his total (or he may stand), but each time he throws, he must leave one more die on the table.

If he makes 24, he neither gains nor loses.

If he fails to make 24, he pays each other player the difference between his score and 24.

If he makes more than 24, the difference between his score and 24 becomes his "point." For example, if he has thrown 26, he has a point of 2.

He then throws all five dice again (but once only), and for every 2 that appears he collects two chips from each of the other players. (If 6 was his point, he would collect six chips for every 6 that appeared.)

SHIP, CAPTAIN, MATE, AND CREW

This game may be played by any number of people. Five dice are used.

Objective Players try to throw 6 (the ship), 5 (the captain), and 4 (the mate) in that order and within three throws.

Order of play is established by a preliminary round, in which each player throws a single die. The highest scorer becomes first shooter.

Play then moves in a clockwise direction around the table.

Play The players each put an agreed stake into the pot.

Each player in turn is allowed not more than three throws of the dice.

If he makes a 6 and a 5 on his first throw, he can set those dice aside. In his second throw he then rolls the other three dice hoping to make a 4. If, however, he makes a 6 and a 4 on his first throw, only the 6 can be set aside, and the remaining four dice

LIAR DICE

The essence of this game, for three or more players, is deception!

Equipment The game may be played with five ordinary dice, 1s (aces) ranking high, but is much more absorbing when poker dice are used. Each player also needs three betting chips (or counters).

Rank of hands is as in poker dice.

Hands of the same rank are also compared as in poker dice, but in liar dice the odd dice are always used as tiebreakers if necessary.

Order of play is established by a preliminary round in which each player throws a single die. The highest scorer becomes first shooter. The second highest scorer sits to his left, and so on.

Play Each player puts three betting chips in front of him. The first shooter then throws all the dice, keeping them covered so that the other player cannot see what he has thrown.

He declares his throw in detail, eg "full house, queens on nines" (q,q,q,9,9). This call may be true or false and it is for the player to his left to accept or challenge the call. The declaring player may call below the actual value of his throw if he wishes.

1) If the player to his left thinks the caller is lying and challenges him, all the dice are exposed.

If the caller has in fact lied, he must pay one chip into the pot; but if the value of the throw is equal to or higher than the call, it is the challenger who pays into the pot.

In either case, it now becomes the challenger's turn to throw.

2) If the player to the left of the caller accepts the call, he takes over the dice (still unexposed). He may now throw all or any of them (or none of them), but he must say truthfully how many he does throw.

Keeping the dice covered, he then makes his call, which must be higher than the call he accepted—but it need not be a higher rank of hand; it can be a higher hand of the same rank. His call may be accepted or challenged by the player to his left, and so play continues round the table.

When a player has lost all three of his chips, he is out of the game. Play continues until all but one of the players has been knocked out. The sole survivor is the winner and he collects the pot.

Start of play rotates one player to the left after each game.

Liar dice

must be rolled again for a 5 and a 4.

If the player makes 6, 5, and 4 in his three throws, the remaining two dice (the crew) are totaled as his score. But if he makes 6, 5, and 4 in his first or second throw, he may, if he wishes, use the remaining throws to try to improve the total of the crew dice.

The pot goes to the player with the highest score in the round. A tie nullifies all scores and a further round has to be played.

Start of play rotates one player to the left after each game.

TWENTY-ONE

This game is based on the blackjack card game. Any number of players may take part.

Equipment: one die, and a supply of chips or counters for each player.

Objective Players try to score 21 without "going bust" (ie throwing more than 21).

Play Each player puts one chip into the pool or kitty. Then each player in turn rolls the dice as many times as he likes in an attempt to make a total of 21 or a number near it. If, for example, a player's first four throws are 4,6,2,6 (totaling 18), it would probably be safer to "stick" on this number than risk a fifth throw that might take his total over 21.

If his total does exceed 21, he "goes bust" and is eliminated from that round.

Players often agree on a minimum number, eg 16, at which sticking is permissible. When all the players have thrown, the player with 21, or the number nearest to it, takes the pool, and a new round commences.

If two or more players have the same score, the pool may either be shared or decided by a play-off.

Start of play rotates one player to the left with each round.

BUCK DICE

This is a game for any number of players, using three dice.

Preliminaries Order of play is established by a round in which each player throws a single die. The highest scorer becomes first shooter. The lowest scorer then throws one die to determine a point number for the first game.

Objective Players aim to score a "buck" or "game" (exactly 15 points). On achieving this score the player withdraws from the game, which continues until one player is left: the loser.

Play Each player in turn takes the three dice, and each goes on throwing for as long as he throws the point number on one or more of the dice. As soon as he makes a throw that does not contain the point number, he passes the dice to the player to his left. Each player keeps count, aloud, of the number of times he has thrown the point number. Each occasion counts one point.

If, when he is nearing 15 points, a player makes a throw that carries his score beyond 15, the throw does not count and he must roll again.

Some throws rate special values. Three point numbers in one throw ("big buck" or "general") count 15 points. A player making this throw withdraws immediately from the game irrespective of any score he has made previously. Three of a kind that are not point numbers count as a "little buck" and score five points.

Variation Some players follow the rule that when a player has scored 13 points, he rolls with only two dice; and when 14 is reached, with only one die.

Continuing play Start of play rotates one player to the left after each game. The right to determine the point number also rotates in this way, so that it is always with the player to the starter's right.

Hooligan score card

Point number	K	J	P	T
1	2	4	1	
2			6	4
3	12	9	3	9
4	12			16
5		10	25	15
6	6	24	18	24
H	20	20		

HOOLIGAN

Hooligan is played with five dice and a throwing cup. Any number of players may take part.

Hooligan is a point-scoring game; the winner is the player making the highest total score.

Preliminaries Aside from a preliminary round to determine the order of play, a scoresheet must be prepared. This sheet should have a column divided into seven sections marked 1,2,3,4,5,6, and H (hooligan), against which the score of each player can be recorded.

The game consists of seven rounds, each player throwing in turn. A turn ("frame") consists of three throws. After his first throw, each player declares which of the numbers on the scoresheet (including H) he is shooting for (ie his point number). He must shoot for H on his final throw, if he has not previously done so.

"Hooligan" is a straight, either 1,2,3,4,5 or 2,3,4,5,6, and counts 20 points.

If he wishes, a player need not declare a point number after his first throw. In this case he picks up all five dice, shoots again, and then declares his point number; but this counts as his second throw, so he has only one throw left in this frame.

If he declares his point number after his first throw, he puts aside all dice bearing that number, then throws a second time with the remaining dice. Once more, any dice bearing the point number are put aside. He then makes his third and final throw with the remaining dice.

His score is determined by multiplying the point numbers he has made by the point number itself.

For example, if he were throwing for 4s and made three of them, his score would be 12.

If a player throws the maximum of five point numbers in his first or second throw, he counts this score and plays the remaining throw(s) of the frame with five dice, setting aside any dice bearing the point number after the first throw if two throws are involved.

The point numbers made on these throws are added to the five made on the first throw.

A player has only one turn to shoot for each point number. He must choose a different point number for each frame. Sometimes games of hooligan are operated by a banker. Players play against the bank, and must pay to enter the game.

The odds and rules of such games vary from place to place.

Two-hand bidou betting sequence

A Bets   B Raises   A Reraises   B Reraises   A Calls

HELP YOUR NEIGHBOR

Help your neighbor, for two to six players, is usually played for fun using counters.

Equipment:
1) three dice and a dice cup;
2) betting chips or counters for each player.

Objective Each player tries to be the first to get rid of all his counters. The winner takes the pot formed during the course of play.

Order of play is determined by a preliminary round in which each player throws a single die. This throw also decides which number(s) each player takes. The highest scoring player in the preliminary round becomes first shooter and takes the number 1. The second-highest scorer becomes the second shooter and, taking the number 2, sits to the left of 1, and so on.

If there are only two players, the higher scoring player takes numbers 1, 2, and 3, and the other the remainder.

With three players, the numbers are paired off: 1 and 2, 3 and 4, 5 and 6.

With four players, numbers 5 and 6 are "dead;" with five players, 6 is dead.

Play begins with each player placing ten counters in front of him, and then proceeds in a clockwise direction from the first shooter.

Each player in turn throws all three dice once. Any player whose number comes up in that throw has to put one counter into the pot for each of his numbers thrown.

For example, if the first shooter throws 4,6,6, the player who has number 4 puts one counter into the pot; and the player with number 6 puts two counters into the pot.

When the pot has been taken by the winning player (the first to lose all his ten counters), the next game is started by the player to the left of the first shooter in the previous game, and he now takes the number 1.

BIDOU

Bidou is a game with the same betting principles as poker— but whereas in poker the player wants to win chips or counters, in bidou his objective is to get rid of them.

Players Any number can take part, but the procedure is different when only two players are involved.

Equipment Each player needs three dice and a throwing cup. The game also requires a supply of chips or counters.

Objective Players aim to get rid of their chips. The last player still holding chips is the loser. If desired, he pays each other player a previously agreed amount, or meets group expenses.

Bidou combinations The ranking of all possible dice throws is shown in the table.

BIDOU COMBINATIONS

Highest listed first
1) 2,1,1 (bidou)*
2) 2,2,1 (bidé)
3) 4,2,1 ("421")
4) 6,6,6
5) 5,5,5
6) 4,4,4
7) 3,3,3
8) 2,2,2
9) 1,1,1*
10) 3,3,6
11) 3,3,5
12) 3,3,4
13) 3,3,2
14) 3,3,1
15) 1,1,6
16) 1,1,5
17) 1,1,4
18) 1,1,3
19) 3,2,1
20) 4,3,2
21) 5,4,3
22) 6,5,4
23–56) The remaining 34 possible combinations are ranked according to their spot total, eg 6,3,2 (=11) beats 4,3,1 (=8). (The maximum is 6,6,5=17.) But all are beaten by any of the combinations listed separately above.
* 1,1,1 beats 2,1,1, but is beaten by all other combinations listed above it.

TWO-HAND BIDOU

Two-hand bidou is played in games made up of three separate rounds. The loser is the player losing at least two of the rounds.

Starting a round Only nine betting chips are used. They are placed on the table between the two players. Each player then throws a die once. The player making the higher score becomes "captain" (first shooter) for the first hand.

Play: first round The captain takes his turn first, then his opponent.

In his turn each player may throw the dice up to three times to achieve the best possible score.

In each throw he must throw all the dice, keeping them concealed beneath his dice cup. He must declare the number of throws he makes. When both players have thrown, betting on that hand begins.

Opening the betting If both players have made the same number of throws, or if the captain has made fewer throws than his opponent, then the captain bets or passes first.

If the captain has made more throws than his opponent, the latter becomes captain and makes the first bet, or passes.

Betting limits The maximum bet or raise is one chip.

Betting procedure Players use the center chips for betting until these run out. As each player states his bet, he moves the appropriate number of chips away from the center pile and slightly toward him.

When all the center chips have been used up, players may use any chips they have received during the round, moving them slightly toward the center as they use them.

Betting A player need not have a strong hand to make a bet; he may choose to bluff his opponent.

Betting is as in poker. If both players pass, the hand ends.

Once one player has bet, the other must call (ie bet an equal amount), raise (ie bet a greater amount), or drop out. If one player raises, the other must call, reraise, or drop out. The betting continues until one player has called or dropped out.

Outcome If one player calls the other, both show their dice. All chips bet are then taken by the loser. The winner becomes the next captain.

If one player drops out, he must take one penalty chip (from the center if possible). All other chips bet are returned to their positions before the hand began.

The player who has not dropped out is the next captain.

If both players pass, neither takes any chips, and the captaincy changes for the next hand.

Play: second round Play is exactly as in the first round, except that on any throw a player may put aside any dice whose score he wishes to keep, and throw only the remainder. The dice put aside must remain hidden from the opponent.

Having put aside dice on one throw, a player may still throw all the dice on his third throw of that turn.

Play: third round Play reverts to the rules for the first round.

"Open throw" occurs when one player has eight chips, leaving one chip with his opponent or in the center. The player with one or no chips is then entitled to not more than three throws of the dice to make the highest possible exposed combination. (Whether he must rethrow all the dice or may select, depends on the rules for the round they are playing.)

His opponent then throws in similar fashion and if he loses the throws he takes the single chip and so loses the game.

If the single-chip player loses, he takes one chip from his opponent and normal play is resumed.

Multihand bidou betting sequence

A Bets

B Drops out C Raises

D Drops out E Stays in

A Calls

The showdown

MULTIHAND BIDOU

When three or more players take part no chips are placed in the center of the table. Instead, each player begins with six chips.

Captaincy A preliminary round decides who is first captain, as in two-hand bidou. Play begins with the captain and proceeds in a clockwise direction. The winner of each round becomes captain of the next.

If all players pass, the player to the left of the captain of that round becomes captain of the next.

Play is as in two-hand bidou. All players must keep their dice hidden from the others until betting has closed.

Opening the betting If all players have made the same number of throws, the same player remains captain. Otherwise, the player making the fewest throws and nearest the original captain's left becomes captain.

Betting limits The maximum bet is three chips, the maximum raise two chips.

Betting procedure Each player uses his own store of chips, and places his bets to the center of the table to form a common pot.

Betting situations

1) On a showdown between two or more players, the loser collects all chips still in the pot.

2) Players dropping out without betting receive no penalty.

3) For players dropping out after betting at least once, the following rules apply:
the first in a round to do so must take from the pot whichever amount he has put in on that hand, plus the same amount for each player still betting, plus one penalty chip;
each player dropping out thereafter on that round must take one penalty chip.
If the players remaining have bet unequal amounts, whichever number of chips is left in the pot is called or raised by the next player in turn.

4) If all players drop out after a player has raised, any chips left in the pot after penalties have been taken are returned to the raising player.

5) A player who bets his last chips has the right to stay in for the showdown, even if other players take the betting further.
If he loses, he receives back his bet and the equivalent amount from each showdown player. Other chips still in the pot are returned to the players who bet them.

6) If, in the same circumstances, there is a tie, the player who bet the last of his chips takes back his bet, and the other players take back all their chips except one each. The remaining chips are removed from the game.
If there is a tie in any other circumstance, each showdown player takes back one chip, and any other chips in the pot are removed from the game.

7) If only one player bets on a round and all the others pass, he can discard one chip even if it is his last.

8) If only two players are left with chips, these two continue until one has lost. Should the two players have more than nine chips between them, each discards one chip whenever he bets and is not called, until the players have a total of nine chips between them. The two then fight out the game as in two-hand bidou.

9) Any player who passes after betting has begun automatically drops out of that round.

Poor fish is a variation that requires all players to expose their last throws, if all have passed.
The player with the highest throw is the "poor fish" and receives one chip from each of the other players.

MONTEVIDEO

Like bidou, this game requires three dice, a throwing cup, and chips or counters for each player.

However, the objective is not to lose chips but to win them on the basis of the winner ultimately taking all. Three or more players can take part.

Ante At the start of play each player has six chips. In each round he antes one chip into the pot before throwing the dice.

Betting After the dice have been thrown, betting proceeds as in poker.

Play resembles poker, but bidou combinations are used. At showdown, the highest combination wins the pot.
If the game reaches a stage where only two players have any chips, it is speeded up by increasing, round by round, the number of chips each must ante into the pot, to a maximum of six. If there are many players, the same process should be made for the last three players.
Any player may, if he wishes, open the betting by "betting the pot," ie stay in without putting up chips. When this happens, any other player—even if he has already passed—may call the pot. The bet may, of course, be raised in the usual way.

CROWN AND ANCHOR

This is a fast game in which any number of players play against a banker.

Equipment Three special dice are used, each marked with a crown, anchor, heart, spade, diamond, and club. These symbols also appear on the layout, which is marked on a cloth or board set in front of the banker.

Play Each player puts a wager on one or more of the symbols on the layout. The banker then throws the three dice from a cup and pays out on the result of the throw.
The usual odds are evens on singles, 2 to 1 on pairs, and 3 to 1 on three of a kind. The advantage always lies with the banker.

ENGLISH HAZARD

This is a centuries old game played with two dice and a throwing cup. Any number may play.

Play begins when a first shooter, called the "caster," puts his stake in a circle marked on the center of the table. Any other player wishing to wager also puts his stake in the center, and the caster accepts his challenge by knocking the table with the throwing cup.
When all betting has finished, the caster throws the dice to establish a "main point," a total of either 5,6,7,8, or 9. If he throws any other total it is "no main" and he must continue throwing until a main point comes up.
Having established a main point, he throws the dice again to establish a "chance point" (a total of either 4,5,6,7,8,9, or 10—but not the same number as the main point number). When he throws to establish the chance point, the caster immediately loses the bet if he throws an "out." An out is any throw of 2 or 3 (called a "crab"); or a throw of 12 if the main point is 5,6,8, or 9.
The caster wins, however, if he throws a "nick." He makes a nick if he throws an 11 when the main point is a 7, or if he throws a 12 when the main point is a 6 or an 8. If he throws the main point itself, this also counts as a nick and he wins immediately.
If he establishes a chance point, he then continues throwing. If he throws the chance point again, he wins the bet. But if he throws the main point again, he loses.

Crown and anchor layout

Crown and anchor die

Professional banking games

These games are found, in some countries, in fairgrounds, cheap casinos, and small gambling parlors. Many of the games flourished in frontier America, but some date back to the European society gaming houses of the eighteenth century.

Barbooth
Losing throws

Winning throws

BARBOOTH

Barbooth, also called barbudi or even-up craps, is often played for high stakes in some parts of the United States.
Equipment: two miniature dice and a dice cup.
Players Any number of players that can be accommodated at an average poker table may play.
House officials include a "cutter," who is responsible for collecting the house percentage of each winning bet. A banker is usually in attendance to take side bets, charging 5 per cent for his services and paying half this percentage to the house.
Play Only two players at a time throw the dice. The first player to throw is the "shooter." The player to his right (the "fader") throws the dice alternately with him. The shooter does not declare any wager. The fader bets whatever he likes (up to the house limit) that he will beat the shooter. If the fader loses, his stake is collected by the shooter. If the fader wins, his stake is returned with an equal amount from the shooter. The other players make side bets on the result of the contest between the shooter and the fader.
Shooter and fader throw alternately until a decision is reached.
Scoring The only meaningful throws are winning throws (3,3; 5,5; 6,5; or 6,6) and losing throws (1,1; 1,2; 2,2; or 4,4).
Continuing play When a shooter loses with a throw of 1,1; 2,2; or 4,4; and when a fader wins with 3,3; 5,5; or 6,6, the dice are taken by the fader, who now becomes the shooter. The player to his right becomes the new fader. But when the shooter loses with 1,2 or the fader wins with 6,5 the dice remain with the shooter.

TWENTY-SIX

This game, especially popular in the American Midwest in the 1950s, is still played today.
Equipment The game is played with ten dice and a throwing cup. Operators usually provide a scoresheet that also states the rules and payoffs.
Play The player chooses any number from 1 through 6 as his point number and then throws the ten dice 13 times. His score is the number of times his point number appears.
Payoffs vary. The average operator pays 8 to 1 for scores of 33 or over; 4 to 1 for 26 through 32; 4 to 1 for 11 or less; and 2 to 1 for an exact 13. No other scores count, and the game always works strongly in favor of the operator.

GRAND HAZARD

Equipment The game is played with three dice, which the operator either throws from a cup or tumbles through a hazard chute. A layout showing the payoff system is provided.
Play Players bet on the total number thrown. They may bet on individual numbers, on "high" (totals of 11 through 17), "low" (totals of four through 10), "odd" (an odd total), "even" (an even total), and "raffles" (three of a kind).
The payoffs on individual numbers are shown on the layout. Even money (1 to 1) is paid on high, low, odd, and even bets; but if the dice show three of a kind on these bets, the bank wins.
Individual raffles are paid at 180 to 1; any raffle (unspecified) at 30 to 1.
The bank's advantage is even higher if the player's stake is included in the payoff count; for example 16 is paid "30 for 1," not "30 to 1."

CHUCK-A-LUCK

Chuck-a-luck, closely related to grand hazard, has had many other names during its long history, including sweat cloth, chuckerluck, chuck luck and, more recently, bird cage.
Equipment:
1) three dice;
2) a chuck cage;
3) a simple layout showing the numbers from 1 through 6.
Play Each player places his bet on one of the six numbers. When all bets have been placed, the operator tumbles the dice in the chuck cage until they come to rest face up or drop down a chute onto the table.
Payoff If a player's number appears on one die, the operator pays him evens; if on two dice, 2 to 1; if on three dice, 3 to 1.

THREE DICE

Equipment: three dice and a throwing cup.

Play is against a banker and begins with all players putting their bets in front of them. The banker covers these bets (ie puts in an equal amount), and then throws first.

If the banker throws three of a kind, any pair plus a 6, or 4,5,6, he wins and collects all wagers. He loses to all players if he throws 1,2,3, or any pair plus a 1.

All other combinations are valueless except a pair plus a 2,3,4, or 5. On such a throw, the number on the odd die becomes the shooter's point number that others then try to beat.

If the banker makes a valueless first throw, he must throw again.

If the banker makes a point-number throw, each player in turn throws to decide whether he or the banker wins.

If the player fails to make a clear-cut winning or losing throw and throws a point number, it is the higher point number—player's or banker's —that wins.

A tie is a no decision.

If a player fails to make a pair, 4,5,6, or 1,2,3, his throw is valueless and he must continue throwing until such a combination appears.

UNDER AND OVER 7

This is a deceptively simple game in which the odds are heavily loaded in the operator's favor.

Equipment:
1) two dice;
2) a throwing cup;
3) a simple layout showing three spaces: "under 7," "over 7," and "7."

Play The player bets on any one of the three spaces and then throws the two dice. If he has bet on "under 7" and throws a total under seven, the operator pays evens. The same odds apply to successful "over 7" bets. If the player bets on the "7" space and wins, the operator pays five times his stake.

HIGH DICE

This is a fast and simple game, also known as two -dice klondike or beat the bank. It is played with two dice and a throwing cup.

The banker and the player each throw once, the banker throwing first. The score is the numerical total of the two dice, and the player must throw a higher total than the banker to win.

Ties count as wins for the banker.

Grand hazard layout

COUNTER KLONDIKE

Equipment Five dice; they are rolled down a stepped chute.

Play The banker rolls first. Each player in turn then rolls, trying to beat the banker's score in a single throw. Ties count as wins for the banker.

Scoring The numbers on the dice rank: 1 (high),6,5,4,3,2 (low). Winning combinations in ascending order of value are: a pair, two pairs, three of a kind, full house (three of a kind and a pair), four of a kind, and five of a kind.

The odd die in a combination does not count. For example, four 3s and a 1 rank equally with four 3s and any other number. Straights, and no pairs, do not count as scoring combinations.

CASINO KLONDIKE

Equipment:
1) two sets of five dice;
2) two throwing cups;
3) a layout with spaces marked "win," "lose," "beat two aces," and "klondike."

Objective Players aim to beat the banker. A player betting on the "win" space has to beat the banker's throw. If he bets on the "lose" space, he must throw less than the banker. To win on "beat two aces," he must throw not less than two pairs.

Play The banker throws first and his throw remains displayed on the "klondike" space throughout the round. Play then goes clockwise round the table, the players using the second set of dice. The banker pays or collects after each player's throw, paying evens to all winners. All ties count as wins for the banker.

Klondike layout

Craps

Craps developed in the early nineteenth century, when American negroes adapted the old English game of hazard. Today, the money wagered at craps in the United States alone makes it the biggest gambling game in history. Its attractions are its speed of action and large element of participation; yet its essence is that of a mathematical game of numbers and odds.

FORMS OF THE GAME
Three forms of craps exist today.
1) Private craps: between two or more people, making bets among themselves.
2) Open (or money) craps: typical of illegal sawdust casinos and big money games. One person banks the game, and certain bets can only be made against the bank.
3) Bank (casino) craps: played on a specially constructed table, and requiring all bets to be made against the house.

GENERAL RULES
Basic equipment is:
1) two matched dice;
2) a playing surface, preferably edged by a wall or backboard;
3) betting chips or cash.
Players: any number over two; one player can play against the house at bank craps.
General procedure
a) Any player by common agreement may shoot the dice first; thereafter the dice are passed around in a clockwise direction.
b) A new player may join a game at any stage and sit anywhere in the circle of players—provided that the house (or the players in a private game) raise no objection at the time. He takes his turn in the normal way when the dice reach him.
c) A player may leave a game at any time, regardless of his gains or losses.

Throw of the dice The shooter shakes the dice in his closed hand and throws them onto the playing area. If there is a backboard, it is usually ruled that the dice must rebound from it before they come to rest. This helps defeat controlled throws.
The two numbers face uppermost when the dice come to rest, added together, give the result of the throw.
Basic play The first throw in a shooter's turn is called a "come-out" throw as is the first throw after each time the dice win or lose.
On a come-out throw:
a) if the shooter throws a 7 or 11 he has thrown a "natural"; the dice "pass" (ie win) immediately. The shooter may keep the dice for another come-out throw.
b) If the shooter throws a 2, 3, or 12, he has thrown a "craps": the dice "miss out" or "crap out" (ie lose) immediately. The shooter may keep the dice for another come-out throw.
c) If the shooter throws a 4, 5, 6, 8, 9, or 10, he has thrown a "point": for the dice to win he must "make the point," ie throw the same number again before he

throws a 7—no other numbers matter.
If the shooter throws the same number again before he throws a 7, the dice pass (win). The shooter may keep the dice for another come-out throw.
If he throws a 7 before he throws the number again, the dice miss out or "seven out" (lose). The shooter must give the dice to the next player in turn.
A sample turn of play
1) First come-out throw: 3 (craps).
2) Second: 11 (natural).
3) Third: 6 (point). Player then throws: (11),(4),(9),(3),6 (makes point).
4) Fourth: 12 (craps).
5) Fifth: 10 (point). Player then throws: (2),(8),(11),7 (sevens out). Player loses dice.

Giving up the dice If the shooter sevens out, he must give up the dice.
He may also, if he wishes, pass the dice if:
a) he has not thrown the dice in his turn; or
b) he has just thrown a "decision:" ie a natural, a craps, or a pass on a point.
Change of dice If more than one pair of dice is being used, any player may call for the dice in use to be changed at any time. This is called a "box-up." The change is made immediately before the next come-out throw.

PRIVATE CRAPS

Private craps games can be played anywhere. Players arrange the bets among themselves, and it is important that they know the correct odds for different bets—in many games hustlers offer short odds that the inexperienced accept. Cheating, with false dice or controlled throws, is also common.

Center bet On each come-out throw, the shooter places the amount he wishes to bet in the center of the playing area. He announces the amount, saying "I'll shoot . . ."

Any of the other players then "fade" (accept) whatever part of the total they wish, by placing that amount in the center alongside the shooter's bet.

Unless agreed at the beginning of the game, there is no set order or amounts in which players fade the center bets. Players simply place money in the center until all the shooter's bet has been faded, or until no one wishes to place any further amount.

(However, it is sometimes agreed that any player who faded the entire center bet on the preceding come-out, and lost, can claim the right to fade the entire present bet.)

If the center bet is not entirely faded by the players, the shooter may either:
a) withdraw the part not faded; or
b) call off all bets, by saying "No bet."

Players may not fade more than the shooter's center bet; but if the players show eagerness to bet more, the shooter can decide to increase the amount of his bet.

Throw of dice and basic play: see the general rules.

Settlement of center bet If the dice miss out (lose), the players who faded the center bet each receive back their money together with the equivalent amount of the center bet.

If the dice pass (win), all the money in the center is collected by the shooter.
The center bet is therefore an even money (1 to 1) bet.
Since the probability of the dice passing is in fact 970 occasions in 1980, the shooter has a 1.414% disadvantage on the center bet.

Continuing play The dice are retained or passed as described in the general procedure. For the new come-out throw, the shooter puts up a new center bet for any amount he wishes.

Other bets are known as side bets. Like the center bet, they must be arranged before the dice are thrown, not while they are rolling.

Note that the shooter himself may make any of the side bets he wishes, in addition to the center bet.

Right and wrong bettors
All these bets require agreement between two players.

One is the "wrong" bettor: he "lays" odds that the dice will not pass or will not make the number(s) bet on.

The other is the "right" bettor: he "takes" odds that the dice will pass or will make the number(s) bet on.

The bet and odds may be proposed by either the right or the wrong bettor; in practice, however, more experienced players tend to be "wrong" bettors and propose odds that the less experienced player will "take."

Flat bet This is a normal bet on whether a shooter's come-out throw will pass, and is made as a side bet between two players (of which one may be the shooter). Flat bets occur especially if one player has faded the entire bet.

Point bet If the shooter throws a point on his come-out throw, players may bet on whether he will "make the point." (The center and flat bets still remain to be settled in the same way.)

Come bet This is a bet on whether the dice will pass—but treating the next throw of the dice, after the bet, as the bet's come-out throw—when in fact the shooter is throwing for a point.

That is: on the shooter's come-out throw he has thrown a point (eg a 6). He continues throwing the dice to see if he makes the point or sevens out.

Before one of these throws, two players agree on a "come bet:" one player lays odds that the dice will not come, the other takes odds that they will. The first throw of the dice after the bet is the "come-out" throw for the come bet. If the shooter rolls a 7, he sevens out on his point—but for the come bet the dice "come," because a 7 on a come-out throw is a natural.

Similarly, 11 is a natural for the come bet, and 2, 3, or 12 is craps—the dice "don't come." (But all these leave the center bet undecided, because they are neither the point number nor a 7.)

If the shooter rolls a point number on the come-out throw for the come bet, this number becomes the point for the come bet. The outcome then depends, in the usual way, on whether the point or a 7 appears first.

If the shooter makes the point on his center bet without making the come bet point, the players making the come bet can agree to withdraw the bet or to continue the number sequence into the shooter's next turn.

Hardway bet (or gag bet)
This is a bet on whether the shooter will throw a certain number "the hard way"—ie as the sum of a double. Hardway bets can be placed on 4 (2+2), 6 (3+3), 8 (4+4), or 10 (5+5).

The right bettor loses if a 7 is thrown, or if the number bet on is thrown any other way before being thrown as a double.

Off-number bet Two players agree to bet on any number they choose. The right bettor wins if the shooter throws the number before he throws a 7. Bettors may call off this bet before a "decision" is reached.

Proposition bet refers to any other kind of side bet agreed upon—limited only by players' imaginations!

Such bets are always offered at odds designed to give the proposing player an advantage. There are two main categories:
a) bets on whether the specified number(s) will appear within a certain number of rolls after the bet: "one-roll bets," "two-roll bets," "three-roll bets;" or
b) bets on whether the specified number(s) will appear before other specified number(s) or before a 7.
In each case, the specified number(s) bet on may be:
a) a certain number to be thrown in any way;
b) a certain number to be thrown in a specified way;
c) any one of a group of numbers (eg a group of specified numbers, odd numbers, numbers below 7, etc).

True odds Table 1 (see p 176) gives the true odds for various bets on or between single numbers, and provides the information from which the true odds for any bet between groups of numbers can be calculated. (A player should particularly avoid accepting 1 to 1 odds on 6 to 5 bets.) Table 2 (see p 176) gives the true odds for hardway bets.

Irregularities at private craps: certain throws are void and the shooter must throw the dice again.
1) If the playing area has been specified at the start of the game, the throw is void if either die rolls out of the area.
2) If either die comes to rest under any object on the playing area or tilted on an obstruction, so that it is not clear which of its faces is uppermost, any agreed neutral player or bystander is nominated to decide the question. If he cannot decide, the throw is void.
3) When there is a backboard and neither die hits it, the roll is void. If only one die hits the board the roll counts, but the shooter must be reprimanded. If it occurs again, the other players may designate a player to complete the shooter's turn for him. They may also bar the shooter from shooting for the rest of the game.
4) If either die hits any object or person after hitting the backboard, the roll is counted.
5) A player may not knock either or both dice aside on the roll and call "No dice." If he does this once, the throw counts as it finally shows; if he repeats it, he may be barred from shooting for the rest of the game.

Throws

7

11

Natural throws

2

3

12

Crap throws

4

5

6

8

9

10

Point throws

Table 1: True odds for bets on or between single numbers

Number	Number of ways	Single roll	Before a 7	Comparative odds
12	1 (a)	35-1 (b)	6-1 (c)	**12** (d)
11	2	17-1	3-1	2-1 **11**
10	3	11-1	2-1	3-1 3-2 **10**
9	4	8-1	3-2	4-1 2-1 4-3 **9**
8	5	31-5	6-5	5-1 5-2 5-3 5-4 **8**
7	6	5-1	—	6-1 3-1 2-1 3-2 6-5 **7**
6	5	31-5	6-5	5-1 5-2 5-3 5-4 1-1 5-6 **6**
5	4	8-1	3-2	4-1 2-1 4-3 1-1 4-5 2-3 4-5 **5**
4	3	11-1	2-1	3-1 3-2 1-1 3-4 3-5 1-2 3-5 3-4 **4**
3	2	17-1	3-1	2-1 1-1 2-3 1-2 2-5 1-3 2-5 1-2 2-3 **3**
2	1	35-1	6-1	1-1 1-2 1-3 1-4 1-5 1-6 1-5 1-4 1-3 1-2 **2**

Table 2: Hardway bets

Bet	Ways of making	Other ways of making	Ways of making a 7	Total ways of losing	Odds against hardway bet
4 (2+2)	1	2 +	6 =	8	8-1
6 (3+3)	1	4 +	6 =	10	10-1
8 (4+4)	1	4 +	6 =	10	10-1
10 (5+5)	1	2 +	6 =	8	8-1

Notes on odds table

a) Number of different combinations of two die faces that will give the number. Total of all possible combinations is 36.

b) Odds against making a number on a single roll—calculated by comparing the number of ways of making the number (x) with the number of ways of making another number (36–x).

c) Odds against throwing the number before throwing a 7: for point and off-number bets.

d) Odds against making the higher number before the lower number (eg 12 before 4: 3–1). Reverse the odds to give odds against making the lower number before the higher (eg 4 before 12: 1–3).

BANK CRAPS

This is the form of the game found in most legal casinos throughout the world. About four-fifths of the turnover of casinos in the United States comes from play at craps. A special table with betting layout is used, and all bets must be placed against the house. The odds paid give the house a mathematical advantage on any bet.

The table is about the size of a pool or billiard table. A wood rail about 10in high runs around the outside edge and forms the backboard. For most of its length the backboard is lined with sponge rubber, embossed so that the dice rebound in a random way. The backboard is faced with a 9in-high mirror over a 6ft length opposite the "stickman" (see the section on croupiers). This enables him to see both sides of the the dice when they have come to rest, and so prevent mis-spotted dice being slipped into play.
Grooves in the top edge of the rail hold players' reserves of chips.

Other equipment: bank craps also requires betting chips; one or more pairs of matched dice; and a "stick" for passing and retrieving the dice.
Players Any number of players from one upward may take part. The role of banker is taken by the house.
Croupiers The "stickman" is the croupier in charge of the dice. He calls out the number thrown, collects the dice, and —when bets have been settled—passes them to the next shooter. His name refers to the curved stick he uses to reach for and pass the dice. Opposite him are two "boxmen," who supervise every aspect of the game. At the table ends (or sometimes in other positions, depending on the layout) stand the two housemen who collect and pay out bets.

Basic rules: see the section on general rules.
Throw of the dice It is often required that the dice rebound from the backboard before coming to rest. With a double-sided layout, there may instead be an elastic cord strung across the center of the table, over which the dice must pass before hitting the table surface. Alternatively, it may be required that the dice travel past the point where the stickman is standing.
Basic play, turn of play, passing the dice, and change of dice: see the general rules for craps.
Betting In bank craps, all bets are placed against the bank; there are no side bets. The shooter must bet that the dice will or will not pass. Any other bets are at the player's discretion.
Note that some of the odds quoted below for place, hardway, and one-roll bets are altered by law in some countries to give the player less disadvantage.

Pass line bet ("Pass," "line," "win," or "do"): placed on the long narrow area marked "pass line," "pass," "line," "win," or "do," and known as the "front line." The bettor wins if the dice pass (ie throw a natural or make a point). The bet is paid at 1 to 1, giving the house a 1.4% advantage.
Don't pass line bet ("Don't," or "lose"): placed on the long narrow area marked "don't pass," "don't," or "lose," followed by the word "bar" and dice symbols, and known as the "back line." The bettor wins if the dice miss out (ie crap out or seven out)—except for a standoff on the barred result shown by the dice symbols (ie when the bettor's stake is returned). The bet is placed at 1 to 1. If 2 (1+1) or 12 (6+6) is the barred missout throw, the house advantage is 1.4%. If 3 (1+2) is the barred throw, the house advantage is 4.4%.
Come bet: placed on the space marked "come." The bettor wins if the dice pass, taking the first throw after the bet as a come-out. The bet is paid at 1 to 1, giving the house a 1.4% advantage.

The layout is printed on green baize stretched across the table surface. There are several designs.
A "double-sided" layout is one with identical patterns at each end and with a smaller central area for proposition bets. The practical differences between layouts are small, except for some of the odds offered.

Betting layout

To calculate the odds between any groups of numbers: add all ways of making the numbers in one group, and compare with the total of all ways of making the numbers in the other group.

True odds for other one-roll bets:
a) against any specified pair (eg 3+3): 35–1;
b) against any specified combination of two different numbers (eg 6+5): 17–1;
c) against any craps (2, 3, or 12): 8–1.

OPEN (OR MONEY) CRAPS

Open craps is played in many parts of the United States. At its highest levels, it brings together the leaders of business and the underworld in games in which bets may be placed in units of $10,000. Winnings of $500,000 in a session are not uncommon.

Betting This form of craps gained its name because originally all bets could be placed, at option, either with the bank or with other players ("open" bets). Today it is much more restricted. Players may bet among themselves on point numbers. All other bets are placed against the bank—including any point number bets not taken up by other players.

Bets are almost always in cash.

The layout if there is one, is usually without any space for proposition bets (see bank craps). Any propositions the bank accepts are memorized. If there is no layout, bets are placed in the same relative positions as if a layout were being used.

The bank The man who is banking the game is called the "book." The percentage he takes is called "vigorish."

Settlement The following bets are paid at bank craps odds:
1) pass/don't pass bets, and come/don't come bets;
2) one-roll bets;
3) hardway bets.
On bets on points or single (place) numbers, the bank pays players at the correct odds, but makes a house charge on the amount wagered.
In some games the bank charges a "wrong bettor" only when he loses. In other games, the charge is made on all point and box numbers.

Don't come bet: placed on the space marked "don't come."
The bettor wins if the dice do not pass, taking the first throw after the bet as a "come-out" —but making one result a standoff, as with the don't pass line bet. The bet is paid at 1 to 1. House advantages are as for the don't pass line bet.

Place bet: is a bet on a single number, either 4, 5, 6, 8, 9, or 10. A right bettor places his bet on the square marked with the number, and wins if the number bet on is thrown before a 7 is thrown.
A wrong bettor places his bet on the space behind the numbered square, and wins if a 7 is thrown before the number is thrown.
Right bets on 4 and 10 are usually paid at 9 to 5 (house advantage 6.6%), on 5 and 9 at 7 to 5 (4.0%), and on 6 and 8 at 7 to 6 (1.5%).
Wrong bets on 4 and 10 are usually paid at 11 to 5 (house advantage 3.0%); on 5 and 9 at 8 to 5 (2.5%); and on 6 and 8 at 5 to 4 (1.8%).
In the United Kingdom, right bets on 4 and 10 are paid at 9½ to 5, and wrong bets at 10½ to 5.

Field bet: placed on the space marked "field." The bettor wins if any one of the following numbers is thrown on the next roll: 2, 3, 4, 9, 10, 11, 12. The bet is paid at 1 to 1, giving the house a 5.5% advantage.
Variants:
a) sometimes 5 is a winning number in place of 4;
b) sometimes higher payments are made on 2 and 12; eg 2 to

1 on both, 3 to 2 on both, or 3 to 1 on 2 only, or (in the United Kingdom) 3 to 1 on 12 and 2 to 1 on 2. These variants reduce the house advantage.

Big six bet: placed on the space marked "big six." The bettor wins if a 6 appears before a 7. It is exactly the same as a place bet on the six, but paid at worse odds, 1 to 1, giving the house a 9.1% advantage—a sucker bet!

Big eight bet: placed on the space marked "big eight." As for "big six," except that the result bet on is 8.
Both "big six" and "big eight" are banned in some countries, for example in the United Kingdom.

Hardway bets: placed on the space marked with the appropriate dice symbol. The bettor wins if the number bet on is made with a double before it is made any other way and before a 7 is thrown. Bets on 4 and 10 are paid at 7 to 1, giving the house an 11.1% advantage. Bets on 6 and 8 are paid at 9 to 1, giving the house a 9.1% advantage.
Payments in the United Kingdom are 7½ to 1 and 9½ to 1 respectively.

One-roll or come-out bets
Layouts usually provide for the following one-roll bets. They are placed on the space marked with the appropriate double dice symbol.
a) 12 (6+6): paid at 30 to 1 (house advantage 13.9%) or at 30 for 1 (ie 29 to 1, house advantage 16.6%). Payment is 33 to 1 in the United Kingdom.
b) 2 (1+1): as for 12.
c) 11 (5+6): paid at 15 to 1 (house advantage 13.9%) or

at 15 for 1 (ie 14 to 1, house advantage 16.7%). Payment is 15 to 1 in the United Kingdom.
d) 3 (1+2): as for 11.
e) 7: paid at 4 to 1 (5 for 1); house advantage 16.6%.
f) any craps (2, 3, or 12): paid at 7 to 1 (ie 8 for 1); house advantage 11.1%. Payment is 7½ to 1 in the United Kingdom.
Note that where payment is quoted as "x for 1" it means that the original betting unit is counted in the winning payment.

Withdrawing bets Come and don't come bets cannot be withdrawn once the dice have rolled.
Pass line and don't pass line bets cannot be withdrawn after a come-out roll.
If the dice make a point, any undecided bet (hardway or place bet) must be declared by the bettor to be "on" or "off," ie it can be withdrawn.

Free odds bets—"do" bets If a player has placed a pass bet, and the shooter comes out on a point number; or
if a player has placed a come bet, and the shooter throws a "new" number, ie a point number for the come bet; then the player may make a further identical bet, up to the amount of his original bet, and —if the dice make the point number—the house will pay off this second bet at the true odds.
This is known as "taking the (free) odds." Accepting it reduces the house advantage on the two bets combined to 0.8%.

Free odds bets—"don't" bets If a player has placed a "don't pass" bet or a "don't come" bet, and the shooter comes out on a point or new number, then the player may make a further identical bet up to a limit that would give him winnings not higher than his original bet. If the dice do not make the point number, the house will pay off this second bet at the true odds.
Accepting the "free odds" on "don't" bets reduces the house advantage on the two bets combined to 0.8%.
Free odds bets may be withdrawn before the bet is decided. Note that (since casinos will only settle in rounded amounts) a player accepting the "free odds" needs to calculate whether the size of bet will allow such payment, at the odds effected. Otherwise, on payment, rounding down may give him worse odds on the two bets than on his original bet.

Betting limits The maximum limit varies in different casinos. The limit on proposition bets (eg one-roll and hardway bets) is usually one-third of the house's pass bet limit. The betting limit on free bets is usually half the normal maximum limit.

Shove ha'penny

Shove ha'penny is an old English game sometimes played in public houses. Two players or pairs attempt to position ha'pennies or metal disks on a marked board. A game is won by the first side to "shove" three ha'pennies into each of the board's nine "beds."

The board Shove ha'penny is usually played on a special board, but can be played on a tabletop marked with chalk or pencil.

A strip of wood under the board keeps it steady when placed over the edge of a table or other level surface.

Boards are 2ft by 1ft 2½in and are made of hardwood or slate. Wood boards have the grain running lengthways and the lines marked by shallow grooves.

Ten lines running across the board at 1½in intervals mark out the nine "beds," and two lines at right angles to them mark the edges of the scoring area.

The squares along the edges of the board are used for recording the players' scores. Some boards have three holes in each square to hold small scoring pegs.

Ha'pennies The game was played in Britain long before decimalization of the currency in 1972. The old ha'penny was 1in in diameter.

Players use very highly polished old ha'pennies, or metal disks of the same diameter.

Each player has five ha'pennies or disks.

Players Shove ha'penny is a game for two players or pairs.

Turns Choice of playing order may be decided by the toss of a coin, or by a preliminary shove for the nine bed (using only one ha'penny except in case of a tie).

Each player shoves five ha'pennies in a turn.

"Shoving" The ha'penny is placed partly over the edge of the board and is then shoved as illustrated. A sharp, light tap is most effective.

Shoving one ha'penny into another ("cannoning" or "caroming") is an important feature of the game.

Objective The game is won by the first side to shove three scoring ha'pennies into each of the board's nine beds.

Short shoves
a) A ha'penny that comes to rest on the nearest line of the first bed must be left in position, but may later be cannoned into the beds by another ha'penny.

b) A ha'penny that fails to reach the nearest line of the first bed after hitting a ha'penny on that line must also be left in position.

c) A ha'penny that fails to reach the nearest line of the first bed without hitting a ha'penny on that line may be retaken.

Dead ha'pennies must be immediately removed from the board and may not be retaken. A ha'penny is dead if:

d) it goes wholly beyond the far line of the ninth bed;

e) it stops wholly or partly beyond the side lines in the area used for keeping the score.

Ha'penny on another If a ha'penny stops wholly or partly on top of another, both are left on the board.

If a ha'penny is on top of another at the end of a turn, neither ha'penny can be scored.

Scoring A player's turn is scored only after he has shoved all his five ha'pennies —hence the importance of cannoning.

A ha'penny is scored if it lies completely within one of the beds for which the player needs a score (f).

There is no score for a ha'penny on a line (g), however slight the overlap.

Scores may be made in any order, but good players usually fill the far beds first.

If a player scores more than three times in any bed, the extra scores may be claimed by the opposition. Except that the score that wins the game must actually be from a shove by the winner.

Penalties A player loses all five shoves for the turn if he: touches a played ha'penny before all are played; or removes his ha'pennies before recording his score.

A player who plays out of turn is allowed no score for that turn and must miss his next turn.

Shovelboard

Table shovelboard is the ancestor of shove ha'penny and of the shovelboard, or shuffleboard, game played on ships' decks and outdoor courts. Players attempt to score points by propelling coins or disks into marked scoring areas. The game can easily be adapted for modern play.

Equipment Each player requires:
a) four coins or disks about 1in in diameter;
b) an implement such as a wood or plastic ruler for propelling the coins or disks.

Table In medieval times shovelboard was played on very long, narrow tables—perhaps 30ft long and 2ft wide. The higher scoring area extended 4in from the end of the table and the lower scoring area 4ft in front of that.
It is, however, possible to play a form of shovelboard on almost any rectangular or square table—by marking off an out of play area and scaling down the dimensions of the scoring areas.

Players Shovelboard is a game for two players or two teams of equal number.
Turns In team games, each player normally plays a round against an opponent from the other team.
The two opponents in a round propel one coin alternately.
Playing a coin Players use their rulers to give the coin one push toward the scoring area. All coins, except those more than half over the out of play lines, are left on the table until the end of the round. This makes hitting one coin into another an important feature of the game.

Scoring Players score:
a) three points for any coin partly over the far edge of the table;
b) two points for any coin completely in the far scoring area;
c) one point for any coin completely in the near scoring area;
d) one point for any coin on the line between the near and far scoring areas.

Result In singles games, the winner is the first person to score an agreed number of points—for example 11.
Team games can be decided in several ways:
the team winning most rounds;
the team with most points after an agreed number of rounds;
the first team to score an agreed number of points.

Shove football

Shove football is a table game for two players or teams based on the rules of soccer. Players use a wood or plastic ruler to propel larger coins—"players"—into a smaller coin—the "ball." Goalposts are marked at each end of the table. The game is won by the team that scores most goals.

Table The game can be played on any rectangular table.

Equipment Players need:
a) a wood or plastic ruler for propelling the coins;
b) a small coin or disk for the "ball";
c) larger coins, marked according to team;
d) matches, pencils, or some other means of marking the goalposts.

Players Shove football can be played by:
two players with two or more coins each;
two teams with one or two coins per player.
(The game is probably best with a maximum of eight coins representing "players.")

Playing the ball A player uses his ruler to shove any of his team's "players" into the ball.

Duration A game consists of two halves of an agreed length of time—usually 2–5 minutes. Teams change ends at half time.

Turns The first turn goes to the team that wins the toss of a coin; the other team has the first turn in the second half. Otherwise turns alternate between teams, with team members playing in the same order throughout.

Kick off The ball is kicked off from the center of the table: at the start of each half; after each goal.
Players may position their "players" by hand before a kick off.
No "player" may be within 3in of the "player" taking the kick.

Play A player is allowed only one kick in a turn unless:
he has been awarded a free kick—in which case he takes the free kick and then his ordinary turn;
he earns an extra kick by hitting the ball into another of his "players."

The "ball"

Free kick

Fouls The following fouls are penalized by a free kick to the opposition:
a) touching the ball directly with the ruler;
b) touching an opposition "player" with the ruler;
c) hitting a "player" into an opposition "player" before hitting the ball;
d) moving a "player" by hand except when specifically allowed in the rules;
e) playing out of turn;
f) interfering with the game in any other way.

Free kick A free kick after a foul is taken from where the offense occurred.
The player taking the free kick may reposition any of his "players" by hand.
Opposition "players" may not normally be moved, except that a "player" less than 3in

from the ball must be moved to that distance.
The free kick is taken as illustrated.

Kick on The opposition is awarded a kick on (a free kick 2in in from where the ball went out of play) if:
the ball is sent over the side edge of the table;
the ball is sent over the opposition's goal line (back edge of the table) without touching an opposition "player."
Both players may reposition any of their "players" for a kick on. Other "players" must be at least 3in from the "player" taking the kick.

Corner kick The attacking side is awarded a corner kick if the ball goes over the opposition goal line after last touching an opposition "player."
The attacker takes a free kick from the corner of the table nearest where the ball went off.
Both players may reposition their "players" by hand. No "player" may be within 3in of the "player" taking the kick.

Scoring A goal is scored when the ball is pushed through the goalposts.
After a goal, play is restarted with a center kick by the team who scored.
The game is won by the team scoring most goals.

Squails

Squails is a type of table bowls that was popular in Britain in the last century. Players are divided into two teams and seek to position wood disks, called "squails," as near as possible to a metal target, called the "process" or "jack." The game can easily be played with improvised equipment.

Table Squails can be played on any kind of table, but a fairly strong, round one is best.

Squails The game was formerly played with wood disks about 1½in in diameter and raised at the center. Coins, wood counters, coasters, or plastic tiddlywinks could all be used. Each team's squails should be clearly differentiated by color or a number.

Each player has an equal number of squails.

Target Old targets were usually made of metal—eg a small medal or a stumpy lead cylinder.

The target is placed in the center of the table at the start of a round.

Players Squails is a game for any even number of players, but four to eight is probably best.

Players are divided into two teams, and team members take alternate places around the table.

Squails

Turns Choice of playing order goes to the player who gets his squail nearest the target in a preliminary play. Turns pass clockwise around the table, alternating between teams.

Each player plays one squail in a turn.

Playing a squail The player places his squail partly over the edge of the table and then pushes it with the palm of his hand—as in shove ha'penny.

Objective Players attempt to position their squails as near as possible to the target. Playing one squail into another to move it toward or away from the target is permitted.

Moved target If a squail pushes the target more than 6in away from the center of the table, the target must be put back in its original position. Two points are generally awarded to the opposition if a player knocks the target off the table or within 3in of the table edge.

Dead squails A squail that goes off the table or stops within 3in of the table edge is dead for that round.

Improvised squails

Scoring Points are scored after all the players have played all their squails for a round.

The squail farthest from the target scores one point, next farthest two points, and so on to the squail nearest the target.

A game consists of an agreed number of rounds.

Bagatelle

The name "bagatelle" is sometimes applied to a billiards game played on a baize-covered table. Better known, however, is the bagatelle game described here, which is played on a wood or plastic board.

Objective Players try to strike the balls in such a way that they score the maximum number of points.

Other equipment Bagatelle is played with small steel or plastic balls. When not in play, they are ranged behind a special partition running along the near end of the board. A stick about the size and weight of a drum stick is used to strike the balls.

The board is made of varnished or painted wood or of plastic.
It is rectangular in shape (approximately 2ft by 1ft) and one of its ends is curved to form a semicircle.
The board has a raised rim—rather like a tray—and slopes very slightly, so that the far (curved) end is higher than the end nearest the player.

A number of small nails are set into the board as shown. (The arrangement of the nails may vary from board to board.) Some of the nails form semicircles (called "cups"); other nails are free standing. There are also a number of shallow depressions or "holes," just big enough to hold a ball and with nails next to them.

The cups and holes are marked with a scoring value, usually ranging from five to 150 points. The free-standing nails act as deflectors and have no score.
The board should be placed on a table or other suitable surface for play.

Burmese caroms

This ancient Burmese game displays most of the techniques and skills associated with billiard games played in the West. It differs significantly in the smaller size of the playing area, the use of disks instead of balls, and in the absence of a cue as a striker.

Players This is a game for two players or for two pairs. Opposing players face each other across the board.

Starting position

Table Burmese caroms is played on a miniature table measuring 2ft square. The playing surface is composed of a highly polished tropical hardwood, such as teak. To reduce friction to a minimum, the surface is lightly coated with French chalk (reapplied after each game).
At each corner of the table there is a netted pocket. The width of each pocket should not exceed $1\frac{1}{2}$ times the diameter of the striker disk. A circle 6in in diameter, with a center spot, is marked on the middle of the board.
Two rectangles, each $21\frac{1}{3}$in by $18\frac{2}{3}$in, are marked out on the board, so that their short edges are equidistant from the four sides of the table. This arrangement forms four

narrow rectangles or "boxes," from which each player makes his strokes.
Equipment There are 19 object disks: nine black, nine white, and one red or "queen" disk. These disks measure 1in across and $\frac{3}{16}$in in depth. They are made of polished hardwood and are designed to fit into the center circle. There is also one striker disk made of bone or ivory, measuring $1\frac{1}{3}$in across and $\frac{3}{16}$in in depth.

Play The participants—of whom there may be any number—each play in turn. In his turn, the player takes a ball and places it at the head of the "guidance channel" that runs part-way along the right-hand side of the board. Holding the striking stick with one or both hands, the player then strikes the ball so that it runs along the channel and into the main area of the board. (In the follow-through, the tip of the stick may not extend beyond the end of the channel.)

If the player strikes the ball with insufficient force—so that it rolls back to the start instead of into the main area of the board—he may strike the ball again.

If, however, the ball is hit so forcefully that it shoots off the board, the player may not take the ball again and his score for that ball is zero.

The number of balls each player may strike in a turn may be determined by the players before the start of the game. The players may also choose whether to remove each ball from the board as soon as it has been played, or to leave all the balls in position until the end of a round.

Scoring A player's score must be noted after each turn. A ball cannot be judged until it has come to an absolute standstill. If it comes to a halt inside a cup or hole, it scores the corresponding number of points.

There is no score if the ball: enters a cup or hole but then rolls out again; becomes lodged against the nails outside a cup or hole; comes to a halt in any non-scoring area of the board, including the near end of the board.

If balls are left in position until the end of a round, points may also be scored by a player managing to dislodge an opponent's ball that has already scored.

For example, if the opponent's ball scored 50 points, the player may add 50 points to his own score—whether or not his ball comes to halt in a scoring area.

End play The players may decide to continue a game until:
a) a set time limit has been reached (in which case the winner is the player with the highest score at that point);
b) one player's score has reached a predetermined number of points; or
c) each player has had a predetermined number of turns—the player with the highest score then being the winner.

Alternative boards come in many different shapes and sizes, sometimes small enough to fit in the hand.

On many of these boards, the balls are fed automatically to the front of a spring-loaded trigger. By pulling and then releasing the trigger, the balls are propelled around the board.

Some of the boards are illustrated with a particular theme.

Bagatelle has also been adapted for play in fairgrounds and amusement arcades on special machines popularly known as "pinball" machines.

Objective Each player (or pair) attempts to pocket the disks of the color allotted to him by knocking them with the striker disk.

All players also attempt to pocket the queen disk—which carries bonus points.

Starting procedure The queen disk is placed on the center spot, with the other disks arranged around it as shown.

Order of play is determined by lot. The player drawing black plays first, and his objective is to pocket the black disks; his opponent's objective is to pocket the white disks.

Play Black places the striker disk anywhere within his box and, by flicking it with his middle finger, attempts to knock one or more black disks into any pocket.

A player must flick the striker disk across the front line of his box at each stroke—although if the striker crosses the front line and then spins off a side of the table in such a way as to hit a disk behind the striker's original position, the stroke is valid. (The striker disk may rebound from a side before hitting a disk.)

A player may hit one of his opponent's disks, using it to pocket one of his own disks.

A player's turn ends when he either:
a) fails to flick the striker across the front line of his box;
b) fails to pocket one of his disks;
c) pockets one of his opponent's disks; or
d) pockets the striker—whether or not he succeeds in pocketing one or more of his own disks. (See also the section on fouls and penalties.)

When the turn passes to a player, the striker disk must be placed in that player's box. All shots must be played from the correct box.

Pocketing the queen disk may be done in either one of two ways (to be agreed on by the players before the start of the game).

1) The queen disk may be pocketed at any time provided that the successful player pockets one of his own disks with his next stroke.

Failure to do so results in the queen being returned to the center, together with any other of the player's disks pocketed with that stroke.

2) In the more difficult alternative, the queen disk may only be pocketed after a player has successfully pocketed all his own disks.

Fouls and penalties In addition to losing his turn, a player may also incur penalties or penalty points.
a) If a player pockets one of his opponent's disks, it remains in the pocket.
b) If a player pockets the striker disk as well as one or more of his own disks, his opponent replaces the disk or disks anywhere within the center circle.
c) If a player pockets the striker disk only, his opponent takes any one of the player's disks from a pocket and places it anywhere within the center circle. If the offending player has no disks pocketed, he has one point deducted from his score.

Scoring No scoring is carried out until one player has pocketed all his own disks, thereby winning the game.

The first player to do so scores the value of his opponent's disks still on the board, plus the value of the queen if it was pocketed by him. No points can be claimed for pocketing the queen disk if it was pocketed by the loser.

Each black and each white disk is worth one point, and the queen is worth five points. Any penalty points are deducted from the players' scores.

Scores are totaled until one player has 30 points—this may take several games.

In match play the first player to score 30 points wins the set, and the winner of two out of three sets wins the match.

English billiards

English billiards is played on a special table by two players or pairs. Three balls are used—white, spot white, and red. Players use a cue to propel their cue ball across the table to score points by pocketing balls ("hazards") or by hitting both other balls ("cannons").

Cue

Starting position

The table is a slate bed covered with green baize. The playing surface of a standard table measures 6ft 1½in by 12ft. Scaled down tables are sometimes used.
Features are:
a) cushion (width 2in);
b) top pocket (width 3½in);
c) center pocket (width 4in);
d) bottom pocket (width 3½in);
e) "the spot;"
f) pyramid spot;
g) center spot;
h) balk line (2ft 5in from the bottom of the table);
i) balk line spot;
j) the "D;"
k) long butt cue (9ft) and long butt rest (8ft);
l) half butt rest (5ft).
The cue must be of the traditional shape and not less than 3ft long. Cues are usually about 7ft long and made of wood.
The balls must all be of equal size ($2\frac{1}{16}$ in in diameter) and weight.
The white and spot white are the cue balls, one used by each player (or pair of players). The red ball is never touched with a cue; it is only hit by knocking other balls against it.

Scoring The striker scores points for winning hazards, losing hazards, and cannons. All points accumulated in a shot are counted.

Winning hazards The player scores:

a) two points if the cue ball hits the other white ball into a pocket;

b) three points if the cue ball hits the red ball into a pocket (the red may be pocketed only five times in succession).

Losing hazards The player scores:

c) two points if the cue ball is pocketed "in off" the white;

d) three points if the cue ball is pocketed "in off" the red. Only 15 consecutive hazards may be scored, whether winning, losing, or both.

Cannons The player scores:

e) two points if the cue ball strikes both other balls.

If the cue ball goes into a pocket after a cannon, it scores an additional two points if the white ball, or three points if the red ball, was struck first. Only 75 cannons may be scored consecutively.

Points to non-striker The striker receives:

one point if the striker's cue ball fails to hit another ball;

three points if the cue ball goes into a pocket after a miss.

Winning hazards

Losing hazards

Cannon

Duration Play lasts an agreed length of time, or until one side reaches an agreed number of points. A game is known as a frame.

Stringing Players "string" for choice of balls and order of play, ie each plays his cue ball up the table from the "D," and the choice goes to the player whose ball stops nearest the bottom cushion. Playing order is retained throughout.

Start The red ball is placed on the spot, and the striker places his cue ball at any point in the "D" and plays the first shot. When his turn is ended, the second player brings his cue ball into play.

When bringing a cue ball into play, no shot may be made directly at any ball within the balk area. If both balls are in this area, the cue ball must

strike a cushion outside the balk before it can touch either ball.

In a break, if the non-striker's cue ball is pocketed, it remains off the table until the end of the break.

When the red ball is sunk, it is immediately replaced on the spot. When the cue ball is pocketed, the striker brings it back into play by playing from the "D."

Balls touching If the striker's ball comes to rest against another ball, the red ball is replaced on the spot. The non-striker's ball, if on the table, is placed on the center spot; if off the table, it is left off, and the striker plays from the "D."

Making a shot The striker uses the tip of his cue to hit his cue ball in the direction of

another ball.

The cue ball must be struck and not pushed; and at the moment of striking, the player must have a foot touching the floor.

Balls must not be forced off the table.

Rests Players may use a rest to support the cue.

Making a break Each time a player scores from a shot he is entitled to another shot. Only when he fails to score does he forfeit his turn. All points scored up to that time count for the break.

Fouls and penalties A striker who makes any foul shot loses his turn and any score he has made in that break. In addition, he concedes points to his opponent for the following fouls:

touching his ball more than once in a stroke, one point;

forcing a ball off the table, three points;

not playing out of balk from the "D" correctly, one point;

making a push shot, one point. The following fouls incur no penalty points:

playing with both feet off the floor;

playing the balls before they are still;

striking the ball with anything but the cue;

playing the wrong ball;

playing out of turn;

playing from outside the "D" when required to play from within it.

Carom billiards

Carom billiard games are played on a billiard table with no pockets. The basic "straight rail" game with three balls is described here. A "carom," scoring one point, is made when the cue ball glances off one object ball onto the other. The first player, pair, or team to reach an agreed number of points wins the game.

The table has a slate base, covered with green baize. There are no pockets. A standard table has a playing surface 5ft by 10ft.
Features are:
a) foot cushion;
b) foot string;
c) foot spot;
d) center string;
e) center spot;
f) head string;
g) head spot;
h) head cushion;
i) side rails;
j) diamond.
(Strings are imaginary lines through the spots and parallel to the table ends.)

Break shot

Cues are similar in size and shape to those used for English billiards.
Balls Three balls are used: a red object ball, a white ball, and a white ball with two small spots. The balls must be of equal size and weight. Each player or side has one of the white balls for a cue ball.
Playing order is usually decided by "lagging."
If pairs or teams are playing, they each choose a player to lag for them.
The red ball is placed on the foot spot. Each player in the lag then takes a cue ball, and plays it against the foot cushion from behind the head string. One player lags to the right, and the other to the left, of the red ball.
Choice of playing order and cue ball goes to the player

whose cue ball at the lag comes to rest nearest the head of the table. Cue balls may touch the side rails during lagging.
A player loses the lag if his cue ball interferes with the red ball on the foot spot, or is clearly out of line and interferes with his opponent's ball.
The lag is repeated if both players are in error or if the result is a tie.
Break shot The break or opening shot is made with the red ball on the foot spot and the white object ball on the head spot. The cue ball is played from the head string, within 6in (center to center) of the white object ball. The cue ball must contact the red ball first.
Rules of play A player's turn continues until he fails to make

a scoring stroke, or commits any foul.
A player scores one point for each carom shot. Failure to make a carom results in the loss of one point unless the player makes a successful "safety" shot.
A game is won by the first player or side to score an agreed number of points.

Playing out of turn If the offender fails to score, it is a foul. He loses one point and ends his turn, and the incoming player must accept the balls is position.
If the offending player scores, his opponent must detect the error before a second shot is played. If the error is detected in time, the offender loses one point and ends his turn.
If the error is not detected in time, all points scored count and the player's turn continues normally. The offender must then wait for his next turn until all the other players have had a turn, and the new playing order is retained throughout the game.

A carom shot is made when the cue ball glances from one object ball to the other. It may do so directly or by way of touching a cushion.

Except at the break shot, the cue ball may contact either of the object balls first or may contact both simultaneously. Only three consecutive caroms may be scored when the balls are "crotched" (in a corner).

A safety shot allows a player to end his turn without penalty. The cue ball must either contact a cushion after striking an object ball (as shown), or drive an object ball to a cushion.

Safety shots are generally not permitted in consecutive innings.

Playing from safety It is a foul if a player fails to make an obvious attempt to score on his return to the table after a safety shot. There is a one point penalty and the player loses his turn. This rule applies until the player opens a turn with a deliberate attempt to score, and additional one point penalties are incurred for each offense.

Kiss shots are all counted, whether they assist in a score or deprive a player of points. The cue ball may kiss from one object ball to another. An object ball already struck by the cue ball may kiss the second object ball either into or away from the path of the cue ball.

Jumped balls If his cue ball jumps off the table, the player loses one point and ends his turn. The cue ball is placed on the head spot, or, if it is occupied, on the foot spot. If both are occupied, the cue ball is placed on the center spot. If the red ball jumps off the table, it is replaced on the foot spot. If the white object ball jumps off the table, it is replaced on the head spot. Any score made before object balls jump off the table is counted and the player continues his turn.

If all the balls jump off the table, it is a foul. The offender loses one point and ends his turn. The incoming player then makes a break shot.

Bounce on rail The cue ball remains in play if it rides the rail and then returns to the table. It is treated as a jumped ball if it remains on the rail.

Lagging

A carom

A safety

Foul: jumped ball

Frozen balls are balls that are touching each other or a cushion.

Frozen object balls remain in play as they are.

If his cue ball is frozen, a player can shoot away from the frozen object ball or have the balls spotted for a break shot. Failure to do either is a foul, resulting in the loss of one point and the end of the turn. If his cue ball is frozen against a cushion, it may be first played against that cushion.

Fouls All fouls cause the loss of one point and the end of the offender's turn. The following are fouls:
a) making a shot when any ball is in motion;
b) touching the cue ball during "warm up" stroking (the offender may not claim that the touch was his stroke);
c) making a push or shove shot, which is defined as a shot in which the cue tip remains in contact with the cue ball after the cue ball has struck an object ball;
d) making a double stroke, defined as a shot in which the cue tip again contacts the cue ball after the cue ball has struck an object ball;
e) touching an object ball with the cue;
f) shooting the wrong cue ball (after which the incoming player must accept the balls in position);
g) not having one foot on the floor when making a shot;
h) causing interference (after which the incoming player must accept the balls in position).

Snooker

The game of snooker is played on a pocket billiard table. Fifteen red balls, six colored, and one white cue ball are used. Points are scored by pocketing balls and by forcing an opponent to give away points through "snookers." It may be played by two persons, pairs, or teams.

Triangle A triangular rack is used to position the red balls for the start of play.
Cues and rests are the same as for English billiards.
Balls Snooker is played with:
a) one white cue ball;
b) 15 red balls;
c) yellow ball;
d) green ball;
e) brown ball;
f) blue ball;
g) pink ball;
h) black ball.
The 22 balls must all be of equal size and weight. English balls are $2\frac{1}{16}$ in in diameter, American $2\frac{1}{8}$ in.

Table Snooker may be played on any pocket billiard table.

Starting position

Starting positions The balls are positioned on the table as shown.
Scoring values Snooker balls score as follows:
red, one point;
yellow, two points;
green, three points;
brown, four points;
blue, five points;
pink, six points;
black, seven points.

Scoreboard

Scoreboard The score is recorded on a board showing units, tens, and hundreds.

Starting play A coin is tossed to decide who will play first. The game begins with the starter playing the cue ball from within the "D" at any red ball.

Rules of play The initial stroke of each turn must strike the cue ball against a red, so long as any red remains on the table.

If the striker succeeds in pocketing a red, he scores that ball and continues his break by attempting to pocket any non-red ball: he must nominate which ball he is aiming for and he must hit the cue ball against that ball. If he pockets it, he adds the value of that ball to his score.

Red balls that are pocketed are not replaced on the table; but colored balls are, at this stage, immediately respotted. The player's break continues, playing alternately a red and a nominated colored ball, until he fails to score on any stroke. The sum of points in his break is then added to his total score for the game to that stage, and it is his opponent's turn to attempt a break.

The opponent plays from wherever the cue ball has come to rest. If the cue ball is pocketed at any time, the break ends, and it is next played from the "D."

Play continues in this way until there are no red balls left on the table. The player pocketing the last red may attempt to pocket any colored ball. If he succeeds, that colored ball is respotted. Thereafter the colored balls must be struck by the cue ball and pocketed only in strict ascending order of value; and once pocketed, they are not put back on the table. A break ends when a player fails to pocket the colored ball of lowest value left on the table.

"On" ball The ball that is next to be struck is referred to as "on."

Duration The player with the highest score when all the balls are cleared from the table is the winner.

When only the last ball (the black) is left on the table, the first score or penalty ends the game—unless this makes the scores equal, in which case the black is respotted and the players draw lots for the choice of playing at the black from the "D." The next score or penalty ends the game.

Pairs and teams play as for singles, with turns alternating between the sides, ie a player of one side is followed, at the end of his break, by an opponent. Order of play within a side must remain the same throughout a game.

Respotting balls Red balls are not respotted, even if illegally pocketed. But any colored ball pocketed while there is a red on the table, or illegally pocketed at any stage, is immediately respotted (ie even during a break).

If the appropriate spot is covered, the ball is replaced on the first available spot in descending order of value, beginning with the black spot. If all spots are covered, any ball except the black or pink is replaced as near as possible to its own spot, on the top cushion side (ie away from the "D"), and without touching any other ball.

Where there are various equally close positions, preference goes to the one that is also nearest the top cushion.

The pink or black is replaced as close as possible to its spot, on the side toward the "D" and on the centerline of the table.

Balls touching If the cue ball comes to rest against another ball, it must be played away from that ball without moving it, or it counts as a push shot.

If it is touching an "on" ball, the striker incurs no penalty for missing the "on" ball or for striking another ball.

Balls touching

"On" ball

A "snooker" A player is snookered when a ball he must not play obstructs a straight line between the cue ball and the ball that is "on."

He must attempt his shot, and will be penalized for missing the "on" ball or for first hitting any other ball.

If he is snookered by an opponent's foul stroke, he may play any ball that he

nominates. If he pockets it, it is treated as a red, unless all the reds are off the table, in which case it is treated as the "on" ball from which he is snookered.

A snooker

"On" ball

192

Fouls

"On" ball

b

"On" ball

c

d

"On" ball

Fouls and penalties After any foul shot, the striker loses his turn and any score that he may have made on that break. His opponent receives the appropriate penalty score, and has the option of playing the balls where they have come to rest or of asking the other player to do so.

The minimum penalty score is four points. The following apply only if they give a higher penalty.

1) For pocketing the cue ball (**a**), missing all the object balls (**b**), or first hitting a ball that is not "on," the penalty is the value of the "on" ball.

2) For striking simultaneously, or pocketing with one shot (**c**), two balls (other than two reds, or the "on" ball and a nominated ball), the penalty is

the higher value of the two balls struck.

3) For a push stroke, jump shot (**d**), or playing out of turn, the penalty is the value of the "on" ball, or of the ball struck or pocketed, whichever is greater.

4) For forcing a ball off the table, or moving a ball when the cue ball is touching it, the penalty is the value of the "on" ball, or of the ball off the table or moved, whichever is greater.

5) For pocketing the wrong ball, the penalty is the value of the "on" ball, or of the ball pocketed, whichever is greater.

6) For playing with other than the cue ball, or playing at two reds with successive shots, the penalty is seven points.

7) For playing with both feet off the floor, or playing improperly from the "D," the penalty is the value of the "on" ball, or of the ball struck, or of the ball pocketed or improperly spotted, whichever is greatest.

8) For playing the balls before they have come to rest, or before they have been spotted, or when they have been wrongly spotted, the penalty is the value of the ball struck, or pocketed, or of the ball wrongly spotted, whichever is greatest.

9) For playing the ball with anything but the cue, the penalty is the value of the "on" ball, or of the ball touched, whichever is greater.

Pool

Pool is played on a pocket billiard table, with one white cue ball and fifteen numbered object balls. It can be played by two individuals, pairs, or teams. Points are scored for pocketing designated balls in designated pockets. The first player or side to reach an agreed number of points wins the game.

Table Pool tables have a slate base covered with green baize. Playing surface sizes range from 5ft by 10ft (standard) to 3½ft by 7ft; the length is always twice the width.
Features are:
a) foot cushion;
b) foot string;
c) foot spot;
d) center string;
e) center spot;
f) head string;
g) head spot;
h) head cushion;
i) long string;
j) side rails;
k) pocket.

Racking It is recommended that the 15-ball is placed in the apex of the triangle at the foot spot. The 1-ball is placed in the left apex of the triangle and the 5-ball in the right apex. The highest numbered balls should be placed near the foot spot apex and the lowest numbered balls near the broad base of the triangle.

Racking

Object balls

Balls Pool is played with 15 object balls numbered from 1 to 15, and a white cue ball. The balls are 2¼in in diameter and must be of uniform weight, between 5½ and 6oz.

Cue ball

©DIAGRAM

Break shot

Objective Players aim to be first to score an agreed number of points.

One point is scored for pocketing a called ball in a called pocket, and an additional one point is scored for every other object ball pocketed in the same stroke.

Duration A match is made up of an agreed number of "blocks." Each block is played to an agreed point requirement —usually 125 or 150 in title play.

Lagging Players "lag" to decide the order of play. The choice goes to the player whose cue ball comes to rest nearest the head of the table after being stroked against the foot cushion from behind the head string. The cue ball may touch the side rails.

The player winning the lag usually chooses to play after his opponent.

Break shot Starting with his cue ball behind the head string, the opening player must either:

a) drop a called ball into a called pocket, in which case his turn continues; or

b) drive the cue ball and two object balls to a cushion, in which case his turn ends and his opponent accepts the balls in position; or

c) scratch the cue ball into a pocket and drive two object balls to a cushion, in which case he loses one point and ends his turn.

He may shoot directly at the object balls or make the cue ball touch one or more cushions before contact with the balls.

Failure to achieve any of these objectives is a foul, and the player loses two points. At the option of his opponent, he then ends his turn or, with the balls reframed, is compelled to break again. Two points are lost for each consecutive failure to meet the break requirements.

Pocketing balls A player must always designate the ball he is aiming to pocket and the pocket in which he is aiming to score.

Combination, carom, and kiss shots are all legal, and the player need not state the type of shot he intends to employ. Illegally pocketed balls are spotted on the long string.

Balls bouncing from pocket If an object ball drops into a pocket and then rebounds onto the table, it is not considered pocketed. If the ball was the called ball, the player ends his turn. The ball remains in play where it comes to rest on the table.

Continuous play

Continuous play A player may pocket 14 object balls successively. After which:

a) the fifteenth object ball is left in position on the table and becomes the "break ball;"

b) the cue ball is also left in position; and

c) the 14 pocketed balls are racked, with space for one ball at the foot spot apex of the triangle.

The player then continues his turn. If he chooses, he may call and pocket one of the racked object balls.

Otherwise, his procedure is to pocket the break ball in a designated pocket and carom the cue ball from the break ball into the triangle of racked balls (as shown).

If he is successful, his turn continues. If not, rules for misses apply.

A player may continue counting 14 balls, having them reracked, and breaking until he misses, scratches, or scores the required number of points for the game.

Miss   Scratch

Interference with the rack
If an unpocketed fifteenth ball interferes with the racking of the 14 balls, the unpocketed ball is placed on the head spot. If an unpocketed fifteenth ball and the cue ball both interfere with the racking of the 14 balls, the 15 object balls are racked and the player has the cue ball in hand.
If the cue ball interferes with the racking of the 14 object balls:
the cue ball is in hand if the break ball is not within the string;
the cue ball is placed on the head spot if the break ball is within the head string;
the cue ball is placed on the center spot if the break ball or the fifteenth ball is resting on the head spot.
In the case of interference with the rack, the player has the option of shooting at a ball in the rack or at the unracked break ball.
If he elects to shoot into the rack, he must either drive an object ball to a cushion, cause the ball to hit a cushion after contacting an object ball, or pocket a ball. Failure is a foul, incurring a one point penalty.

Pocketing the fifteenth ball
If a player by one stroke legally pockets the fourteenth and fifteenth balls of a frame, he scores both balls. The fifteen object balls are reframed, and the player continues play from where the cue ball came to rest.

Misses A player's turn ends if he misses the shot called.
A miss carries no penalty, provided that the cue ball: hits a cushion after hitting an object ball; or
drives at least one object ball to a cushion (as shown); or
drives at least one object ball into a pocket.
Otherwise, the player has fouled, ends his turn, and loses one point.

Scratching
A player may scratch the cue ball into a pocket at the break shot or during continuous play. Scratches are also incurred during safety play on a ball frozen to a cushion, and when a player's cue ball jumps off the table.
At his first scratch, a player ends his turn, loses one point, and has one scratch marked against him on the scoreboard. This scratch may be removed by pocketing a ball at his next turn, or by playing a legal safety.
If he scratches a second time without removing the first scratch, he ends his turn, loses one point, and has two scratches marked against him.

Three scratch 15-point penalty At his third scratch in succession, a player loses one point for the third scratch, plus 15 points for the three successive scratches. The player is then required, with the cue ball in hand, to break the balls as at the start of a game.

End of a block
The first player to reach the point requirement must continue to play until all but one of the object balls on the table are pocketed.
If he fails to clear the table, his opponent attempts to do so. Whichever player clears the table makes the opening shot in the next block.
Subsequent blocks are won by the player who first scores the agreed number of points. But if the winner of the block is behind in total points for the match, play continues until one of the players has a score equal to the point requirement for one block multiplied by the number of blocks played.
In the final block, play ends when a player pockets the ball that brings his total to the specified number of points for the match.

Example of scoring procedure

Player 1	hdcp	1	2	3	4	5	6	7	8	9	10	11	12	13	14	15	Total		
K Dunn	B	3	4 5 6	7	2	5 5	1	0	2 f 1	5	8	1	3 5	2					
		3	7	13	20	22	27	28	28	29	31	36	44	45	48	50	50		

Player 2	hdcp	1	2	3	4	5	6	7	8	9	10	11	12	13	14	15	Total		
P Meier	15	1	3	2 5 1	4	-1 f 4	1	2	2 f 3	0	0	2 5	1						
		16	19	21	23	27	26	30	31	33	34	37	37	37	39	40	40		

Safety play

Safety play In attempting a safety, a player must either:
a) drive an object ball to a cushion; or
b) cause the cue ball to strike a cushion after contacting an object ball; or
c) pocket an object ball.
Failure is a foul with a one point penalty.
The player need not declare his intention to play safe.

Jump shots It is a jump shot if the player causes the cue ball to rise from the bed of the table.
A jump shot is legal if the player causes the cue ball to jump accidentally as the result of a legal stroke, or deliberately, by elevating the butt end of the cue ball in the center or above center.
A jump shot is a foul, with a one point penalty, if the player digs under the cue ball with the tip end of the cue.
Jumped balls If the cue ball jumps off the table, it is a foul. The player ends his turn, loses one point, and has a scratch marked against him. The incoming player has the cue ball in hand.
If the called object ball jumps off the table, it is a miss and ends the player's turn. The retrieved ball is spotted.
If a player scores the called object ball and then, as a result of the stroke, causes another object ball to jump off the table, he scores the ball legally pocketed. The jumped ball is spotted, and the player continues play.
A ball that comes to rest on a rail is considered a jumped ball. But a ball that returns to the table bed after riding a rail or hitting overhead lighting equipment is not considered a jumped ball and remains in play where it comes to rest.

Balls in motion A stroke is not complete until all balls on the table have come to a dead stop.
A stroke made before the balls stop moving is a foul. The offender ends his turn and loses one point. The incoming player can accept the balls in position or insist that conditions prior to the foul be restored.
Object ball within the string If a player has the cue ball in hand and the object balls are within the head string, the object ball closest to the string is spotted on the foot spot. If two balls are equidistant from the string, the lower numbered ball is placed on the foot spot.
The player then plays the cue ball from any point within the head string, shooting at the ball on the foot spot.
Cue ball within the string
It is a foul if a player with the cue ball in hand, fails to shoot from within the head string after a warning.
The offender ends his turn and loses one point. The incoming player can accept the balls in position or insist that all balls are positioned as before the foul.
If a head string foul is not detected until a player shoots and scores, he is credited with all balls pocketed and continues play. If he misses, it merely ends his turn.

Frozen cue ball When the cue ball is in contact with an object ball, a player may play directly at the object ball in contact with the cue ball provided that:
a) the object ball is moved and the cue ball strikes a cushion; or
b) the object ball in contact with the cue ball is driven to a cushion.
Failure to comply with this rule is a foul carrying a one point penalty.
Ball frozen to a cushion A player forfeits one point if he stops the cue ball in front of an object ball frozen against a cushion, whether his cue ball contacts the object ball or not. When playing such a shot (as a safety measure) the player must either:
a) pocket the object ball; or
b) cause the cue ball to contact a cushion after striking the object ball; or
c) drive the object ball to another cushion.
Each player is allowed only two legal shots in safety procedure on a ball frozen to, or within a ball width of, a cushion. On the third shot he must either:
a) drive the cue ball to a different rail; or
b) drive the cue ball to any rail after contact with the object ball.
If a player fails to make this shot correctly, all 15 balls are racked and he must break as at the opening of a game.
(Three scratch 15-point penalty rules apply to scratches acquired through safety play on a ball frozen to a cushion.)

Foot on the floor It is a foul if a player makes a stroke with both feet off the floor. The offender ends his turn and loses one point.
Interference by a player If a player accidentally disturbs a ball with any part of his body or clothing, it is a foul. He ends his turn and loses one point.
Cueing foul If a player touches a ball with any part of the cue but the tip, it is declared a deliberate foul. He loses 15 points and must break as at the start of a game.
Outside interference If anyone other than a player disturbs a ball, it must be replaced as near as possible to its position before the interference.

Eight-ball pool

Eight-ball is one of the officially recognized variants of pool. Unlike pool, the aim is not to score points but to pocket a designated set of object balls. Its appeal lies in the fact that not until the final stroke is made can a player be certain of winning.

Starting position

Objective Unlike its parent game, eight-ball is not won by scoring points. The aim of each player or team is to pocket a designated group of object balls.

The numbered object balls are split into two groups: from 1 to 7 and from 9 to 15. Each player or team chooses, or is allotted, one of the groups; the 8-ball belongs to neither group.

Each player attempts to pocket the balls of his designated group. When all the balls of his group have been pocketed, a player attempts to pocket the 8-ball.

The game is won by the first player or team to pocket the 8-ball.

Starting procedure Players "lag" to determine the order of play (see pool), and the winner of the lag usually allows his opponent to play first.

After the lag, the object balls are "racked" at the foot spot, with the 8-ball in the center of the triangle.

With the cue ball placed behind the head string, the opening player makes his stroke at the racked object balls.

If he pockets an object ball on the break, the group to which this ball belongs is his designated group.

If he pockets one or more object balls from each group, he may designate either group. If he fails to pocket an object ball, turns alternate until someone legally pockets an object ball and so determines his group of balls.

Play The player who pocketed the first object ball continues play. His turn continues until he commits a foul, or fails legally to pocket a ball of his own group.

Except after a successful safety shot, the incoming player starts his turn by playing the cue ball from anywhere within the head string.

Table For championship games, a standard pool table is essential. Informal games can be played on any pocket billiard table.

Cues are as for pool.

Balls One white cue ball and a full set of 15 pool balls are required.

Players The game is for two players or teams.

Pocketing balls A player does not have to call which ball he is trying to pocket, or which pocket he is aiming for. If he pockets one of his opponent's balls, even with a foul stroke, that ball remains pocketed and is credited to his opponent.

A ball from a player's own group is legally pocketed only if the player's cue ball first strikes a ball from his own group. A legally pocketed ball remains pocketed; an illegally pocketed ball is replaced on its spot.

A player may legally pocket more than one of his own balls with one stroke.

If a player legally pockets an opponent's ball along with one of his own balls, both balls remain pocketed and the player's turn continues.

A player loses the game if he pockets the 8-ball before he has pocketed all the balls of his group.

Safety play A player may end his turn by playing to safety. For a successful safety shot, the cue ball must contact a ball from the player's own group and then either the cue ball or a ball from the player's group must be driven to a rail.

After a successful safety shot, the incoming player must play the cue ball from wherever it rests.

End play When a player has pocketed all the balls in his group, he must attempt to pocket the 8-ball in a designated pocket.

A player makes a foul stroke and loses the game if, when attempting to pocket the 8-ball he:

a) fails to drive the 8-ball or the cue ball to a cushion if the 8-ball is not pocketed;
b) pockets the 8-ball in a pocket not designated before the stroke;
c) pockets the cue ball;
d) fails to hit the 8-ball if the cue ball was bounced off the cushion;
e) hits a ball from his opponent's group before the cue ball strikes the 8-ball.

Fouls and penalties General rules of conduct are the same as for other pool games. Similarly, the rules applying to balls bouncing from pockets, jump shots, jump balls, balls in motion, etc are substantially the same as for pool.

However, as the eight-ball game is not a game in which points are scored, the usual penalty for a foul stroke is for the player to end his turn and for any advantage derived from the foul stroke to be canceled.

Groups of object balls

8-ball

Table tennis

Table tennis is a fast-moving game that has achieved worldwide popularity. Rackets are used to hit a small, light ball backward and forward across a special table divided by a low net. Players win points by making shots that an opponent is unable to return. It is a game that can be enjoyed by experts and beginners alike.

Table A standard table measures 9ft by 5ft, with the playing surface 2ft 6in from the ground.
The playing surface is usually dark green and has the white marking lines illustrated. The sides of the tabletop are not considered part of the playing surface.

The net is made of fine mesh and is suspended across the center of the table by a cord attached to two supports. The net is 6in high and extends 6in beyond the sides of the tabletop.

A good service

A good return

Choice of ends and the right to serve or receive is usually decided by tossing a coin.
If the winner of the toss decides to serve or receive first, the loser has the choice of ends, and vice versa. The winner of the toss may require the loser to choose first.
In doubles, each pair decides which of them is to serve and receive first in the first game.
Change of ends The players or pairs change ends after each game until the end of the match. They also change ends in the last game when the first player or pair scores 10 points.
Wrong ends If the players are playing from the wrong end they must change ends as soon as the error is discovered, unless a game has been completed since the error, in which case the error is ignored. In any circumstances, all points scored since the error are counted.

Order of play The period when the ball is in play is termed a "rally."
The player who first strikes the ball in a rally is termed the "server"; the second is the "receiver."
"Struck" means hit with the racket or the racket hand below the wrist.
A stroke made with the hand alone, after dropping the racket, is not good; nor is a stroke made by the racket alone after it is dropped or thrown.
In singles the server must first make a good service, the receiver must make a good return, and then server and receiver make good returns alternately.
In doubles the server must make a good service, the receiver a good return, the server's partner a good return, the receiver's partner a good return, the server a good return, and so on in this sequence.

Service The ball is placed on the palm of the free hand, which must be stationary, above the level of the playing surface, and not cupped. The fingers must be kept together, with the thumb free.
The ball is then thrown by hand only, without giving it spin, nearly vertically upward, so that it is at all times visible, and so that it visibly leaves the palm.
On descent, the ball is struck to touch the server's court first and then, passing directly over or around the net, to touch the receiver's court. (Around the net is defined as under or around the projection of the net and its supports outside the side line.)
The ball must be struck at the first attempt. At the moment of striking, the racket must be behind the end of the table or an imaginary continuation of it.
In doubles the ball must touch the right-hand half of the court on the serving side and then the diagonally opposite court or line.

Returning service The ball must be struck to pass directly over or around the net to touch the opponent's court. If the ball, in passing over or around the net, touches the net or its supports, it is considered to have passed directly.
The ball must not be allowed to bounce twice before return, nor must it be struck by a player or side more than once consecutively.
Volleying—striking the ball in play before it has touched the playing surface on that player's side of the table—is not allowed, and loses a point.
The ball is considered out of play once it has touched any object other than the net, supports, playing surface, racket or racket hand below the wrist. A stroke made with the hand alone, the racket having been dropped, also puts the ball out of play.

Players The game is for two players (singles) or four players (doubles).

The ball is made of white or yellow plastic, has a matt surface, and weighs approximately 2.5g.

Racket International table tennis rules permit any size, weight, or shape of racket but most players use a racket of the type illustrated.
Racket blades are normally made of wood and must be continuous, of even thickness, flat, and rigid.
Blades may be covered with pimpled rubber or with a sandwich of cellular and pimpled rubber.
Each side of the blade must be of a uniform dark color, but the two sides need not be of the same color.

A game is won by the first player or pair to score 21 points, except that if both sides have scored 20 points the game is won by the first side to score two points more than the opposition.
A match consists of one game, the best of three, or the best of five games.

A player fails to make a good service

A player fails to make a good return

Points are scored by a player when his opponent:
fails to make a good service;
fails to make a good return;
deliberately strikes the ball out of sequence in a doubles game;
touches the playing surface with his free hand when the ball is in play.
A player also scores when: anything his opponent wears or carries comes into contact with the ball before it has passed over the end line or side lines while not having touched the playing surface; his opponent (or his racket or something he wears or carries) touches the net or its supports or moves the playing surface while the ball is in play.
Under the expedite system, a server also scores when he has received 13 good returns from his opponent.

A let is a rally from which no point is scored. It occurs when:
a) the ball touches the net or its supports in service, provided the service is otherwise good or has been volleyed by the receiver;
b) a service is delivered when the receiver or his partner is not ready, provided no attempt has been made to return the ball;
c) a player fails to make a good service or return through an accident beyond his control, such as a movement by a spectator or a sudden noise;
d) the ball is broken during play;
e) a rally is interrupted to correct a mistake in playing order or ends;
f) a rally is interrupted to apply the expedite system.

Change of service With certain exceptions, the service in singles and doubles passes from one player to another after every five points scored.
The service sequence in doubles is as follows:
the player to serve first of one pair (1a) serves to the player who serves first of the second pair (2a);
2a then serves to 1a's partner, 1b;
1b then serves to the fourth player 2b; and
2b serves to 1a.
From the score of 20-all, or under the expedite system, the serving sequence is unchanged, but each player serves only once in succession until the game ends.
The player or pair who served first in one game receive first in the next game.
In each game of doubles the initial order of receiving is opposite to that of the previous game.
In the last game of a doubles match the receiving pair changes its order of receiving when the first pair scores 10 points.
Any error in serving or receiving must be corrected as soon as it is noticed; all points scored after the error count.

The expedite system is introduced in match play if a game is unfinished 15 minutes after the start. It then applies to the rest of that game and to all remaining games of the match.
The umpire interrupts play after 15 minutes by calling "let." If the interruption occurs between rallies the game is restarted by a service from the player who is due to serve next.
The return strokes of the receiving player or pair are counted out loud, from one to 13, by an official other than the umpire. After 13 good returns the point goes to the receiving player or pair.

Baccarat and Chemin de fer

Games of the baccarat and chemin de fer family originated in the baccarat that became popular in French casinos in the 1830s. In the present century they have traveled from Europe to the United States, from the United States back to Europe, and from both points to casinos throughout the world. This process has resulted in wide variations in playing rules, and what is called "baccarat" in one casino may more nearly resemble the "chemin de fer" of another. Three basic forms of play are described here.

Value of cards

0
0
0
0
9
8
7
6
5
4
3
2
1

Players: at least two, but usually seven or more. Often persons without seats may also bet.

Croupier The casino provides a croupier, who assists players in making and settling bets, advises on rules and odds, and takes the casino's cut.
The croupier also plays the "bank" hand when the game is banked by the casino.
The casino makes an hourly charge for the croupier and his assistants, and for supervising the game.

The objective is to bet on a winning hand, ie on a hand with a higher point value than the other hand(s).

Hands are of two or three cards.
Cards score as follows:
a) face (court) cards and 10s, zero;
b) aces, one point;
c) any other card, its numerical value.
When scoring a hand tens are ignored—eg five plus seven counts as two not 12. Hence the highest possible score for a hand is nine.

The basic sequence of play is:
1) placing of bets;
2) dealing of hands;
3) receipt of another card on request;
4) comparison of hands and settlement of bets.

Equipment Several standard decks of playing cards are used.
Other equipment is:
a) a heavy table, padded and covered with green baize, and marked with a layout for nine or 12 players;
b) a card-holding box or "shoe," from which the cards are dealt one at a time;
c) a discard box, positioned beneath a slot in the table;
d) wooden palettes for distributing cards and payments to the players.

CHEMIN DE FER
The distinctive features of the "chemin de fer" game are that:
the role of banker rotates rapidly among the players;
only a bank hand and one non-bank hand are dealt;
bets can only be placed against the bank.
Cards Six or eight standard decks of cards are used.

The shuffle
1) The croupier places the decks face down on the table.
2) Players and croupier take groups of cards and shuffle them, and then shuffle the groups of cards into each other.
3) The croupier gathers the cards, gives them a final shuffle in large groups, gathers them all into a single

Chemin de fer

deck, and cuts the deck several times.

4) The croupier asks one of the players to make a final cut. (Often the croupier makes the actual cut, after the player has inserted an indicator (a blank or advertising) card at the point where the cut should be made.)

5) Often the croupier then inserts a second indicator card into the deck, around eight or ten cards from the bottom, to give warning of the end of the shuffled cards.

6) The croupier places the deck face down in the shoe.

7) The croupier deals three or four cards from the shoe, shows them, and discards them.

First choice of banker is either:
a) by lot;
b) by auction, with the players bidding the amounts they are prepared to put forward as the "bank";
c) by acceptance, the bank being offered first to the first player to the croupier's left or right (according to house rules), and then on around the table, clockwise or counterclockwise, until a player accepts the bank.
The croupier passes the shoe to the first banker.

Amount of the bank On the first play of a turn as banker, the bank is:
a) what the player bid for it if the bank was gained by auction;
b) any figure the banker wishes to put at risk if he gained the bank by lot or acceptance.
On all subsequent plays of a turn as banker, the bank is the amount stated on the first play plus subsequent winnings.

Betting takes place before any cards are dealt.
Players can only place bets against the bank—ie they bet that the bank will lose.
The total of bets on a single play is limited to the amount of the bank—the banker is never liable for payment of bets in excess of this.
The player to the banker's right (or left, according to house rules) has first bet.
Any amount of the bank he does not bet against ("fade"), may be bet against by the next player in turn.
Betting passes around the table until the entire bank is covered by several bets, someone has called "banco," or everyone has bet who wishes to.
Bystanders may bet if there is part of the bank left to cover or if one of them calls "banco."
If the bank is not completely covered, the amount not faded is safe for the hand and is kept by the banker whether he wins or loses.

"Banco" A player or bystander who wishes to bet against the entire bank makes this known by calling "banco." A call of "banco" makes all other bets void.
When two or more wish to banco, a player who bancoed on the preceding hand has precedence over all others. Otherwise, a seated player has precedence over a bystander and the order of priority among players belongs to the player who is earliest in the betting order.

Play is as follows.

1) The banker deals two hands of two cards each. The cards are dealt singly and face down, alternately to the table and to the banker himself. The "table" hand represents all players betting against the bank. It is played by whoever made the highest bet against the bank. If there are two equal bets, the player nearer the banker in the betting order has priority.

2) The player and banker examine their hands without showing them.

3) If the player's hand totals eight or nine, it is a "natural," and is immediately declared and turned face up. If it is an eight hand, the player calls "la petite;" if a nine he calls "la grande."

4) If the player's hand is a natural, the banker shows his own cards. If only the player's hand is a natural, all bets against the bank win. If both hands are naturals, a nine beats an eight. If both hands are naturals of the same number, it is a "stand-off" and all bets are returned.

5) If the player's hand does not contain a natural, he says "pass." The banker then examines his own hand, and if it contains a natural he declares it immediately and wins all bets.

6) If both hands have been examined, and neither contains a natural, the player may "draw" (request another card, face up) or "stay" (not request another card). His decision must be based on the rules of mathematical advisability (see table), except that in some games a player who has bancoed is allowed to ignore these rules.

7) Whether the banker then draws another card or stays depends on the card that he has just given to the player (see table), except that in some games the banker is allowed the option when holding a five hand and having given a four. If a player has bancoed and is allowed to use his judgment, the banker may also ignore the rules for drawing or staying.

8) The hands are shown. If there has been any error, the banker must reconstruct the play as it should have been.

Player

Player holding	Action
0, 1, 2, 3, or 4	draw
5	optional
6 or 7	stay
8 or 9	face

Banker

After giving	Banker stays on	Banker draws on
0 or 1	4, 5, 6, or 7	3, 2, 1, or 0
9	4, 5, 6, 7, (or 3)	2, 1, 0, (or 3)
8	3, 4, 5, 6, or 7	2, 1, or 0
7 or 6	7	6, 5, 4, 3, 2, 1, or 0
5 or 4	6 or 7	5, 4, 3, 2, 1, or 0
3 or 2	5, 6, or 7	4, 3, 2, 1, or 0
Player has stood	6 or 7	5, 4, 3, 2, 1, or 0

Natural 8s

Natural 9s

Winning The hand totaling nine or nearest nine wins.
a) If the totals are the same, all bets are returned.
b) If the banker has won, he collects all bets less any casino levy. In most countries the casino levies a percentage (usually 5%) on bankers' winnings. Sometimes the winnings on a player's first hand as banker are exempt from the levy. (In countries where a percentage levy is illegal, all casino profits come from the hourly rate charged by the casino.)
c) If the banker has lost, each player collects the amount of the bank that he had covered.

Keeping the bank If the banker has won a hand, he may keep the bank for the next hand.
In this case, the new bank comprises the original bank plus the winnings after any levy.
A player who keeps the bank is not permitted to remove any of his winnings between hands.
If the original bank plus winnings exceeds the house limit on bets, the excess is not at stake.

Passing the bank If the banker has won a hand but chooses not to keep the bank, he may take his winnings and pass the bank.
In this case:
a) the bank is offered to the players in turn until one of them accepts it, after which the new banker decides the amount of his bank; or
b) the house croupier holds an informal auction, and the bank passes to a player who will put up a bank equal to the one that has just been passed.

Losing the bank If the banker loses a hand, the bank is offered to the players in turn—as when the banker chooses to pass the bank. (An auction is not held.)
Reshuffling The cards are not reshuffled until at least ⅚ of the deck has been used— and usually not until the last few cards are reached.

BACCARAT BANQUE

Also known as *baccarat à deux tables* (double table baccarat), baccarat banque is the oldest European form of the game.

The distinctive features of baccarat banque are that: the role of banker rotates more slowly among the players or may be held permanently by the casino or concessionaires; one bank hand and two non-bank hands are dealt; bets can be placed only against the bank.

Except when specifically described here, the rules are the same as for chemin de fer.

Cards Three standard decks are used.

Banker Sometimes the role of banker is held permanently by the casino—or by concessionaires who pay the casino a percentage of their takings.

Otherwise the procedure is as follows.

a) The bank is auctioned to the highest bidder, who pays 2½% of his bid to the casino.
b) The banker does not lose the bank if he loses a hand, but holds it until he loses the whole bank or passes.

BACCARAT-CHEMIN DE FER (LAS VEGAS)

The distinct Las Vegas form of the game may be called baccarat, chemin de fer, or baccarat-chemin de fer.

The distinctive features of the Las Vegas game are that: the role of banker is usually held permanently by the casino, although it may rotate slowly among the players; one non-bank hand is dealt; bets can be placed either with or against the bank.

Cards Six or eight standard decks are used.

Banker When the role of banker rotates among the players, the rules for the bank are the same as for baccarat banque.

More usually the casino keeps the bank, and the procedure is as follows.

a) The limit on bets on a hand is not the size of the bank but the house betting limit. (The house betting limit will, however, sometimes be raised when a player requests this.)
b) There is no banco bet and no need for rules of precedence in betting.
c) A single player can play.
d) The casino takes a cut (usually 5%) from winning bets that have bet the bank to win.

c) The banker cannot withdraw any money from the bank unless he passes—but any part of the bank not bet against on a hand is not at risk.
d) When a bank is lost or passed, the bank is again auctioned. As before, the casino takes a 2½% cut from the winning bidder.

Betting and play differs from chemin de fer in the following ways.

a) The banker deals three hands—one to his right, one to his left, and one to himself.
b) Bets against the bank may be placed on either the right or the left hand, or on both hands. Betting on both hands is called betting "*à cheval*" (on horseback).
c) Priority for betting on the right table hand begins with the player sitting to the banker's right; for the left table hand, with the player to the banker's left. Calling "banco" is usually allowed, but not always.
d) Each hand is played by a player on the appropriate side of the table. The player playing the right hand always plays first. On the first deal, the hands are played by the players nearest the dealer on his right and left sides. Thereafter, a player continues playing one of the table hands until he loses a hand. After a player has lost a hand, the right to play that side's hand passes to the next player in rotation.
e) Table players are bound by the same staying and drawing rules as in chemin de fer. The banker may stay or draw on any hand, and will obviously concentrate on beating the hand on which most money has been bet.
f) Players betting *à cheval* lose only if the bank wins both hands, and win only if the bank loses both hands. Otherwise their bets are returned.

Baccarat banque layout

Baccarat – Chemin de fer layout

Betting Players may bet with or against the bank.
A player betting the bank to win places his bet on the appropriate numbered section at the table center.
A player betting the bank to lose places his bet on the numbered section in front of him.

A player may also back the bank to have a natural eight or nine, and if successful, he is paid the odds of nine to one.

Play is as in chemin de fer, except that all player's and banker's options are removed to become draw plays. Thus:
a) a player must draw if holding a hand totaling five;
b) the banker must draw if holding a three hand when he has given a nine, or a five hand after giving a four.

Faro

Faro or farobank is a very old banking card game. It was known as pharaon in the French court of Louis XIV. In the 1700s it was the most popular gambling house game in England. The following century it became equally popular in the United States, where it was often called "bucking the tiger."

Casekeeper

Equipment
a) A table covered with green baize, bearing the faro layout. The complete spades suit is usually used for the layout.
b) A dealing box from which one card can be slid at a time.
c) A casekeeper. This is a frame like an abacus used to show which cards in the deck have been played.
d) A standard deck of cards.
e) Betting chips.
f) Faro "coppers"—round or hexagonal chips of either red or black—used for betting a denomination to lose.
g) Bet markers—small flat oblongs of ivory or plastic—used to make bets over the limit of a bettor's funds.

Players
Up to ten can play. House officials are a dealer, a lookout who supervises betting, and a casekeeper official.
The house always banks.

Objective
Players try to predict whether the next card to appear, of the denomination bet on, will be a winning or a losing card.
Cards appear in play two at a time. The first in each pair is always the losing card, the second the winning card.

Shuffle, cut, and bet The dealer shuffles the cards, cuts them, and puts them in the dealing box face up. The exposed top card is called the "soda." It is ignored for betting.
Bets are now placed.

First turn The dealer puts the soda card face up to one side to start the discard pile or "soda stack."
He then takes the next exposed card from the box and places it face up to the right of the box. This card is the losing card. The card now exposed in the box is the winning card.

Between turns Any bets on the two exposed denominations are settled. Other bets may be changed and new bets made. The casekeeper is altered to show the cards that have already appeared.

Continuing play Play continues through the deck. In each turn:
1) the dealer removes the last winning card from the box and places it face up on the discard pile;
2) a new losing card is taken from the box as in the first turn;
3) the new winning card is exposed at the top of the box.

The casekeeper has pictures of the 13 denominations, with four large wood buttons on a spindle opposite each picture. At the beginning of the deal all the buttons are positioned at the inner ends of the spindles. As a card is taken from the box, one of the buttons on the relevant spindle is moved along toward the outer edge of the frame.
How far it is moved depends on whether it represents a winning or a losing card:
a) for a losing card it is moved until it touches the outer frame or an earlier button on the same spindle;
b) for a winning card a gap of about ½in is left between the button and the frame or between this and an earlier button.
When the fourth card of a denomination appears, whether it is a winning or a losing card, all four buttons are pushed together against the outer frame to show that betting on this denomination is at an end.

The last turn Three cards are left in the box for the last turn. The casekeeper shows which cards they are. The last card in the box is called the "hoc" or "hock" card.
For the last turn players may normally:
a) bet on any one of the cards to win or lose as usual;
b) "call the turn"—ie try to predict the precise order of all three cards (eg, queen first to lose, 6 second to win, ace last).
The turn is played in the usual way, except that when the winning card has been removed from the box the losing card is half slid out to confirm the denomination of the hoc card.
A player's bet is returned if the card that he bet to win or lose appears as the hoc card.

Continuing the game After the last turn all cards are gathered and shuffled for the next deal.

Betting There are three kinds of bet apart from bets on the last turn:
a) bets on a single denomination;
b) bets on a set of denominations;
c) bets that take action in every turn.

Bets on a single denomination are settled when a card of that denomination appears. To make the same bet again a player places a new stake on the layout.

Bets on a set of denominations are bets on groups of different numbers that appear close together on the layout (see placing of bets). They are settled as soon as any one of the denominations bet on appears. To make the same bet again, a player places a new stake on the layout.

Bets that take action in every turn remain on the layout until removed by the player. There are two such bets: a "high card" bet and an "even or odd card" bet.
a) In a high card bet the player bets that the higher denomination card of each pair will win in each turn, or, if he has "coppered" the bet, that the higher card will lose. (For this bet ace ranks low.)
b) In an even or odd card bet the player bets that either the even card or the odd card will win in each turn. (For this bet ace, jack, and king count as odd, and queen as even.)
With these two bets the player wins or loses on every turn. Each time he loses he gives the dealer a number of chips equal to his stake. Each time he wins he receives an equal number. The actual stake remains on the table until the player stops making the bet.

Placing of bets

HIGH CARD

Explanation of placing of bets diagram:
a) bets a single denomination (5);
b) bets two denominations horizontally adjacent (2+3);
c) bets two denominations diagonally adjacent (6+9);
d) bets two denominations vertically adjacent (2+q);
e) bets 6+7;
f) bets 7+8;
g) bets two denominations horizontally adjacent and separated by one other denomination (j+k);
h) bets three denominations horizontally adjacent (8,9,10);
i) bets three denominations in a right angle (3,10,j);
j) bets 6,7,8;
k) bets adjacent denominations in a square (4,5,9,10);
l) bets the even denomination card in each turn (the chip position is between the 2 and the table edge);
m) bets the odd denomination card in each turn (the chip position is between the 5 and the table edge);
n) bets the higher denomination card in each turn.

Bets to win using one or several chips All bets may be made with one chip or several chips.
If several chips are used, they are stacked vertically except for bet (c). For that bet they are tilted or "heeled," by moving the bottom chip in to rest on the corner of one card and tilting the remainder toward the other card.

Bets to lose using one or several chips In general these bets are placed as for bets to win but are "coppered" —ie a faro copper is placed on top of the betting chip(s). The only exception is where bet (c) is made with a single chip. In this case the copper is placed in the usual position not far from the tip of one of the cards, with the chip on top of it tilting toward the other card.

Betting one card to win and one to lose This bet can be placed on any two adjacent denominations or on bet (g).
a) If made with a single chip, a copper is placed on the edge or corner of the lose card and the chip is tilted toward the win card.
b) If made with several chips, one chip is placed on the edge or corner of the lose card and the remaining chips are tilted on it in the direction of the win card.

This bet is settled as soon as one of the denominations appears as a winning or losing card.
Last turn bet: "calling the turn" The stake is placed on the card bet to lose and angled toward the card bet to win.
a) When made with a single chip, a copper is placed on the card bet to lose on the edge nearest the card bet to win. The single chip is placed on it, tilted toward the card bet to win. Another copper is placed on top of the single chip.
b) When made with several chips, one chip is placed on the card bet to lose on the edge nearest the card bet to win. The remaining chips are tilted on the bottom chip so that they point toward the card bet to win.
When the third card lies between the winning and losing cards, the bet is tilted toward the outside of the layout. This shows that it avoids the middle card, ie the middle card is bet to be the hoc card.
Last turn bet: "cat hop" The stake is placed as for calling the turn.
Bet markers are used when a player wants to place on the layout at one time more bets than he has funds for.
For each marker placed on the layout the player must have staked an equal value in chips elsewhere on the layout.
If one of the player's bets loses, the dealer takes payment in chips. The player must then withdraw his marker bet unless the value of his chips on the layout still exceeds the value of the markers he has used.
If one of the player's bets wins, the player wins an equivalent amount in chips.
A "split" occurs in a turn when a single bet has covered both winning and losing cards.
a) A split on a single denomination occurs when two cards of the same denomination appear in a turn. The house takes half of any bets on that denomination; the other half is returned to the bettor.
b) A split on a set of denominations occurs when two cards of a group bet on by a player appear in a single turn. The bet is returned to the bettor.
c) A split on bets that take action in every turn occurs when both cards in a turn are of the same denomination or are both odd or both even.

The bet remains on the table and the bettor neither makes nor receives any payment.
Betting on "cases" When only one card of a denomination is left in the box, this is called "cases"—eg, "cases on the queen."
Most houses forbid a player to bet on cases until after he has bet on a denomination that could be split.
"Cat hop" bet On the last turn the casekeeper may show that the three cards left are not all of different denominations. "Calling the turn" is then replaced by the "cat hop" bet. It may be made on denominations or on colors.
a) If two of the three cards are of the same denomination, a player may make a cat hop on denominations, predicting the order of denominations as usual—eg, 10,6,10. (A player may still bet one denomination to win or lose as usual.)
b) If all three cards are of the same denomination, a player may make a cat hop on color, predicting the order of suit colors—eg, red, black, red. Cat hop bets are placed in front of the dealer according to whatever temporary regulations he states.
Settlement A player who calls the turn successfully is paid at 4 to 1. A player who makes a successful cat hop bet is paid at 2 to 1. All other bets are paid at even money (1 to 1).

STUSS

Stuss is also known as Jewish faro. It is a simplified form of faro, with a larger percentage in the house's favor.
Equipment:
a) a table;
b) a dealing box similar to the faro box, but with a recess ("pocket") at the bottom of the box, deep enough for the thickness of four cards. This prevents the last four cards of the deck appearing in play.
c) a standard 52-card deck;
d) betting chips of various colors.
Players and officials are as for faro, except that there is no casekeeper or casekeeper controller.
The objective is for a player to bet on a denomination that subsequently appears as a winning card before it appears as a losing card.
Cards appear in play two at a time. The first in each pair is always the losing card, the second is the winning card.

Shuffle, cut, and bet The house dealer shuffles the cards, cuts the deck, and puts it face-down in the box. Bets are then placed.
Betting A player may place as many bets as he wishes, but each bet is on one denomination only.
A bet is always for a denomination to win—ie that the next card of that denomination to appear will be the second (winning) card in a turn.
A turn
1) The dealer removes the top card from the box and places it face up to the right.
2) Any bets on the denomination of this (losing) card are collected by the house.
3) The dealer removes the next card from the box and places it face up to the left.
4) Any bets on the denomination of this card are won by the bettors. Their bet is returned together with an equal payment by the house.
Between turns Other bets may be changed and new bets placed.
Continuing play Play continues in this way through the deck. The two cards in play in each turn are added to those played previously, to form a winning and a losing pile.
Eventually no more cards can be dealt. There will then have been 24 two-card turns, and four cards still remain in the pocket of the box.
Pocket cards The dealer opens the box and shows the four remaining cards. If any bets had been placed on their denominations, they are all won by the house.
Splits If two cards of the same denomination appear on a turn (a "split"), any bets on that denomination are won by the house.
Second bets are bets on a denomination of which one card has already been dealt; usually they are bet on in the normal way. Some casinos, however, do not allow second bets. In this case, the last four cards are not "pocketed" but appear for play and for betting in the normal way.
Variants
1) In a very simple form of stuss, the cards are dealt from the hand.
2) Stuss is sometimes played as a private banking game; the role of banker is taken by the player willing to put up the largest bank.

Ziginette

Ziginette is the Italians' favorite way of seeing money change hands at cards. The rules given here are those played in gaming houses in the United States.

Cards used

Equipment:
1) one standard 52-card deck from which all the 8s, 9s, and 10s have been removed, leaving 40 cards;
2) a metal card box that allows only one card to be removed at a time.

Players Two or more people can play. One person is banker.
There are also two house officials. One, the "cutter," collects and pays bets for the banker and takes the house's percentage cut. (The house never banks the game.)
The other, the "lookout," keeps a watch on proceedings and transfers dead cards to the discard pile.

The objective is for a player to bet on a table card that is not matched by the time the banker's card has been matched. A card is "matched" when another card of the same denomination becomes visible at the top of the card box.

Choice of first banker is by deal—the first ace to appear (see p80). The cutter carries out the deal after he has shuffled the cards and had them cut by any player.

Shuffle and cut See p80. Any player other than the banker cuts the cards. The banker places the deck face up in the card box.

Deal The banker deals two cards from the box face up onto the table. The next card in the box is now visible: this is the banker's card.
If all three cards are of different denominations, players may now bet; if they are not, special rules govern further procedure (see the section on "playette").

Opening bet Any player other than the banker may place a bet on one or both of the table cards.

Betting limits The banker decides the minimum and maximum allowable bets and can alter them at will between stages of play.

Opening play The banker takes the banker's card from the box and places it so that one end rests beneath the card

Table card matched

box but most of it is visible. It stays in this position for the rest of the deal.
This exposes the next card in the box. If the card now exposed matches any card on the table (including the banker's card), any bets involved are settled. But if it does not match any card on the table, there is no further action in this turn, unless any player wishes to place a further bet.

Settlement of bets If at any time a card exposed in the box matches the banker's card, the banker loses all unsettled bets, ie he pays all outstanding bets by players on all table cards. Settlement is at even money—a winning player gets back his stake plus an equal amount from the bank. Play on this deal then ceases and the bank and deck pass one player to the right.
If a card exposed in the box matches a table card on which bets have been placed, these bets are won by the banker and he continues to operate the bank.
The house cutter pays out the banker's losses and collects his winnings for him. He takes a 10% house cut from each bet won by the bank.

Next turn of play If the banker's card has not been matched, then any settlement of bets and placing of new bets ends the turn of play. The exposed card is then taken from the card box.
1) If the exposed card has matched a table card, then the exposed card and the table card it matched are now dead (even if the table card had no bets placed on it).
The cutter takes both cards and places them to one side out of play. They are dead for the remainder of the deal, as are the other two cards of the same denomination still in the card box. When cards appear in the box that are the same denomination as cards already matched, they are removed and added to the discard pile. The discard pile is kept fanned out so that the denominations

of dead cards can be seen.
2) If the exposed card has not matched a table card, then it is placed face up on the table alongside the other table cards. It is now available for players to bet on in the usual way at the end of a turn of play, provided it is not immediately matched by the new exposed card in the box. If it is immediately matched, both it and the matching card are transferred to the discard pile in the usual way and the other cards of the same denomination are also dead.

Continuation of play Play continues in this way until the banker's card is matched.
At each turn of play:
1) The top card is removed from the card box.
2) If, on the previous turn, it had matched a table card, it is placed on the discard pile together with the card it matched.
If it was the same denomination as a card already matched, it is added to the discard pile.
If it had matched neither a table card nor a dead card, it is added to the table cards.
3) If the card now exposed in the box matches a table card, any bets involved are settled. If it matches the banker's card the banker collects all bets and the deal ends.
4) If the banker's card has not been matched, players can bet on any card now on the table. This includes any card just added to the table, providing that this card has not been immediately matched by the new card exposed in the box.

Playette This is the term used when two cards of the same denomination appear in the opening deal. It is usually ruled "no deal." The cards are removed from the box and reshuffled. Sometimes the rule is that the duplicate cards are "doubled up."

Doubling up—opening deal If two table cards match, they are placed together, and the top card from the box is dealt to fill the empty table position.

If a table card and the box card match, the box card is added to the table card's position. In either case, the next card in the box becomes the banker's card.

Doubling up—settlement of bets When any two cards have been doubled up then, with all denominations, no bets are settled until three cards of the denomination have appeared. For example, the bank does not win the bet on the 6s until a further 6 has been exposed;
the bank does not win the bet on the queen of hearts until two further queens have been exposed;
the bank does not lose until two further 10s have been exposed.

Tripling If all three cards of the opening deal are of the same denomination, then (providing "doubling up" is allowed) they are all placed together on one of the table hand positions.
No decision is reached on any bet, or on the bank, until four cards of a denomination have been exposed.

Change of banker A banker may pass the bank at any time that there are no unsettled bets on the table.
When the banker's card is matched he must pass the bank.
All cards are collected, shuffled, and cut before the new game begins.

Skinball

Skinball is a very fast action game played in the South and Midwest United States. It is very similar to ziginette and seems originally to have been a black American version of that game. It is also called skin or skinning.

Equipment:
a) one standard deck of 52 cards;
b) a card box that allows only one card to be removed at a time.

Players The game is played by three or more people. One person is banker.
There is also a house official who keeps a watch on proceedings, transfers dead cards to the discard pile, collects and pays bets for the banker, and takes the house's percentage cut. (The house never banks the game.)

The objective is for a player not to have his card matched before the banker's card has been matched. Also, if the player has made side bets, he aims not to have his card matched before the card of any player that he has bet against has been matched.
A card is "matched" when another card of the same denomination is dealt from the card box.

Choice of first banker is by deal—the first ace to appear (see p 80).

Shuffle and cut See p 80. After the cut, the banker places the deck face down in the card box.

Betting limits are decided by the banker and can be altered by him at will.

Opening play The banker slides the top card from the card box and deals it face up to the first player to his right. The player may accept the card or may refuse it for any reason. If a player refuses a card he is out of the game until the next turn of play. The card that has been refused is offered to the next player to his right.
As soon as a player accepts this first card, the banker deals a second face-up card from the box to himself: this is the banker's card.

Opening bet The player who has accepted the card states his bet. This may be for any amount within the betting limits.
Even if the bet is within the limits, however, the banker need not accept it. He may reduce it to any amount he chooses. If the banker does this, the player must accept the decision; he cannot withdraw.
Whichever bet the banker accepts, he places the corresponding amount of money in the center of the player's card.
The player then makes his bet by literally "covering" the banker's money with his own.

Next card in play The banker deals a third card from the box. If this card's denomination matches either the banker's or the player's card, then the bet involved is settled.
If the card matches the banker's card, the amount on the player's card is won by the player.
If the card matches the player's card, the amount on his card is won by the banker.
If the third card does not match either of the earlier cards, it is dealt to the next player in turn. He may accept or refuse it. If he refuses it, it is offered to the next player in turn. Once the card is accepted, a bet is placed against the banker in the usual way.

Bets between players When more than one player has a card, bets may be made between them.
A player bets that the other player's card will be matched before his own.
Either of the two players may suggest the bet; the other player must be in agreement for the bet to take place.
Money involved in bets between players is stacked to one side.

Matched cards Each time a card is matched, the houseman takes both cards and puts them in a discard pile. The other two cards of the same denomination still in the deck are not allowed to enter play. When one appears it is put directly into the discard pile and a further card is dealt.

Continuation of play As long as the banker's card is not matched, the deal and betting continue as above until each player has been offered a card. The banker then continues to deal further cards (one at a time and face up) to the table. Any card that appears that does not match either a player's card, a discarded card, or the banker's card is called a "fresh" card.
If there is a player without a card—either because he refused an earlier card or because his card has been matched—he is offered the first fresh card to appear.
If there is more than one player without a card, the fresh card is offered first to the player without a card who is nearest the banker's right.
If he refuses it, it is offered to the next player to his right without a card.
Any fresh cards that appear when every player is holding a card are placed face up in the center of the table. A player may accept any one of them as soon as the card he holds has been matched.
Each time a player accepts a card, he makes a bet against the banker in the usual way. A player with a card will often have side bets against every other player, but he must bet against the banker first.

Banker's card matched Whenever the banker's card is matched, all the players betting against him at the time win the amounts on their cards. If there are no unsettled side bets, the bank passes to the next player to the right. All cards are collected and shuffled for the next deal.
If there are unsettled side bets, the banker chooses either:
a) to continue to deal for the betting players only—he does not enter into any further bets himself and does not give out any fresh cards; or
b) to take the first fresh card dealt from the deck as his new banker's card.
Any player's cards that are matched while the banker has no card become dead without the players losing their bets.
After the banker has a new card, players without cards may take fresh cards as they appear, and place new bets. Although players with outstanding side bets may make new bets against the banker, they are not obliged to do so.
When the bank is exhausted, the bank must pass.

House percentage The house takes either:
a) 25% of the last winning bet of each deal; or
b) 2% from each bet won by a player against the banker, plus 2% of the banker's winnings, if any, at the end of his deal.

Trente et quarante

Trente et quarante is one of the most popular games in French and Italian casinos, although it is rarely found elsewhere. It originated in seventeenth-century Europe and is also known as rouge et noir.

Equipment:
a) regulation table with trente et quarante double layout;
b) six standard 52-card decks shuffled together to form a single deck of 312 cards;
c) an indicator card for cutting the deck.

Players Any number of people can play up to the limit that the table will accommodate.
Five croupiers operate the game: four control the bank and one acts as dealer ("tailleur"). A supervisor sits on a stand overlooking the table.

Value of cards Face cards count 10. All other cards count their face value, with aces counting one.

The objective is to bet which of two rows of cards will give a total points count nearer 31.

Shuffle and cut At the start of a round of play the dealing croupier spreads all six decks on the table. (If it is not the first round of play, the cards must first be taken from the discard receiver and sorted until they are all face down.) All croupiers and players each take a group of cards and shuffle them.
The croupier then gathers all the cards and gives them a further shuffle. He offers one player the whole deck to cut. The player inserts the indicator card at the point at which he wants the cards cut. The dealer cuts the deck at this point and the indicator card and all cards above it go to the bottom of the deck.

Play The players place their bets (see the section on betting).
The dealing croupier then takes about 50 cards from the top of the deck and deals one card face up onto the table. He then deals further cards face up, placing them alternately to the right and left of this first card. After each card he announces the total number of points now contained in the row. When the total equals or passes 31 points he stops dealing. This first row is called the "black" row whatever the suit color of the cards it contains.
The dealing croupier in exactly the same way then deals a second row below the first. This is the "red" row. He again stops dealing when the total equals or passes 31 points.
The row with the points total nearer to 31 is the winning row. (In the example illustrated, the black row totals 33 and the red row 37. Black therefore wins.)
The winning total will always be in the range 31 to 39 inclusive—ie between 30 and 40. It is from this that the game takes its name.

Betting All bets are placed against the bank. Before the play players bet in one or both of the following ways, placing their bets on the layout.
a) Players bet which row will win, either black (N for "noir" on the layout) or red (R for "rouge").
b) Players bet whether the suit color of the very first card dealt will or will not match the color of the winning row. If they want to bet that it will match they bet on C for "couleur" on the layout. If they want to bet that it will not match they bet on I for "inverse." (In the example illustrated bets on C win since the first card was the black 3 of spades and the total for the black row was nearer 31.)

Settlement of bets After the deal the dealing croupier announces the result. Traditionally he calls the results for red and color only, ie "Rouge gagne" (red wins) or "Rouge perd" (red loses), and "Couleur gagne" (color wins) or "Couleur perd" (color loses).
The croupiers collect all losing bets. All winning bets are paid off at even money (1 to 1).
If both rows tie at more than 31 (a "refait"), all bets are returned.
If both rows tie at 31 ("refait de trente et un") the bank takes half of all bets and returns the remainder; or, rather than lose half of his bet, a player may decide to leave his bet in "prison" (P on the layout) for the next deal. If his original bet is successful in this next deal, his bet is returned but earns no money. If it is unsuccessful he now loses all his bet. (Sometimes with a bet in prison the player may choose whether to maintain his original bet or transfer it to its opposite.)

Insurance bet Before a hand is dealt, a player can indicate that he wishes to insure against a tie at 31. The charge for this is 5% of his wager.

Card values

10
10
10
10
9
8
7
6
5
4
3
2
1

Black   33

Red   37

Card craps

This game was created to bypass laws banning dice craps. It is necessary to understand the game of dice craps (see page 174) before attempting card craps.

Equipment:
a) a special deck of 48 cards. It is made up of six denominations only—ace, 2, 3, 4, 5, and 6. In each denomination there are eight cards, two in each suit. For example there are eight 6s made up of two hearts, two spades, two diamonds, and two clubs;
b) betting chips.
Players Any number can play from two upward. One person is dealer and is known as the "shooter."
Choice of first shooter is by any agreed method.
Shuffle See p 80.
Cut Any player may cut; but the player to the dealer's left has the right to cut last. If he does not wish to do so, the right to cut last passes clockwise.

Play The shooter deals two cards from the top of the deck face up onto the table. This constitutes a "throw." The value of the two cards added together gives the score for the throw in just the same way as the two dice in dice craps.
Play follows the basic rules for craps. The first two cards on a come-out give either a natural (7 or 11), a craps (2,3, or 12), or a point (4,5,6, 8,9, or 10) that must be repeated before a 7 is thrown. After every come-out throw the two cards are shuffled back into the deck by the shooter and the deck is cut by him. This happens even if no decision has been reached (ie if a point has been thrown). If the shooter then still has to make a point, he deals further throws but does not shuffle these back into the deck. This continues until he makes the point or sevens out. The entire deck is then shuffled together and cut. If, on a point, the whole deck is used without a decision, the deck is reshuffled and cut by the shooter; he then continues, trying for the same point.

Change of shooter If the shooter sevens out he must give up the cards. He may also give up the cards if:
a) he has not made any throw in his turn; or
b) he has just thrown a decision.
The cards pass to the next player to the left.
Change of deck When two decks are available, any player may request a change of deck at any time. The change is made immediately before the next come-out throw.
Betting and odds See rules for private craps, p 175-176.

Double hardway Players may arrange bets on the "hardway" as usual. A "double hardway" is not a bet but a double payment made when the shooter throws a point number (4,6,8, or 10) with two cards that are pairs of the same suit, eg 8 with two 4s of hearts.
The payment is made by wrong bettors to those who have taken a normal "right bet" on the shooter making the point. This serves to equalize the right and wrong bettors' chances on even number points. Otherwise point number payment is as in private craps (see table on p176).
Open card craps is played as in open dice craps, with the "book" accepting bets and making a 5% (or 3%) charge.

Cards used

Payment by wrong bettor when cards make point

Point number	Point made normally	Point made "double hardway"
4	2-1	4-1
5	3-2	-
6	6-5	12-5
8	6-5	12-5
9	3-2	-
10	2-1	4-1

©DIAGRAM

Monte bank

Monte bank is the major banking card game of illegal gambling clubs in America. It is also called monte or Spanish monte.

Cards used

Cards A 40-card deck is used —a standard deck with the 10s, 9s and 8s removed.

Players From two to as many as can get around the gaming table. One of the players is banker.

There is also a non-playing house official called a "cutter." He assists the banker and collects a 25% cut from certain bets. When the bank passes, the amount collected by the cutter is divided equally between the house and the retiring banker.

The objective for a player is to bet on the layout card or cards that will first be matched in play.

Normally a card is "matched" when another card of the same denomination appears at the top of the deck.

Pair in top layout   Triple in top layout

Top layout

Bottom layout

Choice of first banker/ dealer is by low cut (see p 80).

Bank The banker places in front of him, in cash, the total amount he wishes to put at risk. The banker does not have to pay out an amount greater than this on any one hand. If the result of a hand presents a banker with losses exceeding the bank total, he pays off the highest bet first, then the next highest, until the bank is exhausted. Other bets are then void and are returned to the players.

Betting limits The minimum bet is governed by house rules. The maximum bet is the amount of the bank. A player betting the maximum on a hand does not prevent other players betting because his bet may lose.

Shuffle and cut The dealer shuffles. Any other player may claim the right to shuffle before the cut but the dealer shuffles last.

The dealer then places the cards in front of the player to his right. Any other player may claim the right to cut but the player to the dealer's right must cut last.

Dealing the layout Holding the deck face down, the banker deals two cards from the bottom. He places them face up on the table, slightly apart. These form the "top layout." He then deals two cards from the top of the deck and places them face up on the table just below the first two cards and slightly apart. These form the "bottom layout."

Pairs and triples If the two cards of the bottom layout are of the same denomination, the deal is void. The cards are collected and reshuffled. The same applies if two cards, one in each layout, are of the same denomination.

If the two cards of the top layout are of the same denomination (**a**), the dealer places them one on top of the other and deals another card alongside (**b**).

If this card is also of the same denomination, it is placed with the others and a further card is dealt (**c**).

If this card is the fourth of the the same denomination, the deal is void.

The cards are collected and reshuffled.

Betting involves predicting which of two cards or two groups of cards on the layout will be matched earliest. Players back a certain card or cards to be matched before another specified card or cards. Normally a card is "matched" when another card of the same denomination appears at the top of the undealt portion of the deck.

Bets are placed in cash on the layout. The position of a bet shows the card(s) bet and the card(s) bet against. There are four types of bet:
1) circle bet;
2) crisscross bet;
3) doubler bet;
4) Monte carlo bet.

Circle bet The player bets that a specified card will be matched before any of the other three cards on the layout. A successful circle bet is paid at 3 to 1.

Crisscross bet The player bets that the specified card will be matched before another one specified card on the layout.

A successful crisscross bet is paid at evens (1 to 1).

Doubler bet The player bets that one of the cards (unspecified) in the top layout will be matched before either one of the cards in the bottom layout, or vice versa. Alternatively, he bets that one of the cards (unspecified) to the dealer's right will be matched before either one of the cards to the dealer's left, or vice versa.

A successful doubler bet is paid at evens (1 to 1).

Monte carlo bet This is a combination of the other three types of bet.

Sample betting
a) bets 7 of spades;
b) bets ace of diamonds;
c) bets 7 of spades against 3 of clubs;
d) bets king of hearts against ace of diamonds;
e) bets 3 of clubs against king of hearts;
f) bets ace of diamonds against 7 of spades;
g) bets left layout;
h) bets bottom layout.

Sample play with pairs
Cards turned up:
1) jack of clubs, no action;
2) ace of hearts, bet (d) loses (crisscross bet not involving pair); all other bets undecided;
3) 7 of hearts, bet (a) wins, paid 3—1; bets (c) and (g) win, paid evens; bets (b), (f), and (h) lose; bet (e) undecided;
4) 6 of clubs, no action;
5) king of diamonds, bet (e) loses.

Matching with pairs and triples in the layout When cards of the same denomination have been dealt to the top layout, they are placed together (see the section on pairs and triples). A pair or triple is matched as usual when a further card of the same denomination appears from the undealt part of the deck.

But other cards on the layout are not necessarily matched when a card of their own denomination appears. To give all cards an equal chance, the color of the cards appearing at the top of the deck is taken into consideration.

Matching with pairs in the layout When a denomination in the top layout has been paired, then another card on the layout is matched only by a card which is of its own denomination and of a different color.

Matching with triples in the layout When a denomination on the layout has been tripled, another card on the layout is matched only by a card which is of its own denomination and of the same color.

Crisscross bets An unmatched pair or triple will be involved in some way in all bets on a layout, with the exception of those crisscross bets in which neither of the two cards bet is the pair (or triple).

Such crisscross bets are settled as soon as one of the two cards involved is matched in the normal way, ie by the appearance of any other card of its denomination.

For other purposes the card is not considered matched.

Play After bets have been placed the cutter says "That's all."

The dealer then turns the deck face up, showing the bottom card only.

If the card matches any of the cards on the layout, all bets involved are settled and the matched card is removed from the layout.

If the card does not match any card on the layout, or if there are still other bets unsettled, the dealer removes the bottom card and places it to one side, exposing the next face–up card. This continues until all bets have been won or lost, each exposed card being added to the discard pile.

The deal is complete as soon as the last bet on the layout has been settled. (This will happen before all cards on the layout have been matched.) The dealer then gathers all cards and shuffles them for the next deal.

House cut and banker's cut When a player wins because the card he has backed is matched by the very first card exposed, the house takes a 25% cut from the player's winnings.

When the bank passes, the total collected is divided equally between the house and the retiring banker.

House cuts are collected by the cutter.

Change of banker A banker may hold the bank for as long as he wishes, or he may be limited to a set number of deals agreed by players beforehand. However, a banker may pass the bank at any time that there are no unsettled bets on the table. He indicates that he is passing the bank by saying "Aces."

If the bank becomes exhausted, the role of banker passes immediately.

The role of banker always passes to the next player to the left.

Variant Sometimes the dealer adds unmatched cards from the deck to the layout. Players may place further bets on them as in ziginette (see p 208).

Sample betting

Matching with pairs

Does not match

Match

Matching with triples

Do not match

Matches

Sample play

Blackjack

Blackjack is the world's most widespread banking card game. It is also known as BJ, twenty-one, vingt-et-un, pontoon, and vanjohn. There are two main forms: that with a "changing bank"—the usual private game; and that with a "permanent bank"—the casino game. The two forms of the game have many features in common.

Examples of hands totaling 21

Card values

11
10
10
10
10
9
8
7
6
5
4
3
2
1

GENERAL FEATURES
Players Games are played by a banker/dealer and from one to six or seven or more other players (private games can have as many as 14 other players).
Value of cards Standard playing cards are used.
a) An ace counts as 1 or 11, at the option of the holder.
b) A "face" or "court" card counts as 10.
c) All other cards count their numerical face value.
A joker, if used, is only an indicator card and does not enter play.

Objective Each player tries to get a higher point count in his hand than the dealer—but the value of his hand must not exceed 21. A hand whose point count exceeds 21 is immediately lost.
A two-card hand with a value of exactly 21 (a face card, or 10, and an ace) is called a "natural" or a "blackjack."

Betting With the exception of the dealer, each player bets at the beginning of each hand. Only bets against the dealer are allowed.
At the end of each hand, the dealer pays those with point counts higher than his own. Onlookers may be allowed to bet on any player's hand, but not on the dealer's hand.
Basic sequence of play
1) Betting, and deal of two cards to each player.
2) Receipt of further cards on request by each player in turn —with the dealer last.
3) Settlement of bets.

BLACKJACK WITH A CHANGING BANK

Cards A standard deck of 52 cards (or sometimes two decks shuffled together), plus a joker that does not enter play.

Choice of first banker/ dealer is by deal: usually the first ace, but in some versions the first black jack, decides (see p 80 for procedure.)

Change of banker/dealer There are two alternative systems.

1) Each player has five deals as banker/dealer, after which the role passes to the next player to the left.

2) The deal passes whenever there is a hand in which a "natural" is dealt—ie when a player's first two cards total 21. The player with the natural has the option of becoming the new banker/ dealer on the completion of that hand.

When two or more players hold naturals, the player nearest the dealer's left has the first option.

If all players with naturals refuse the option, the present banker/dealer continues— unless he also refuses, in which case the role is offered around the table clockwise, beginning with the player to the immediate left of the present banker/dealer. If all refuse, a new banker/dealer is chosen in the same way as the original one.

Auctioning the bank
Private games are occasionally run so that the banker/dealer is always decided by auction. In all private games, however, a player who no longer wants to be banker/dealer may, between hands, put the bank and deal up for auction. However, if there are no bids he loses the bank and deal to the first player to his left (or, if that player refuses, the bank and deal are offered clockwise around the table until accepted or until a new dealer has to be chosen in the original way).

Shuffle and cut

1) The dealer shuffles the cards. (Any player has the right to shuffle at any time but the dealer has the right to shuffle last.)

2) Any other player cuts the cards. If several players want to cut, each of them must be allowed to do so.

3) The deck is placed, face down, on an upturned joker, which acts as an indicator card. (If no joker is available, the dealer "burns" a card—ie he takes the top card from the deck, shows it to all players and places it face up at the bottom of the deck. An ace may not be burned, and if an ace is turned up the deck must be reshuffled and cut again.)

Betting limits The dealer decides the minimum and maximum allowable bets, and can alter them at will between hands.

Bet and deal for the two forms of the private game

The betting and dealing stage of the private game takes two main forms.

a) As in the casino blackjack game, the players place their bets before they have seen any of their own cards.

b) As in the pontoon game of the British Commonwealth, the players bet after looking at their own first card.

There is no standard way of distinguishing between these: American rules for private blackjack games may quote the pontoon form, while a few Americans use "pontoon" to mean standard blackjack. We have used the name "blackjack" for form (a), and "pontoon" for form (b).

Bet and deal: "blackjack"

1) Before any cards are dealt, each player but the dealer puts his bet in front of him in full view.

2) The dealer deals one card to each player but himself, face down, beginning with the player to his immediate left and going clockwise. He then deals one card to himself, face up.

3) A second card is then dealt to each player, including the dealer, face down.

4) If the dealer's face-up card is an ace or a card worth 10 points, the dealer looks at his face-down ("hole") card to see if he has a natural. If he has, he immediately announces this and turns his cards face up. The other players then show their own cards. The dealer collects the bets of all players not having naturals; players with naturals usually have their bets returned, but in some versions of the game they also pay the dealer.

5) If the dealer's face-up card is not an ace or a 10 point, or if he finds that he does not have a natural, then the player to the dealer's left commences play.

Bet and deal: "pontoon"

1) The dealer deals one card face down to each player, including himself, beginning with the player to his immediate left and going clockwise.
Each player, including the dealer, looks at his own card.

2) Each player, except the dealer, puts his bet in front of him in full view.
The dealer may call for all bets to be doubled. Any player refusing to double drops out of the hand and loses his original bet.
If the dealer has doubled, any other player may then redouble his own individual bet.

3) The dealer deals a second card, face up, to each player including himself.

4) The dealer then considers if he has a natural, as in the "blackjack" game. If he has a natural, he collects from each player twice the amount of that player's current bet—except that from any other player with a natural he collects only that player's bet.

5) If the dealer's face-up card is not an ace or a 10 point; or if he finds that he does not have a natural, then the player to the dealer's left commences play.

© DIAGRAM

First player's hand The player to the dealer's left looks at his hand and commences play.
a) If he has 21 points, he shows his cards, claims a natural, and is paid by the dealer unless the dealer also has a natural.
b) If his card total is less than 21 points, he has the option of taking further cards.
If he feels that the points count he already holds is closer to 21 than the dealer is likely to achieve, then he can say "I stand," and he receives no further cards.
If he decides to attempt a total closer to 21, he can say "I draw" or "hit me," and receives another card face up. He can repeat this until he is satisfied with his hand, when he says "I stay." However, if his point count goes over 21, he must announce this immediately by saying "bust." If a player goes "bust," he turns his cards face up, the dealer collects his bet, and the player's cards are placed face up at the bottom of the deck. He is then out of the game until the next hand.
Subsequent player's hands Once a player has said "I stand," "I stay," or "I bust," play passes to the player to his left. This continues until all players have had the chance of drawing further cards.

Dealer's hand The dealer plays last.
If all players have bust, he simply discards his cards and begins the next hand. Otherwise he turns his hidden card face up, and decides to stay or to "draw" (giving himself further cards, face up) until he is satisfied or he exceeds 21 (busts).
Once the dealer's hand is completed, all hands still in the game are shown.

Doubling down is a procedure allowed in the "permanent bank" game and often incorporated in the "blackjack" form of the "changing bank" game.
In his turn a player may, after looking at his first two cards, decide to "double down"—ie with his original two cards face up, he doubles his original bet and receives one further card only, face down. He may not look at this card until the dealer turns it up after all other players and the dealer have completed their turns of play. (Sometimes doubling down is allowed only when the first two cards total 10 or 11.)

Buying is a procedure sometimes played in the "pontoon" form of the "changing bank" game.
At his turn, a player may "buy" a card: instead of receiving a further card face up, he adds to his original bet and receives a further card face down. The amount of the additional bet must be at least the minimum, but not greater than the original bet.
Buying can be repeated for further cards if the player wishes; or he may "twist"— ie draw further cards face up in the normal way. However, once a player has twisted he is not allowed to buy.

Player 4: bust

Player 3: buying (pontoon)

Player 3: doubling down (blackjack)

Irregularities
a) If a player is missed on the first round of dealing, he must ask for a card from the top of the deck before the second round of dealing begins, or must stay out for that deal.
b) If a player receives two cards on the first round of dealing, he has the choice of: discarding either one; or playing both hands with his original bet on each.
c) If a player in the "pontoon" game receives his first card face up, he can either:
bet, and receive the next card face down; or
drop out of that hand.
d) If a player receives two cards on the second round of dealing, he discards either one.

e) If a card appears face up in the deck, a player has the choice of accepting or refusing it.
f) If a player receives a card that he did not ask for, he may either keep or discard it.
g) If a player has stood on a total of over 21, he pays the dealer twice his original bet even if the dealer has bust. (All discards are placed face up at the bottom of the deck. They may not be claimed by the next player in turn.)

Settlement If the dealer goes bust, he pays all players who have not bust.
If he does not bust, he collects the bets of all players with a lower total, and pays out to all players with a higher total who have not bust.
Where a player and the dealer have the same total, rules vary. Sometimes the player's bet is returned, but often (more commonly in the "pontoon" game) the dealer collects.
All winning bets are paid off by the dealer at even money, except that a player who has beaten the bank with a natural is paid off at two to one.

Continuing play As each bet is settled, the player's cards are given to the dealer and placed face up at the bottom of the deck.
Play of further hands then continues from the same deck, without a shuffle, until the face-up cards are reached. All face-up cards are then shuffled by the dealer, cut by another player, and a joker or burnt card is used as an indicator as before.

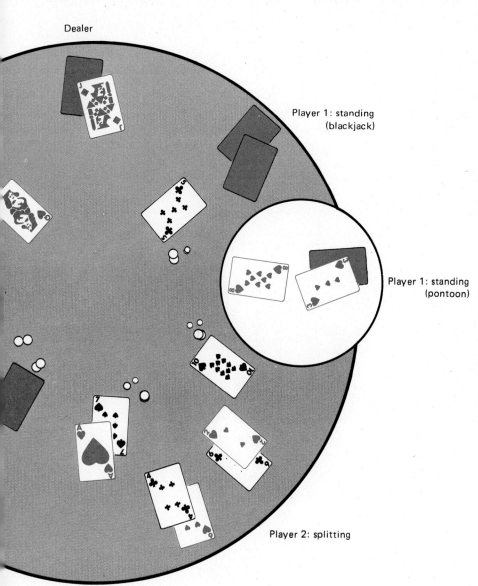

Dealer

Player 1: standing
(blackjack)

Player 1: standing
(pontoon)

Player 2: splitting

Splitting pairs is a procedure allowed in the "permanent bank" game, and often incorporated in both the "blackjack" and "pontoon" forms of the "changing bank" game.

If a player's first two cards are a pair (eg two 6s or two kings), they may be "split" if the player wishes—ie they may be treated as the basis of two separate hands.

In his turn of play, the player with the pair turns it face up—one card to his right and one to his left. He places his original bet by one of the cards and an equal amount by the other. The dealer then deals one card, face up, to the card to the player's right—after which the player plays this hand off in the normal way. When he has finished (stood, stayed, or bust), he receives another face-up card, dealt to the card to his left, and then plays off this hand.

If, on splitting and receiving a new card other than an ace, a player forms a further pair, he may split the pair again if he again puts out an amount equal to his original bet. Any further pairs may also be split. If aces are split, one card may be drawn to each split ace. A 21 point count made in two cards after splitting does not count as a natural—it is paid off at even money and the bank does not change hands.

Bonus payments In the "pontoon" game, a player other than the dealer can win his bet with certain special hands. These hands are declared and paid off as soon as they have been achieved.
a) A hand with five or more cards totaling 21 or under: for a five-card hand, a player receives double his bet; for a six-card hand, a player receives four times his bet; for a seven-card hand, eight times his bet, and so on. The win stands even if the dealer achieves a total nearer to 21.
b) Triple 7s: for a 21 made with three 7s, a player receives three times his bet.
c) 8,7,6: for a 21 made with an 8,7, and 6, a player receives double his bet.

None of these is a special hand if held by the dealer. They are then judged only according to their points count: a banker's five-card hand is beaten by a player's hand with a higher point count, and a player's win on a natural stands against a banker's triple 7s or 8,7,6.

a

b

c

BLACKJACK WITH A PERMANENT BANK
Equipment:
a) a regulation blackjack table, with six or seven betting spaces on the layout;
b) a rack containing betting chips;
c) a card-dealing box ("shoe");
d) a discard receiver;
e) one, two, or four standard 52-card decks, shuffled together;
f) two blank or advertising cards to be used as indicator cards—one to cut the deck and one to mark the end of the shuffled cards.

Participants:
1) a permanent house dealer/banker;
2) one to six or seven active players.
There is also a casino observer/supervisor, who controls play and whose decision is final.
Shuffle and cut
1) Only the dealer shuffles. He may reshuffle at any time.
2) After he has shuffled, he offers the deck to a player to cut. (Casino regulations may require an "indicator card" cut, in which the dealer holds the deck and the player inserts a blank or advertising card to indicate the point where he wants the deck cut. The dealer then cuts the deck, with the indicator card going to the bottom.)

3) In many casinos, the dealer then inserts a second indicator card about 40 cards from the bottom of the deck to prevent the last cards of any shuffle coming into play.
4) If a shoe is being used, the dealer places the deck in it, face down.
5) The dealer then deals a few (usually three) cards from the top of the deck and places them to one side, out of play.

Betting limits The casino sets the minimum and maximum bet limits. (A casino will often agree to raise the maximum at a player's request.)

Dealer's play

a Stay on 17   **b** Draw on 16

Bet and deal

1) Before any cards are dealt, each player but the dealer puts his bet on the layout in the betting space directly in front of him.

If empty betting spaces are available, players are allowed in most casinos to bet on and receive more than one hand.

2) The dealer deals one card to each player, beginning with the player to his immediate left and going clockwise, and then deals one card to himself. Then in the same way he deals a second card to each player and to himself. Whether cards are dealt face up or face down varies from casino to casino; possibilities are illustrated here.

3) If the dealer's face-up card is a 10 point or an ace, he looks at his face-down card to see if he has a natural, exactly as in the "changing bank" game. If he has a natural, he immediately collects the bets of all players who do not have naturals; players with naturals always have their bets returned.

(In some casinos, to prevent cheating by the collaboration of a player and a crooked dealer, the dealer is not allowed to look at, or sometimes even to deal, his own face-down card until all other players' hands are completed.)

4) If the dealer's face-up card is not a 10 point or an ace; or if he finds that he does not have a natural; or if he may not look at his face-down card: then the player to the dealer's left commences play.

Dealing possibilities:

a) dealer and all players: first card received face down, second face up.

b) Dealer's first card face up, second face down; players' first and second cards face down.

c) Dealer's first card face up, second face down; players' first and second cards face up.

d) Dealer's first card face down, second face up; players' first and second cards face up.

e) Dealer's first card face up, second face down; players' first card face down, second face up.

Insurance bet If the dealer's face-up card is an ace, players are in many casinos allowed to place an insurance bet against being beaten by a dealer's natural.

Before the dealer looks at his face-down card, a player wishing for insurance puts out an amount equal to half his present bet. If the dealer has a natural, the player receives two to one on his insurance bet; otherwise the insurance bet is lost.

Play If a player is playing more than one hand, he must play out the hand farthest to his right before looking at his next hand or hands.

Play is as for the private game, with splitting and double downing but no buying allowed.

Dealer's play In the "permanent bank" game, the dealer has no decisions to make:

a) if his count is, or reaches, 17 or more—he must stay;

b) if the count is 16 or less he must draw;

c) when he holds an ace he must accept a count of the ace as 11 and not draw if this gives him 17 or more without busting.

(As the dealer has no option in his play, it does not matter if he sees the players' hands. For this reason players' hands are dealt face up in some casinos.)

Settlement is as for the "changing bank" game, except that:

a) when a player and the dealer have the same total, the player's bet is always returned;

b) naturals are paid at odds of three to two, not two to one;

c) there are no bonus payments.

Irregularities are treated in the same way as in the "changing bank" game.

VARIANTS OF BLACKJACK

There are a number of games whose basic differences from blackjack are the card values and the points count that the players are attempting to reach.

SEVEN AND A HALF

This is an Italian-American variant of blackjack. The rules are as for blackjack with the following exceptions.

Cards The 8s, 9s, and 10s are removed from a standard deck to give a deck of 40 cards. No indicator card is used.

Objective Players aim to get a total points count of $7\frac{1}{2}$:
non-court cards count their numerical face value, with aces counting 1 point;
the king of diamonds can be given the value of any card the holder chooses;
other court cards each count $\frac{1}{2}$ point.

Play The player receiving the king of diamonds in a preliminary deal becomes the dealer for the first hand.
The dealer decides and alters betting limits at will. A player not wishing to bet on a round can say "Deal me out."
The deal is one card face down, after which a player stands or draws one or more cards face up.
$7\frac{1}{2}$ in two cards is announced and settled immediately. Unless the dealer also has $7\frac{1}{2}$ in two cards, it is paid double and wins the bank (If two or more players have $7\frac{1}{2}$ in two cards, the bank goes to the player nearest the banker's left).
Bust—8 or more with any number of cards—is also settled immediately.
The dealer then plays, and pays surviving players with a higher total. He returns the bet of any player with the same total as himself.
The dealer shuffles the deck after every round.

TEN AND A HALF

Ten and a half or "*saton pong*" is the Dutch equivalent of seven and a half. The rules are as for seven and a half, with the following exceptions.
It is played with a standard 52-card deck.
Players aim for a total points count of $10\frac{1}{2}$. A count of $10\frac{1}{2}$ is always announced immediately. $10\frac{1}{2}$ in two cards is paid double.
The dealer places discards at the bottom of the deck, face up. The deal changes by passing to the left when the whole deck has been used—though the current dealer is allowed to reshuffle used cards to complete a half finished hand.

Card values

½
½
½

Any value

7
6
5
4
3
2
1

Card values

½
½
½

10
10
9
8
7
6
5
4
3
2
1

MACAO

Macao or "three naturals" is a variant of blackjack that was popular in the 1920s and 1930s.

It is played with a standard 52-card deck.

Players aim for a total points count of 9 in one or more cards.

Card values are:

zero for court cards and 10s; the numerical face value of all other cards (with aces counting 1).

The deal is one card, face down.

A player with a 9,8, or 7 in one card announces it immediately. The dealer then shows his own card, and pays if the player's card is higher.

For a 9 in one card a winning player is paid three times his bet, for an 8 twice, and for a 7 one for one.

Players and dealer without a 7,8, or 9 in one card, then draw one or more cards toward a total of 9.

The dealer then collects and pays out on remaining bets.

A player who ties with the dealer has his bet returned.

Card values

0 0 0 0 9 8 7 6 5 4 3 2 1

FIFTEEN

Fifteen, also called quince, cans, or ace low, is a blackjack variant for two players with one acting as dealer.

Players aim for a points count of 15. Court cards count 10; other cards their numerical face value (with ace as 1). Dealer and non-dealer place equal amounts in a pool before the deal.

The deal is one card face down. The non-dealer stands, or draws one or more cards face up. He does not announce if he busts—he says only "I stay." The dealer then stands or draws.

Both players then show their face-down cards. The player nearer 15 without busting wins. If both players tie or bust, bets are left in the pool for the next deal.

The loser of one hand deals for the next.

Card values

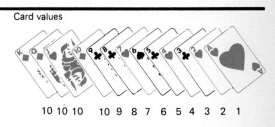

10 10 10   10 9 8 7 6 5 4 3 2 1

FARMER

This is an interesting variant of blackjack for two to eight players.

One player, the "farmer," is the equivalent of the banker/dealer in other games of the blackjack family, but in this game players also make an ante bet into a central pool or "farm."

The money in the farm is won only when a player has a points count of exactly 16; other settlements are made between player and farmer after each round.

Cards 45 cards are used: a standard 52-card deck with all the 8s and three of the 6s removed (the 6 of hearts is retained in the deck).

Objective Players aim for a total points count of 16: court cards count 10 points; other cards their face value (with aces counting 1).

Choice of first farmer is as for the banker/dealer in blackjack, except that the deciding card is the 6 of hearts.

Ante bet Each player puts one unit into the farm.

Shuffle The farmer shuffles. Any other player has the right to shuffle, but the farmer has the right to shuffle last.

Cut The player to the farmer's right is offered the cut. If he does not wish to cut, any other player may do so. If no other player wishes to cut, the farmer must cut.

Deal The farmer deals one card face down to each player, including himself, beginning with the player to his left and going clockwise.

Play The player to the farmer's left begins. He looks at his card and then receives one further card from the farmer.

If his total now exceeds 16, he does not announce this but says "I stay" and receives no further cards. He does not show his hand.

If his card total is less than 16, he can either stay or receive further cards as he wishes. When he is satisfied with his hand or when his total exceeds 16, he says "I stay," receives no further cards, and keeps his hand concealed.

Play then passes to the player to the first player's left, and play continues as described until all other players, including the farmer, have received at least one further card and had the chance to draw others.

Settlement At the end of the round, all hands are shown and settlement is as follows.

a) Each player who has a count of over 16 points must pay one unit to the farmer who dealt the hand. (The farmer does not have to pay anyone if his hand exceeds 16 points.)

b) A player holding 16 points wins the farm (the central pool) and becomes the next farmer. If more than one player holds a total of 16, the order of precedence when deciding the new farmer is:

the player with the 6 of hearts;
the player with fewest cards;
the current farmer if he has 16 points;
the player nearest the farmer's left.

c) If no-one holds a total of 16, the farm is not won. The player with the total nearest 16 then receives one unit from each player with a lower total (but not from players who have bust).

If two or more players have equal totals, they divide the units won from the other players. The same farmer then deals the next hand, and all players put a further ante into the farm.

Farmer

Player 3: loses

Player 1: bust, pays one unit

Player 2: wins the farm

10
10
10

6

10
9
7
5
4
3
2
1

Card values

Poker

Poker is played all over the world. It has been called the national card game of the United States of America, where it developed its present form. Poker ranks with blackjack among card games. Although the betting element is central to both games, they also allow for great skill; it is this that sets them apart from most pure gambling games.

GENERAL RULES
Equipment
1) One standard deck of 52 cards (see also the section on arrangements p 229).
2) One or two jokers as "wild" cards if desired (see also the section on wild cards p 226).
3) Betting chips or cash.

Players: two to eight or more. Certain forms of poker can be played by up to 14 people. No alliances are allowed; a player may play only for himself.

Basic terms The usage of some poker terms is not standard. In the following text a "hand" means the cards, or the particular combination of cards, held by a player.
A single game, from one shuffle to the next, is here called a "play" (rather than a "hand").

Objective Each player tries to maximize his winnings.
On each play all bets are put into a common pool (the "pot").
One player wins the pool on a play if:
a) he holds a higher ranking hand than anyone still betting at the end (the "showdown"); or
b) all other players drop out of the betting before the showdown in the belief that they cannot win (see also the section on bluffing p 227).

Rank of cards Cards rank in the normal order (see p 80). Ace ranks high, except in the 5,4,3,2,ace sequence; in a "high-low" game it may rank either high or low (see p 233). Sometimes low-ranking cards (2s, 3s, and even 4s and 5s) are removed from the deck to speed up the game. The suits are not ranked.

Poker hands In standard poker all hands must, for scoring (showdown) purposes, contain five cards, although fewer or more than this may be held at different stages of the game.
The following hands are universally recognized. Each hand loses to the one listed before it, and defeats the one listed after it. This order derives from the mathematical probabilities involved.

1) **Straight flush** Five cards in sequence of the same suit. (A, k, q, j, 10 of the same suit is known as a "royal flush.")
2) **Four of a kind or "fours"** Four cards of the same denomination, and one unmatched card.
3) **Full house** Three cards of one denomination, and two cards of another denomination.
4) **Flush** Five cards of the same suit, but not in sequence.
5) **Straight** Five cards in sequence, but not of the same suit.
6) **Three of a kind or "threes"** Three cards of the same denomination, and two unmatched cards.
7) **Two pairs** Two cards of one denomination, two cards of another denomination, and one unmatched card.

Straight flush

Four of a kind

Full house

Flush

Straight

Three of a kind

Two pairs

Pair

8) One pair Two cards of the same denomination, and three unmatched cards.
9) High card Five unmatched cards.
Other hands are sometimes accepted locally (eg a "blaze" denotes any five court cards). Their inclusion and their ranking should be agreed before the game begins.

High card

Hands of the same rank
When poker hands are of the same rank, the winning hand is decided by the rank of the cards involved.
The following rules apply where no wild cards are used.
1) Straight flush: the highest ranking card in a sequence decides the best hand. Thus a royal flush is the highest when there are no wild cards. Note that the ace in a 5, 4, 3, 2, ace sequence ranks low, so this hand would be beaten by 6, 5, 4, 3, 2. The same rule applies to straights.
2) Four of a kind: the hand with the highest ranking matched cards wins.
3) Full house: the hand with the highest ranking "three of a kind" wins.
4) Flush: the hand with the highest ranking card wins. If the highest cards are the same denomination, the next highest are compared. This continues down to the lowest, until a difference is found.
5) Straight: as for straight flush.
6) Three of a kind: as for four of a kind.
7) Two pairs: the hand with the highest ranking pair wins. If the higher pairs in two hands are the same, the lower pairs

are compared. If both pairs in two hands are the same, the hand with the best-ranking unmatched card wins.
8) One pair: the hand with the highest ranking pair wins. If the pairs in two hands are the same, the highest unmatched cards are compared. If these are the same, the next highest are compared. This continues down to the lowest, until a difference is found.
9) High card: as for flush.

Hands tie if they contain exactly the same denominations: the suits are irrelevant. Hands that tie as highest in a showdown divide the pool between them. If the pool is not exactly divisible, the amount left over goes to the player who was "called" (ie the player who first made the highest bet).

Wild cards Sometimes players agree at the beginning of a game to designate certain cards "wild." A wild card is one that may represent a card of any denomination.
Any card or group of cards may be agreed on, but the following are popular choices:
the joker (or two jokers);
the "deuce" (2) of spades if no joker is available;
all the deuces;
all the deuces and "treys" (3s);
red 10s.
In some forms of the game, a card that occupies a particular position in the game may count as wild, for example each player's "hole" (concealed) card in some stud poker games.

Wild cards

Two alternative rules govern the use of a wild card. The holder may either:
a) use it to represent any card (denomination and suit) he does not hold; or
b) use it to represent any card even if he holds that card.
In either case, a wild card ranks the same as the card it represents.

If a joker is used as a wild card, it may be used either like any other wild card, or alternatively as a "bug." The bug may be used to represent only an ace or any card the player needs to complete a straight or a flush. Again, the use of the joker as the bug may or may not be limited to cards that the player does not hold.

Hands with wild cards
Wild cards rank exactly the same as the cards they stand for, so when comparing hands of the same rank, ties are possible between same-denomination fours, full houses, and threes. With fours and threes, the rank of the other cards in the hands decides the winner where possible.
If hands with wild cards are of identical rank, the hand with no or fewer wild cards wins. If there are the same number of wild cards, the hands tie.

A Checks | B Opens for 1 | C Drops out | D Stays in | E Raises 2

Example of a betting interval

Betting intervals In a single play there will be at least one betting interval, and normally two or more.
These always follow receipt of cards by players, but the precise number and when they occur depend on the form of poker being played.
In each betting interval, a certain player will have the right to bet or not to bet first. (How he is chosen depends on the form of the game.)
Thereafter players bet or do not bet in clockwise rotation.

Principles of betting All bets on a play are placed together near the center of the table to form a pool. One player bets first ("opens the betting"). Thereafter, each player in turn must either "drop out," "stay in," or "raise."
In his turn, a player announces what he is doing before he places any chips in the pool. For a first bet or a raise, he also announces the amount of the bet or raise.
A bet is not considered made until the better has removed his hand from the chips bet: until then it can be withdrawn.

a) Drop out (or "fold"): the player discards his hand and gives up his chance of winning the pool on this play.
A player may drop out at any time, even if he has previously bet on this play in an earlier interval or in this interval; but any chips he has already bet remain in the pool and go to the pool winner.
A player who has dropped out is no longer "active," and may not take further action in this play.
b) Stay in (or "call" or "see"): the player puts in just enough chips to make the total he has bet so far in this play exactly equal to the total bet by the player with the highest total bet.
c) Raise (or "up" or "go better"): the player puts in enough chips to stay in, plus an additional number. The additional amount is that by which he "raises the last bet." Every other player in the game must then either stay in (by bringing his total bet up to the raised amount), drop out, or raise again ("reraise").

Checking is allowed in many games of poker. A player who checks at the beginning of a betting interval stays in the game for the moment without making a bet. If all active players check, the betting interval ends. But if one player bets, the interval continues as usual: all other players (including those who have checked) must now stay in, drop out, or raise. To stay in, a player who has checked must equal the highest bet made so far.
If all players check on the first betting interval, the play is void and ends. The next player in turn deals the next round (see the section on pattern of play, p 228).

A betting interval ends
when either:
a) all players have checked;
b) only one player is still active (and therefore wins), all the others having dropped out; or
c) the bets of active players are equalized. This happens when all players still active have put equal amounts in the pool, and the turn has come round again to the last person to raise (or, if no one raised, to the person who opened the betting): he may not then raise again. As long as the bets are unequal any player may raise, but as soon as the bets are equal, no one may raise.

Where wild cards are used for any card (even one held by the player) two new hands are possible.

1) Five of a kind Five cards of the same denomination. This ranks as highest hand, above a straight flush.

2) Double ace high flush Flush including two aces. This ranks above flush and below full house.

Sometimes, a wild card may be used only to make five of a kind—but not to make double ace high flush. This must be decided before the start of play.

Five of a kind

Double ace high flush

Prohibitions A player may not:
a) attempt to make a private agreement with any other player (eg divide the pool without a showdown);
b) waive his turn as dealer, unless physically unable to deal;
c) look at the discards (either before or after showdown), at undealt cards, at another player's hand, or at a hole card (in stud poker);
d) take chips or money from the pool during play, except as correct change for a verbally stated bet;
e) leave the table taking his cards with him (he should ask another player, preferably a non-active one, to play his hand for him—if he fails to do so and misses his turn, his hand is dead).

Bluffing is allowed (ie trying to mislead other players by actions, statements, gestures, or manner). Bluffing may include:
making announcements out of turn about one's hand or plan of play that are not true or are not subsequently kept to; playing so as to make one's hand seem weaker than it is. Sarcasm, heckling, and derision are allowed—genuine help is not!

A Stays in

B Raises 1

D Drops out

E Stays in

A Stays in

Example of a betting interval

Player	bet	action	total bet
A	0	checks	0
B	1	opens for 1	1
C	0	drops out	(0)
D	1	stays in	1
E	3	raises 2	3
A	3	stays in	3
B	3	raises 1	4
D	0	drops out	(1)
E	1	stays in	4
A	1	stays in	4

The betting interval ends. The only three players still active have bet equal amounts; B may not raise the betting again.

Passing may mean either: to drop out; or to check (where checking is allowed).

In games where checking is allowed, a player who says "Pass" is assumed to be checking, if checking is available to him. (A player shows that he is dropping out by discarding his hand.) Games in which no checking is allowed are referred to as "pass and out" (or "pass out" or "bet or drop").

Sandbagging is poker slang for either:
a) checking to disguise a good hand—this is sometimes considered unethical, but is better accepted as a regular part of bluffing; or
b) constant raising and reraising by two players, forcing a third along with them if he wishes to stay in the play.

Raising to force out other players is an essential part of poker, but beyond a certain point it can spoil the game's character. Two optional rulings can keep it in check: limiting raises, and freezing raises.

A limit on raises is often agreed beforehand. Possible limits are:
a) three (or sometimes two) by one player in one betting interval;
b) a total of three by all players in one betting interval.

Freezing the raise is becoming accepted procedure. If there have been two or more raises (whether by one or several players) in a single betting interval, any player who has not raised in that interval may "freeze the raise." In addition to betting sufficient to stay in, he bets a previously agreed amount, usually two to five times the normal maximum bet (see the section on betting limits). Other active players must then drop out or stay in by equaling his bet.

The action only freezes the raise for that betting interval.

Side bets are sometimes made between players. For example, in a "high card bet" in stud poker, players bet on who will have the highest first upcard.

Bonuses It is sometimes agreed before play that, on showdown, a player holding a royal flush, straight flush, or four will receive a payment from each player, whether active or not. The amount agreed is usually three to five times the maximum bet.

Prohibitions A player may not:
a) bet for another player;
b) borrow money or chips from another player during a play;
c) take back a bet once it has been placed in the pool and the better's hand removed. An inadequate bet must be added to, otherwise it is lost and the player's cards are dead.

Betting limits The system to be used must be decided upon before play. The betting limits are also the raise limits.

Note that a player forced to bet, for example, the maximum amount to stay in, may still in that turn raise by the maximum (or by any lesser amount).

1) Specified limits: fixed Minimum and maximum amounts are specified before play starts. Sometimes it is agreed that either:
a) any amount between the limits is acceptable as a bet or raise;
b) only specified amounts between the limits are acceptable as a bet or raise; or
c) no amount between the limits is acceptable as a bet or raise.

2) Specified limits: varying The minimum and maximum limits change during a play; for example, limits for the final betting interval are always twice the earlier limits.

3) Last bet limit The opening bet is governed by agreed limits. Thereafter, the maximum bet or raise is the amount put in the pool by the previous bettor's action. Players must decide either:
a) that each betting interval recommence at the original limits; or
b) that continuous growth be allowed over a single play.

4) Pot limit The opening bet is governed by agreed limits. Thereafter, the maximum bet or raise is the total amount in the pool at the time. To calculate this, a player wishing to raise may include in the pool total the amount needed for him to stay in.

Agreement on an absolute maximum (eg 50 chips) is still necessary.

5) Table stakes Before the session, each player puts any amount of money he wishes onto the table, or buys chips to that amount. (A minimum is agreed beforehand, and sometimes a maximum too.) Any amount a player wins is added to his table amount. He may also, from his own pocket, increase his table amount— but not during a play, and only by at least the agreed minimum.

During a play, a player may not:
borrow from, or owe money to, the pool;
decrease his table amount or withdraw chips from it;
sell chips back to the banker until he withdraws from the game.

The maximum betting limit for a player is his table amount at the time (the minimum is the amount agreed beforehand). If a player's table amount is used up in a play, he has the right to remain in for the main pool showdown. Any amounts bet by other players, above the amount he has bet, are put into a side pool.

In the example shown: of three active players, player B has only 30 units left on the table. Player A bets 40 units: 30 go into the main pool; 10 start a side pool.
Player B bets his 30 units, if he wants to stay in the main pool.
Player C bets 50 units: 30 go into the main pool, the rest into the side pool.
Betting between A and C then continues until their side pool bets have been equalized.

B makes no further bets, and there are no further payments into the main pool, on this or any further betting intervals in this play.
At the showdown, B wins the main pool if he has the best hand. The side pool can only be won by A or C.

6) No limit A player can bet or raise any amount. He may borrow during a play, if he can, but he may not put IOUs in the pool. To stay in, he must equal the highest bet.
In the old no limit games, a player had 24 hours to raise money for a bet.
No limit games have now virtually disappeared.

Table stakes:
a player's table amount is used up.

Freeze-out This can be played with any limits system except table stakes.
Before the session, each player puts an equal number of chips on the table in front of him. Winnings are added to this amount, but no player may add new chips, lend chips, or remove chips from the game. As soon as a player has lost all his chips, he drops out. The session continues until one player has won all the chips.

Jackpot This ruling can be played with any limits system. It applies if all other players drop out in a play, after one player has opened the betting. In the next play and before the deal, the others must each "ante" (put) into the pool an amount equal to the single bet made in the previous play. The new maximum limit (for this play only) is the total amount now in the pool before play starts (providing that this is higher than the normal maximum).
The minimum is as usual.

Whangdoodle This ruling can be played with any limits system. After the appearance of any very good hand (eg full house or better), the usual or opening limits are doubled for the next play.
Sometimes the special limits hold for the next round of play, ie one deal by each player.

PATTERN OF PLAY

Rotation of play is clockwise. No player acts until the active player nearest to his right has acted.
Choice of first dealer is by deal: the first jack to appear (see p80).
Shuffle and cut See p 80.

The deal is clockwise to active players only, beginning with the active player nearest the dealer's left.
Play varies from one form of poker to another.

Showdown After the final betting interval, players still active expose their hands (in draw poker) or hole card(s) (in stud poker), beginning with the player being called, and in a clockwise direction. Each player announces the rank of hand he is claiming. In any discrepancy the cards "speak for themselves"—this includes giving the hand a higher rating than claimed, except if there are wild cards (when the player's announcement cannot be improved on).
The hand of highest rank wins. Tied hands divide the pool equally.

Change of dealer After each play, the deal passes one player to the left of the previous dealer.

Play rotates clockwise

Deal passes to left

ARRANGEMENTS

Banker Poker is not a banking game. Bets are made as contributions to a pool. The "banker" simply supervises the supply of betting chips. He records how many have been issued to each player, including himself, and keeps the payments and the unissued stock to one side.

Players must not make exchanges or transactions among themselves. A player needing more chips must purchase them from the banker's stock; a player with surplus chips may sell them back into stock.

The banker is either the host; or any player chosen by lot (eg high cut) or agreement.

The kitty is a fund for buying new cards or refreshments, set up by agreement before the game starts.

Usually, one betting unit is contributed to it from any pot in which there has been more than one raise or, alternatively, where the winner holds a hand of a specified rank or better. The banker arranges all this. Any chips in the kitty at the end of the game are divided equally among those still playing. (A player who leaves before the end loses the right to any part of the kitty.)

Betting chips are almost always used rather than cash. Usually different colors represent different values, for example: white, one unit; red, five units; blue, 10 units; and, sometimes, yellow, 25 units. A game with seven or more players needs about 200 chips. The best value distribution depends on the maximum betting limit.

At the start of play, each player buys chips to the same total value, for example 50 units.

A player's stock of chips must always be kept in full view of other players, and not taken from the table except for cashing in.

Two decks of cards with contrasting backs are usually used in club play. At the end of one play, one deck is collected and shuffled by the player who dealt last, while the other is dealt into play by the new dealer.

New deck(s) of cards may be called for by any player at any time.

Seating at the start of a session is random, unless a player demands a reseating after the first dealer has been chosen but before play begins.

On reseating, the first dealer has first choice of seat. He then shuffles the deck, has it cut by the player to his right, and deals one card face up to each player in rotation, beginning with the player to his left.

The player with the lowest ranking card sits to the dealer's left, the player with the next lowest card to that player's left, and so on. Of two cards of the same denomination, that dealt first ranks higher.

The dealer then gathers the cards and has them shuffled and cut for play.

After play starts, or after a reseating, no one may demand a reseating for at least an hour, provided no one joins or leaves the game.

If a player joins the game after it starts and someone questions the seat he takes, the dealer, between plays, deals a card to each existing player, and the new player takes his seat to the left of the player with the lowest card. This is done separately for each player joining.

If a player replaces another player, he must take the seat vacated, provided no one objects.

Two players may exchange seats just before any play, provided no one objects.

Time limit The time at which the game will end should be agreed before play starts, and be strictly observed.

Any players who then wish to continue can do so, but should set a new time limit.

Time limit for a decision by a player during play (eg how many cards to draw, how to bet) is five minutes. This is important in a high-limit game. If a player fails to act within this time, his hand is dead.

Rules to be agreed before the start of a game (and best written down) are:
a) the form of game to be played;
b) wild cards and their use;
c) any special hands and rulings;
d) the value of chips;
e) betting limits and checking;
f) limits on raises and/or payment for freezing a raise;
g) bonus payments and payments to the kitty.

Club and casino poker The management supplies table, chips, cards, dealer and/or inspector. It takes a cut—usually as a direct charge on the winner of each pool, but sometimes rents tables at an hourly rate and supervises the game to prevent cheating.

Irregularities Because poker can be played for very high stakes, innumerable rules govern irregularities of play, both accidental and deliberate. It is impossible to treat all these here. The reader who wishes to play poker for high stakes should consult an advanced book on the subject.

FORMS OF POKER

There are two main forms of poker.
1) Closed poker, usually played in the form of draw poker. Players receive their cards face down. After a betting interval, they discard the cards they do not want, and receive replacements from the deck.
A second betting interval is followed by a showdown if more than one player is still active.

2) Open poker, known as stud poker. Players receive some cards face down, some face up. Betting intervals interrupt the deal. After the deal, players cannot receive replacements, but (in versions where more than five cards per player are dealt) each chooses only five cards to form his final hand.
A final betting interval is followed by a showdown if more than one player is still active.

The form of poker chosen may be decided by the host or by club rules; but if a decision has to be made, two factors should be taken into account.
1) Number of players. The best games for a particular number of players are as follows.
Four or under, stud poker; five to eight, any form of poker; nine or ten, five card stud; more than ten, any variant with fewer than five cards per player—or split into two tables.
2) Relative experience. If some players are considerably more experienced than others, it is best to choose one of the less common variants in which the element of skill is lower.

Dealer's choice If it is agreed to play "dealer's choice," the dealer chooses the game to be played: a standard form, a known variant, or any new and easily explained variant he can devise.

He designates any wild cards. He may not, however, alter the betting limits, add cards to or remove them from the deck, or alter basic poker rules.

His choice of game holds by agreement, either:
a) for his deal only; or
b) for a complete round of dealing. The next dealer in turn then chooses for the next complete round.

Sometimes, a play or round of dealer's choice is played whenever a very good hand appears (eg full house or better).

STUD POKER

Stud poker is a faster game than draw poker and allows for greater skill. As there is no exchange of cards, the average rank of winning hands is lower than in draw poker.

STANDARD GAME: FIVE-CARD STUD

Players Up to ten may play.

Ante Usually, a small compulsory bet is made by all players; alternatively no ante is made.

Opening deal One card is dealt face down to each player (the "hole" card), then one card face up. Each player examines his hand.

First betting interval The player with the highest ranking face-up card must open or drop. A wild card is considered higher than an ace. If two players hold equal-ranking cards, the player nearer the dealer's left opens. After the opener, each player drops, stays in, bets, raises, or reraises in the normal way until betting is equalized.

Continuing play Further rounds of dealing one card face up to each player alternate with betting intervals, until the end of the fourth interval (when each player has one face-down and four face-up cards).

On these deals, the dealer leaves the deck resting on the table and takes cards one at a time from the top.

On the betting intervals, the player with the right to open is the one with the highest ranking completed hand in exposed cards—the dealer announces the player and also announces exposed pairs or better hands, possible flushes and straights, and the last deal. The showdown follows the fourth betting interval; all active players expose their hole cards.

Additional rules

1) If all the players check, the betting interval ends and the play continues.

2) If a player drops out, he turns all his cards face down and does not reveal his hole card.

3) If on any betting interval only one active player is left, he wins and the play ends. He need not show his hole card.

4) A "four flush" is often ruled a ranking hand in stud poker, ie four cards of the same suit plus one other. At showdown (and in deciding the start of a betting interval) it beats a pair but loses to two pairs.

Deal

Player 2

Player 1

Player 3

Dealer

End of betting

Player 3, dropped out

DRAW POKER

The basic pattern of the game is as follows:

1) Ante: a small compulsory bet is made by all players.

2) Deal: five face-down cards are dealt to each player in the normal way. Players count their cards, then look at them.

3) First betting interval: the player to the dealer's left has the right to bet first; if he does not bet, the other players may bet in turn.

4) Draw: each active player in turn may discard one or more cards and receive from the dealer the same number, face down, from the undealt part of the deck. A player need not draw—he may "stand pat."

5) Second betting interval: the player who made the first bet in the first interval has the right to bet first. If he has dropped out, the first active player to his left may bet.

6) Showdown takes place if more than one active player is left at the end of the second betting interval.

STANDARD GAME

Players Up to ten may play. No more than six should play in high-betting games, since with more players it may be necessary to use discards to complete the draw.

Ante Either:

a) each player puts an equal agreed amount into the pool; or

b) only the dealer antes ("dealer's edge").

The ante amount is usually the same as the minimum bet.

First betting interval There are two forms:

1) "Jacks or better." A player may not open the betting unless he holds a pair of jacks or any better hand. (Before betting is opened, players may check.)

After betting has opened, a player may bet on any hand, and must bet or drop out.

At the end of the play, the opener must show the cards he opened on.

2) "Pass and out" (or "pass out" or "bet or drop"). A player may open the betting on any hand. Each player must bet or drop out; no one may check.

In either case, the player to the dealer's left is the first to "speak."

Once the betting has opened, it proceeds in the normal way. If no one opens, all players ante again, and the next dealer deals for the next play.

The draw occurs if more than one player is still active after the first betting interval. The dealer offers the draw to each player in turn in normal rotation, beginning with the player to his left and ending with himself.

Each player in his turn either:

a) states the number of cards he requires and places that number from his hand face down on the table in full view —the dealer then gives him the same number from the undealt part of the deck; or

b) says "I stand pat," or knocks on the table, to indicate that he wishes to keep the hand that he has.

In his turn, the dealer also either states the number of cards he has drawn (exchanged), or indicates that he is "standing pat."

Normally it is ruled that a player may draw one, two, or three cards at his discretion. With four or fewer players, four and five card draws are sometimes allowed.

A player may use the draw to bluff in any way he wishes about the value of his hand. The dealer must answer truthfully how many cards he himself drew. No other question need be answered

VARIATIONS OF STUD POKER

Six-card stud This is like five-card stud, except that after the fourth betting interval each player receives a sixth card face down. This is followed by a fifth (final) betting interval.

At the showdown, each active player chooses five cards from his six to form his final hand.

Seven-card stud (or seven-toed Pete or down the river) This game is for two to eight players.

The opening deal is of three cards: two hole cards, then one face up. Betting intervals and rounds of dealing face-up cards then alternate as usual, until each player has seven cards (including the two hole cards).

After a final betting interval, each active player chooses five cards from his seven to form his showdown hand.

Seven-card stud: low hole card wild As above, but each player's lower ranking hole card is wild—as, for him, is any other card of that denomination. Sometimes players are allowed to choose either one of their hole cards (and its denomination) as wild.

Mexican stud is like five-card stud, except that all cards are dealt face down.

After the second and each subsequent dealing round, each player turns up any one of his face-down cards, leaving one chosen card as hole card. Sometimes a player's final hole card is ruled wild, together with any other cards of that denomination that he holds.

Other five-card stud variants

1) Last card down: the last card is dealt face down, giving two hole cards.
2) Last card optionally down: a player may turn up his hole card before the last dealing round and receive his fifth card face down.

Low-hand stud The lowest hand wins the pool. The lowest exposed hand begins each betting interval. Other rules are as for the form of stud being played.

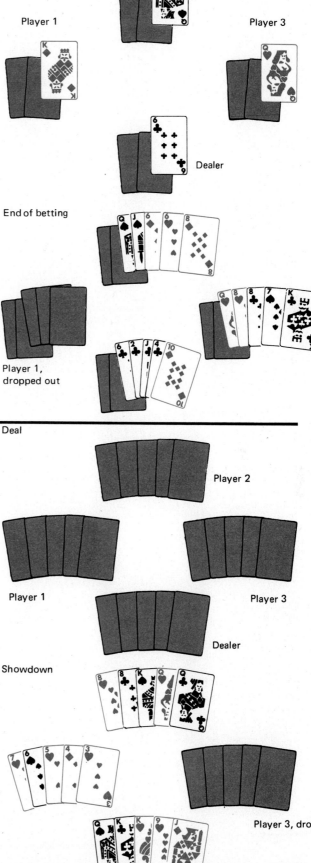

Seven-card stud Deal

Player 1 Player 2 Player 3

Dealer

End of betting

Player 1, dropped out

truthfully by anyone.
The bottom card of the deck is not used. If further cards are required, the bottom card and the cards discarded so far are shuffled together and cut to allow the draw to continue. The usual rules apply, but the player who is due to draw next cuts last.

No other shuffling or cutting on the draw is allowed. Sometimes, in "jacks or better," the opening bettor discards one of his "openers" (ie one of the cards that gave him the right to open). If he does so, he must state this, and the discarded opener is kept to one side to be inspected at the end of the play. It is not used if the discards are reshuffled.

Second betting interval This follows the usual rules. All players may check, even if "pass and out" was enforced for the first interval. If all the players check, the interval ends. If all the players except one drop out, that player wins without showing his hand (except for showing his openers in "jacks or better," if he opened the betting).

Showdown Each active player in turn must place all his five cards face up on the table, to be seen by all players

(active or otherwise). At the same time he announces the value of his hand—he must do this even if he sees he is beaten.

If all players checked in the second betting interval, the opener shows his hand first; but if bets were placed in the second betting interval, the player who was called shows first.

In either case, other active players then follow in normal rotation.

Dropping out In draw poker a player indicates that he is dropping out by placing his cards face down on the table when his turn in the betting interval arrives.

As long as a player wishes to remain in the game he must keep his cards in his hands, above table height, unless he is forced to put down the cards temporarily for some reason, in which case he must state this.

Deal

Player 1 Player 2 Player 3

Dealer

Showdown

Player 3, dropped out

VARIATIONS OF DRAW POKER

"Jacks or better" variations

1) Progressive openers: if no one opens on a play, two queens or better are required to open on the next play. If again no one opens, two kings or better are required on the next play; then two aces or better; then back down to two kings or better, two queens or better, and two jacks or better.

Each time, players must ante again; and sometimes the limits are doubled. Once a player opens, the next play reverts to jacks or better (and limits go back to normal).

2) "Jacks or bobtail" to open. This is like "jacks or better" but a player may also open on a "bobtail" (four cards of the same suit plus one other card) or a "bobtail straight" (four cards in sequence plus one other card—but the sequence may not be a,k,q,j or 4,3,2,a). These hands have no showdown value.

Blind opening (or "blind tiger" or "blind and straddle").

In this variation, players bet "blind," ie before receiving their hands.
Before the deal:
1) the dealer antes only one chip;
2) the player to his left bets one chip blind ("edge");
3) the next player raises him, betting two chips blind ("straddle").
After the deal, the next player after the blind raiser has the first voluntary bet. He may call (two chips), drop out, or raise (three chips). The betting interval then proceeds as normal. The maximum raise before the draw is one chip. (Note that the dealer's ante does not count toward staying in, but the two players' blind bets do.)
In the second betting interval, the bet and raise limit is two chips. Betting begins with the first blind bettor or the (still active) player nearest his left. Players may check until a bet is made.
Sometimes, in the predeal betting, up to three voluntary blind bets—each doubling the last bet—are allowed after the blind raise. These bets count toward staying in the game in the first interval.

Shotgun
Play is as in the standard game, except for an additional (first) betting interval during the deal, after each player has received three cards.
Any hand can open. There is no checking.

Spit in the ocean
There are many versions of this; some are given in the section on closed poker games.
1) Basic game: each player receives four cards. The next card is dealt to the center of the table. The game proceeds as usual, but at showdown each active player must count this table card as the fifth card in his hand.
2) Pig in the poke: as above, but the face-up card and all the others of the same denomination are wild (or sometimes only cards of the same denomination as the face-up card, but not the face-up card itself).

Stormy weather
Each player receives four cards. Three face-down cards are dealt to the table, one each after the second, third, and fourth dealing rounds.
There is then a betting interval. A player may open on any hand. There is no checking. In the draw, each player may change up to four cards. After the draw, the dealer turns up the table cards one at a time, with a betting interval as each one is turned up.
At the showdown, a player uses any one of the table cards as his fifth card. None of the table cards is wild.

Sequence of play

Draw poker
Deal

Betting

The draw

Betting

Showdown

CLOSED POKER GAMES
These are variants in which there is no draw.

Showdown straight poker
(or cold hand poker) There is one betting interval before the deal. The deal is normal, but the cards are dealt face up and the best hand dealt wins.

Double barrel shotgun
Each player receives five face-down cards. Beginning with the player to the dealer's left, all the players then expose any one of their cards.
Betting intervals then alternate with further rounds of exposing one card each. On the fifth and final round of exposure, the best hand wins.

Spit in the ocean variants
1) Criss-cross (or X marks the spot): each player receives four cards. Five cards are then dealt face-down to the center of the table in the shape of a cross.
Players examine their hands. The dealer then turns up any one of the table cards except the one at the center of the cross. A betting interval follows.
Exposure of the cards in the cross alternates with betting intervals until all but the central card of the cross have been exposed.
After the fourth betting interval the center card is exposed; showdown follows immediately.
The center card of the cross is wild, as are all other cards of the same denomination.

Each player mentally selects his final five-card hand from any cards in his hand and the table cards. (Sometimes, he is only allowed to choose table cards from any three that form a straight line in the cross.)
2) Cincinnati: five cards are dealt to each player, and the next five cards are dealt face down to the center of the table.
The game is the same as criss-cross, but without the cross pattern. None of the table cards is wild; a player may use any of the table cards in his final hand.
3) Lame brain Pete: this is played like Cincinnati, but the lowest-ranking table card is wild, as are all the other cards of that denomination.

Three-card poker
Each player receives three face-down cards, and there is a betting interval after each round of cards is dealt. Showdown follows immediately after the third interval.
The rank of hands (with the highest given first): threes; three–card straight flush; three–card flush; three–card straight; pair; high card.

Two-card poker
(usually played with wild cards) comprises: a deal of two face-down cards to each player; a single betting interval; and a showdown.
Pairs and high cards are the only hands.

Spit in the ocean

Deal

Player 2

Player 1   Player 3

Dealer

Stormy weather

Deal

Player 2

Player 1   Player 3

Dealer

Stud poker
Deal   Betting   Further dealing   Betting   Showdown

Lowball is often played during "jacks or better" sessions. When no one has openers for "jacks or better," lowball is played for that play only.

In lowball the lowest hand wins. Rules are as for the standard game, with the following exceptions.

1) Ante: the dealer and the player to his left (sometimes also the second player to his left) ante.

2) First betting interval: the player to the left of the last player to ante must open or drop out. No checking is allowed. The limit is the ante amount. Antes count toward staying in.

3) Draw: before the draw the dealer "burns" (exposes and then discards) the top deck card.

4) Second betting interval: this begins with the active player nearest the dealer's left. Checking is allowed, but a player who checks cannot later raise on that play. Limits are agreed beforehand.

5) Showdown is won by the lowest hand.

Ace always counts low, and straights and flushes do not count. Therefore a,2,3,4,5 (known as a "bicycle") counts as five low cards and is the lowest hand—regardless of suits.

The joker can be used for any card not in the player's hand.

Low ball: lowest hand

HIGH-LOW POKER

Almost any standard game or variant, draw or stud, can also be played as a high-low game. Especially popular is seven-card high-low stud. At showdown, the highest and lowest hands split the pool. Usually a player must declare, just before showdown, whether he is competing for highest hand, lowest hand, or both.

It is possible to declare for both in any game where a player has more than five cards from which to select his final hand, for he is then allowed to select two different hands.

Rank of cards is as usual. If a player is competing for the lowest hand, ace ranks low; if for the highest hand, high or low, as he wishes; if for both,

both high and low, if he wishes.

Rank of hands is as usual. Hence the lowest possible hand, without wild cards, is 6,4,3,2,a, in different suits (5,4,3,2,a would be a straight).

The usual rules for comparing hands apply—highest card first, then next highest, until a difference is found. Thus, 9,7,6,5,4 ranks lower than 9,8,4,3,2.

Wild cards A wild card can only be given one denomination and suit at showdown.

If declaring for lowest hand, a wild card ranks the same as a low ace, without pairing any ace in the hand. Thus, 4,3,2,a, wild card becomes the lowest possible hand.

Declaring follows the last betting interval. There are two methods.

a) Beginning with the player to the dealer's left, each active player in turn declares himself as competing for highest hand or lowest or both.

b) Each player takes one of his chips in his hand, without revealing its color. He takes a white one if declaring low, a red one if declaring high, or a blue one if declaring both. When all the players have decided, they show their chips.

The highest hand and lowest hand divide the pool equally (if an exact division is impossible, the highest hand receives any odd chips).

A player can only win the part of the pool for which he has declared. If more than one

player has declared the same way, the player with the best hand wins that part of the pool. If all the players have declared the same way, the player with the best hand wins the whole pool.

If a player has declared for both high and low, he must at least tie each way at showdown, or his hand is dead and he receives nothing.

High-low: lowest hand

Brag

THREE-CARD BRAG

This is the basic form of the game.

Players: from three to 12.

The objective on each deal is to win the pool by holding the best ranking hand on a showdown or by having all the other players drop out of the betting.

Betting limits are agreed beforehand. Typical limits would be:

1) maximum one unit bet or raise;

2) one to five or one to ten units bet or raise.

Ante Sometimes rules specify that, before each deal, each player must contribute one unit to the pool.

Deal The dealer deals one card face down to each player, including himself, beginning with the player to his left and going clockwise, and continuing until each player has three cards.

Play Players look at their hands and bet accordingly, beginning with the player to the dealer's left and going clockwise. Bets are placed in a central pool. Players may bet on any hand—bluffing is unrestricted.

There is only one betting interval. A player cannot "pass" and stay in the game—he must bet or drop out. If all the players but one drop out the remaining player wins the pool.

Otherwise betting continues until there is a showdown, when the player with the best hand wins. A showdown is not allowed until all players but two have dropped out. Dealt cards are replaced at the bottom of the deck, face down. The cards are reshuffled for the next hand only if a pryle has just appeared on showdown.

GENERAL RULES

Brag was one of the ancestors of poker and still remains very popular in Britain. There are many forms and variants but basically the game is a form of three-card poker with no "draw."

Equipment:

a) one standard deck of 52 cards;

b) betting chips or cash.

Rank of hands A "hand" at brag contains only three cards. Originally only threes and pairs scored but today, through poker influences, all the following are generally recognized (with the highest listed first).

a) "Pryle": three cards of the same denomination.

b) "On a bike" run: three cards in sequence from the same suit.

c) Run: three cards in sequence.

d) Flush: three cards of the same suit.

e) Pair: two cards of the same denomination and one unmatched card.

f) "High card": three unmatched cards.

Rank of cards The cards rank in normal order, with ace high, except:

a) ace can rank low to make a 3,2,ace run or on a bike run—which then counts as the highest hand of that rank, beating a,k,q.

b) for pryles only, a specified denomination varying with the game played (eg three 3s) is ranked above three aces.

Wild cards Today brag is usually played with no wild cards, or sometimes with 2s (deuces) wild.

However, the traditional wild cards for the game, listed in order of rank, are:

ace of diamonds;

jack of clubs;

9 of diamonds.

Hands of the same rank are valued according to the denomination of cards used—as in poker. For two special cases, see "rank of cards." Otherwise:

1) for pryles, on a bike runs, flushes, and high cards, the hand with the highest denomination card wins;

2) for pairs, the hand with the higher denomination pair wins or, if these match, the hand with the higher ranking odd card wins.

Rank of hands with wild cards A hand using wild cards is valued in the usual way (with the wild card valued according to the card it represents). However, a hand using wild cards loses to a hand that uses none.

Note that a pair using a wild card loses to the same pair in natural cards even if the wild card hand has the higher odd card.

Arrangements:

1) choice of first dealer is by low cut (see p 80).

2) shuffle and cut are normal (see p 80).

a Pryle   b On a bike run   c Run

Betting principles There are several alternatives:
a) "round the table";
b) "bet or raise";
c) poker betting.

Round the table betting
Each time it is his turn to bet a player must bet one unit or drop out.
This continues even when there are only two players left, but then either player may in any of his turns pay a double amount to "see." Both players then show their cards without further betting.

Bet or raise In this system limits are agreed beforehand and affect only the opening bet and raises.
In the betting interval betting is as for the round the table system, but in any turn a player may choose to bet more than one unit.
All active players must then bet exactly the same amount each time their turn comes around—or must drop out or raise again.
Raises are therefore not like the raises in poker. Instead of players just having to "call," they set a new minimum contribution to the pool per turn.
Each player must contribute at least that full amount in subsequent turns—regardless of his previous contributions to the pool—or must drop out.
Each time the bet is raised only the increase is limited.
The total bet of a player in a turn can therefore exceed the "limits."
As in the round the table system this can continue when only two players remain—until one of them pays double the amount at that time to see.

Poker betting is sometimes used (see poker, p226). In this system the interval ends when bets are equalized.
However, unless modified, poker rules can leave more than two active players at showdown. This can be accepted, or the following rules may be observed:
a) when there are three or more active players, a player may not call if this equalizes all players' bets (he must raise or drop out);
b) if a player drops out and so equalizes the bets between the remaining three or more active players, the last player to raise must raise again.

"Blind" betting It is sometimes ruled that a player may bet without looking at his cards.
In this case, any player who has looked at his cards must in each turn pay double the blind bettor if he is to stay in.
When only two active players are left an "open" bettor cannot double his stake to see a blind bettor. To remain in the game he must continue to bet until the blind bettor doubles his bet to see him.
When the last two active players are both blind bettors either of them can pay double to see the other.

Covering the kitty If a player runs out of money during a betting interval he places his hand face down on the pool.
Subsequent bets by other players are then placed in a side pool.
Showdown is then between three players: between the last two active players for the side pool and between these two and the player who covered the kitty for the main pool.

SEVEN-CARD BRAG
This version is for two to seven players.
Before each deal, players contribute equal amounts to a pool.
Each player then receives seven cards, looks at them, discards one face down, and visibly splits the remainder into two unexposed three-card brag hands.
When all are ready, each player in turn exposes one hand, beginning with the player to the dealer's left.
Then each player in turn exposes his other hand, beginning with the player whose first hand was highest.
A player has complete discretion on how he splits his cards between the two hands, but he must expose the best hand first.
The rank of cards is as in three-card brag, except that the highest pryle is three 7s, followed by three aces. (Three 3s rank normally—below three 4s and above three 2s.)
If the same player has the highest hand both times, he wins the pool.
Alternatively, a player whose original seven cards contain four cards of the same denomination wins the pool if he declares this at once without discarding.
Otherwise the pool is not won, but players still contribute again before the next deal.
A deal is usually one card at a time, face down. It may, however, be three cards to each player, followed by another three, and then by a single card.
In the latter case, dealt cards are usually not shuffled between hands but replaced face down at the bottom of the deck with no shuffle or cut.

NINE-CARD BRAG
This is similar to seven-card brag. A maximum of five can play, as nine cards are dealt to each player. The deal is usually in ones, but sometimes in threes.
Players divide their cards into three brag hands, exposing the highest hand first.
Any player with the highest hand in all three exposures wins the pool (or, under some rules, the pool is won by a player with two out of three highest hands).
Alternatively, as in seven-card brag, the pool is won immediately by a player with four cards of a kind.
The rank of hands is as in three-card brag, except that the highest pryle is three 9s, followed by three aces. (Three 3s rank normally—below three 4s and above three 2s.)
If no one wins the pool, players still contribute again before the next deal.
Sometimes a pool may not be won for many hours—by which time it can be very large.

STOP THE BUS
This British students' game is a variant of three-card brag.
All players start with an equal number of betting chips. An additional three-card hand—the dummy—is dealt face up onto the table.
In play, each player in turn may exchange one card in his hand for one from the dummy. The discarded cards go into the dummy face up.
This continues until one player does not wish to alter his hand.
All players then show their cards, and the lowest hand pays a previously agreed amount into the pool (eg five units).
Further hands are played until only one player has any chips remaining. He then wins the whole pool.

Flush

Pair

High card

Wild cards

Private banking card games

The following private betting games are "banking games," in which one person takes on the wagers of all other players. He also has a different role to other players in play. But unlike in casino banking games, no one person is banker continuously. Instead, to equalize players' chances, the role of banker moves around—often after every hand

CARD PUT-AND-TAKE
Equipment:
1) one standard deck of cards;
2) betting chips.
Players: from two to eight.
Objective On the "take" deal each player aims to hold, and on the "put" deal not to hold, cards of the same rank as those turned up by the banker.
Choice of first banker/dealer is by high cut (see p80).
Shuffle and cut are standard (see p80).
Deal The banker deals five face-up cards to each player but himself, dealing them one at a time in a clockwise direction.
Betting limits Payments are one to 16 chips. One chip's value is agreed beforehand.
Play
1) Players look at their cards.
2) The put deal is made. The banker deals five face-up cards one at a time onto the table.
After each card is dealt, any player holding a card of the same rank must pay chips into a pool. The payment doubles with each card: one chip for the first card turned up; two for the second; four for the third; eight for the fourth; and 16 for the fifth. A player with two or more cards of the same rank as the banker's card must pay for each one.
The banker makes no payments.
3) The banker takes the five cards from the table and places them face up at the bottom of the deck.
4) The take deal is made, for which the banker deals five more cards as before. This time each player takes chips from the pool for each of his cards of the same rank. The number of chips taken increases exactly as in the put deal.
5) Any chips left in the pool after the five cards have been played go to the banker. Any chips still owing are paid by the banker from his own chips.
Change of banker/dealer After each hand the bank and deal pass to the player to the banker's left.

VARIANTS
Ante payment Sometimes each player but the banker puts one chip into the pool before each hand.
Easy go has an additional payment and claim. Players pay—and take—one additional chip for each card that, besides being of the same rank as the card played by the banker, is also of the same color.
Red and black has an additional payment and claim for any player with three or more cards of the same suit as the card played by the banker. Players pay—and take—one chip for the first card the banker turns up; two for the second; three for the third; four for the fourth; and five for the fifth, in addition to the regular payments.
Up and down the river has a different payment and claim system. Each player pays—and takes—according to the rank of the matching cards, not according to whether it is the first, second, third, fourth, or fifth card turned up. Payment for an ace is one chip; for a jack, 11 chips; for a queen, 12 chips; and for a king, 13. Payments on other cards match their face value.

Put-and-take   Player 2

−16+21

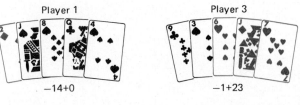

Player 1   Player 3

−14+0   −1+23

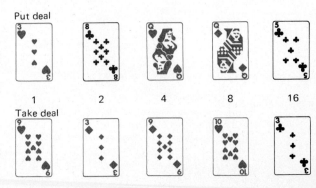

Put deal

1   2   4   8   16

Take deal

RED AND BLACK
Equipment:
1) two standard decks of 52 playing cards;
2) betting chips.

Players: two or more.

Objective Each player tries to forecast correctly whether he will hold more red or more black cards in his hand.

Choice of first banker is by high cut (see p 80).

Shuffle and cut are standard (see p 80)—with the two decks shuffled together to form a single deck.

Betting limits are agreed beforehand.

Betting Each player bets on red or black. He bets any amount within the limits. A player bets on black by placing his bet in front of him to his left; he bets on red by placing it in front of him to his right.

(Alternatively each player may be given two colored tokens: one red and one black. He places one of these beside his bet.)

Play The banker deals five cards, one at a time, face up, to the player to his left.
He deals them directly in front of the player, so that it is clear whether the player's bet lies to the right or left.
If the first four cards consist of two red and two black cards, the player may double his bet before he receives his fifth card.
After the first player's bet is settled, the banker deals to the next player to the left. He continues dealing until all players but himself have received a hand.

Settlement of bets A player wins from the banker if he is dealt three or more cards of the color bet on. If he has three of that color, he wins the amount of his bet. If he has four, he doubles his bet. If he has five, he wins four times his bet.
A player loses to the banker if he is dealt three or more cards of the color not bet on. If he has three, he loses his bet. If he has four, he pays the banker twice his bet (his original bet and a further payment equal to it). If he has five cards, he pays four times his bet (his original bet plus a payment equal to three times his bet).

Change of banker After the banker has dealt a hand to all the other players, the bank and deal pass one player to the left.

HORSE RACE
Equipment:
1) one standard deck of 52 cards;
2) betting chips.

Players The game is for three or more players.

Objective Players try to "win the race" by betting on the first suit to appear eight times in a deal.

Choice of first banker is by high cut (see p 80).

The "horses" The banker takes the four aces from the deck and lines them up in any order.

Shuffle and cut are standard (see p 80).

The "course" After the shuffle and cut, the banker deals seven face-up cards in a line at right angles to the horses. If five or more of the cards dealt are of the same suit, the banker takes them all up, reshuffles, and deals the course again.

Betting limits are decided by the banker for each race.

Betting The banker declares the odds on each horse (suit), taking into account the cards that have appeared to form the course. If one suit has appeared predominantly in the course, there will be fewer cards of that suit to appear in the race.
The table gives an example of the odds that a banker might offer. He will choose odds that give him some degree of advantage; it is up to each player whether or not to place a bet at those odds.
The players then state their bets, placing their stakes in front of them. The banker makes a note of how much each player bets on each horse and what the odds are.

The "race" The banker deals the top card from the deck face up onto the table. The horse (ace) of the same suit as the dealt card is then moved up the course one space. The banker then deals another card face up on top of the first, and again moves the horse of the corresponding suit one space. This continues until one horse has passed the end of the course. This horse is the winner.

Settlement of bets The banker collects all bets placed on the losing horses. He pays at the quoted odds each bet on the winning horse.

Change of banker After each hand, the bank and deal pass one player to the left.

Horse race

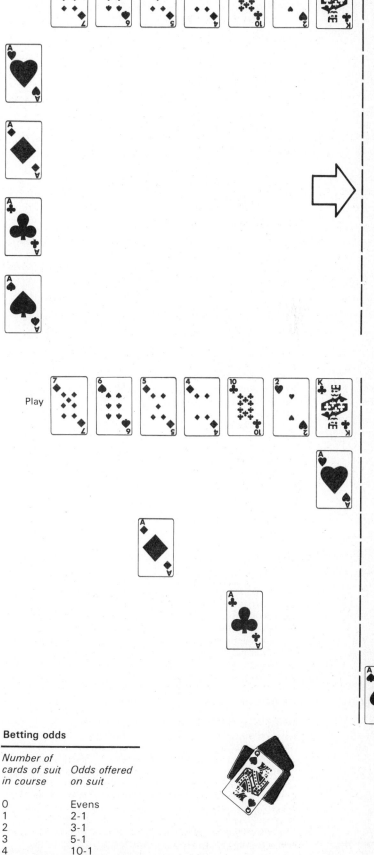

Deal

Play

Finish line

Betting odds

Number of cards of suit in course	Odds offered on suit
0	Evens
1	2-1
2	3-1
3	5-1
4	10-1
5 or more	Layout redealt

SLIPPERY SAM

This game is related to red dog (p247).

Equipment:
1) one standard deck of cards;
2) betting chips or cash.

Players: ideally six to eight but two or more can play.

Rank of cards is normal (ace high). Suits are not ranked.

Objective Players aim to hold a card in the same suit but of a higher rank than the banker's card.

Choice of first banker is by high cut (see p80).

Shuffle and cut are normal (see p80).

Bank The banker places in the center of the table the amount he wishes to put at risk. This is any amount above an agreed minimum.

Deal The banker deals three cards to each player, dealing them one at a time and face down. He then deals one card face up to himself.

Play Players bet without looking at their hands. Play begins with the player to the banker's left. He may agree or refuse to bet against the exposed banker's card.

1) If he agrees, he bets any amount he chooses, above an agreed minimum, up to the total amount in the bank. He then looks at his cards. If he holds a card in the same suit but of higher rank than the banker's card, he wins; if not, he loses.

2) Alternatively, he refuses to bet against the exposed banker's card. In this case he says "Deal me another card." For this privilege he must pay into the bank an amount equal to one fifth of the bank (or, under alternative rules, he pays a previously agreed amount).

The exposed banker's card is then discarded and another card dealt from the top of the deck face up onto the table. This becomes the new banker's card. The player either bets against this card in the usual way, or pays again for a new banker's card to be dealt. A player may reject the banker's card up to three times on a single hand, paying the same amount each time. After the third rejection, the player may either bet in the usual way against the banker's card now exposed, or he may pass his turn without betting.

3) If the player has bet and won, he shows his winning card only. His bet is returned plus an equal amount from the bank.
If he has bet and lost, he shows all his hand and his bet is added to the bank.
Whether he has won or lost, his hand is then added face down to a discard pile.

4) Bet and play then pass one player to the left, and continue in the same way. Each player's turn begins with the banker's card on which the last player bet or passed: a new banker's card is dealt only when paid for.
When all players except the banker have had a turn, the banker collects whatever amount is now in the bank. Bank and deal then pass one player to the left.
If the bank is emptied ("bust") before each player has had a turn, the bank and deal pass immediately.

Deal

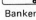

Player 2

Player 1

Player 3

Banker

Play

Player 1, wins

Banker's card

Player 2, loses

Player 3, wins

Banker's new card

LANSQUENET

This game is said to have been popular with German mercenaries in the 1600s. Its name derives from *Landsknecht*, the German word for mercenary. It is closely related to ziginette and skinball.

Equipment:
1) one standard deck of cards;
2) betting chips.

Players: two or more.

Objective Players aim to bet on a card that has not been "matched" by the time the banker's card is matched.
A card is matched when a card of the same denomination is dealt from the deck.

Choice of first banker is by deal: first ace to appear. (See p80.)

Shuffle and cut are normal (see p80).

Dealing the layout Provided that none of the cards dealt for the layout matches, the procedure is as follows. The banker deals the top two cards from the deck (the "hand" cards) face up onto the table. He then deals one card face up to himself (the "banker's card"), followed by another one face up (the "players' card").

Matching cards in the layout The following procedure must be observed if matching cards are turned up while dealing the layout.
1) If the card dealt for the second hand card matches the first, it is placed on top of it. A further card is then dealt as the second hand card. If necessary this process is repeated until the hand cards do not match.

2) If the card dealt as the banker's card matches one of the hand cards, it is placed on top of that card and a new banker's card dealt. This process is repeated if necessary until the banker's card is of a different denomination from those of the hand cards.
3) If the card dealt as the players' card matches one of the hand cards, the procedure is as for the banker's card. If the players' card is the same denomination as the banker's card, the deal is void and a new deal made.

Betting limits are decided by each banker for the duration of his hand.

Betting Each player places his bet alongside the players' card. If all chips are of the same color, the bets may be placed at different corners of the card to distinguish them.

First turn The banker deals one card from the top of the deck face up onto the table. If the dealt card does not match any card on the layout, it is placed face up next to the players' card. It is now a further players' card, on which players may place bets. If the dealt card matches one of the hand cards, it is placed on top of the matched card. This denomination is now out of play. The hand cards have no effect, except to remove two denominations from the betting.
If the dealt card matches the players' card, the banker wins the players' bets. There is then no further betting on the matched denominations for the rest of the deal.

POLISH RED DOG

This game is also known as stitch and Polish pachuk.

Equipment:
1) one standard deck of 52 cards;
2) betting chips (or cash).

Players The game is for two to ten players.

Rank of cards is normal, with ace high. The suits are not ranked.

Objective Players aim to hold a card in the same suit but of a higher rank than the banker's card.

Choice of first banker is by deal: first ace to appear. (See p80.)

Shuffle and cut are normal (see p80).

Bank The banker places in the center of the table the amount he wishes to put at risk. A minimum is usually agreed before the game.

Deal The banker deals three face-down cards to each player but himself, dealing one card at a time.

Play Players bet without looking at their cards. Play begins with the player to the banker's left. He places his bet in front of him: this may be any amount up to half the total of the bank.

The banker then "burns" the top card of the deck, ie he turns it face up, shows it to all players, and places it face up at the bottom of the deck. He then turns up the next card and this becomes the banker's card.

The first player then turns his own cards face up. If he holds a higher ranking card of the same suit as the banker's card, he wins; if not, he loses.

If he has won, he receives back his bet and twice that amount from the bank.

If he has lost, his bet is added to the bank.

His cards are then placed face up at the bottom of the deck. Bet and play then pass one player to the left. After the player has bet, the banker burns one card before exposing a new banker's card.

Change of banker If the bank is emptied at any time, the bank and deal immediately pass one player to the left and a new round is begun.

If the bank is not emptied at the end of a round, the same banker continues to deal.

If, at the end of any round, the bank has increased to three or more times the size it was when the present banker began, then the banker declares a "stitch" round. He deals one more round, and, at the end of this, collects anything left in the bank. Bank and deal then pass one player to the left.

A player must continue to act as banker until the bank is emptied or a stitch round has been completed.

Deal

Play

Player 1, wins

Banker's card

Player 2, loses

Player 3, wins

The matched and matching cards are dead, but are left on the layout, on top of each other, as a reminder that this denomination is out of play. Any further cards of that denomination are placed on top of the matched cards.

If the dealt card matches the banker's card, the banker pays all bets at even money, ie each winning player receives his stake plus an equal amount from the bank. Play on this deal then ceases and the bank and deal pass one player to the left.

Continuing play If the banker's card is not matched immediately, play continues in the same way until it has been matched—when the banker pays all outstanding bets.

A card is dealt in each turn—

and either matches a card on the layout or becomes a new players' card.

Each time one of the players' cards is matched, the banker collects the bets on that card. Between turns, players may place new bets on the players' cards. But a bet that has once been placed may not be removed or transferred to another card.

Explanation of play diagram
a) The 8 was dealt first, and became a players' card.
b) The king was dealt, matching a hand card and having no effect on play.
c) The 6 was dealt. It matches the banker's card—so players win all bets and the deal ends.

Betting

Players' card

Hand cards

Banker's card

Play

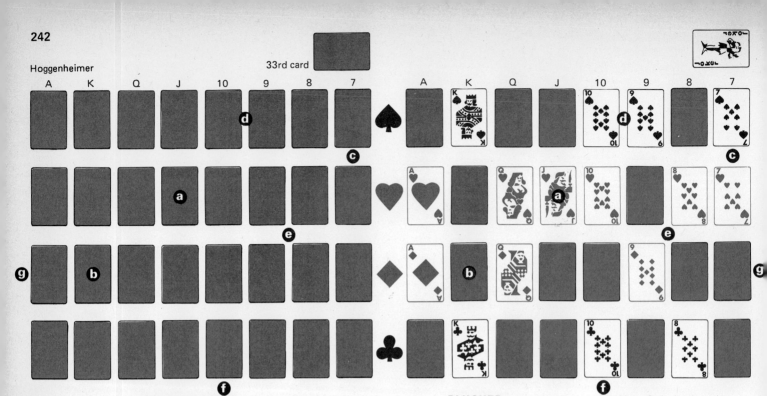

33rd card

HOGGENHEIMER
Equipment:
1) one standard deck of 52 cards from which the 2s, 3s, 4s, 5s, and 6s have been removed.
2) one joker (or any one of the discarded cards if a joker is not available);
3) betting chips.

Players The game is for two or more players.

Objective Players try to bet on a card (or cards) exposed before the joker is exposed.

Choice of first banker is by high cut (see p 80).

Shuffle and cut are normal. (See p 80).

Dealing the layout The banker deals four rows of eight cards face down, and the 33rd card face down to one side. He takes care that no card's face is seen during the deal.

Betting limits are agreed beforehand.

Betting Each player but the banker places as many bets as he wishes.

The card bet on is shown by the position of the bet on the layout. The top row represents spades, the next hearts, the next diamonds, and the bottom row clubs. The column furthest to the right represents 7s, the next 8s, and so on; the column furthest to the left represents aces.

Examples of betting are shown in the illustration:
a) is a bet on the jack of hearts;
b) on the king of diamonds;
c) is on two adjacent cards— the 7s of spades and hearts;
d) is on two adjacent cards— the 9 and 10 of spades;
e) is on four cards in a square —the 8s and 9s of hearts and diamonds;

f) is on a column of cards of a single denomination—all the 10s;
g) is on a row of cards of the same suit—a bet on all the diamonds.

Play The banker turns the 33rd card face up.

If it is a joker the deal ends and the banker collects all bets.

If it is any other card the banker places it face up in its correct position on the layout. Any bet on that position is replaced on top of the card. The face-down card that was in that position is removed, turned face up, and placed in its correct position in the layout.

Play continues in this way until the joker appears.

Settlement A player's bet wins if all the cards bet on are turned up before the joker. The banker collects all other bets.

In the example illustrated: bets (**a**),(**c**), and (**d**) win; bets (**b**),(**e**),(**f**), and (**g**) lose.

Bets on single cards are paid 1 to 1.

Bets on two cards are paid 2 to 1.

Bets on four cards in a square or column are paid 4 to 1.

Bets on eight cards in a row are paid 8 to 1.

Continuing play The bank and deal pass one player to the left. This rotation overcomes any bias in the settlement odds. All cards are collected for the next hand.

BLUCHER
This game is named after a German general who fought against Napoleon. Modified rules are given here.

Equipment:
1) one standard deck of cards;
2) betting chips;
3) a betting layout with areas representing each denomination of card (it can be made up of cards from another deck, or may be drawn on paper).

Players: three or more.

Objective Players aim to bet on a denomination on the layout that is not matched during the hand.

A denomination is matched when the dealer, having called that denomination, turns up a card of that rank.

Choice of first banker is by high cut (see p 80).

Shuffle and cut are normal (see p 80).

Betting limits are agreed beforehand.

Betting Each player but the banker places as many bets on the layout as he wishes. Each bet must be placed on only one denomination.

Play The banker turns up cards one at a time from the top of the deck to form a face-up pile on the table. As he turns the first card up he says "Ace." He says "Deuce" for the second, and so on. For the eleventh, he says "Jack," for the twelfth, "Queen," and for the thirteenth, "King."

For each card, if the denomination of the exposed card matches the rank called, the bank collects any bets placed on that denomination on the layout.

For example, if the eighth

card is an 8, the banker wins the bets on section 8; if the twelfth card is a queen, he wins the bets on the queen's section.

Each time the banker wins a bet on the layout, he is paid an additional equal amount by the player who made that bet. When the banker has counted to king he begins again from ace, still turning up a card from the deck for each rank he calls. The players may not add to, remove, or change their bets. The banker collects bets as before, if rank and card match. Play continues in this way until the banker has counted from ace to king four times. All the deck has then been dealt.

Doubling This occurs if at any time the banker counts from ace to king without any of the 13 cards matching the rank called. The banker must then, with his own chips, double all players' bets that are then on the layout. However, the bets stay on the layout and are still at risk. This doubling only takes place once in a single deal. If the banker counts from ace to king again without any cards matching, he does not add again to the players' bets. If the banker wins a player's bet that has been doubled, he wins all the doubled bet plus an equal amount from the player.

Final settlement Any bets still on the layout at the end of the game are returned to the players who placed them.

Continuing play Bank and deal pass one player to the left. All the cards are collected for the next deal, and new bets are placed.

CHINESE FAN-TAN

This simple game works on the same principle as the Chinese bean game of fan-tan (p 272). It was once an American gambling house game but disappeared because it gives no advantage to the banker.

Equipment:
1) one standard deck of cards;
2) one joker to be used for the betting layout;
3) betting chips—preferably a different color for each player.

Players The game is for two or more players.

Objective Players aim to guess how nearly the number of cards in a section cut from the deck will be divisible by four.

Choice of first banker is by high cut (see p 80).

Betting limits are agreed beforehand.

Bank Because each player may make more than one bet, the betting limits do not limit a bank's losses. A banker therefore places to one side, before his first hand as banker, any of his fund of chips he is not prepared to put at risk. The remainder constitutes the bank. Any winnings gained during a player's turn as banker must remain at risk in the bank until the role of banker passes to the next player.

The betting layout consists of the joker, turned face up in the center of the table. The card is placed so that one of its short sides is facing the banker.

Each of the joker's corners is allocated a number. As the banker looks at the card, the bottom left hand corner is 1, the top left hand corner 2, the top right hand corner 3, and the bottom right hand corner 4.

Bets at the corners of the joker are on one number only. Bets along the side of the joker are on the numbers of the two adjacent corners.

In the example illustrated, bet (**a**) is on 3, bet (**b**) on 3 and 4, and bet (**c**) on 4 and 1.

A player may place as many bets as he likes, provided each bet is within the betting limits. For each bet, he puts down the number of chips he wishes to put at risk.

More than one player may make the same bet. The banker does not bet.

Shuffle The player to the banker's left shuffles the deck thoroughly and gives it to the banker.

Play The banker cuts a section of at least one third of the cards from the deck, and then counts them out face down onto the table in groups of four. If the section divides exactly into groups of four, 4 is the winning number.

If a number of cards is left over after counting out in fours, the number left over is the winning number.

In the example illustrated, the section comprised 19 cards—four groups of cards and three over.

Settlement of bets The banker first collects losing bets and then pays winning ones. Bets on single numbers are paid at 3 to 1—bet (**a**) in the example illustrated. Bets on two numbers are paid at evens —bet (**b**). (Bet (**c**) loses.) The banker first pays any winnings due to the player to his left and then those due to the other players in turn.

If the bank is emptied before all winnings have been paid, the winning bets that remain unpaid are simply returned to the bettors.

Change of banker Unless the bank has been emptied, bank and deal remain with one player for a set number of hands agreed beforehand. After this the banker receives all the chips then in the bank, and bank and deal pass one player to the left.

The bank and deal pass immediately if a bank is emptied.

Betting

Settlement

Private monte bank

Top layout

Bottom layout

"Gate"
Gate matches
bottom layout

Rank of cards

MONTE BANK (PRIVATE)

This is a simple version of the gambling club game (p 212). Cards are matched by suit not by denomination.

Equipment:
1) one standard deck of 52 cards with all 10s, 9s, and 8s removed to leave a 40-card deck;
2) betting chips.

Players The game is for two or more players.

Objective Players bet that one of two cards on a "layout" (pair of cards) will be matched.
A card is matched when the next card exposed from the deck is of the same suit.

Choice of first banker/ dealer is by low cut (see p 80).

Shuffle and cut are normal (see p 80).

Dealing the layouts
Holding the deck face down, the banker deals two cards from the bottom. He places them face up on the table, slightly apart. These form the "top layout."
He then deals two cards from the top of the deck and places them face up on the table, slightly below the first two cards. These form the "bottom layout."
The deal is valid whatever suits appear—even if all four cards are of the same suit.

Betting Each player but the banker may bet on the top or the bottom layout or on both. A bet on a particular layout is shown by placing the chips between that pair of cards.

Betting limits are agreed beforehand.

Play The banker turns the deck face up, exposing the bottom card. This card is known as the "gate."
If the gate card's suit matches one (or both) of the cards in a layout, the players win any bets on that layout.
If the gate card matches cards in both layouts, the players win their bets on both layouts.
If no layout card is matched all bets are lost.

Settlement The banker collects all losing bets. Winning bets are paid at 1 to 1, even if both cards in a layout were matched.

Continuing play The banker collects together the layout cards, and places them to one side to form a discard pile.
He then turns the deck face down, takes the next gate card from the bottom of the deck and puts it on the discard pile.
He then deals the layout cards for the next hand. There is no shuffle or cut.

Change of banker Bank and deal remain with one player for a previously agreed number of hands (up to a maximum of six). At least 10 cards of the deck should remain unplayed to prevent players calculating which suits remain.
The bank and deal then pass one player to the left. All cards are collected, and the deck shuffled and cut as before.
If the bank and deal is emptied at any time bank and deal pass immediately.

BANKER AND BROKER

This simple game has very fast betting action. Also known as Dutch bank and blind hookey, it is played in a number of slightly different ways.

Equipment:
1) one standard deck of cards;
2) betting chips (or cash).

Players: two or more.

Rank of cards is normal (ace high). Suits are not ranked.

Objective Players try to bet on a card of higher denomination than that bet on by the banker.

Choice of first banker is by high cut (see p 80).

Shuffle and cut are normal (see p 80).

Betting limits are as agreed.

Basic form of play
1) The banker cuts a number of sections from the deck: one for himself and one for each of the other players.
2) The other players lay bets on their sections by placing chips (or cash) beside them.
3) The banker turns all the sections face up to show the bottom cards.
4) The banker collects the bets on sections showing a lower denomination card than his own. He pays 1 to 1 on sections showing a card of higher denomination.

Points of variation

1) Discarding the bottom card: either the banker removes and discards the bottom card from the deck before cutting; or, he leaves an unused bottom section after cutting.
2) Timing of bets: bets are placed either before or after the sections are cut.
3) Number of sections cut: either the banker cuts one section for each player and one for himself (up to a limit of seven), and each player may only bet on the section cut for him;
or, the banker cuts three sections, two for the players and one for himself, and each player bets at will on either or both of the players' sections;
or, the banker cuts as many sections as he likes, varying the number from deal to deal if he wishes, and the players bet as they please but leave one section for the banker.
4) When the banker's denomination is the same as that bet on by a player: either the bank wins or the player's bet is returned.
5) Change of banker: either the bank passes one player to the left after each deal or set number of deals; or, players cut for the bank after each deal or set number of deals;
or, the bank is passed when a player bets on an ace.
If two players (or player and banker) both have an ace, or if two players have bet on the same ace, the deck is cut and the bank goes to the player with the higher card.

Banker and broker

Deal

Play

A HUSTLER'S GAME: ACE-DEUCE-JACK

The odds in this game are so heavily loaded that it is found only as a hustler's game.

Equipment:
1) one standard deck of cards;
2) cash for betting.

Players Two or more can play. One player is banker.

WITH THE HUSTLER AS BANKER

Objective Players bet that none of the three cards exposed in play will be an ace, deuce (2), or jack.

Betting limits are agreed beforehand.

Shuffle and cut The banker shuffles. Any player has the right to shuffle but the banker has the right to shuffle last. Any player other than the banker then cuts the deck.

Preparation
1) The banker takes three cards face down from the bottom of the deck, making sure that no one sees their denominations. These three cards are ruled "dead," and are put to one side.
2) The banker then cuts two groups of cards from the deck, taking care that no one sees the bottom card of each cut. He places each group face down alongside the deck, so that there are now three groups of cards on the table.

Bet and play Each player but the banker may place a bet. The banker then turns the three sections face up, exposing the bottom card of each section.

Settlement If any one of the three cards is an ace, deuce, or jack, the banker takes all bets. If none of the cards is one of these denominations, the banker pays 1 to 1 on all bets.

Continuing play All cards in the deck are collected, shuffled, and then cut for the next turn of play.

WITH THE SUCKER AS BANKER

Sometimes the sucker wants to be banker. The hustler then suggests the following version, in which players bet on which denomination will appear. "You bank, and we'll do the guessing too," says the hustler. "You can't help but win."

On a big hustle, with a planned victim, the hustler may set up this version from the beginning.

Objective Players bet that one of the three cards exposed in play will be one of three specified denominations.

Betting limits are agreed beforehand.

Shuffle, cut, and preparation are as for the version with the hustler as banker.

Betting Each player but the banker may place a bet. Sometimes the betting denominations are as in the first version, ie ace, deuce, jack.

But usually the three denominations change for each hand, and are chosen by the players as they place their bets.

This "guessing" process gives the banker the impression that the odds are with him.

Play The banker turns the three sections face up, exposing the bottom card of each section.

Settlement If none of the three cards is one of the three denominations bet on, the banker takes all bets.

But if any one or more of the denominations appear, the banker pays 1 to 1 on all bets. (Note that he pays only 1 to 1 even if two or three denominations appear.)

Continuing play is as in the first version.

The hustle There are high odds that the three exposed cards will include one of any three specified denominations. This will occur on average nearly 60 times in 100 plays—which is enough to ruin anyone betting against these odds.

The hustler simply has to ensure that the sucker is on the wrong side of the appropriate version of the game.

Ace-deuce-jack

Dead cards

Deal

Show

Pool games

In the private gambling games that follow, there is no banker. Instead, all players' bets take the form of contributions to a central pool. In many games the entire pool is then won by a single player—usually at the end of every hand—but in other games the pool acts as a reservoir of chips, from which payments are made to players according to their success.

INJUN

This fast, amusing game is very simple to play. But it can see a lot of money change hands very rapidly, and offers opportunities for skillful judgment to anyone familiar with mathematical odds.

Equipment:
a) a standard deck of 52 cards;
b) betting chips or cash.
Players: from two to about 15.
Rank of cards The cards rank in normal order, with ace high. The suits are not ranked.
The objective is to bet on holding a higher ranking card than any other player.

Choice of first dealer is by deal: first ace to appear (see p 80).
Shuffle and cut are normal (see p 80).
Ante Before each deal, each player, including the dealer, puts an equal amount into the center of the table to form a pool. This amount is known as the "ante."
Deal The dealer deals one card face down to each player including himself, beginning with the player to his left and going clockwise.
Play Players are not allowed to look at their own cards. Each picks up his own card and puts it against his forehead.
He holds it there, face outward, so that all the other players in the game can see the card.
Players should watch carefully at this stage of play to check that no player glimpses his own card.

Betting begins with the player to the dealer's left, and goes clockwise.
Each player bets according to his judgment of whether his own card, which he cannot see, is likely to be higher in rank than all the other players' cards—which he can see.
A player must bet to stay in the game. If he drops out at any time, he places his card face down on the table in front of him.
All bets are placed in the pool.
Betting principles There are two alternatives:
a) poker betting;
b) brag betting.

Poker betting In this alternative each player in turn bets, calls, raises, or drops out until the bets are equalized. When this happens, betting ends and there is a showdown between all active players.
Brag betting In this alternative, betting is as in the "round the table" system in brag. Each player in each of his turns contributes one unit to the pool, or drops out. No one can raise and betting continues until all but two players have dropped out. These last two active players then continue to put bets of one unit each into the pool, until:
a) one of them drops out leaving the other player the winner; or
b) one of them pays two units to "see the other" and there is a showdown between these two players.

Showdown On showdown all active players look at their own cards.
The player with the highest card wins the play and takes the pool.
Ties for highest card divide the pool.
"Covering the kitty" If a player runs out of money during betting he places his card face down on the pool—allowing all other players to remind themselves of its rank before he does so.
Subsequent bets of other players are then placed in a side pool.
Showdown is then between three players: between the last two active players for the side pool, and between these two and the player who covered the kitty for the main pool.
Continuing play After the pool has been won the deal passes one player to the left and all players ante for the next play.

RED DOG

This fast betting game, also known as high card pool, is very popular among American news reporters. It needs little skill and is usually played for low stakes.

Equipment:
1) one standard deck of cards;
2) betting chips (or cash).
Players: from two to ten.
Rank of cards is normal (ace high). Suits are not ranked.
Objective Players aim to hold a card in the same suit but of higher rank than a card dealt from the deck.
Choice of first dealer is by deal: first ace to appear. (See p 80.)
Shuffle and cut are normal (see p 80).

Ante Before each deal, each player, including the dealer, puts an equal amount into the pool. This amount is known as the "ante."
Deal The dealer deals five face-down cards to each player including himself, beginning with the player to his left and going clockwise. (Four cards each are dealt if players prefer or if more than eight are playing.)

Betting All players look at their cards. Play begins with the player to the dealer's left. He must bet if he wants to stay in the game. To bet he places his stake in front of him, near the pool.
The minimum bet is equal to the ante. The maximum bet is equal to the total in the pool at the time. The dealer must keep note of all bets.
If a player does not wish to stay in the game, he must pay a forfeit equal to the minimum bet but may then place his hand face down on the table without showing it.

Red dog

Deal

Play

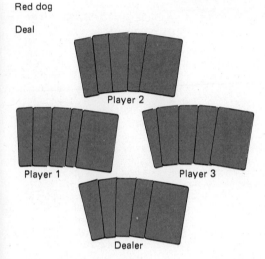

Play The dealer deals the top card from the deck face up onto the table in front of the bettor. If the player holds a card of higher rank in the same suit, he wins; if not, he loses. If he has won, he shows the winning card only (**a**); he receives back his bet and an equal amount from the pool. If he has lost, he shows all his hand (**b**), and his bet is added to the pool.
In either case, his hand is then placed face down in front of him.
Bet and play then pass one player to the left.
When all players including the dealer have had a turn of play, the deal passes to the next player to the left. Any money in the pool remains, but all players ante again before the next round is dealt.
Empty pool If the pool is emptied during a round, all players ante again to allow the round to continue. They must still ante again before the next round begins.

Division of the pool
Sometimes the pool becomes too large for the level of betting. It is best if a limit for the pool is agreed beforehand. If the pool passes that limit, it is divided among the players at the end of that round.
Irregularities
1) If a player receives no hand, or too many cards in his hand, he may not take part in the round. The dealer is not penalized.
2) If a player receives too few cards in his hand, he may bet if he wishes, or he may discard his hand without showing it and without betting or paying a forfeit. The dealer is not penalized.
3) If the top card of the deck is accidentally exposed, it is discarded.
4) Once a player has stated his bet, he cannot alter it. A bet paid into the pool in error cannot be returned. A bet received from the pool in error cannot be taken back once the top card for the next player has been dealt.

VARIANTS OF RED DOG
Burning card version The dealer "burns" a card from the top of the deck before each card that he exposes to settle a bet. That is, at each bettor's turn, the dealer discards the topmost card after turning it face up and showing it to all the players. The next card is then turned up to decide whether the bettor has won or lost.

Banking version Red dog can also be played as a banking game. The current dealer acts as banker. He does not deal himself a hand. Before the hand, the dealer places in front of him the money or chips he wishes to put at risk. This can be any amount he wishes. The players do not ante.
Each player in turn, excluding the banker, bets any amount he wishes up to the total then in the bank.
Any amount left in the bank at the end of the hand is returned to the banker. The bank and deal then pass one player to the left.
If the bank is emptied before all the players have had a turn, the hand ends and the bank and deal pass at once.

Deal

Play

SIX-SPOT RED DOG
Equipment:
1) one standard deck of 52 cards;
2) betting chips (or cash).
Players The game is for two to 15 players.
Rank of cards is normal (ace high).
Objective Players aim to hold a card in the same suit but of higher rank than the pool card.
Choice of first dealer is by deal: first ace to appear. (See p80.)
Shuffle and cut are normal (see p80).
Ante Before each deal, each player including the dealer puts an agreed equal amount into the pool.
Deal The dealer deals three face-down cards to each player including himself, beginning with the player to his left and going clockwise. The dealer then deals one card from the top of the deck face up to the center of the table.
If it is a 6 or lower (6,5,4,3 or 2) it becomes the pool card. If it is a 7 or higher, it is discarded and the next card from the top of the deck is dealt face up onto the table. This procedure is repeated until a 6 or lower card is dealt to become the pool card. If there is no such card left in the deck, the hand is redealt.

Betting All players including the dealer bet immediately without looking at their cards. The minimum bet is one chip (or a previously agreed amount of money). The maximum bet is the amount then in the pool. More than one player may bet the maximum.
Play Players then turn their hands face up. If a player has a card of the same suit but ranking higher than the pool card, he has won. If not, he has lost.
Settlement of bets is supervised by the dealer. He first adds to the pool the bets of all the players who have lost. Then he pays out to those players who have won, beginning with the player to his left and going clockwise. Winning bets are returned together with an equal amount from the pool.
If the pool is emptied before all winning players have been paid, the remaining players receive back only their bets.
If anything remains in the pool after all bets have been settled, this amount is carried over to the next round.
The deal then passes one player to the left, and all players ante again to begin the next round.

VARIANT: BANKING VERSION
Six-spot red dog can also be played as a banking game. The dealer acts as banker. He does not deal himself a hand or bet.
Bank Before the hand, the banker places in front of him the money or chips he wishes to put at risk. This can be any amount he wishes. The players do not ante.
Deal The banker deals to the players as usual but excludes himself. He then deals one card at a time to the table in the usual way, until a 6 or lower card is dealt. This is now referred to as the banker's card.
Betting begins with the player to the banker's left. He may bet ("cover") any amount up to the total of the bank. Subsequent players may only bet against any amount of the bank that has not yet been "covered." The total of bets against the bank cannot therefore exceed the amount in the bank.
If all the bank has been covered before all players have bet, the remaining players are not allowed to bet on that hand.
Any part of the bank that is not covered when all players have bet is not at risk in that hand.
Play and settlement of bets takes place in the usual way. When all bets have been settled, any amount left in the bank is returned to the banker. The bank and deal then pass one player to the left.

THIRTY-FIVE
Thirty-five is a modern version of the Italian game of trentacinque.
Equipment:
1) one standard deck of 52 cards;
2) betting chips (or cash).
Players The game is for two to five players.
Rank of cards Court cards count 10 points; others count their pip value.
Objective Each player aims to hold a total of 35 points or more in one suit.
Choice of first dealer is by high cut (see p80).
Shuffle and deal are normal (see p80).
Ante Before each hand, each player including the dealer places an agreed equal amount in the center of the table to form the pool.
Deal
1) The dealer deals one card face down to each player including himself and then one card face down to the center of the table. He continues in this way until each hand, including the hand on the table, contains four cards. He then deals no further cards to the center of the table, but continues dealing to each player,

THIRTY-ONE (SCHNAUTZ)
Equipment:
1) one standard deck of cards;
2) betting chips (or cash).
Players: from three to 15.
Value of cards Aces count 11, court cards 10, and all other cards their pip value.
Rank of cards is normal, ace high. Thus although court cards all count 10, king beats queen and queen beats jack.
Objective Players aim to obtain the highest points count from three cards of the same suit or rank.
Choice of first dealer is by low cut (see p80).
Shuffle and cut are normal (see p80).
Ante Before each hand, each player including the dealer puts an agreed equal amount into a pool.
Deal The dealer deals one card face down to each player including himself, beginning with the player to his left and going clockwise; and then one card to the center of the table. This continues until all players and the table hand (the "widow") each have three cards.

including himself, until each has a further five cards. Thus the hand at the center of the table contains four cards and the other hands nine cards each.

2) The remaining cards of the deck are placed to one side and do not enter subsequent play.

3) The players then examine their cards. A player who holds cards in any one suit to the value of 35 or over announces this and takes the pool. If two or more players have 35 or more, the pool is divided between them.

4) If no player claims the pool, bidding begins.

Bidding for the "buy"
Betting takes the form of bidding for the table hand—the "buy."

Bidding begins with the player to the dealer's left. His opening bid may be any amount up to the total in the pool. (If he does not wish to bid, he throws in his cards.) Thereafter, each player may raise the bid or throw in his cards until only one player is left prepared to bid. He then takes the table hand and adds it to the nine cards he already holds.

Settlement involves only the pool and the player who has taken the table hand. If the player now holds cards to the value of 35 or over in any one suit, he declares this, shows his cards, and takes an amount from the pool equal to his bid. If his bid exceeded the amount of the pool, he takes all the pool but has no further claim. If the player does not hold cards in one suit to the value of 35 or more, he pays into the pool an amount equal to his bid.

Division of the pool
Sometimes the pool becomes too large for the level of betting. It is best if a limit for the pool is agreed beforehand. If the pool passes that limit, it is divided among the players.

Change of dealer The deal passes one player to the left after each hand.

Deal

Value of cards

End of play

Making 35 — in hearts

Play Each player examines his cards and announces immediately if he holds:
a) three cards of one suit—with a points total of 31 ("31 points");
b) any three cards of the same rank ("three cards");
c) three cards of one suit—with a points total that he feels is high enough to win ("x points").
If a player announces immediately, all players show their hands and the highest point count wins.
If no player announces immediately, the player to the dealer's left must exchange one of his cards with any face-up card on the table. (Sometimes it is agreed that two or even three cards may be exchanged in one turn.) He is not allowed to pass.
The next player then does the same. Cards that have been put out by a player may subsequently be picked up. Play continues around the table in this way until one player has 31 points or is satisfied with his cards.
If a player has 31 points he must announce it immediately, and all exchanging ends. All players then show their hands. If a player is satisfied with his

hand he knocks on the table instead of exchanging a card in his next turn. In this case, hands are not shown until each of the other players in turn has had the option of exchanging one more card. The pool is won by the player who shows the best hand. The deal then passes to the next player to the left.

Scoring of hands A hand with three cards of the same rank scores 30½; all others score their points count. Illustrated examples are:
a) 31 point hand comprising ace, queen, 10;
b) 30½ point hand comprising three 6s;
c) 30 point hand comprising king, jack, 10;
d) 29 point hand comprising king, queen, 9;
e) 28 point hand comprising ace, king, 7.
Where two or more players have hands scoring the same number of points, the hand containing the higher ranking card wins. For example: ace, king, queen beats ace, queen, jack; and three 6s beats three 5s. (Note that a score of 25 or 26 points often wins.)

a

31 points

b

30½ points

c

30 points

d

29 points

e

28 points

Deal

Play

"Widow"

14 points

27 points

13 points

"Widow"

Value of cards

250

Deal

Play

Player wins

Player loses

Consecutive cards: no bet

YABLON

This game is also called in between and ace-deuce.

Equipment:
1) one standard deck of cards;
2) betting chips (or cash).

Players: from two to eight.

Rank of cards is normal, ace high. Suits have no significance.

Objective Each player hopes to draw a card ranking between his first two cards.

Choice of first dealer is by deal: first ace to appear. (See p 80.)

Shuffle and cut are normal (see p 80).

Ante Before each deal each player including the dealer puts an equal agreed amount into the pool.

Deal The dealer deals two face-down cards one at a time to each player including himself.

Play begins with the player to the dealer's left.
1) He examines his cards and decides whether to bet.
2) If he does not wish to bet he says "No bet," and returns his cards to the dealer to be placed on a discard pile. Play then passes to the left.
If the first player does wish to bet, he places his bet in front

of him near the pool. The minimum bet is the same amount as a player's ante; the maximum is the total amount then in the pool.
3) The dealer deals him the top card from the deck, face up. This is called the player's draw card.
4) The player turns his two original cards face up.
5) If his draw card ranks between his original two cards, the player wins. For example, if he has a 5 and a 9 he must draw a 6, 7, or 8 to win; if he has a 2 and an ace he can draw any card except a 2 or an ace to win. Note that if a player holds two identical cards (eg two 6s) or two consecutive cards (eg 10 and jack), he cannot win and will not bet.
6) If the player has won, he retains his bet and takes from the pool an amount equal to his bet. If he has lost, his bet goes into the pool.
7) Each player including the dealer has a turn of play, with turns passing to the left.

Continuing play After each player has had a turn, the deal passes to the player to the dealer's left. He collects all the cards, shuffles them, and has them cut for the next hand.

Any money left in the pool remains for the next hand, but players also ante again.

Division of pool If the pool passes a limit agreed beforehand it is immediately divided among the players.

YABLON VARIANT

Yablon can also be played as a banking game. The dealer acts as banker and does not deal himself a hand.

Before the hand, the dealer places in front of him the money or chips he wishes to put at risk. This can be any amount he wishes. The players do not ante.

Each player in turn bets any amount he wishes, up to the amount then in the bank. The dealer does not have a turn. Any amount left in the bank at the end of the hand is returned to the banker. The bank and deal then pass one player to the left.

If the bank is emptied before all the players have had a turn, the hand ends and the bank and deal pass at once.

BANGO

Equipment:
1) two standard decks of cards, with different backs;
2) betting chips.

Players The game is for three to ten players.

Objective Each player aims to be the first player to turn all his face-up cards face down.

Choice of first dealer is by deal: first ace to appear. (See p 80.)

Shuffle and cut The dealer and the player to his left each shuffle one deck of cards. Each deck is then offered separately to the player to the dealer's right to be cut in the usual way (see p 80).

Ante Before each deal, each player including the dealer puts an equal agreed amount into the pool.

Deal From one deck, the dealer deals five cards to each player including himself, dealing them face up and one at a time. The rest of this deck is then put to one side out of play.

Play The players arrange their cards face up in front of them. The dealer then takes the second deck of cards and deals the top card face up onto the table, stating its rank and suit

as he does so.
If any player including the dealer has the identical card from the first deck face up in front of him, he now turns that card face down.
The dealer then takes the next card from the top of the second deck and deals it face up onto the table, stating its rank and suit as he does so.
Play continues in this way until one player has turned all his cards face down. He announces this by calling "Bango."

Checking The dealer checks the hand of the player who called against the cards that have been dealt from the second deck, and if no mistake has been made that player wins the pool.

Change of dealer The deal passes one player to the left after each hand.

BANGO VARIANT

In this game players take into account only the rank of the cards turned up by the dealer. The dealer calls the rank and players turn face down all cards of that rank in their hands.

Deal

End of play

KENTUCKY DERBY

Also called pasteboard derby, this game has a varied race and simple betting.

Equipment:
1) one standard deck of cards;
2) betting chips (or cash).

Players: three or more.

Objective Players try to bet on the winning "horse."

Choice of first dealer is by high cut (see p 80).

Shuffle and cut The four aces are removed from the deck. The rest of the deck is shuffled and cut in the normal way (see p 80).

The "course" After the shuffle and cut, the dealer forms the course by dealing seven face-down cards in a line.

The "horses" The four aces are the horses—they can be given the names of favorites. They are lined up just below the first course card, in the order: hearts, diamonds, spades, clubs.

To make judging easier, the two red aces are put to one side of the course and the two black aces to the other.

The player to the dealer's left lines up the aces and moves them during the race.

Ante Before the game, each player including the dealer puts an equal agreed amount into the pool.

Betting Each player decides which horse he will back. A player may only bet on one horse; more than one player may bet on the same horse. A horse still runs even if no one bets on it.

It is best to write down the selections if there are several players. This is done by the player to the dealer's right. He also has charge of the pool and pays out the winnings at the end.

Starting the race The dealer deals the top card from the deck face up onto the table just behind the ace of hearts.

The player to the dealer's left moves the ace of hearts the appropriate number of spaces up the course, if any (see moves table).

The dealer then deals a card behind the ace of diamonds, and so on.

Running the race How far a horse moves depends on the card dealt. The dealer deals one card to each ace in turn, in the order: hearts, diamonds, spades, clubs, and then starts again.

Further cards dealt to each ace are placed face up on top of the cards first dealt, forming four discard piles.

Finishing the race A horse finishes when it passes the last course card.

But the winner is only decided when all horses have had an equal number of turns. The winner is then the ace that has gone furthest over the finishing line.

If the second place horse is to be decided too, and only the winning horse has crossed the finishing line, then the winner's discard pile is turned face down, and play continues with the remaining aces.

Splitting "dead heats"

Sometimes two aces have gone an equal distance over the finishing line on the same turn.

Each is then dealt a further card from the deck. This continues until, with an equal number of cards dealt, one horse has gone further past the post than the other.

Settlement: winning horse only With fewer than six players, races are run for first place only.

The pool is won by the player or players betting on the winning horse.

If there are two or more successful bettors, the pool is split equally between them.

If the pool does not divide equally, any chips over stay in the pool for the next race.

Settlement: winner and second place With six or more players, races may be run for first and second places.

Bettors on the second place horse receive back their ante from the pool.

The remainder of the pool is won (and divided if necessary) by the player(s) who bet on the winning horse.

Preparing for the next race

The deal passes to the player to the dealer's left. He collects all the cards (except the aces) and reshuffles them.

The player to the new dealer's left controls the horses, and the player to his right bets.

Finish line

2 lengths

1½ lengths

1 length

The moves

	Card played	Distance moved
Ace moves forward	king	2 lengths
	queen	1½ lengths
	jack	1 length
	7, 8, 9, or 10 same color as ace	1 length
	3, 4, 5, or 6 same color as ace	½ length

Any card dealt of same suit as ace adds ½ length

Ace moves back	2 of same color as ace	½ length back
	2 not of same color as ace	1 length back

2 dealt while ace still on starting line — No move

Word games

Play with words is a popular form of amusement, newly devised games taking their place alongside old favorites. Word games range from straightforward spelling games to more complex games requiring verbal dexterity or skilful guesswork. Most of the games can be played by any number of people.

STANDARD SPELLING BEE

One person is chosen as leader, and the other players sit facing him.

The leader is either given a previously prepared list of words or he makes one up himself. It is a good idea to have a dictionary to hand in case of disputes.

Play The leader reads out the first word on his list and the first player tries to spell it. He is allowed ten seconds in which to make an attempt at the correct spelling.

If he succeeds, he scores one point and the next word is read out for the next player.

If he makes a mistake, the leader reads out the correct spelling. The player does not score for that word, and the next word is read out for the next player. (Alternatively, the player is eliminated from the game for an incorrect answer.)

Play continues around the group of players until all the words on the list have been spelled.

The winner is the player with the most points at the end of the game.

GREEDY SPELLING BEE

In this version of standard spelling bee, if a player spells a word correctly he is given another word to spell. Only when he makes a mistake does the next player take a turn—and he starts with the incorrectly spelled word.

One point is scored for each correct spelling, and the player with the highest score at the end of the game wins.

BACKWARD SPELLING BEE

In this more difficult version of the standard game, players must spell their words backward.

Scoring is the same as in standard spelling bee.

RIGHT OR WRONG SPELLING BEE

The players should form two teams of equal size, and get in line opposite each other.

The leader calls out a word to each player in turn, alternating between teams. Each time a player spells a word, the player standing opposite him must call out "Right" or "Wrong." If he calls a correctly spelled word wrong or a misspelled word right, he is eliminated from the game and must leave the line. (Players may move around once their numbers have been depleted, so that there is a caller for each player in the other team.)

If the caller makes a correct call, he gets the next word to spell.

The last team to retain any players wins the game.

GRAB ON BEHIND

Also called last and first or alpha and omega, this is another good game for a lot of players.

Players decide on a specific category, such as flowers, cities, or insects.

The first player calls out a word in the chosen category. The next player then follows with another word in the category—but it must begin with the last letter of the previous word. Play continues in this way around the group.

For example, if the category were flowers the words might be: mimosa, anemone, edelweiss, sweet pea, and so on.

Players have only five seconds in which to think of a word and may not repeat a word that has already been called.

Anyone failing to think of a word or calling an incorrect word drops out of that round. The last player to stay in wins.

GHOSTS

Ghosts needs concentration and a good vocabulary to win. The players sit round in a circle and take it in turns to contribute a letter to an unstated word. They try to keep the word going for as long as possible—any player who completes a word loses one of his three "lives."

For example, the first player thinks of any word (about) and calls out its first letter (A). The second player thinks of a word with more than three letters starting with the letter called (agree) and calls out its second letter (G). The third player thinks of a word that begins with AG (agate) and calls out its third letter (A). The next player, thinking of "again," calls out "I." The fifth player, unable to think of anything other than "again" is forced to add N and thus complete a word. He may also try to bluff his way out of the situation by calling out a letter of an imaginary word, in the hope that none of the others will notice—if they do notice, they may challenge him.

Challenging If a player hesitates for too long or the other players suspect that he has no particular word in mind they may challenge him. The challenged player must state his word, and if he cannot do so he loses a "life."

If his explanation is satisfactory, however, the challenger loses a life.

Scoring Whenever a player completes a word he loses a life and becomes "a third of a ghost." Losing a second life makes him "two-thirds of a ghost," and if he loses a third life he becomes a whole ghost and must drop out of the game.

The player who survives until the end is the winner. (For a longer game, the number of lives may be increased to four or five.)

I-SPY

I-spy is an excellent game for children learning to spell. It is also fun for older children, who can try and outwit each other by "spying" (seeing) inconspicuous objects.

Objective Each player tries to be the first to guess which visible object one of them has spied.

Play Two or more people can play, and one of them is chosen to start.

He says "I spy, with my little eye, something beginning with . . ." and gives the first letter of an object that he has secretly chosen, that must be visible to all the players. (They may have to turn their heads in order to see the object, but they should not need to move about.)

For example, if he chose a vase, he would give the letter V or, if he chose a two-word object, the first letter of each word (eg PF for picture frame).

If the player chooses an object, such as a chair, of which there may be more than one in the room, the other players must guess the particular chair he has in mind.

The game ends as soon as someone has spotted the object that was chosen—he may then spy the next object.

Variation I-spy may be played by very young children if colors rather than first letters are given.

For example, a player may say "I spy, with my little eye, something red" and the others then look for the red object that he has in mind.

INITIAL LETTERS

The players sit in a circle. One of them puts a question—it may be as farfetched as he likes—to the others. Each of them in turn must reply with a two-word answer, beginning with the initials of his or her name. Players have only five seconds in which to think of an answer.

For example, if the question were "What is your favorite food?" Bruce Robertson could reply "Boiled rice," and Robert Chapman might say "Roquefort cheese."

When all the players have answered, the second player asks a question.

Any player who fails to answer after five seconds or who gives a wrong answer drops out of the game; the winner is the last person to stay in.

INITIAL ANSWERS

This is a good game for a large group of people. The players sit in a circle and one of them starts by thinking of any letter of the alphabet (eg S). He must then think of a three-letter word beginning with that letter and give a definition of his word, for example "S plus two letters is a father's child."

The second person in the circle has to try and guess the word ("son"), and he then thinks of a word of four letters also beginning with S. He might choose "soup" and define it as "S plus three letters makes a tasty start to a meal" for the person sitting next to him to guess.

This next person, after guessing the word correctly, must think of a five-letter word—perhaps "snail"—defining it as "S plus four letters carries a house on its back."

The game continues in this way, with each person having to think of a word beginning with the chosen letter, and each word having one letter more than the previous word. Any player who fails to think of an appropriate word, or who fails to guess a word must drop out.

The last person left in the game is the winner.

A different letter of the alphabet should be chosen for the next round.

TRAVELER'S ALPHABET

In this game, the first player says "I am going on a journey to Amsterdam," or any other town or country beginning with A.

The next person then asks "What will you do there?" The verb, adjective, and noun used in the answer must all begin with A; for example, "I shall acquire attractive antiques."

The second player must then give a place name and an answer using the letter B, the third player uses the letter C, and so on around the players. Any player who cannot respond is eliminated from the game.

If the players wish to make the game more taxing, they may have to give an answer that is linked with the place they have chosen. For example, a player might say "I am going to Greece to guzzle gorgeous grapes."

If a player gives an inappropriate answer he may be challenged by another player. If that player cannot think of a more fitting sentence, the first player may stay in the game. Should the challenger's sentence be suitably linked, the first player is eliminated.

BUZZ

This game should be played as briskly as possible for maximum enjoyment.

The players sit in a circle. One player calls out "One," the next player "Two," the next "Three," and so on.

As soon as the number five, or any multiple thereof, is reached, the players must say "Buzz." If the number contains a five but is not a multiple of five, only part of it is replaced by buzz. (For example, 52 would be "buzz two.")

If a player forgets to say buzz or hesitates too long, he drops out; the last player to stay in the game is the winner.

FIZZ

This is played exactly like buzz, except that players say "Fizz" for sevens or multiples of seven.

BUZZ-FIZZ

Buzz-fizz combines the two games, so that 57, for example, becomes buzz-fizz.

I LOVE MY LOVE

In I love my love, players have to think of an adjective beginning with each letter of the alphabet to complete a given statement.

The first player starts by saying "I love my love because she is . . ." using any adjective beginning with A. The next person repeats the phrase, but his adjective must begin with B, the next person's with C, and so on through the alphabet.

Alternatively, each player must say a different refrain, as well as using an adjective with a different letter. The refrains may be:
"Her name is . . . ;
She lives in . . . ;
And I shall give her . . ."
Players may write down the refrains decided upon if they wish, but there must be no hesitation over the answers. Any player who hesitates or gives an incorrect answer drops out of the game, and the winner is the last person left in.

A WAS AN APPLE PIE

This is a similar game to I love my love, but players must think of a verb instead of an adjective.

The first player says: "A was an apple pie, A ate it," and other players might add "B baked it," "C chose it," "D dropped it," and so on.

TABOO

In taboo—sometimes called never say it—players try to avoid saying a particular letter of the alphabet.

One player is the questioner and chooses which letter is to be "taboo."

He then asks each of the players in turn any question he likes. The respondent must answer with a sensible phrase or sentence that does not contain the forbidden letter—if he does use the taboo letter, he is out.

The last player to stay in the game wins and becomes the next questioner.

I—spy

© DIAGRAM

6 *Fizz* 8 9 *Buzz* 11 12 13 *Fizz Buzz* 16 1 *Fizz* 18 19 *Buzz Fizz* 22 23 24

JOIN THE CLUB

This game needs players who have not played it before. Only when they guess a secret solution, known only to the leader, are they allowed to "join the club."

The leader says: "Mrs Pettigrew doesn't like tea, what does she like?"

The other players suggest different things and the leader tells them whether they are right or wrong—if they are wrong they must drop out. Play continues until all the players have dropped out, or until one of them guesses the solution; "tea" is really the letter T, so that any answer given should not contain it. For example, answers like "chocolate," "tomatoes," or "tequila" would eliminate a player.

If a player guesses the solution, the leader says "Join the club!"

Other questions the leader could ask are:

"Our cook doesn't like peas, what does he prefer?"; or "The G-man never takes his ease, what does he take?"

COFFEEPOT

Coffeepot is a word substitution game that is easily learned and a lot of fun.

The objective is for one player to guess an activity chosen by the other players. He does so by asking questions in which he substitutes the word "coffeepot" for the unknown word.

Play One player leaves the room while the others choose a verb or participle describing an activity—for instance "laugh" and "eat" or "laughing" and "eating." The player then returns to the room and puts a question to each of the players in turn, saying something like "Do you often coffeepot?" The players must answer truthfully, with either a straight "Yes" or "No," or with answers like "Only sometimes" or "When it rains."

As the guesser does not know what the activity is, some of the questions will be hilarious —which is where the fun of the game lies.

If he manages to guess the word, the player whose answer enabled him to do so becomes the next guesser. If he cannot guess the word within a reasonable time, he must take another turn at guessing.

TEAKETTLE (TEAPOT)

As in coffeepot, one of the players leaves the room while the others think of a word for him to guess.

The choice of word might be quite tricky, as it must be one with several meanings. Examples are: rain, reign, rein; or way, weigh, whey.

The player comes back into the room and listens to the others as they make conversation; he may join in if he likes. Sentences must have "teakettle" in place of the chosen word, so that a player might say: "It always seems to teakettle(rain) when I take my baby for a walk."

As soon as he guesses the word, another player takes a turn at guessing a new word.

A variation of teakettle is for the first player to select the word, and the other players to guess what it is as he makes up different sentences. The first person to guess the word correctly may then take a turn at choosing a word.

ASSOCIATIONS

Associations needs quick thinking, as the slightest hesitation eliminates a player from the game!

One person starts by saying any word (preferably a noun). As quickly as possible, the player next to him says the first word that the first player's word brought to mind, and so on around the group, beginning again with the first player.

If a player hesitates before saying a word, he drops out— if he manages to stay in the game longer than all the other players, he wins.

ASSOCIATION CHAIN

This game can be played as a continuation of the last game. As soon as the chain has been formed, the last player to have called out a word starts to repeat the chain backward. If he makes a mistake, he drops out, and the player before him continues to unravel the chain. This goes on until either the first word is reached, or only one player is left.

The more obvious or striking the associations, the easier it is to unravel the chain.

NUMBER ASSOCIATIONS

Number associations needs a person to call out any number between 1 and 12.

As soon as he has said a number, the players call out an appropriate association. For example, if the number called is seven, a player could call "Deadly sins."

The first player to call out a correct association scores one point. Other players may challenge a reply if they feel it is inappropriate. If the leader agrees with the challenge, that player loses one point from his score.

An association may not be repeated.

At the end of the game, the winner is the person with the highest number of points.

I WENT ON A TRIP

Each player tries to remember and repeat a growing list of items.

One of the players chooses any article he likes—for example an umbrella—and says "I went on a trip and took my umbrella."

The next player repeats that sentence and adds a second item after "umbrella." In this way the players gradually build up a list of articles. Each time his turn comes, a player repeats the list and adds another item. Whenever a player cannot repeat the list correctly, the list is closed and the next player in the group begins a new list.

CITY OF BOSTON

City of Boston is very similar to I went on a trip, but the additions are made at the beginning of the sentence. Thus the first player might say "I shall sell you a nosegay of violets when you come to the City of Boston," and each of the other players repeats that sentence, adding an item he will "sell" to the list.

ONE MINUTE PLEASE

One minute please calls for quick wits and imagination as players try to speak for one minute on a given topic.

One player is chosen as timekeeper, and also picks a topic for each player to talk about.

When it is his turn to speak, the player is told his topic. This may be anything from a serious topic such as "The current political situation" to something frivolous like "Why women wear hats."

The player may choose to treat the subject in any manner he pleases and what he says may be utter nonsense, provided he does not deviate from the topic, hesitate unduly, or repeat himself.

Other players may challenge the speaker if they feel he has broken a ruling. If the timekeeper agrees, then that player must drop out and the next player is given his topic. The winner is the player who manages to speak for an entire minute. If two or more players achieve this, the others decide which of the speeches was the best, or alternatively further rounds may be played.

Associations

WHAT IS MY THOUGHT LIKE?
This is a game for those with a lively imagination and the ability to bluff.
Any number of players may take part. One of them thinks of a thing or a person and asks the other players "What is my thought like?"
Each of them then makes a totally random guess (as no clues have been given) as to the object thought of.
Once all the players have made their guesses, they are told the object and are given a moment or two in which to think of a way of justifying the relationship between the object and their own guesses.
For example, if the object were a tiger and the first player had suggested a fire engine, he might legitimately explain "A fire engine is like a tiger because they both roar down the road!"
As some of the explanations may be rather farfetched they may be discussed among the other players. Any player whose explanation is disallowed must pay a forfeit. If all the players give satisfactory answers, the questioner must pay a forfeit. A different questioner is chosen for each subsequent round.

WHO AM I?
This is a fairly simple game, in which one player does all the guessing.
He leaves the room while the other players think of any well-known personality— real of fictional, dead or alive. The guesser returns to the room and asks "Who am I?" The other players each reply with a clue to the character's identity.
If the character is Napoleon, for example, answers given might be:
"You are rather short and stout;"
"You are a great strategist at war;"
"You underestimated the Russian winter."
When each of the players has given a reply, the guesser may make three guesses as to the identity of the person.
If he fails to guess correctly, he is told the answer.
Another player is always chosen for the next round.

PROVERBS
In this guessing game, one player has to discover a proverb hidden in the other players' answers to his questions. (It is sometimes called hidden proverbs, or guessing proverbs.)
While he is out of the room the other players select a proverb. He returns to the room and asks each player in turn a question—it may be about anything at all, such as "What did you have for breakfast today?"
Each answer must contain one word from the proverb in the correct order. As soon as all the words have been used up, the players begin again with the first word of the proverb. The questioner may make as many guesses at the proverb as he likes within a time limit of, say, ten minutes. If he cannot guess the proverb, he is told the answer and another player takes over as guesser in the next round.

BOTTICELLI
This is another game featuring famous people, and requires a good general knowledge.
One person chooses a personality, and tells the other players the initial of his surname. For example, he might say "M" for Groucho Marx.
Taking turns, each player must think of a character whose name begins with that letter, and give a description of him without naming the person he has in mind. If he thought of Mickey Mouse, he would ask "Are you a Walt Disney cartoon character?"
If the first player recognizes the description, he answers "No, I am not Mickey Mouse," and another player may make a guess.
If the first player does not recognize the description, however, the player who gave it may then ask a direct question that will give him and the other players a lead, such as "Are you in the entertainment business?" The first player must give a truthful "Yes" or "No" reply.
The first person to guess the personality wins the round and may choose the next character.
If nobody succeeds in guessing the personality after a reasonable length of time, the first player tells them the answer and may choose again for the new round.

ANIMAL, VEGETABLE, OR MINERAL
Sometimes called twenty questions, this game is one of the oldest and most familiar word guessing games. It may be made as simple or as difficult as the players wish, and can provide plenty of scope for intellectual dexterity as the players try to guess an object thought of by one of the others.
Players The game needs two or more players, or two teams. It is often helpful to have a non-playing person to act as referee.
Play One of the players thinks of an object. It may be general (eg "a ship"), specific (eg "the Lusitania"), or a feature (eg "the bridge of the Lusitania").
Sometimes the player then tells the others the composition of his chosen object (ie animal, vegetable, or mineral)—in an alternative version the players must guess it themselves.
The three categories may be defined as follows:
1) animal: all forms of animal life or anything of animal origin, eg a centipede, a tortoiseshell comb;
2) vegetable: all forms of vegetable life or anything of vegetable origin, eg flax, a wooden mallet;
3) mineral: anything inorganic or of inorganic origin, eg soda water, a mirror.
Objects are often a combination of categories, for example a can of beer or a leather shoe (The referee may be consulted if the player is unsure as to the category of an object.)
The player usually indicates the number of words in the object—excluding the definite or indefinite article.
The other players then ask anything up to 20 questions to try to guess the object. They should ask questions of a general nature rather than make random guesses, until they feel confident that they are near to knowing the object.
As each question is put to the player, he must reply either "Yes," "No," or "I don't know" as appropriate. In one version of the game, he may be allowed to qualify his answer if necessary by saying, for example, "Yes, in certain conditions."
The referee may intervene if he feels the player has given a wrong or misleading answer; he may also be consulted for guidance on a particular point.

End The first player to guess the object correctly may choose an object for a new round of play.
If no one has guessed the object by the time 20 questions have been asked (usually the referee keeps a count) the players are told what it was, and the same person may choose an object for the next round, or—if two teams are playing—a person in the other team may choose.

MAN AND OBJECT
In man and object, a player thinks of a person and something identified with him.
The person may be someone known personally to all the players, or a famous personality or fictional character. Examples might be an eskimo and his igloo, or Dante and the Inferno.
Playing procedure is the same as for animal, vegetable, or mineral—except that the players may be allowed to ask more than 20 questions.

Acting word games

In charades, "the game," dumb crambo, and in the manner of the word, one team mimes a word for the other team to guess. All these games are old favorites requiring only a lively imagination and a little acting ability. Amusement derives not only from the players' acting attempts but also from the often bizarre guesses made by the other team.

Players Acting guessing games can be played by any number of players divided into two teams.

One team chooses a word or phrase according to the rules of the particular game and then the other team attempts to guess it.

The teams change roles whenever a correct guess is made.

Costumes and other props are not necessary for these games but they can add to the players' enjoyment.

CHARADES

Charades is probably the best known and most popular of all acting and guessing games.

The objective is for one team to guess a word with several syllables that is acted out in mime by the other team.

Play The acting team leaves the room and decides on a suitable word. Usually words of three syllables are chosen, but players may choose words of only two syllables or of four or more.

This word is then presented to the other team in mimed scenes representing the different syllables, and then in a final scene representing the whole word.

Usually there is one scene for each syllable, although players may choose to represent two syllables in a single scene. (For example, the word "decorate" could be broken down as "deck-or-rate" or as "decor-ate.")

A member of the acting team must announce the number of scenes before miming begins. The actors usually leave the room between scenes and the guessing team is then free to discuss its ideas.

It is advisable for players to agree on a time limit for guessing words after the final scene.

An example of the sort of word that might be chosen is "nightingale," which was used in a charade scene in the book Vanity Fair by the nineteenth-century English novelist, William Thackeray.

Nightingale breaks down into three syllables and could be represented by:
a) a "night" scene with people going to bed or sleeping;
b) an "inn" scene with people drinking and making merry;
c) a "gale" scene with people being blown down a street;
d) a "nightingale" scene with people flapping their arms and imitating bird song.

CATEGORY CHARADES

This game is played in the same way as standard charades except that teams must choose words that belong to a previously agreed category and there is no miming of the full word.
Ideas for categories are:
a) towns (eg "came-bridge," "prince-ton");
b) people's names (eg "rob-in," "car-row-line");
c) animals (eg "lie-on," "buff-a-low");
d) flowers (eg "snow-drop," "butter-cup").

PROVERB CHARADES

Proverb charades is played in the same way as standard charades except that teams choose a proverb or well-known quotation, which they then act out word by word or in groups of several words. A good proverb for this game would be "a bird in the hand is worth two in the bush."

SPOKEN CHARADES

This game is played in the same way as standard charades except that the actors speak. Instead of miming scenes representing the syllables and then the full word, players must mention them while acting in the different scenes. This game is easier to play than most charades games, and for this reason is particularly popular with younger children.

THE GAME

This is a fascinating variation of charades. It is called "the game" because its early enthusiasts claimed that it was truly the game of all games. The players are divided into two teams, and each team nominates a different person to be its actor for each round.

Objective Using conventional gestures and free mime, the actor must convey to his teammates a well-known phrase chosen by the opposing team. The teams compete on a time basis.

Categories Phrases for this game must belong to one of a number of categories previously decided by both teams. Typical categories are the title of a book, play, television series, song, or painting, or a quotation, slogan, or proverb.

Play One team chooses a phrase and whispers it to the actor from the other team. The actor then begins miming, and a person appointed as timekeeper makes a note of the time. The actor should use conventional gestures where possible.

His teammates are allowed to speak, and make guesses as the acting proceeds. The actor, however, is only allowed to reply to their guesses with gestures.

If a correct guess is made, the timekeeper records the time and the teams change roles. (It is advisable to have a time limit, after which the teams must change roles even though the phrase has not been guessed.)

a

b

c

d

e

Gestures Players may improvise in their miming, but "the game" is characterized by the use of previously agreed gestures.

Firstly the actor indicates the category of the phrase. For example he can mime holding a book (**a**) for a book title. To indicate the number of words in the phrase the actor then holds up that number of fingers (**b**).

If the actor is going to mime the entire phrase he forms a circle, either with his thumb and forefinger (**c**) or with his arms.

If he wishes to mime only part of the phrase, he indicates a word by tapping the appropriate finger (**d**). He then counts his fingers to show how many letters there are in this word (**e**). If he wishes to use only part of a mimed word, he must make chopping actions to divide the word into syllables.

When his team makes a correct guess, the actor nods his head. If a guess is along the right lines, he beckons; if totally wrong, he makes a brushing away gesture.

Scoring The game is always scored on the basis of the time taken to guess the phrases. There are, however, two different scoring systems:
a) a round is won by the team that guesses its phrase most quickly and a game is won by the team that wins the most rounds;
b) times for the different rounds are added together and the game is won by the team with the shortest total guessing time.

THE GAME (SIMULTANEOUS)

Some players prefer to have both teams acting the same phrase simultaneously.

In this case it is necessary to appoint a referee, who thinks of a phrase, writes it on two slips of paper, and hands the slips to an actor from each of the teams.

Acting takes place in different rooms—so that players cannot hear the guesses of the opposing team.

A round is won by the team that is first to guess the phrase correctly. A game is won by the team that wins the most rounds.

THE GAME (RELAY)

This is played in the same way as the simultaneous version except that it is organized like a relay race.

The teams must be of equal size and each team member has a turn at being the actor. As soon as a team guesses a phrase, its next actor goes to the referee, tells him the last phrase, and is given a new one. A game is won when a team guesses its last actor's phrase.

DUMB CRAMBO

Dumb crambo is a very old game of the charades family. It was particularly popular in the nineteenth century.

Objective After receiving a rhyming clue, a team attempts to guess and mime a word, usually a verb, chosen by the opposing team.

Play The first team chooses a word, for example "feel," and then tells the second team a word rhyming with it, for example "steal."

It is obviously best for this game to choose a word that has several words rhyming with it. For example, other words that rhyme with "feel" are "heal," "keel," "reel," "deal," and "peel."

The second team then attempts to guess the chosen word and must mime its guesses. A maximum of three guesses is allowed.

If a guess is incorrect, members of the other team hiss or boo; if a guess is correct, they clap their hands.

A team scores one point each time it guesses a word. Teams change roles after a word is guessed or after three incorrect guesses.

The game is won by the team with most points when play ends.

IN THE MANNER OF THE WORD

This is an amusing acting guessing game in which players attempt to guess adverbs.

Play One player chooses an adverb, such as rapidly, quietly, or amusingly.

The other players, in turn, then ask him to carry out some action "in the manner of the word." For example, a player might say: "eat in the manner of the word," "walk in the manner of the word," or "laugh in the manner of the word."

The player who chooses the adverb must do as the other players ask, and the other players may make guesses as soon as acting begins.

The first player to guess an adverb correctly scores one point. If no one guesses the word after each of the players has asked for an action, the player who chose the adverb receives one point.

The game is won by the player with most points after each of the players has had a turn at choosing an adverb.

Pencil and paper games

Pencil and paper games need only the simplest equipment, yet they can provide great scope for the imagination, increase a player's general knowledge, and—above all—be a highly enjoyable way of passing time. Pencil and paper games fall basically into two categories: word games and games in which pictures or symbols are drawn.

KEYWORD
Keyword, sometimes called hidden words, can be played by any number of people. The players choose a "keyword" containing at least seven letters. Each player then tries to make as many words as possible from the letters in the keyword. The letters may be used in any order, but a letter may be used in any one word only as many times as it appears in the keyword. Generally, proper nouns (capitalized words) or words with fewer than four letters are not allowed; nor are abbreviations or plurals. The game may be played just for interest, with players working together; or it may be made into a contest, with individuals competing to find most words in an agreed length of time.

JUMBLED WORDS (ANAGRAMS)
Any number of players may take part. One of them prepares a list of words belonging to a particular category (eg flowers, cities, poets) and jumbles up the letters in each word. Each of the other players is given a list of the jumbled words and their category, and tries to rearrange the letters back into the original words. For example, "peilmidhun" should be "delphinium" and "wodronsp" should be "snowdrop." The first player to rearrange all the words correctly, or the player with most correct words after a given time, wins the game. More experienced players may like to make up anagrams of their own by rearranging the letters in a word to make one or more other words, eg "angered" is an anagram of "derange."

ACROSTICS
Acrostics is another word-building game. A word of at least three letters is chosen. Each player writes the word in a column down the left-hand side of a sheet of paper; he then writes the same word, but with the letters reversed, down the right-hand side of the page. The player fills in the space between the two columns with the same number of words as there are letters in the keyword—and starting and ending each word with the letter at either side. For example, if the keyword is "stem," a player's words might read: scream, trundle, earliest, manageress. The winner may be either the first person to fill in all the words, or the player with the longest or most original words.

TRANSFORMATION
Two words with the same number of letters are chosen. Each player writes down the two words. He tries to change the first word into the second word by altering only one letter at a time, and each time forming a new word. For example, "dog" could be changed to "cat" in four words as follows: dog, cog, cot, cat. It is easiest to begin with three or four letter words until the players are quite practiced—when five or even six letter words may be tried. The winner is the player who completes the changes using the fewest number of words.

FILL INS
A list of 30 to 40 words is prepared and kept hidden from the players. Each player is then given the first and last letters and the number of letters missing from each word on the list. The winner is the first player to fill in all the blanks correctly. Alternatively, the players may be allowed an agreed length of time and then the winner is the player with the most correct words.

CATEGORIES
Perhaps one of the best-known pencil and paper games, categories can be played at either a simple or a sophisticated level.
Preparation Each player (there may be any number) is given a pencil and a piece of paper. The players decide on between six and a dozen different categories; these may be easy ones for children (eg girls' or boys' names, animals, colors) or more difficult for adults (eg politicians, rivers, chemicals). Each player lists the categories on his piece of paper. One of the players chooses any letter of the alphabet—preferably an "easy" letter such as "a" or "d" if children are playing. Experienced players can make the game more challenging by choosing more difficult letters such as "j" or "k."
Players may decide to play to an agreed time limit of say 15 minutes.
Play The players try to find a word beginning with the chosen letter for each of the categories (eg if the chosen letter is "p" all the words must begin with that letter). They write down their words next to the appropriate category. The more unusual or original the word, the better—thus even if simple categories have been chosen, there is still plenty of scope for ingenuity.
Scoring Writing must stop as soon as the time limit is up, or as soon as one player has finished.
Each player in turn then reads out his list of words. If he has found a word not thought of by any of the other players, he scores two points for that word. If, however, one or more of the other players has also chosen the same word, each of them scores only one point. If the player could not find a word at all, or if his choice of word did not correctly fit the category, he gets no points. (Any disagreement about the relevance of a word to a category must be solved by a vote among the other players.) The winner is the player with the highest score for his list of words.
Subsequent rounds Any number of rounds may be played, using either the same or different categories; the chosen letter, however, must be different for each round. Players may take it in turns to choose a letter at the start of a round.
Players make a note of their scores at the end of each round. The winner is the player with the highest points total at the end of the final round.

GUGGENHEIM
Guggenheim is a slightly more complicated version of categories. Instead of choosing only one letter for each round of play, the players choose a keyword of about four or five letters. The letters of the keyword are written spaced out to the right of the list of categories, and players try to find words for each of the categories beginning with the letter heading each column.

CROSSWORDS

This intriguing game can be adapted for play by any number of people.

If up to five people are playing, each of them draws a square divided into five squares by five on a sheet of paper.

If more people take part, or if players wish to lengthen the game, the number of squares can be increased to, say, seven by seven.

Each of the players in turn calls out any letter of the alphabet. As each letter is called, all players write it into any square of their choice, with the objective of forming words of two or more letters reading either across or down.

Generally, abbreviations or proper nouns (names, etc) may not be used.

Once a letter has been written down, it cannot be moved to another square.

Players continue to call out letters until all the individual squares have been filled.

The number of points scored is equal to the number of letters in each word (one-letter words do not count). Thus a three-letter word scores three points. If a word fills an entire row or column, one bonus point is scored in addition to the score for that word.

No ending of a word can form the beginning of another word in the same row or column. For example, if a row contains the letters "i, f, e, n, d" the player may score four points for the word "fend" but cannot in addition score two points for the word "if." Each player adds together each of his horizontal and vertical totals; the winning player is the one with the highest score.

SYNONYMS

A list of 10 to 20 words is prepared, and a copy given to each player.

The objective is to find a synonym (word with the same meaning) for each word on the list. If a player can think of more than one synonym for any word he should write down the shortest one.

After an agreed length of time, the players' lists are checked.

The winner is the player who finds a synonym for the most words, or, if two or more players have an equal number of synonyms, the player with the lowest total of letters in his synonyms.

GEOGRAPHY RACE

This is an ideal game for a large group of players, and a good way of brushing up one's knowledge of geography! The players are formed into two teams, and one person acts as umpire. If possible, the teams should sit in parallel rows. The first person in each team is given a piece of paper and something to write with.

The object of the game is for each person in a team to write down the name of a town or city that lies in a specified direction of the last town on the list.

Play The umpire chooses the name of any well-known town or city and specifies in which compass direction the other towns must lie.

For example, he might say "Towns to the east of Berlin." He gives a start signal, and the first person in each team must write down a town that lies to the east of Berlin.

The player then hands the pencil and paper to the next person in his team, who writes down a town to the east of the town chosen by the first player.

Play continues in this way until the last member in the team has written down a town.

Scoring As soon as one team has finished, the umpire checks both teams' answers. The team that finished first scores a bonus of five points. In addition, each correct answer scores one point, and one point is deducted for each incorrect answer.

The team with the highest number of points after one or more rounds wins.

TELEGRAMS

Players are given a list of 15 letters, and must use each of them—in the order given—as the initial letter of a word in a 15-word telegram. (Alternatively, the players are given a word of about 10–15 letters, eg blackberries, so that the first word must begin with "b," the second with "l," and so on.)

The telegram may include one or two place names and may— if the player wishes—have the name of the "sender" as the last word.

Stops (or periods) may be used for punctuation.

The winner is the first player to complete his telegram, or, if a time limit has been set, the player whose telegram is judged to be the best at the end of the time set.

Consequences

Hangman

CONSEQUENCES
Consequences is a favorite among children and is a game purely to be enjoyed—there are no winners or losers.
Any number of players can take part, and each of them is provided with a sheet of paper and a pencil.
The objective is to write as many stories as there are participants, with each person contributing to each of the stories.
Play One person is chosen as "caller" (this does not exclude him from taking part). He calls out the first part of the story. Each person writes down an appropriate name, phrase, or sentence, making it as humorous as possible. He then folds over the top of the piece of paper to hide what he has written, and passes the paper to the player to his left.

Squiggles 1

The caller then says the next part of the story, and the players write something on the paper they have just received from their neighbors.
This procedure is repeated until the story is complete. Any theme may be used, but the one decribed here is perhaps the best known.
a) "A girl . . ." (players write the name of someone known to them, or alternatively a famous personality or fictional character);
2) "met a boy . . ." (again, the players may choose any name of their choice);
3) "at . . . beside . . . in . . ." (the players may choose any location);
4) "he said . . .";
5) "she said . . .";
6) "the consequence was . . .";
7) "and the world said . . ."

When the story is complete, each player passes the piece of paper on which he wrote the last sentence to the person to his left. The pieces of paper are unfolded and the stories read out one by one—they may not be fictional masterpieces but are sure to provide a lot of fun!

PICTURE CONSEQUENCES
This game follows the same principle as standard consequences, but instead of writing words the players draw parts of the human figure dressed in funny clothing—starting with the head and finishing with the feet.
When the pieces of paper are folded over, a part of the last drawing is left showing, so as to give a lead to the next player. For example, after drawing the head, the paper should be folded so that the edge of the neck is showing. Parts of animals or birds can also be drawn in addition to (or instead of) humans.
After drawing the feet, players may write down the name of the person whom they want the figure to represent!

Picture consequences

| I GR | I GR | I GR | I GR | I AGRA | I AGRA | I AGRAM | I AGRAM |
| EUBCWF | EUBCWFT | EUBCWFTO | EUBCWFTOS | EUBCWFTOS | EUBCWFTOSL | EUBCWFTOSL | EUBCWFTOSLP |

PICTURES

Pictures is best played by two teams of at least three players each. In addition, there must be an organizer who belongs to neither team.
The organizer makes a list of half a dozen or so book titles, proverbs, or other subjects (they need not be in the same category).
The organizer whispers the first title on the list to one player from each team. This player returns to his team (the teams should preferably be in separate rooms) and must draw a picture representing the title. He may add to his drawing or make further drawings—until one of his teammates has correctly guessed the answer. (No verbal clues may be given, however!)
As soon as one player has guessed the title, he may go to the organizer for the next title on the list.
The winning team is the first one to guess all the titles on the organizer's list.

HANGMAN

Hangman is a popular game for two or more players. One person thinks of a word of about five or six letters.
He writes down the same number of dashes as there are letters in his word.
The other players may then start guessing the letters in the word, calling one letter at a time. If the guess is a successful one, the letter is written by the first player above the appropriate dash—if it appears more than once in a word it must be entered as aften as it occurs.
If the guess is an incorrect one, however, the first player may start to draw a hanged man—one line of the drawing representing each wrong letter.

The other players must try to guess the secret word before the first player can complete the drawing of the hanged man.
If one of the players guesses the word (this should become easier as the game progresses) he may take a turn at choosing a word. If the hanged man is completed before the word is guessed, the same player may choose another word.
To make the game more difficult, longer words may be chosen, or even a group of words making a proverb or title of a book or film—the player gives the others a clue as to the category.

SQUIGGLES

This is a game for two people, each of whom should have a piece of paper, and a pencil different in color from the other player's.
Each player scribbles very quickly on his piece of paper— the more abstract the squiggle, the better.
Players then exchange papers and set themselves a time limit of, for example, two minutes, in which they must use every bit of the squiggle to make a picture. Ingenuity is more important than artistic ability—a third person could be asked to judge which of the players has used his squiggle more inventively.

Squiggles 2

Tick-tack-toe

TICK-TACK-TOE

A favorite for generations, tick-tack-toe (or noughts and crosses) is a game for two people that may be over in a matter of seconds!

Two vertical lines are drawn with two horizontal lines crossing them, forming nine spaces.

Players decide which of them is to draw noughts (circles) and which of them crosses. Taking alternate turns, the players make their mark in any vacant space until one of them manages to get three of his marks in a row (either horizontally, vertically, or diagonally). He then draws a line through his winning row and the game comes to an end. If neither player succeeds in forming a row, the game is considered drawn.

As the player who draws first has a better chance of winning, players usually swop their starting order after each game.

THREE-DIMENSIONAL TICK-TACK-TOE

Based on the standard game, the three-dimensional version offers a lengthier and more challenging alternative.

Three-dimensional tick-tack-toe can be bought as a game, but can equally well be played with pencil and paper.

The cube may be represented diagrammatically by 64 squares—as shown. For actual play, each "layer" of the cube is drawn out individually.

Playing procedure is similar to standard tick-tack-toe, but the winner is the first player to get four of his marks in a row (see illustrations).

Three-dimensional tick-tack-toe

The cube

Boxes

Playing layout

Nine winning rows

Crystals

BOXES

This is a simple but amusing game for two players. Any number of dots is drawn on a piece of paper—the dots are drawn in rows to form a square. Ten rows by ten is a good number.

Players take alternate turns. In each turn they may draw a horizontal or vertical line to join up any two dots that are next to each other.

The objective is to complete (with a fourth line) as many squares or "boxes" as possible. Whenever a player completes a box he initials it and may draw another line. He may continue his turn until he draws a line that does not complete a box.

As soon as there are no more dots to be joined—all the boxes having been filled—the game ends. The player with the highest number of initialed boxes is the winner.

Another way of playing is to try to form the lowest number of boxes—the players join up as many lines as they can before being forced to complete a box. The winner is the player with the fewest initialed boxes.

Sprouts

SPROUTS

Sprouts has certain similarities with boxes, but needs rather more ingenuity to win!

Two players take part. About six or so dots are drawn—well spaced out—on a sheet of paper (more may be drawn for a longer game).

Taking alternate turns, each player draws a line joining any two dots or joining a dot to itself. He then draws a dot anywhere along the line he has just made, and his turn ends.

When drawing a line, the following rules must be observed:

1) no line may cross itself or cross a line that has already been drawn;

2) no line may be drawn through a dot;

3) a dot may only have three lines leaving it.

The last person able to draw a legitimate line is the winner.

Disallowed sprouts

CRYSTALS

In this sophisticated pattern visualizing game, each player tries to form symmetrical shapes known as "crystals."

Equipment All that is needed is a sheet of squared (graph) paper and as many differently colored crayons as there are players.

The number of squares used for each game depends on the number of players: if two take part (the best number) about 20 rows of 20 squares each would form a suitable area.

Objective Each player attempts to "grow" crystals on the paper with the aim of filling more squares than his opponent.

A player does not score points for the number of crystals he grows, but for the number of squares his crystals cover.

A crystal is made up of "atoms," each of which occupies a single square. In growing crystals, players must observe certain rules of symmetry that determine whether or not a crystal is legitimate.

The symmetry of a crystal can be determined by visualizing four axes through its center: horizontal, vertical, and two diagonal axes. Once the axes

have been "drawn," it should theoretically be possible to fold the crystal along each of the four axes to produce corresponding "mirror" halves that, when folded, exactly overlay each other (ie are the same shape and size).

In addition to the rules of symmetry, players must observe the following:

a) a legitimate crystal may be formed from four or more atoms drawn by one player only;

b) the atoms forming a crystal must be joined along their sides—they may not be connected only by their corners;

c) a crystal may not contain any empty atoms (ie holes).

Play Players decide on their playing order and each one in turn shades in any one square of his choice—each player using a crayon of a different color.

In their first few turns, players rarely try to grow a crystal. Instead, they place single atoms around the playing area in order to establish potential crystal sites. As play progresses, players will see which atoms are best placed for growing crystals and add to them as appropriate.

When a player thinks he has grown a crystal, he declares it, and rings the area that it covers.

A player with a winning advantage will try to retain the lead by either blocking his opponents' attempts at growing crystals, or by growing long narrow crystals that—although not high scoring—restrict the playing area.

Play ends when no blank squares are left, or when the players agree that no more crystals can be formed.

Scoring Players work out which of the crystals are legitimate, and count the number of squares each crystal covers.

Any crystal that does not demonstrate symmetry around each of the four axes is not legitimate and does not score. The number of squares in the legitimate crystals that each player has grown are added, and the player with most squares wins the game.

Disallowed

Allowed

©DIAGRAM

Battleships

HOME FLEET   ENEMY FLEET

ENEMY FLEET   HOME FLEET

BATTLESHIPS

This is an extremely popular game for two players, each of whom needs a pencil and a sheet of squared (graph) paper.

The players should sit so that they cannot see each other's papers. Each of them draws two identical playing areas, ten squares by ten squares in size. In order to identify each square, the playing areas have numbers down one side and letters across the top (thus the top left-hand square is A1; the bottom left-hand square is A10, etc). Each player marks one playing area his "home fleet" and the other playing area the "enemy fleet."

Each player has his own fleet of ships that he may position anywhere within his home fleet area.

His fleet comprises:
a) one battleship, four squares long;
b) two cruisers, each three squares long;
c) three destroyers, each two squares long; and
d) four submarines, each one square only.

He "positions" his ships by outlining the appropriate number of squares.

The squares representing each ship must be in a row, either across or down. There must also be at least one vacant square between ships.

The players' objective is to destroy their opponent's entire fleet by a series of "hits." Players take alternate turns. In each turn, a player may attempt three hits: he calls out the names of any three squares—marking them on

his enemy fleet area as he does so.

His opponent must then consult his own home fleet area to see whether any of these three squares are occupied. If they are, he must state how many and the category of boat hit.

In order to sink a ship, every one of its component squares must have received a hit. The game continues with both players marking the state of their own and their enemy's fleets—this may be done by shading or outlining squares, or in some other manner of the players' choice.

There is no limit to the number of hits each player may attempt—the game comes to an end as soon as one player destroys his opponent's fleet.

Buried treasure

Drawing the boundaries

Positioning the armies

BURIED TREASURE

This is a very much simpler version of battleships and is particularly suitable for young children. It is a game for two, with a third person needed to help at the beginning of the game.

Each player draws an area nine squares by nine and marks it in the same manner as for battleships, so that each square has a name.

The third person designates any four of the letters from A to I to one player, and any four of the remaining letters to the other player; he then does the same thing with the numbers from 1–9.

Neither player may know which letters and numbers have been designated to his opponent, nor which letter and number are left over—this is the square in which the treasure is "buried" and which the players must try to identify.

Players take turns to ask each other whether they hold a particular letter or number. Although a respondent must always give a truthful answer, a player may—if he wishes— enquire about a letter or number that he holds himself, so as to mislead his opponent. The first player to locate the treasure by this mixture of bluff and elimination, wins the game.

AGGRESSION

Aggression is a game in which players fight imaginary battles in a bid to occupy the maximum amount of territory. Two players are ideal— though the game can also be played by three or more, who may choose to form teams. Each player must have a crayon of a different color.

Playing area A large sheet of paper is used. One player begins by drawing the boundaries of an imaginary country; each player in turn then draws the outline of an imaginary country adjoining one or more other countries. Any number of countries may be drawn (20 is an average number if two play) and they can be any shape or size. When the agreed number of countries has been drawn, each is clearly marked with a different letter of the alphabet.

Armies Each player is allotted 100 armies. Taking turns with his opponent, he chooses a country that he intends to occupy and writes within it how many armies he is allocating to it. (Once a country has been occupied, no player may add further armies to it.) This procedure continues until all the countries have been occupied, or until each player has allocated all his armies.

Play The player who chose the first country has the opening move. His objective is to retain more occupied countries than his opponent; to achieve this he "attacks" enemy armies in adjacent countries. (Adjacent countries are defined as those with a common boundary.) A player may attack with armies from more than one country— provided they are all in countries that have a common border with the country under attack.

If the number of armies located in the attacking country or countries is greater than those located in the defending country, the defending army is conquered—its armies are crossed off and can take no further part in the game. (The armies used to conquer a country may be reused.) Players take it in turns to conquer countries until one or both of them cannot mount any further attacks.

Scoring At the end of the game the players total the number of countries each of them retains. The winner is the player with the highest number of unconquered countries— he need not necessarily be the player who made the greatest number of conquests.

Conquering:
P conquers R but is then conquered by LOT

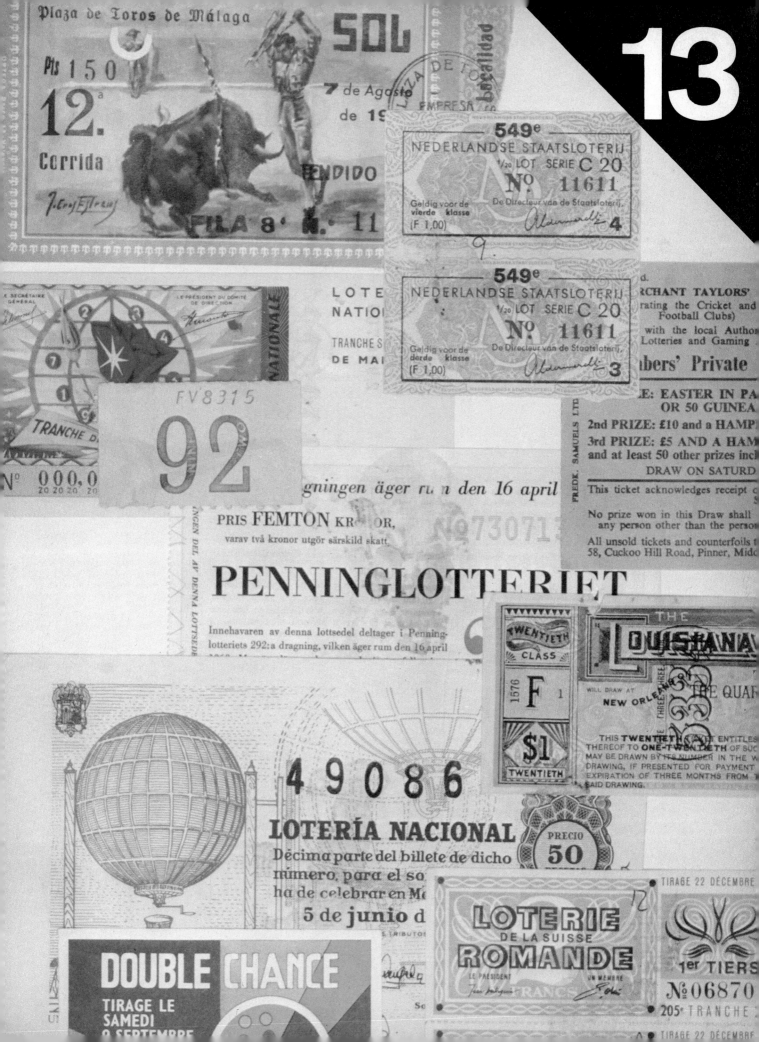

Games of chance

There are numerous theories as to why gambling should always have held so much fascination. Perhaps the only certainty is that man will never run short of things on which to make a wager, be it on the roll of a die or the outcome of a political election. Some forms of betting involve a degree of skill or judgment, but the games described here are games of pure chance—ranging from simple guessing games played for fun to highly organized games on which vast sums of money are gambled each year.

Scissors cut stone

Paper wraps stone

Stone blunts scissors

a Scissors   **b** Paper   **c** Stone

SCISSORS, PAPER, STONE

This ancient game, also known as hic, haec, hoc and by many other names, is played all over the world.
It is a game for two players.
Three objects (scissors, a piece of paper, and a stone) are indicated by different positions of the hand:

a) two fingers making a V shape represent scissors;
b) an open hand represents a piece of paper; and
c) a clenched fist represents a stone.
Each player hides one hand behind his back and adopts one of the three positions.
One of the players calls "One, two, three" (or "Hic, haec, hoc") and as the third word is

called the players show their hands.
The rule of the game decides the winner: scissors can cut paper, paper may be wrapped around a stone, and a stone can blunt the scissors.
Thus if one player chooses scissors and the other player paper, the player who chooses scissors wins the round. If both players decide on the

same object, the round is a draw.
Players usually play a predetermined number of rounds.

SPOOF

This is an intriguing game of bluff for at least two players, in which each person tries to guess the total number of objects the players are concealing in their hands.
Each player requires three small objects, such as coins or matches. He hides any number of them (or none if he wishes) in his outstretched fist.
One by one, in a clockwise direction, the players call out the number of objects they think are contained in the players' hands—but no two players may say the same number.

When all the players have guessed, they open their fists and the objects are counted.
The player who guessed correctly, or whose guess was nearest the correct number, wins the round.

Obviously, much depends on the ability to determine whether a player is bluffing when he calls a number. For example, guessing high might indicate that the caller has a full hand of three objects (especially if he happens to be the first caller in a round). Similarly, guessing low could mean a low number of objects —or an attempt to deceive the other players as to the contents of a hand.

Spoof: two players

3 + 3 = 6   3 + 2 = 5   2 + 3 =

6   **5**

MORA

Mora, also known as fingers, is another finger guessing game for two players.

The object of the game is to guess the number of fingers that will be "thrown" (displayed).

The players stand facing each other, each with a closed fist against his chest. At a given signal they throw a chosen number of fingers (or extend their clenched fist to indicate zero) and simultaneously call out the total number of fingers that they think will be thrown by both players (thumbs count as fingers). A call of "Mora!" indicates that the player is betting on ten fingers.

If neither player guesses correctly, the round is considered void. If one player guesses correctly he wins that round; if both players guess the right number, the round is a draw.

A mora session usually comprises 10 or 15 rounds.

SHOOT

Shoot is rather like mora, except that the two players must guess not the number of fingers thrown, but whether it will be an odd or an even total. The players may throw the fingers on one or both hands (ie each player may throw any number from zero through ten).

As they show their hands, the players call out "Odds!" or "Evens!" The fingers are counted (zero is considered an even number) and the winner is determined as in mora.

Mora

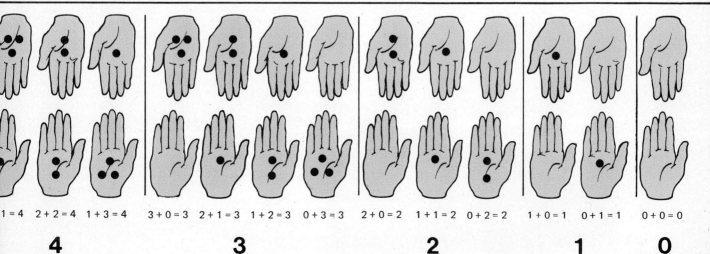

1 = 4 2 + 2 = 4 1 + 3 = 4 3 + 0 = 3 2 + 1 = 3 1 + 2 = 3 0 + 3 = 3 2 + 0 = 2 1 + 1 = 2 0 + 2 = 2 1 + 0 = 1 0 + 1 = 1 0 + 0 = 0

4　　　**3**　　　**2**　　　**1**　　　**0**

FAN-TAN

Fan-tan is a gambling game that originated in China several centuries ago. It is still very popular in Asia and in Chinese communities throughout the world.

Fan-tan is played on a board or table with the corners numbered 1, 2, 3, and 4 (**a**). The players bet on the numbers, placing their stakes on the appropriate corner of the playing area.

When the bets have been made, the banker takes a random handful of beans or other small objects and places them in the middle of the playing area (**b**).

Using a small stick as a rake, he then counts off the beans in groups of four (**c**).

The groups are disregarded until the last batch—the one that determines the winner. If it contains four beans, the players who bet on 4 win; if it contains three beans (**d**) those who backed 3 win, and so on. The banker takes a percentage of all the stakes, usually 25 per cent.

DOLLAR POKER

No relation to card poker, dollar poker is a betting game played with one-dollar bills. Its other names are money poker and liar poker.

Objective The game is based on the eight digits contained in the serial number on the bill (its two letters are ignored). Players bid the total number of any one digit that appears on all the dollar bills held by the players. The player with the highest successful bid is the winner, and collects one dollar from each player. If he fails to justify his bid, he loses and pays each player one dollar.

Deal The best number of players is about five or six, and one of them is chosen as dealer.

Each player gives the dealer five or more one-dollar bills. The dealer shuffles the bills with their serial numbers face down, and deals them out one at a time in a clockwise direction to all the players including himself, beginning with the player to his left.

Each player selects any one bill from those he has just been dealt, and the other bills are put to one side for later games.

Play Bidding is started by the player to the dealer's left and then passes from player to player in a clockwise direction. Each player has the option of bidding or passing (ie missing his turn). If he passes, he may reenter the bidding whenever it is his turn to play.

The player who bids first may bid (call out) any digit and amount he chooses; but thereafter each bid must be successively higher, either in the amount of that digit or in the same amount of a higher-ranking digit. Rank is 0 (high), 9, 8, 7, 6, 5, 4, 3, 2, 1 (low).

For example, if the opening bid is two 4s, the next bid must be either two 5s (or two of any higher ranking digit), or three 1s, 2s, 3s, or 4s.

If only one player bids and all the other players pass, he is the winner if he justifies his bid at the "showdown," or the loser if he fails to do so.

Showdown When bidding stops, the last bidder (inevitably the player who made the highest bid) must try to justify his bid. He declares the quantity of the bid number on his own bill, and then each player in turn does likewise.

If the sum total of the bid number is equal to or exceeds the amount called, the bidder is paid one dollar by each player. If it is less, he loses and must pay one dollar to each of the other players.

For example, if the bidder called ten 7s and his dollar bill has three 7s, he calls "Three," and each of the other players calls out the number of 7s on his bill. If the final total of 7s equals ten or more, the bidder wins—but if it is less than ten he loses.

Any player is entitled to see the serial numbers of all the bills in play at the showdown in order to verify the outcome of the game, but it is more usual to assume that the players have been honest in their declarations.

a

b

c

d

Subsequent rounds Each player selects another dollar bill from his stock for the next round of play.
The first bid is made by the player to the left of the previous round's winner. If, however, the last bidder in that round lost, it is he who must make the first bid.
Play continues as before.

PUT AND TAKE TOP

Around 1940 this was a big gambling craze in the United States of America but "loaded tops" and rampant cheating meant it soon died out. However, it now seems to be coming back into fashion. An eight-sided top is used, with sides marked as shown. Any number can play and each player contributes an agreed amount to a pot. Players then take it in turns to spin the top. If the top falls with a put side uppermost, the spinner puts the amount indicated (1, 3, 4, or all) into the pot. For put all, the spinner doubles the amount in the pot. If the top falls with a take side uppermost, the spinner takes the amount indicated. For take all, he takes all the money in the pot.

PUT 1

TAKE 1

PUT 3

TAKE 3

PUT 4

TAKE 4

PUT ALL

TAKE ALL

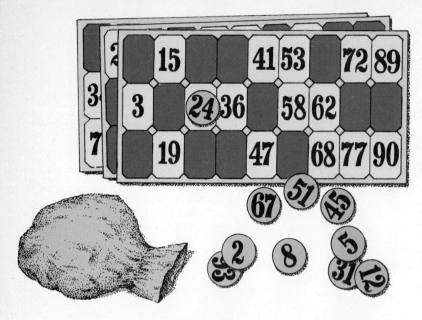

LOTTO

This family game—the forerunner of games like bingo —originated in Italy. Other names by which it is known are housey housey, tombola, and bolito.

Equipment Lotto is played with special rectangular cards divided into either three or five horizontal and nine vertical rows.

Each horizontal row has five numbered and four blank squares in random arrangement. The vertical rows contain, from left to right respectively, numbers selected from 1 to 10, 11 to 20, 21 to 30, and so on up to 90. No number is duplicated on any other card, and no two cards are alike.

Complementary to the cards is a set of 90 small card counters, numbered from 1 to 90.

Play As many players may take part as there are cards. Each player is given one card —or more than one if there are any left over.

One player (who may take part in the game if he wishes) is the caller. He puts the card counters into a sack or other container and mixes them well. The caller takes out one counter at a time, calls its number, and gives it to whichever player has the card on which the number appears. That player places the counter on the appropriate square.

End As soon as one player has covered all the numbers on his card in this way, he calls out "Lotto!" His card and counters are checked, and if they are correct he wins the game.

BINGO

This descendant of lotto has developed into a commercial bonanza. Millions of people play regularly at bingo halls and parlors all over the world, lured by big cash prizes in return for only a modest financial outlay. Many bingo sessions are organized to raise money for charities or community projects.

Equipment resembles lotto equipment but is much more sophisticated.

Bingo cards The typical North American bingo card is divided into five rows of five squares each and has the letters B, I, N, G, O printed at the top of the card, one letter relating to each column. Numbers selected from 1 to 75 fill all the squares except the one at the center, which is specially marked and called the "free-play" square. In the United Kingdom two types of bingo are played. "Prize" bingo—usually played at fairgrounds or at non-commercial sessions—is played for prizes other than cash, using the type of card described above (but without a free-play square).

The more usual "cash" bingo (for cash prizes) is played with cards of three rows of ten squares each. Each row has five numbered and five blank squares, arranged at random. The numbers are selected from 1 to 99. There is no free-play square.

At commercial bingo sessions cards are sometimes pasted on a piece of cardboard called a lapboard— this forms a convenient table and ensures that players do not take their cards home at the end of the session.

Cardboard or plastic markers may be used to cover the numbers, and sometimes cards have slides that can be finger-tipped across the numbers.

Bingo balls Like the cards, bingo balls in North America are both numbered and lettered. B-balls are for numbers 1 to 15, I-balls 16 to 30, N-balls 31 to 45, G-balls 46 to 60, and O-balls 61 to 75. Sometimes a colored "wild" ball with neither letter nor number is added, giving some special advantage to the player when it is drawn. For example, it might allow him to cover any number on his card, or perhaps the final number needed to complete a line. In the United Kingdom, the bingo balls usually bear only numbers, from 1 to 99.

Machines to mix and select the numbers may be either wire mesh cages, or glass or plastic "blower" machines. Many are partly or fully automatic.

The balls are released from the machines one at a time. Many establishments have a master board connected to a lighted signal board; this displays the numbers as they are placed on the master board and can also be used to check previously called numbers.

PICTURE LOTTO

This is a variation of standard lotto, using pictures instead of numbers. It is an excellent test of recognition for young children.

The cards used in picture lotto are usually divided into six or eight squares, each showing a different symbol or picture, eg flowers, animals, or household objects.

Each picture has a matching card. At the start of the game the caller gathers these small cards together, mixes them thoroughly, and picks out one at a time for the players to see. The player who claims the small card takes it and covers the appropriate picture on the large card with it. As in lotto, the first player to cover all the pictures on his card wins the game.

Play At the start of each round of calling, the players buy one or more cards. Often they hope to increase their chances of success by buying as many as ten or more cards. As each ball emerges from the selector machine, the caller announces its number (and letter) and places it on the master board.

Any player whose card shows the drawn number covers the appropriate square. (The same number may appear on more than one card, although no two cards are exactly alike.) The first player to complete a line of numbers—vertically, horizontally, or diagonally—calls "Bingo!" His card is then read back aloud to the caller by a floor attendant, and if it tallies with the master board, he gets a prize.

But the single line rarely brings in the big money! Most players have their sights set on the jackpot. This is won by the first player to achieve a "blackout" or "coverall" (ie covering all the numbers on his card). Some bingo halls place a limit on the amount of the jackpot; others let it accumulate from week to week until it is won.

Other winning variations include:
covering the eight numbers around the central free play square;
covering the numbers at the four corners of the card;
covering specific lines, or lines that intersect to form a stated letter of the alphabet.

When a game has been won, any player may keep or exchange his card(s) for a further game, or buy additional cards, but the selection of numbers starts afresh.

Drawing the lucky number

LOTTERIES

Organized lotteries as we know them today probably began in the fifteenth century. Then as now, they provided an attractive and easy means of raising money—be it for the benefit of the community or for less philanthropic reasons. Nowadays, many countries have lotteries that are organized or supervised by the state. Tickets or bonds are sold to the public and a small percentage of the income raised from their sale is used in prize money. The winning tickets are drawn by lot.

After the deduction of the running costs, the profit goes to the government—as revenue, for charity, or for other purposes.

The manner in which money is raised and given out in prizes may vary; occasionally the lottery may also be linked to an event such as a horse race. But in all lotteries, no skill or judgment is involved and the winners are determined solely by chance.

Many people—including those who would never consider themselves gamblers—are happy to spend a small amount on what may turn out to be a ticket to fortune!

Roulette

Spinning wheels have fascinated gamblers ever since ancient Greeks wagered on the turn of a battleshield spun on the point of a sword. Today roulette is one of the great casino games—being simple to play and yet offering the hope of dazzling success. The impersonality of the turning wheel lures players who believe that magical numerologies or "scientific systems" can help them "break the bank."

American wheel

French wheel

Equipment for roulette is:
a) a table, marked with the betting layout;
b) a roulette wheel;
c) a roulette ball;
d) a rake for the croupier;
e) betting chips.

The table is usually mahogany. A standard table has the betting layout at one end and the wheel at the other. A "double ended" table has a wheel at the center and layouts at each end.

The "wheel bowl" is a wood bowl-shaped recess in the table. It forms a stationary surrounding to the wheel. High on its side is a groove known as the "back track." Below the back track is the gently sloping "bottom track" —lined off into eight equal arcs, each with a diamond-shaped metal obstacle. At the bowl's center, hidden by the wheel, is the steel spindle on which the wheel spins.

The wheel (or "wheel head") is a solid wood disk. At its center is the "spinner"—a metal ornament used to spin the wheel.

The wheel's perimeter is divided by paint lines into 37 or 38 numbered sections of equal size.

The French wheel has sections numbered 1 through 36, plus one 0 section. There are never more than two odd or two even numbers consecutively. The American wheel has sections 1 through 36, plus 0 and 00 sections. Any number always has a consecutive number directly opposite it. On both types of wheel the sections are numbered in gold. They are colored alternately red and black, except that 0 and 00 sections are green. Directly next to each numbered section is a pocket painted the same color as the section. Pockets are divided by metal partitions known as separators.

The roulette ball is about $\frac{1}{2}$in–$\frac{3}{4}$in in diameter and made of ivory or plastic.

The betting layout is painted on green baize. Gold lines divide it into a large number of sections, each bearing a number, symbol, or label.

Players place chips in different positions on the layout according to the bets they wish to make.

Sections numbered 1 through 36 are colored black or red to match the corresponding section of the wheel.

French and American layouts differ in shape and labeling, but the only difference that affects the game is the 00 section on American layouts. (The addition of this section increases the casino's mathematical advantage.)

Players The number of players varies from one to as many as can get around the roulette table.

0		
1	2	3
4	5	6
7	8	9
10	11	12
13	14	15
16	17	18
19	20	21
22	23	24
25	26	27
28	29	30
31	32	33
34	35	36

PASSE   PAIR   ◆

MANQUE   IMPAIR   ◇

12P 12M 12D   12D 12M 12P

French layout

The objective for a player is to anticipate and bet on:
a) the winning number, ie the number of the pocket in which the ball comes to rest;
b) a group of numbers including the winning number;
c) a characteristic of the winning number, ie red or black, even or odd, high or low; or
d) any combination of these.
Betting chips are of various colors. Often a player is assigned a color when he joins the game. Several players may have the same color chips if large numbers are playing.
Stacks of chips are bought from the croupier. High value chips are usually inscribed with their value while low value chips are unmarked.

If a player buys unmarked chips he pays according to the value he wishes each chip to have. If they are to be bet above the house minimum the croupier generally uses an inscribed marker to indicate their value.
Croupiers The game is staffed by croupiers provided by the house.
One croupier runs the game—selling betting chips, spinning the wheel, throwing the roulette ball, announcing the winning number, raking in losing bets, and paying winning bets.
He is assisted by one or more other croupiers whose job is to sort and stack the chips.
In large casinos a house inspector watches the game and intervenes if necessary.

Playing procedure is as follows.
1) Players place bets on the layout.
2) The head croupier sets the wheel spinning and throws the ball.
3) Players may continue to bet if they wish.
4) When the ball is about to fall from the back track, the croupier calls "Rien ne va plus" or "No more bets."
5) The ball comes to rest in one of the pockets.
6) The croupier calls the winning number and color, and points to the number on the layout.
7) The croupier rakes in the losing bets and pays the winning ones. Unless the player removes it, a winning bet is left on the layout for the next throw.

Change of croupier Some casinos allow the wheelman to be changed if one player requests it and no other player objects. The change is not permitted until the croupier has made five throws.

Throwing the ball

Throw of the ball The croupier first takes the ball from the pocket in which it last came to rest.
If the wheel's spin has slowed, or if the casino requires the wheel's direction of spin to change for every throw, he then turns the wheel's spinner with whichever hand is most visible to the players. (If the direction of spin does not change, the spin is usually counterclockwise.)
Using the same hand, the croupier next throws the ball at speed into the wheel bowl so that it travels in the opposite direction to the wheel.

The path of the ball is as follows:
1) It travels at speed high against the bowl's side, in the groove known as the back track.
2) As its speed slows, it drops to the gently sloping bottom track.
3) On the bottom track the diamond-shaped obstacles can make it ricochet unpredictably.
4) It passes onto the outer wheel perimeter, where the contrary motion slows it abruptly and then carries it around with the wheel.
5) The ball may hover over two or three neighboring numbers, be hit by one of the separators, or go into a pocket and bounce out again.
6) Eventually it settles into one of the pockets.

Betting There are three types of bet:
a) single numbers;
b) groups of numbers;
c) all numbers of a specified characteristic (red or black, odd number or even, high number or low).
Bets on a group of numbers are paid if any one of the numbers comes up.
Bets on a characteristic are paid if any number with that characteristic comes up.

Betting on American layout

Bets available

Coverage	American term	French term	Payment	Numbers bet
1	Straight bet	En plein	35-1	Any one number (a)
2	Split bet	A cheval	17-1	Any two adjacent numbers (b)
3	Street bet	Transversale plein	11-1	Three numbers in a row; or 0, 1, 2; or 0, 2, 3; 00, 2, 3 (c)
4	Square/quarter	En carré	8-1	Four numbers in a square; or 0, 1, 2, 3 (d)
5 (US)	Line bet		6-1	0, 00, 1, 2, 3 (e)
6	Line bet	Transversale simple	5-1	Six numbers in two adjacent rows (f)
12	Column bet	Colonne	2-1	All 12 numbers in a vertical row (g)
12	Dozens bet	Douzaine	2-1	All 12 numbers in block 1-12, or 13-24, or 25-36 (h)
24	Two column bet	Colonne à cheval	2-1 on	All 24 numbers in adjacent vertical rows (i)
18	Black bet	Noir	1-1	All black numbers (j)
18	Red bet	Rouge	1-1	All red numbers (k)
18	Even number	Pair	1-1	All even numbers (l)
18	Odd number	Impair	1-1	All odd numbers (m)
18	Low number	Manque	1-1	All numbers 1 to 18 (n)
18	High number	Passe	1-1	All numbers 19 to 36 (o)

Betting on French layout

Placing bets on the layout
a) Single number bet: on any number, not touching any lines.
b) Two number bet: on the horizontal or vertical line separating any two numbers.
c) Three number bet: on the outside vertical line of the layout alongside any line of numbers. Or (on the French layout) to bet the 0, 1, 2 or 0, 2, 3: on the intersection of the three numbers.
d) Four number bet: on the intersection where any four numbers meet. Or (on the French layout) to bet 0, 1, 2, 3: on the outside vertical line of numbers against the line separating the two lines of numbers.

e) Five number line bet (American): on the outside vertical line of the layout against the lines separating 00 and 3.
f) Six number line bet: on the outside vertical line of the layout against the line separating any two lines of numbers.
g) Vertical 12 number bet: on any one of the three spaces at the base of the number columns.
h) Black 12 number bet: on the appropriate space on the layout. American: first, second, or third dozen. French: P¹², M¹², D¹²—either one of the pairs of these.
i) Vertical 24 number bet: on the line between any two of the three spaces at the base of the number columns.

j) Black number bet: on the space containing the black diamond.
k) Red number bet: on the space containing the red diamond.
l) Even number bet: on the space marked "even" (American) or "pair" (French).
m) Odd number bet: on the space marked "odd" (American) or "impair" (French).
n) Low number bet: on the space marked "1–18" (American) or "manque" (French).
o) High number bet: on the space marked "19–36" (American) or "passe" (French).

Boule

Boule is a simple version of roulette played in European casinos. It first appeared in the eighteenth century and remains popular because of its simplicity and low minimum stake.

Boule wheel

Zero and double zero The 0 and 00 may be bet as single numbers in the usual way.
They may also be included in a two or three number bet with adjacent numbers, ie 1, 2, and 3. (On the American layout 0 cannot be bet with 3 or 00 with 1.)
They may also be included in a four number bet (French) or the five number bet (American).
They are not, however, covered by any other bet—either on a group of numbers or on characteristics of numbers. 0 and 00 are therefore known as house numbers.
If there is a bet on a group of numbers and the 0 (or 00) comes up, the bet is lost.
If there is a bet on a characteristic and the 0 (or 00) comes up, the bet is lost (American rules), put "in prison" (some European casinos), or half lost (other European casinos).
Bet in prison A bet in prison must be left on the layout, and its fate is decided by the next throw of the ball.
If the characteristic bet (eg red) comes up next, the bet is returned to the player but with no winnings. If the opposite characteristic (eg black) comes up, the bet is lost.
If the 0 comes up again, rules vary (since these are European casinos there is no 00):
a) in some casinos the player loses half the bet and the other half is returned;
b) elsewhere the player loses half the bet, while the other half remains in prison to have its fate decided by the next throw of the ball in exactly the same way (the bet in prison is halved for each further 0 that appears consecutively).
Betting limits House regulations lay down the minimum and maximum bets allowed.
The house advantage derives from the difference between the true odds and the odds offered.
The house advantage where there is both 0 and 00 is 5.26% on all bets—except for the five number line bet, which has a 7.8% house advantage.
When there is only a single 0, the general house advantage is 2.7%. If 1–1 bets are put in prison when the 0 appears (or if half the stake is returned), the house advantage on even money bets is only 1.35%.

Equipment consists of a table, bowl, ball, betting layout, and betting chips or cash.
The table has at one end an area of polished wood centering on the bowl. At the other end there is an area of green baize printed with one or two layouts.
The bowl is a wood recess in the table; it contains no wheel or moving part.
Since the bowl is set slightly below the table's surface it is edged by a low rim. A groove cut into this rim runs right around the bowl's circumference.
The surface of the bowl itself slopes gently down toward a slightly raised hub at its center. This surface is divided into 18 segments, numbered consecutively in a clockwise direction from 1 to 9 twice.
At the point of each segment, just before the raised hub, are one or more holes to catch the ball. The holes are marked with the number of the segments to which they belong.
The holes are colored alternately black and red, except that the two 5s are any contrasting color (usually yellow).
Holes of segments with the same number are always the same color.
The ball is made of rubber. Ball sizes vary.
The betting layout is an oblong area divided into sections and printed in gold on the green baize.
One section is printed with one or more red diamonds and another with one or more black diamonds. All other sections are labeled in gold.
Players place bets on different positions on the layout according to the bets they wish to make.
Players The number of players may be from one to as many as can get around the table.

Croupiers The game is staffed by one or more croupiers provided by the house. If there are two croupiers, one controls the play of the ball and the other supervises the betting.
The objective for a player is to anticipate and bet on:
a) the winning number, ie the number of the hole in which the ball comes to rest; or
b) a characteristic of the winning number, ie red or black, even or odd, high or low.
Playing procedure is as follows.
1) Players place bets on the layout.
2) The croupier calls "Rien ne va plus," after which no more bets may be placed.
3) The croupier throws the ball into the bowl so that it travels at speed around the groove in the bowl's rim.
4) The ball slows, descends toward the bowl's hub, and comes to rest in one of the holes.
5) The croupier calls the winning number and color.
6) The croupier rakes in losing bets and pays winning ones.
Betting There are two types of bet:
a) single numbers;
b) all numbers of a specified characteristic (red or black, even or odd, high number or low).
Bets Players may make the following bets.
a) Single number bet: bets the number shown on the section of the layout on which the bet is placed.
b) Black numbers bet: bets all black numbers.
c) Red numbers bet: bets all red numbers.
d) Odd numbers bet: bets all odd numbers except the 5.
e) Even numbers bet: bets all even numbers.
f) Low numbers bet: bets all numbers below 5.
g) High numbers bet: bets all numbers above 5.

Betting on boule layout

f) MANQUE 1234		
1	d) IMPAIRS 1379	2
3	5	4
6		7
8	PAIRS 2468 e)	9
PASSE 6789 g)		

b) a) c)

The five Players may bet on the 5 as a single number, but it is not covered by any bet on a characteristic.
Betting limits are usually low.
Settlement A successful single number bet is paid at 7 to 1. All other bets are paid at 1 to 1.

Musical games

These are all active games in which players move around to music. When the music stops, the players must immediately stand still or change what they are doing. All the games require someone to organize the music.

MUSICAL CHAIRS
Play Chairs are placed around the room in a large circle. There should be one chair fewer than the number of players.

The players stand in the circle and, when the music starts, all dance around.

When the music stops, each player tries to sit on a seat. The player left without a seat is eliminated.

One chair is then removed from the circle and the music is restarted.

The last person to stay in the game is the winner.

MUSICAL BUMPS
This is like musical chairs, except that it is played without the chairs.

When the music stops, players sit down on the floor. The last person to sit down is out.

OWNERSHIP MUSICAL CHAIRS
In this version of musical chairs there is one chair per person.

Before the music starts each player sits on a chair and marks it as his own.

When the music starts, the players dance around the circle in the same direction.

When the music stops, the players continue moving around the circle. As each player comes to his own chair he sits down. The last player to sit on his chair is out and remains seated.

The organizer may vary the game by calling directions to the players as they move around—eg walk backward, or turn to the right.

The last person to stay in the game is the winner.

MUSICAL BLACKOUT
This is played like musical chairs except that when the music stops, the lights are switched off for five seconds. When the lights are switched on again, any player who has not found a chair is eliminated.

MUSICAL HOTCH POTCH
In this game, players race for objects instead of chairs.

Play A pile of objects, numbering one fewer than the number of players, is placed in the center of the room.

When the music starts, players hop or dance around the pile.

When the music stops, each player dives for an article from the pile.

The larger the objects, the less likely are the players to bump their heads!

The player left without an object is out.

One object is removed from the pile and the game continues.

MUSICAL MAGIC CARPET
The organizer chooses a part of the floor as a "magic patch" but keeps its position a secret.

Play When the music starts the players dance in pairs. When the music stops, they stop dancing.

The pair nearest the magic patch wins a prize, and the game continues until all the prizes are won.

Alternatively, the game can be played for points. The pair nearest the magic patch scores a point, and the game is won by the pair with most points after an agreed time.

HIGH STEPPERS
Preparation Pairs of chairs with their fronts touching are placed around the room to form a circle of hurdles.

Play The players space themselves around the room in pairs.

When the music starts, they march around the room and must climb over the hurdles as they come to them.

When the music stops, any pair touching a hurdle is eliminated.

The music starts again and the game continues.

The winning pair is the last one left in the game.

Musical hotch potch

High steppers

Musical chairs

MUSICAL STATUES
Players dance around the room to music.
When the music stops, the players immediately stop dancing and stand as still as statues.
Any player seen moving after the music stops is eliminated.
The music is started again fairly quickly and the game continues.
Eliminated players can help to spot moving statues.
The last player to remain as a dancer is the winner.

Statues

MUSICAL RINGS
This is a game for a large room and many players.
Play Players space themselves around the room. When the music starts, they dance around.
When the music stops, the organizer announces a number and players quickly arrange themselves into groups of this size.
Any spare players unable to form a group of the right size are out.
The game ends when only two players remain. These players are the winners.

MUSICAL ISLANDS
This is another game for a large room.
Preparation Small mats, newspapers, pieces of cardboard, etc are scattered over the floor to form "islands."
Play When the music starts, players walk around in a circle.
When the music stops, players must stand on an island. More than one player may stand on one island.
Anyone unable to get onto an island or falling off into the "water" is eliminated. The music starts again and the game continues.
Islands are gradually removed during the game.
The last player left in the game is the winner.

Musical islands

GODS AND GODDESSES
This is a game requiring fairly slow and gentle music.
Play Each player is given a book. When the music starts, the players walk around the room balancing the books on their heads.
When the music stops, each player goes down on one knee. If a player's book falls off, he is eliminated.
The music starts again and the game continues.
The last player left in the game is the winner.

Gods and goddesses

©DIAGRAM

Blindfold games

In these games the blindfolded player's movements are a source of much amusement. It is a good idea if an adult ties on the blindfold and checks that it is tied neither too tight nor so that the blind man can peep out.

Blind man's buff

BLIND MAN'S BUFF
Objective A blindfolded player tries to catch and identify another player.
Play A "blind man" is chosen and blindfolded. He is turned around three times in the center of the room and then left on his own.
The other players dance around, taunting him and dodging out of his way to avoid capture.
When the blind man catches someone, he has two or three guesses at the name of his prisoner.
If he guesses correctly, the prisoner becomes the new blind man.
If wrong, he continues to be the blind man and tries to catch another player.

TEN STEP BUFF
Objective As in blind man's buff, a blindfolded player tries to catch and identify another player.
Play The blind man stands in the center of the room.
The other players scatter around him and stand still.
The blind man takes ten paces and stretches out his hands.
If he touches a player, that player becomes the blind man.
If not, he takes another ten paces and tries again.

SQUEAK-PIGGY-SQUEAK
Objective A blindfolded player attempts to identify another player by getting him to squeak.
Play One player is blindfolded, given a cushion, and turned around three times in the center of the room.
The others sit down around the room.
The blind man must then place his cushion on another player's lap and sit on it.
He then calls "squeak-piggy-squeak" and the person he is sitting on squeaks like a pig.
If the blind man recognizes the person, he changes places with him.
Once the new person is blindfolded, the players all change seats before he tries to sit on a player's lap.

BLIND MAN'S STICK
Objective A blind man tries to identify a player from the noises he makes.
Play One player is blindfolded and given a stick. The others form a circle and slowly move around him.
If the blind man touches a player with his stick, the player must grasp the stick. The blind man then asks the player to imitate a noise—for example a creaking door.
If the blind man guesses the player's name, that player becomes the new blind man.
If he guesses incorrectly, the blind man must touch another player.

BLIND POSTMAN
Objective A blindfolded player tries to sit in a vacant seat while two players are changing places.
Preparation One person is chosen to be postmaster. All the others choose a town, and the postmaster makes a list of their choices.
Play One player is blindfolded and becomes the first postman. All the other players sit in a circle. The postman stands in the center of the circle, and is turned around several times by the postmaster.
The postmaster then announces that a letter has been sent between two of the towns on his list, for example from Cambridge to Birmingham.
The two players whose towns are called then try to change places before the postman sits in one of their empty seats.
If the postman gets a seat, the player without a seat becomes the new postman.
More than one letter may be sent at a time.
Mode of travel The postmaster can also say how the letter traveled—and so indicate how the players should move. For example, if the letter went:
a) by air, they hop;
b) by sea, they walk backward;
c) by train, they crawl; and
d) by Pony Express, they bunny hop.

The donkey's tail

Jailer

Squeak-piggy-squeak

THE DONKEY'S TAIL

Objective Blindfolded players try to pin a tail in the correct position on a drawing of a tailless donkey.

Preparation The organizer draws a large picture of a donkey without a tail and fastens it onto a pinboard propped upright.

He also makes a donkey's tail out of cardboard or wool and sticks a large pin through the body end.

Play Each player in turn is blindfolded and turned around so that he is in front of and facing the donkey.

He is then given the tail and attempts to pin it on the correct part of the donkey.

The organizer marks the position of each player's attempt.

The player who pins nearest the correct place is the winner.

DRAW THE ELEPHANT'S TAIL

This is similar to the donkey's tail but instead of pinning on a tail players draw one.

Each blindfolded player is given a crayon and draws a tail on a picture of an elephant (or any other animal).

BLIND MAN'S SORT OUT

Objective Blindfolded players race to sort a collection of objects into categories.

Preparation The organizer collects a selection of buttons, screws, nails, beans, beads, etc.

Play The game is usually organized as an elimination contest—with two players competing at a time.

The objects are divided into two similar piles. The first two players are then blindfolded and each placed in front of a pile of objects.

When the organizer calls "Go!" each of the blindfolded players starts sorting his objects into groups of buttons, screws, etc.

The first player to finish sorting his objects into categories goes forward into the next round of the contest. All the other players then compete in pairs, and the winners all go into the next round.

Further rounds are held until only two players remain for the final. The winner of the final wins the game.

A BLIND JUDGMENT

Play One player is blindfolded and placed on a "seat of judgment."

Another player then stands quietly in front of him, and the player in the judgment seat gives a brief description of whoever he thinks might be standing in front of him.

If the other players think that the "blind judgment" was reasonably accurate, the player in front of the

blindfolded player becomes the new blind man.

If his judgment was inaccurate, the original blindman must pass judgment on another player.

MURALS

Preparation The organizer cuts out large pieces of paper for drawing on.

Play Each player in turn is blindfolded, given a crayon, and asked to draw a picture on a piece of paper pinned on the wall.

The subject for the picture is chosen by the other players— good examples are a house, a person, or some kind of animal.

The artist feels the edges of the paper and has one minute in which to draw the chosen subject.

When everyone has had a turn, the drawings can be judged by an adult or by all the players together.

Murals

THIEVES

Objective A blindfolded player tries to catch players stealing from him.

Play One player is blindfolded and given a rolled newspaper to hold in his hand. The blindfolded player sits in the middle of a circle made by other players, and a pile of treasure—necklaces, brooches, bracelets, etc—is placed in front of him.

Players in the circle quietly take it in turns to steal a piece of treasure.

If the blindman hears a thief, he strikes at him with the newspaper and calls "thief, thief."

If he touches a thief, the thief must return empty-handed to his place to await his next turn.

The thief who collects most treasure wins the game.

JAILER

This is similar to thieves except that the blindfolded man is guarding a bunch of keys.

The organizer names a player, who then has to take the keys from the jailer and carry them around the outside of the circle and back to his place. The jailer listens for the thief and if he hears him points at him.

If the jailer locates the thief the thief takes over as jailer.

BLIND MAN'S TREASURE HUNT
Objective Each player chooses a parcel by touch and tries to identify the contents before opening it.
Preparation Objects of different shape and feel are wrapped up—one parcel per player. The parcels are piled on a table.
Play Each player in turn is blindfolded and led to the table to choose a parcel. He then takes off his blindfold and waits until all the players have chosen a parcel.
Each player then guesses what is in his parcel before opening it.
Presents This game is an excellent way to give out small presents at a party.

SWEET TOOTH
Objective Each player tries to identify foods that he has eaten while blindfolded.
Play Each player sits down and is then provided with a plate of goodies such as chocolate, fudge, nuts, liquorice, and pieces of orange.
When all the players have eaten or tasted all their goodies, any leftovers are taken away and the blindfolds are removed.
The children then write down what they think they have eaten.
If the players are too young to write, they can whisper their answers to an adult.

MURDER IN THE DARK
Although players are not blindfolded for this game, a "detective" attempts to identify an unseen "murderer." The opening stages of play take place in the dark.
Preparation One small piece of paper per player is folded and placed in a hat. One is marked with a cross, another with a D, and all the others are blank.
Play Each player draws a piece of paper from the hat. The player who gets the paper with the cross is the murderer and the one with the D the detective.
The detective first leaves the room and the lights are switched off.
The other players then dance slowly around the room in the dark. The murderer catches a victim and puts his hands on the victim's shoulders. The victim must scream and fall to the ground.
The lights are then switched on and the detective is called in.
The detective tries to identify the murderer by questioning everybody except the victim. All the players except the murderer must answer his questions truthfully.
After the questioning the detective accuses his prime suspect of the murder, saying "I charge you (name of suspect) with the murder of (name of victim)."
If the accusation is correct, the murderer must admit his guilt.

Hunting and observation games

Hunting games have always been popular and there is a great variety of games of this type. In some, players hunt for hidden objects. In others, they hunt for another player who may or may not himself be hidden. Observation is obviously a vital part of hunting, but there are also games of pure observation and memory.

HUNT THE THIMBLE
This very popular game is usually played with a thimble, but any other small object will do just as well.
Play All the players but one leave the room while this player hides the thimble somewhere in the room or on his person.
He then calls the other players back into the room to look for it.
The game is won by the first player to find the thimble and take it to the player who hid it. The finder then has a turn at hiding the thimble.

SIT DOWN HUNT THE THIMBLE
This is played in the same way as the last game except that when a player sees where the thimble is hidden he sits down on the floor.
The last person to see the thimble and sit down must pay a forfeit.
The player who sat down first has the next turn at hiding the thimble.

SINGING HUNT THE THIMBLE
This is played like hunt the thimble except that only one player leaves the room while one of the others hides it. On his return, the players who stayed in the room try to guide him to the thimble by singing. They sing more loudly as he moves closer to the thimble and more quietly as he moves away.

HOT AND COLD THIMBLE
As in singing hunt the thimble, only one player leaves the room while the thimble is hidden.
The other players help him find the thimble by telling him how "hot" he is in different parts of the room.
If he is in the wrong part of the room he is "very cold" or "cold." As he approaches the thimble he is "getting warmer"—until he becomes "warm," "hot," and finally "very hot" just before he touches the thimble.

Hunt the ring

Hunt the thimble

BLINDFOLD OBSTACLE WALK

Preparation Everyone lays out obstacles—a pile of books, a glass of water, cushions, etc—from one end of the room to the other.

Play Several of the players volunteer to walk the course. They then leave the room to be blindfolded.

Meanwhile the others quickly and quietly remove all the obstacles.

Each of the blindfolded volunteers is then brought in one at a time.

The blindfolded player then attempts to walk across the room without hitting the obstacles. To add to the fun all the onlookers utter appropriate gasps and shudders.

When he has completed the "course" the blindfold is removed.

NELSON'S EYE

This game plays on a blindfolded person's heightened imagination.

Play Several volunteers who do not already know the game are asked to leave the room. They are blindfolded and brought back into the room one at a time.

One of the other players begins by asking the blind man to feel "Nelson's good leg"—and the blind man's hands are guided so that he can feel someone's leg.

He is then asked to feel Nelson's bad leg—and his hands are guided to a chair leg. Next the blind man must feel Nelson's good arm—and feels someone's arm. Then he must feel Nelson's bad arm, which can be a stuffed stocking.

This is followed by Nelson's good eye, which can be a marble.

Finally he is asked to feel Nelson's bad eye—and is presented with a squashy pickled onion or a soft flour and water mixture.

The blind man usually becomes rather squeamish at this point—much to the amusement of the other players!

Nelson's eye

HUNT THE SLIPPER

In this game one player tries to find which of the others is holding the slipper. A little acting greatly adds to the fun of this game.

Play All the players but one sit with their feet touching in a circle on the floor. These players are the cobblers.

The other player has a small slipper (or shoe) which he says is in need of repair. He then gives the slipper to the cobblers and asks them to mend it.

He walks away and returns several times to see if it is ready. Each time the cobblers pretend that it is not quite finished. Finally, however, they admit that they have lost it.

The hunt The cobblers now pass the slipper from one to another under their knees. The customer tries to touch a cobbler while he is holding the slipper. When he succeeds, the slipper is "found" and the customer and the cobbler holding the slipper change places.

HUNT THE RING

This is another game in which one player tries to find which of the others is holding an object.

Preparation A curtain ring is threaded onto a long piece of string. The two ends of the string are then tied together with a knot that is small enough to allow the ring to pass easily over it.

Play One player stands in the middle of the room and the others form a circle around him.

The players in the circle each hold the string with both hands—and one of them also holds the ring so that the player in the middle cannot see it.

When the player in the middle says "Go!" the others pass the string through their hands— passing the ring from hand to hand at the same time.

The player in the center tries to locate the ring by touching any hand he thinks conceals it.

A player must open his hand if it is touched. If it concealed the ring, he must change places with the player in the center. If his hand is empty, the original player stays in the middle.

UP JENKINS!

This game is similar to hunt the ring but is played with any small object instead of a ring on a string.

Play One player sits on the floor in the middle of a circle formed by the other players sitting around him.

The players in the circle sit with their hands behind their backs and one of them holds the small object.

When the player in the middle says "Go!" the players in the circle all pass, or pretend to pass, the ring around the circle behind their backs.

When the player in the middle says "Up Jenkins!" the players in the circle, including the one with the object, must all raise their clenched fists.

When the player in the middle says "Down Jenkins!" the players in the circle must put their hands palms down on the ground—and the player with the object must, of course, do his best to keep the object concealed at this stage of the game.

The player in the middle then tries to identify which of the players is hiding the object.

Jigsaw hunt

Easter egg hunt

© DIAGRAM

Finding the thimble

BEAN HUNT
Preparation The organizer hides a large quantity of beans around the room. A small container such as a paper cup is needed for each player.
Play Each player collects as many beans as he can within a given time limit. The player who finds most beans is the winner.

BUTTERFLY HUNT
This game is played in the same way as bean hunt except that players look for paper butterflies hidden by the organizer. The winner is the player who finds most butterflies after an agreed time limit.

HIDDEN OBJECTS
In this game players look for objects hidden all around the house.
Preparation The organizer hides about 20 objects in different rooms. It should be possible to see the objects without moving anything. A list of the objects is prepared for each of the players.
Play Each player is given a list and tries to locate the objects, noting down wherever he finds one.
The game is won by the first player to locate all the objects and take his list to the organizer.

JIGSAW HUNT
Preparation One "jigsaw" is needed for each player. The organizer makes the jigsaws by cutting picture postcards into four irregular pieces.
Three pieces from each jigsaw are hidden in the room.
Play Each player is given one of the jigsaw pieces that was not hidden.
The first player to find the three pieces missing from his jigsaw wins the game.

PRESENT HUNT
Each player is given a piece of paper with a written clue to guide him to his present.

COLOR HUNT
This game is played in the same way as present hunt except that each player is given a small piece of wrapping paper and then hunts for and keeps the present wrapped in the same sort of paper.

EASTER EGG HUNT
Each player hunts for a chocolate Easter egg wrapped in a particular color of paper. Alternatively, a tag with the name of one of the players may be attached to each hidden egg.

DETECTIVE TREASURE HUNT
This game requires more preparation and ingenuity than most hunting games.
Preparation The organizer thinks up a series of clues such that the solution of each clue will lead players to the hiding place of the next one. The solution of the last clue may lead to:
a) a prize for the first player or pair to find it;
b) a pile of presents, one for each player; or
c) the party table.
Play Sometimes players take part on their own. Alternatively they may play in pairs.
The organizer gives each player or pair the first clue. As the other clues are discovered, they should be left in their places for the other players to find.

CARD HUNT
In this game players form two teams and look for playing cards hidden around the room.
Preparation Two decks of playing cards are needed. The cards from one deck are hidden around the room within reach of the players. The other deck is divided into two piles—one of red cards and one of black cards.
Play Each member of one team is given a black card and each member of the other team is given a red one.
Each player searches for the hidden card that matches the card he has been given.
When a player finds the card he is looking for he takes it to the organizer who gives him another card of the same color.
Play continues in this way until one of the teams has found all its cards.

STOREKEEPERS
This is another team hunting game. It is best if there are about four teams each with three or more members. Each team represents a different store.
Preparation The organizer takes a number of plain cards and writes the names of a commodity on each one. These commodities should be items sold in the stores that will be represented. There should be an equal number of cards for each store. These cards are hidden around the room.
Play The players form teams and each team is given the name of a store—for example the bakery or the grocery store.
The players are told how many commodities are missing from the stores.
Each team chooses a "storekeeper," who stands in the middle of the room. The other players then look for the cards and when they find a card for their own store take it to their storekeeper.
The game is won by the team that first finds all its hidden commodities.

CUT-OUT PAIRS
This is a good game for introducing players to each other at the start of a party.
Preparation All sorts of pictures are cut out of magazines, comics, etc. Each picture is pasted onto cardboard and cut into two oddly shaped pieces. (Picture postcards may be used to save time.) There should be one picture for each pair of players.
Play Each player is given one piece of a picture. He then tries to find the player with the other half of the same picture. When two players have a complete picture they write a suitable caption for it. Pictures and captions are displayed and the writers of the funniest caption may win a prize.

MOTHERS AND BABIES
This is another pairing game along the lines of cut-out pairs. For this game players are given a card showing a mother or a baby animal—for example a cow or a calf, a frog or a tadpole. Players then have to find the player with the card showing the other member of their family.

HIDE AND SEEK
Children enjoy organizing this game themselves.
Play Players choose somewhere to be "home"— for example a chair or a door. They also choose someone to be the first "seeker." The seeker then shuts his eyes and counts to 40 while all the other players hide.
When he reaches 40, he shouts "Ready!" and goes and looks for the other players. When he finds a player, that player must try and reach home before the seeker can touch him.
The first player to reach home untouched becomes the next seeker.

SARDINES
This is a type of hide and seek usually played in the dark.
The more rooms the children can play in the more exciting the game becomes.
Play One player is chosen as the first sardine. He then leaves the room and finds a place to hide—preferably somewhere big enough for most of the others to squeeze in too.
When the first sardine has had time to hide, the other players split up and look for him. When a player finds the hiding place he creeps in and hides with the first sardine.
The last sardine to find the others usually becomes the first sardine for the next game.

KIM'S GAME
Sometimes called memory test or the memory game, this is an excellent test of the players' powers of observation.
Preparation The organizer puts about 20 small objects on a tray. He then covers them with a cloth until play begins.
Play The organizer uncovers the objects and allows the players about 3 minutes in which to memorize them. The players are not allowed to make any notes.
At the end of the time limit the organizer covers the tray with the cloth and gives each player a pencil and paper.
The players are then asked to write down as many of the objects as they can.
The winner is the player who remembers most objects.

MISMATCHES

This is a team observation game, in which one team tries to spot all the "mismatches" made by the other.

Play Players divide into two teams. One team leaves the room while the other makes its mismatches by altering things in the room.

For example the team making the mismatches might change the position of objects—such as turning a vase upside down—or might change something about a person—such as putting a cardigan on inside out.

At the end of a time limit the other team returns and tries to spot the mismatches.

At the end of another time limit, any mismatches that have not been noticed score one point to the team that made them.

The teams then change roles, and the winning team is the team that scores most points.

RUMORS

This is a competitive form of the popular old game of Chinese whispers.

Objective Each player tries to pass on a message that has been whispered to him.

Play Players divide into two equal teams and each team sits down in a circle. Players take it in turns to be team leader. The organizer decides on a message and whispers it to the two leaders.

Each leader then whispers the message to the player to his right. This player then whispers the message as he heard it to the player to his right, and so on around the circle. Whisperers are not allowed to give the message more than once.

The last player of each team tells the leader the message as he heard it. The leader then tells the message as it began. The team that kept the message most intact wins the game.

WRONG!

In this game players try to spot deliberate errors in a story that is read to them.

Preparation The organizer writes a short story in which there are numerous errors of fact—for example he might say that he went to the antique shop and bought a new clock.

Play The organizer reads out the story.

If a player spots a mistake he shouts "Wrong!" The first player to call out a mistake scores one point. A player who shouts when there has been no mistake loses one point.

The player with most points at the end of the story wins the game.

HAPPY TRAVELERS

Each player tries to be the first to sort the pages of a newspaper into the correct order.

Preparation For each player the pages of a newspaper are put together in the wrong order—some pages may be upside down or back to front—and then folded.

Play Players sit facing each other in two rows. They should sit very close together like passengers on a crowded train.

Each player is given one of the newspapers.

At the word "Go!" each player tries to rearrange the pages of his newspaper into the correct order.

The first player to succeed wins the game.

PRINTERS' ERRORS

In this game players try to set out jumbled lines of a printed article into their correct order.

Preparation A jumbled article is needed for each player. The organizer makes as many copies of the article as he needs and then jumbles each one by cutting it into pieces after each line.

Play Each player is given his jumbled article. When the organizer gives the signal players start to sort out their articles.

The winner is the first player to put his article into the correct order.

Hide and seek

Trickery games

In these games players try to trick others into carrying out some action for which they will be penalized. As these games are usually played, a player must drop out if he makes a mistake. Alternatively, players may be allowed to stay in the game if they carry out a forfeit.

Simon says

SIMON SAYS

Simon says is an old party game that remains a great favorite. It is sometimes called O'Grady says.

Play One player is the leader and the others spread around the room in front of him.

The leader orders the others to do various actions—such as touching their toes or raising their arms.

Whether or not they must obey his orders depends on how the orders are given.

If the leader begins the order with the words "Simon says," the players must obey.

If he does not begin with these words, they must not do the action.

If a player makes a mistake he is out of the game.

The leader encourages mistakes by:

a) giving rapid orders;

b) developing a rhythm with a repeated pattern of movements and then breaking it;

c) doing the actions himself for the others to follow.

The last person left in the game is the winner and becomes the next leader.

DO THIS, DO THAT!

This is played like Simon says except for the way in which the leader gives his orders.

If the leader says "Do this!" the players should mimic his action.

If he says "Do that!" they should remain still.

IN THE DITCH

This game is simpler than Simon says but calls for a lot of energy.

Play A line is marked along the floor with cushions or two parallel strands of yarn.

One player is the leader and the others space themselves out down one side of the line. One side is called "the bank" and the other side "the ditch."

The leader orders the players to jump from side to side by calling out "In the ditch!" or "On the bank!" He can try to trick the players by calling the orders very quickly and repeating an order instead of alternating them.

A player must drop out if he makes a mistake. The winner is the last person left in the game.

Parcel games

Everyone loves to unwrap a parcel and find a present inside. Pass the parcel is an old party favorite and is enjoyed by children of all ages. There are also a number of entertaining variations on the parcel-opening theme.

Pass the parcel

PASS THE PARCEL

Preparation A small present is wrapped in layer after layer of paper. Each layer should be secured with thread, glue, or a rubber band.

Music is needed for this game —and a non-player to start and stop it.

Play Players sit in a circle and one of them holds the parcel. When the music starts, players pass the parcel around the circle to the right.

When the music stops whoever is holding the parcel unwraps one layer of wrapping. The music is then restarted and the parcel passed on again.

The game continues in this way until someone takes off the final wrapping and so wins the present.

MY LITTLE BIRD

This game is played in countries all over the world. Other names for it include flying high and birds fly.

Play One player is the leader and the others stand in a row in front of him.

Alternatively everyone sits around a table.

The leader starts by saying "My little bird is lively, is lively," and then goes on to name something followed by the word "fly"—for example he might say "eggs fly."

If whatever he names can fly—for example cockatoos—the players raise their arms and wave them about.

If it cannot fly—as with eggs—the players should remain still.

A player who makes a mistake is out. The last player left in the game wins.

YES-NO BEANS

In yes-no beans players must guard against being tricked while at the same time trying to trick others.

Play Each player starts with five beans or any other unit of exchange.

The players circulate round the room, asking each other questions and replying to any questions that another player asks them. Players must not use the words yes or no in any of their replies.

Whenever a player succeeds in tricking another into saying yes or no, he gives that player one of his beans.

The first player to get rid of all his beans wins the game.

LAUGHING HANDKERCHIEF

This game is often a riot of infectious laughter. It will be won only by a player who can start and stop laughing at will.

Play One player is the leader and stands in the center of a circle formed by the others. The leader has a handkerchief which he drops as a signal for the other players to laugh. They must start laughing as soon as he lets go of the handkerchief and must stop when it touches the floor.

A player is out if he does not laugh the whole of the time that the handkerchief is falling or if he continues laughing after it has landed.

The last player left in the game wins and becomes the next leader.

In the ditch

FORFEITS PARCEL

This game is the same as pass the parcel except that a forfeit is written on each layer of wrapping.

A player who is holding the parcel when the music stops must carry out the next forfeit before taking off the next layer of wrapping.

MYSTERY PARCEL

Preparation A parcel is prepared as for pass the parcel but with a message written on each layer of wrapping. Typical messages are "Give to the player with the whitest teeth!" and "Pass to the person to your left!"

Music is needed.

Play The parcel is passed around to music as in pass the parcel.

When the music stops, the player holding the parcel reads out the message and hands the parcel to the player who fits the description in the message. This player then unwraps the next layer of paper before the music is restarted.

HOT PARCEL

Preparation A present is given a single strong wrapper.

Music is needed.

Play is as for pass the parcel except that when the music stops the person holding the parcel drops out of the game. The last player left in the game unwraps the parcel and wins the present.

LUCKY CHOCOLATE GAME

Preparation A chocolate bar is wrapped in several layers of paper. Each layer should be secured with thread.

The parcel and a knife and fork are then put on a breadboard on a table.

A chair with a hat, scarf, and gloves on it is then placed at the table.

One die is also needed.

Play The players sit in a circle on the floor and take it in turns to throw the die.

If a player throws a 6, he puts on the hat, scarf, and gloves, sits on the chair, and uses the knife and fork to remove the wrappings.

If another player throws a 6 he changes places with the player at the table.

When the chocolate is unwrapped, players at the table use the knife and fork to eat the chocolate.

The game continues until all the chocolate has been eaten.

Lucky chocolate game

Contests

In these games players perform various feats of skill. Some of the games are a test of physical strength or ability, others need ingenuity in order to outwit opponents. It is a good idea in case of dispute for someone to act as referee.

Card and bucket contest

Balloon flights

Limbo

BALLOON FLIGHTS
Objective Each player tries to flick a balloon the farthest distance.
Play Players form a straight line. Each person balances a balloon on the palm of one hand. Balloons should all be a different color, or marked with the players' initials.
The referee counts "One, two, three, go," and each player then flicks his balloon with the first finger and thumb of his other hand.
The player whose balloon makes the longest flight is the winner.

STATIC ELECTRICITY
Objective Each player tries to have the most balloons clinging to a wall at the end of a time limit.
Preparation Plenty of balloons are inflated and their necks tied.
Play The balloons are placed in a pile in the center of the room and each player is allocated an area of wall.
On the word "Go," each player takes a balloon, rubs it on his clothing to create static electricity, and then tries to make it cling to the wall.
If he succeeds, he takes another balloon and does the same, and so on with as many balloons as possible.
If a balloon falls off the wall any player may use it again.
End At the end of a time limit, the player with the most balloons still clinging to the wall wins.

CARD AND BUCKET CONTEST
Objective Players try to flick all their cards into a bucket or other large container.
Play Each player is given ten playing cards—preferably old ones—and writes down which ones they are.
The players then form a large circle around a bucket. At a call of "Go!" each player tries to flick his cards into the bucket.
When all the players have flicked all their cards, the cards in the bucket are identified.
The winner is the player who gets most cards into the bucket. Several rounds may be played.

APPLE PARING
Objective Each player tries to peel the longest unbroken paring from an apple.
Play Each player is given an apple, a knife, and a plate. All the apples and all the knives should be of similar quality.
The players then peel their apples.
The winner is the one to produce the longest and narrowest paring.

Apple on a string

CANDY WRAPPER

This game is similar to apple paring, but instead of fruit the children get a candy to eat.

Objective Each player aims to tear a candy wrapper into a long, thin, spiral strip.

Play Each player is given a candy, which he unwraps. While eating the candy, he tears its wrapping paper, starting at the outer edge and tearing round and round towards the center.

The player with the longest unbroken strip of paper wins.

HOPPIT

Objective Each player tries to hop the farthest while making progressively larger hops.

Play Using strands of yarn, two straight lines are marked on the floor. The lines are about 1ft apart at one end of the room and fan out to about 6ft apart at the other.

Players take turns at hopping back and forth across the two lines. They start at the narrow end and move down the room.

The player who gets the farthest down the lines before failing to hop right across the two lines, is the winner.

SINGING HIGH JUMP

This is a test of vocal range—each player aims to sing the most widely spaced low and high notes.

Play The referee stands by a "take-off" line ready to score each player's attempt.

In turn, each player runs up to the take-off line, stops, and sings two notes: the first as low as possible, the second as high as possible.

The player who makes the highest musical "jump" is the winner.

APPLE ON A STRING

An old favorite for Halloween, players try, without using their hands, to eat apples suspended from strings.

Play A piece of string is hung across the room, well above head height.

One apple (or currant bun) per person is suspended from it, also on a string.

The players try to eat their apples or buns without using their hands.

The first player to eat the apple down to its core, or to completely eat the bun, is the winner.

LIMBO

Originally a West Indian acrobatic dance, this is a test of suppleness and sustained contortion.

Play Two people gently hold a long stick horizontally and at chest height.

Each player in turn bends backward and edges himself under the stick.

He must neither touch the floor with his hands nor touch the stick.

If a player, after two attempts, fails to pass under the stick he is eliminated.

After each round the stick is lowered a little.

The last person to stay in the game is the winner.

GRANDMOTHER'S FOOTSTEPS

Objective Each player tries to be the first one to creep up behind the "grandmother" without her seeing him move.

Play One person is chosen as the grandmother and stands with his face against a wall and eyes shut.

The other players line up across the opposite wall. When everyone is ready, the players start to creep up behind the grandmother—but whenever she looks round they must "freeze" into statues.

The grandmother may look round as often as she likes. If she sees anyone moving, she points to him and he has to go back to the start. The grandmother turns round to face the wall, and the players move forward again.

End The first player to touch the grandmother's wall wins and takes the next turn at being grandmother.

TWO-MINUTE WALK

Objective Each player tries to walk from one end of the room to the other in exactly two minutes.

Play Players line up along one wall.

On the word "Go," they set off across the room. Without using a watch or a clock, each player tries to reach the other side of the room in exactly two minutes.

The organizer times the players' walks.

End When all the players have finished, the player whose time was nearest two minutes wins.

STORK FIGHTING CONTEST

Play Two players tie their left ankles together with a scarf, and hop on their right feet. Each player then tries to make his opponent's left foot touch the ground—without putting down his own left foot. If a player's left foot touches the ground, or if his hands touch the ground, his opponent scores a point.

The winner is the player with the most points at the end of a time limit.

COCK FIGHTING CONTEST

Objective Each player tries to tip over his opponent.

Play Two players crouch on the floor facing each other. Each brings his knees together under his chin and clasps his legs with his arms.

A walking stick is then passed under his knees and over his arms.

The two players then try to tip each other over.

The first player to succeed is the winner.

TRIANGULAR TUG-OF-WAR

This is a game for three players.

Play A circle is made from a rope about 3yd long.

Three players space themselves around the rope and hold it taut, forming a triangle.

A handkerchief is placed at each corner of the triangle, out of reach of the player.

On the word "Go!" each player tries to pick up the handkerchief nearest him without letting go of the rope.

The first player to pick up his handkerchief is the winner.

ARM WRESTLING

Objective Each player tries to prove he has the strongest arm muscles!

Play Two players sit facing each other at either side of a table.

Resting their right elbows on the table and with crooked arms, they clasp each other's right hands. (Both players may use their left arms if they prefer.)

On the signal to begin each player tries to force his opponent's right hand back until it touches the table. Elbows must be kept firmly on the table.

The winner is the first to succeed.

Stork fighting

Cock fighting

Triangular tug-of-war

Arm wrestling

© DIAGRAM

Goal scoring games

Although goal scoring games are often based on energetic outdoor sports, they can safely be played in the home if a balloon, soft ball, or large rag is used. Playing with balloons is particularly enjoyable as they are difficult to control and unlikely to cause damage.

AVENUE GOALS

Players try to score goals by patting a ball or balloon so that it goes beyond their opponents' end of the avenue.

Players The players form two lines about 5ft apart, and sit facing each other on the floor. Counting from one end, the odd-numbered players in one line belong to the same team as the even-numbered players in the other line.

Each team is allotted one end of the avenue as its goal.

Play The organizer puts the ball into the center of the avenue.

Each team tries to score by patting the ball by hand down the avenue into its opponent's goal. Players are not allowed to hold or throw the ball.

The ball is put back into the center of the avenue after each goal.

The winning team is the one with most goals at the end of a time limit.

OVERHEAD GOALS

Players try to score goals by patting a balloon over their opponents' heads.

Players The players form two teams in rows about 4ft apart, and sit facing each other on the floor.

Play The organizer tosses the ball into the center.

Each team tries to score goals by knocking the balloon over the heads of the opposing team and onto the ground behind them.

The winning team is the one with most goals at the end of a time limit.

Avenue goals

Scoring races

In all these games players are in some way singled out from their teams to take a turn at competing for points. In each case, the competition takes the form of a race between members of opposing teams.

NUMBER PARADE

Objective Each team tries to be the first to parade a number called by the organizer.

Preparation Single digits from zero to nine are drawn on separate pieces of card. The digits should be several inches high.

There may be either one or two cards for each player but there should be the same set of digits for each team.

In addition, a list of numbers using the digits available to each team is drawn up.

Play The teams form lines and each player is given either one or two of the cards.

The organizer calls out a number—for example he might call "469."

Immediately the players in each team with the digits 4,6, and 9 rush to the front and line up holding their digits so that they read "469."

The first team to parade the number correctly scores a point.

Players return to their teams and another number is called. To make the game more interesting the organizer can set easy sums for the players to solve and parade.

WORD PARADE

This is played like number parade except that letters are written on the cards and words are called out to be spelled and paraded by the players.

BALLOON VOLLEYBALL
In balloon volleyball players hit a balloon over a piece of string held taut by two players standing on chairs.
Players The players divide into two teams, one on either side of the string. Players within a team take turns at serving (hitting the balloon into play at the start of play or after a break).
Play Players hit the balloon back and forth over the string with the aim of making a shot that their opponents will not be able to return.
A team scores a point whenever it hits the balloon over the string onto the floor on its opponent's side.
If the ball goes under the string, the opposing team serves it.
The winning team is the one with most points at the end of a time limit.

BLOW VOLLEYBALL
This is played in exactly the same way as balloon volleyball except that the balloon is blown rather than hit, and the string held lower.

ASTRIDE BALL
This is a goal scoring game without teams.
Players One player stands in the center of a circle formed by the other players standing with their legs apart.
Play The center player has a ball to be rolled along the ground. If he rolls it between the legs of a player in the circle, he "scores a goal" and changes places with that player.
The players in the circle should keep their hands on their knees except when trying to prevent a goal.

HOCKEY RAG TIME
In this game team members take turns at trying to shoot a goal.
Players The players form two rows about 6ft apart and sit down facing each other on the floor. Each team member is given a number, starting with one.
A rag and two walking sticks are laid on the floor between the two rows of players. A chair is placed at each end of the avenue as a goal. Each team is allotted one of the goals.
Play The organizer calls out a number.
Each player with that number picks up a walking stick and uses it to maneuver the rag into his opponent's goal.
The successful player scores a point for his side.
The rag and walking sticks are replaced and the organizer calls another number.
The winning team is the one with most goals at the end of a time limit.

Balloon volleyball

MYSTERY NUMBERS
Objective Each team's players try to be fastest at solving clues and running around their teams.
Preparation It is a good idea to prepare a list of clues indicating particular numbers. If there are seven players in a team, clues for numbers one through seven will be needed. For example for number six the clues might be: half a dozen, a hexagon, an insect's legs, June, the sides of a cube.
Play Players line up behind their leaders and sit down. In each team players are numbered off starting with the leader as number one.
The organizer calls out a clue. As soon as a player recognizes that it refers to his number, he jumps up, runs around his team, and sits down in his place again.
The first player back scores a point for his team.
When all the players are seated again, the organizer calls out another clue.
End The team with the most points at the end of a time limit wins the game.

SIMPLE NUMBERS
This is played in the same way as mystery numbers except that the numbers are not hidden in clues. The organizer simply calls out each number.

LADDERS
Ladders can be played like either mystery numbers or simple numbers.
The difference is that the teams sit in two rows facing each other. It is recommended that players take off their shoes for this game. Each player sits with his legs outstretched and his feet touching those of the opposing player with the same number as himself.
When a player's number is called or indicated he runs up between the lines over the other players' legs, back down behind his team, and then up between the lines to return to his place.

MY MOTHER'S CAKE
This is played in the same way as ladders except that players are given the name of an ingredient instead of a number.
The organizer then tells a story about how the cake was made and while telling it he mentions all the various ingredients. When a player hears the name of his ingredient he must race around as in ladders.

Mystery numbers

©DIAGRAM

Passing races

These are all games in which teams of players race to pass objects to each other in different ways. In each game, the contestants need to strike a balance between speed and skill.

Nose in the matchbox

Switchback

Passing the orange

PICK AND CUP

Objective Each team tries to be the first to pass assorted objects down its line of players.

Preparation Identical piles of various objects—eg fruit, beans, buttons, pebbles, etc—are collected together, one pile for each team.

Play Players divide into teams and sit down beside their leaders.
One pile of objects is placed beside each leader.
On the word "Go!" each leader picks up an object and drops it into the cupped hands of the player next to him.
The third player in the line picks the object out of the cupped hands and places it into the fourth player's cupped hands.
This continues down the line to the last player, who puts the object on the floor.
The leader can then pick up the next object and pass it down the line as before.

End The first team to transfer all the objects down the line wins.

NOSE IN THE MATCHBOX

Play Players divide into teams and line up beside their leaders.
A matchbox lid is given to each leader.
On the word "Go!" he lodges it on his nose and passes it onto the next player's nose without using his hands.
In this way the matchbox lid is passed down the line.
If a player touches the lid with his hands or drops it, it is returned to the leader to start again.

End The first team to successfully pass the matchbox lid down the line wins.

DOUBLE PASS

Objective Players in each team try to pass objects behind them and in front of them in two directions.

Preparation Two identical piles of objects are collected, one for each team.
Alternatively, a deck of cards may be divided between the teams.

Play Players divide into teams and sit in a line to the left of their leaders.
One pile of objects, or cards, is placed beside the leader.
On the word "Go!" he starts passing the objects, one after the other, down the line.
Only right hands are used until the object reaches the end of the line. Then the left hands are used to return the objects behind the players' backs.
As objects arrive back at the beginning again, the leader makes a pile of the returned objects.

End The first team to return all the objects wins.

SWITCHBACK

Objective Each team tries to be quickest at passing through a hoop.

Play Players divide into teams and line up behind their leaders. A hoop is given to each leader.
On the word "Go!" the leader puts the hoop over his head, drops it to the ground, and steps out of it.
The next player steps into the hoop, lifts it over his head, and hands it to the next player.
The hoop is passed down the line in this way, players putting the hoop over their heads and stepping into it alternately.
When the last player has passed through the hoop, he runs with it to the front of the line and passes it back as before.
This continues with each player taking a turn at the head of the line.

End The first team with its leader at the front again wins.

BALLOON PASS
Objective Each team tries to be quickest at passing a balloon overhead.
Play Players divide into teams and form lines behind their leaders.
Each leader is given a balloon. On the word "Go!" he passes it over his head to the player behind him. This player in turn passes the balloon back over his head.
In this way the balloon is passed down the entire line. When the last player gets the balloon, he runs to the front of his line and passes the balloon back in the same way as before.
Thus each player takes a turn at the head of the line.
The winning team is the first one to have its leader at the front of the line again.

TUNNEL BALL
This is played like balloon pass except that players stand with their legs apart and pass the balloon back between their legs.

STRAWS AND BEANS
Objective Each team tries to be quickest at using straws to pass beans from player to player.
Play Players divide into teams and sit in a line beside their leaders.
A saucer with six beans on it is placed next to each leader, and an empty saucer is placed at the other end of each team.
Every player is given a drinking straw.
On the word "Go!" the leader picks up a bean and transfers if from his hand to the next player's cupped hand by sucking the bean onto the end of his straw and holding his breath.
In this manner all the beans are passed down the line and placed in the empty saucer. If a bean is dropped, it is returned to the beginning again.
End The first team to successfully transfer all its beans wins.

SUGAR AND SPOONS
This is played like straws and beans, except that players hold teaspoons in their mouths and tip sugarlumps from spoon to spoon.

PASSING THE ORANGE
Objective Seated players try to pass an orange down the line using their feet, or (in an alternative version) by using their chins!
Play Players divide into teams and sit in a line on the floor beside their leaders.
Each leader is given an orange and, with his legs together, cradles it on his feet.
On the word "Go!" he passes the orange onto the feet of the next player.
(Alternatively, the leader tucks the orange under his chin. The next player takes the orange from him, also using his chin—neither player may use his hands.)
Using either one of these ways, the orange is passed from player to player.
If the orange drops onto the floor, or if a player uses his hands, the orange is returned to the leader to start again.
End The first team to successfully pass the orange down the line wins.

PALMS
Objective Each team tries to be quickest at passing coins with flat hands.
Play Players divide into teams and form rows to the left of their leaders.
Each leader is given six large coins that he holds in his left hand.
On the word "Go!" he places one coin on the flat palm of his right hand and slaps it onto the flat palm of the next player's right hand.
In this manner each coin is passed down the row.
If a coin is dropped, it is returned to the leader to start again.
End The first team to successfully pass all six coins from one end to the other wins.

Tunnel ball

Balloon pass

Straws and beans

Sugar and spoons

Passing the orange

Strange races

Individuals, pairs of players, and sometimes larger teams compete in these races. They can all be run in heats leading to a final if there is not enough room or equipment for everyone to compete at once.

Newspaper walk

Rabbit race

NEWSPAPER WALK
Each player tries to be the first to walk the length of the room on two sheets of newspaper.
Play Players stand in a line at one end of the room.
Each player is given two sheets of newspaper to stand on, one sheet under each foot.
At the word "Go!" he starts to move across the room on his newspaper.
If he touches the floor with any part of his body he must go back to the beginning again.

TORTOISE RACE
Each player tries to be the last to finish.
Play Players line up along one side of the room.
At the word "Go!" they each start to move across the room as slowly as possible. They must head straight for the opposite wall.
A player is disqualified if he stops moving or changes direction.

FISHERMEN
Each player tries to be the first to wind in his "fish."
Preparation Each player requires a fishing line and fish —made by tying a teaspoon to a length of strong thread wrapped around a spool.
Play Players stand in a line at one end of the room.
Each player is given a spoon and spool. He places the spoon on the floor and then unwinds the thread in a straight line to the other end of the room.
At the word "Go!" each player starts to wind in his spoon by turning the spool round and round in his hands. He is not permitted to hold the thread in one hand and wind it around the spool.

RABBIT RACE
Each player tries to be the first to jerk his "rabbit" along his piece of string.
Preparation One rabbit shape for each player is cut out of heavy card. A small hole is made in its center and a piece of string about 6ft long threaded through the hole and tied to a chair.
Play Each player holds the free end of one of the pieces of string and moves the rabbit to that end.
At the word "Go!" each player, without touching his rabbit, must jerk it along the string to the chair.

BOTTLE FISHING
Each player tries to be the first to ring his bottle.
Preparation Several bottles of the same size and shape are needed, together with an equal number of rings large enough to slip over the necks of the bottles. Each ring should be tied to a length of string.
Play Players sit or stand in a line, with a bottle in front of each of them. Each player then tries to "catch" his bottle, by getting his ring over his bottle's neck.

BACK TO BACK RACE
Pairs of players try to be the first to run the course.
Play Players form pairs and line up at one end of the room. Each pair of players stands back to back with their arms linked.
At the word "Go!" the linked players race to the other end of the room. Pairs who become unlinked must go back to the beginning and start again.

PIGGY BACK RACE
This is another race in which pairs of players try to be the first to run a course.
Play Players form pairs and line up at one end of the room. One player from each pair gets on the other's back to be carried.
At the word "Go!" the pairs race to the other end of the room, where they must change places so that the carrier becomes the carried. They must then race back to the original end of the room. If a player touches the floor while he is being carried, that pair must start again.

Bottle fishing

NECKLACE RACE

Each pair tries to be the first to thread all its beads.

Preparation 12 beads on a saucer, a needle, and a length of thread are needed for each pair of players.

Play Players line up in pairs along one side of the room. Each saucer of beads is placed opposite a pair of players at the other end of the room. One player in each pair is given a needle and length of thread.

At the word "Go!" each player with needle and thread must thread his needle and tie a large firm knot at one end of his thread.

At the same time his partner runs to the saucer, picks up two beads, and returns with them.

When the first player in each pair has threaded his needle he takes the two beads from his partner and threads them while his partner goes back to the saucer for two more beads. Play continues in this way until all 12 beads have been threaded. If any beads are dropped they must be picked up and threaded normally.

When a player has threaded all 12 beads, he removes the needle and ties the bead necklace around his partner's neck.

The game is won by the first pair to finish its necklace.

YARN TANGLES

Teams of four players try to be first to untangle balls of yarn wrapped around chairs.

Preparation A chair and four different colored balls of yarn are needed for each team.

Play Players form into teams of four. Each team is given four balls of yarn and a chair. Teams are then allowed about one minute in which to tangle their yarn around their chairs. They are not allowed to lift up their chairs or to make deliberate knots in the yarn.

At the end of the time limit the organizer calls "Stop!" and teams must move around to a different chair.

At the word "Go!" teams start to disentangle the yarn from their new chair. Each player winds one of the balls of yarn. Players are not allowed to pick up the chair or deliberately break the yarn.

The game is won by the first team to untangle the yarn into four separate balls.

DUMB ARTISTS

Each pair tries to be the first in which one player recognizes an animal drawn by the other. Players are not allowed to speak to each other during this game.

Play Players form pairs, and partners stand opposite each other at different ends of the room.

The players at one end are each given a pencil and a card with the name of an animal written on it.

At the word "Go!" each of these players runs to his partner and, with the animal's name face down, tries to draw the animal.

When his partner thinks that he recognizes the drawing, he takes the pencil and writes down the animal's name.

If his answer is correct, his partner nods his head and both players run to the other end of the room.

If his answer is incorrect, his partner shakes his head, takes the pencil back, and continues drawing.

The game is won by the first pair to reach the other end of the room after the animal has been guessed.

CROCODILE RACE

This is an amusing race for teams of players.

Play Players divide into teams and line up behind their leaders at one end of the room. Players then squat on their heels, each with his hands on the shoulders or waist of the player in front of him.

At the word "Go!" the "crocodiles" move forward by little jumps or bounces.

If a player loses contact with the player in front of him, his team must stop and reassemble. For reassembling, the hind end of the crocodile must stay where it is while the front end moves back to join it.

The first team to reach the other end of the room intact wins the race.

THREE-LEGGED RACE

Pairs of players try to be the first to run from one end of the room to the other.

Play Players form pairs and line up at one end of the room. A scarf is needed for each pair so that the right leg of one of the players in the pair can be tied to the left leg of his partner.

At the word "Go!" pairs race to the other end of the room.

PATCHES

Players race to sew patches on their partners' clothes.

Preparation A square of material, a needle, and thread are needed for each pair of players.

Play Each player finds a partner and one of them is given a square of material, a needle, and a length of thread.

At the word "Go!" a player from each pair quickly sews his patch on his partner's clothes. (Big stitches are allowed!)

The first player to finish wins the heat.

The other player in each pair then has a turn at sewing.

Back to back race

Three-legged race

Piggy back race

©DIAGRAM

Relay races

In relay races players in each team take it in turns to perform the same action one after the other. Two or more teams can take part in any of the races described here. Relay races are particularly enjoyable for large numbers of players.

Flying fish

Burst the bag

FLYING FISH

Objective In this game (also known as kippers in the United Kingdom) teams race each other at fanning "fish" across the room.

Preparation A "fish" about 10in long is made for each player out of fairly thick paper—the plumper the fish, the better it will "fly."
Each team is given a folded newspaper or magazine.

Play Players line up behind their leaders at one end of the room. A plate is placed on the floor at the other end of the room opposite each team.
At the word "Go!" each leader places his fish on the floor and fans it with the newspaper, down the room and onto the plate.
As soon as he has done this, he races back to his team and hands the newspaper to the next player in line.
Each player in turn fans his fish across the room and onto the plate, and the first team to finish wins the game.

BURST THE BAG

Objective Teams race each other to be the first to blow up and burst paper bags.

Play Players line up behind their leaders.
Paper bags, one for each player, are placed on chairs opposite each team leader.
At the word "Go!" each leader runs to the chair, takes a paper bag, blows it up, and bursts it with his hands.
As soon as he has done this, he runs back to his team and touches the next player. As soon as this player is touched, he takes his turn at bursting a bag.
Play continues in this way until each player has burst a bag—the first team to finish being the winners.

FRUIT COLORS

Objective Each team tries to be the first to color in pictures of fruit.

Preparation For each team, outlines of fruit (one per player) are drawn on a large sheet of paper. The drawings should be the same for each team.
The sheets of paper are attached to a wall or laid out on a table.

Play Teams line up behind their leaders at the opposite end of the room to the drawings.
Each leader is given a box of crayons.
At the word "Go!" he runs to his team's sheet of paper and colors in one of the pieces of fruit.
He then goes back to his team, hands the box of crayons to the next player and stands at the back of his team.
As soon as the second player gets the crayons, he goes and colors in another fruit and so on down the line of players.
If a crayon is dropped on the floor, the player with the box must pick it up.

End The first team to color in all its fruit wins.

SURPRISE SENTENCES

Objective Each team tries to write a sentence, with each player in the team writing one word of it.

Preparation For each team, a large sheet of paper is attached to a wall or to a board propped upright.

Play Each team lines up opposite its sheet of paper and the leader is given a pencil.
At the word "Go!" he runs up to his paper and writes any word he likes.
He then runs back to his team, hands the pencil to the next player, and goes to the end of his team.
As soon as the next player gets the pencil, he goes to the paper and adds a second word either in front of, or behind the leader's word.
Play continues in this way with each player adding one word. The words should be chosen and put together so that they can be part of a grammatically correct sentence.
Each player, except the last, must avoid completing the sentence. The last player should be able to complete the sentence by adding just one word, and he also puts in the punctuation.
Players may not confer and choose a sentence before writing their words.

End The first team to construct a sentence with one word from each player wins the game.

EMPTYING SOCKS

Objective Each team tries to be the first to remove a variety of objects in their correct order from a long sock.

Preparation Identical groups of small objects are put into long socks, one sock for each team. There should be only one item of each kind in each group. The objects might be buttons, beans, coins of different sizes, hairpins, pebbles, etc.

Play Teams line up opposite their leaders. Each leader is given a sock to hold.

The organizer announces the first object to be found. Immediately the first player in each team runs to his leader and puts his hand in the sock. He feels for the object and picks it out of the sock.

If he makes a mistake, he returns the object that he took and tries again.

If he is right, he gives the object to the organizer and is told the next object to be retrieved.

He returns to his team, tells the next player what to search for and stands at the back of his team.

As soon as the next player knows what to find, he takes his turn at feeling for an object in the sock.

Play continues in this way until each object has been retrieved, and the first team to finish wins.

EGG CUPS

Objective Each player tries to blow a table tennis ball from one egg cup to another without dropping it.

Play Players divide into teams and line up beside their leaders.

Two egg cups and a table tennis ball are given to each leader.

At the word "Go!" the leader blows the table tennis ball from one egg cup to the other. He may hold the egg cups so that they touch, but he may not merely tip the ball from one cup to the other.

As soon as the leader has finished, he hands the cups and the table tennis ball to the next player; and so on down the line, until each player has blown the ball from one egg cup to the other.

If the ball is dropped, handled, or tipped instead of blown, it is returned to the leader who must start again.

End The first team whose players have all correctly blown the table tennis ball from one cup to the other wins.

HAT AND SCARF

Objective Players of each team try to be the quickest at dressing up and running around the team.

Preparation A hat, a scarf, a coat, and a pair of gloves are collected for each team.

Play Teams line up behind their leaders and a set of clothes is placed on a chair in front of each team.

At the word "Go!" each leader runs to the chair, puts on the clothes, and runs around his team.

He then takes off the clothes and gives them to the next player to dress up in.

Play continues in this way down the line. When the last player has run around his team, he places the clothes on the chair.

End The first team with its set of clothes back on the chair wins the game.

BALLOON HOP

Objective Teams try to be the first to find and inflate all the balloons belonging to them.

Preparation Balloons of as many different colors as there are teams should be bought, and each player in each team will need a balloon.

Play Players line up behind their leaders. Each team is allotted a color.

The balloons are placed in a pile at the other end of the room.

At the word "Go!" each leader hops across the room, finds a balloon of his team's color and hops back with it to his team.

When he returns, the next player hops across to find a balloon; and so on, until each player has a balloon.

When players return to their teams, they inflate the balloons and fasten the necks.

If a player has a lot of difficulty tying his balloon, another player in his team may help him.

End The first team with all its balloons blown up and tied wins.

HURRY WAITER!

Objective This game also needs a table tennis ball for each team, and the players try to balance it on a plate as they weave in and out of a line of their teammates.

Play Players divide into teams and stand in a line behind their leaders.

Each leader is given a table tennis ball on a plate.

At the word "Go!" he weaves in and out between the players in his team as quickly as he can without dropping the table tennis ball.

When he reaches the end of the line, he runs straight to the head of the line again and hands the plate and ball to the next player, saying "Here is your breakfast Sir (or Madam)" as he does so.

This procedure is repeated, with each player beginning at the head of the line and returning to his place as soon as he has handed the "breakfast" to the next player in turn.

If a player drops the ball, he must go back to the head of the line and start again.

The first team to finish wins the game.

Hat and scarf

©DIAGRAM

Children's card games

All the card games in this chapter are fast-moving and easy to learn. Some old favorites like snap and happy families are primarily games for children. Others—like racing demons, cheat, and memory— are enjoyed by adults and children alike.

SNAP

Amusing and noisy, snap is among the most familiar of all children's card games.

Players Two or more can play.

Cards Special snap cards can be bought but the game is just as much fun with standard playing cards.

It is best to use old cards in case of damage, and it does not matter if any of the cards is missing.

If there are more than three players it is a good idea to use two decks of cards.

Objective Players aim to win all the cards.

Deal One player deals out all the cards in a clockwise direction—one at a time and face down. It does not matter if some players have one card more than the others.

Each player puts his cards into a neat pile face down in front of him.

Players are not allowed to look at their cards.

Play The player to the dealer's left turns over the top card of his pile and places it face up to start a face-up pile of cards next to his face-down pile.

The next player to his left does the same, and so on around the players until any player sees

that the cards on the top of any two face-up piles have the same value (eg two 10s).

Snap The first player to shout "snap" when there are matching cards on the top of two face-up piles, collects both these piles of cards and puts them at the bottom of his own face-down pile.

Players now continue turning cards over as before, beginning with the player to the left of the last player who turned over a card.

Snap pool If two players shout "snap" together, the matching face-up piles are put face up in a pool in the center. Players then continue to turn over cards, and the pool is won by the first player to shout "snap pool" when the top card of any player's face-up pile matches the top card of the pool.

No more cards When a player runs out of face-down cards he simply turns over his face-up cards when it is next his turn to play.

Penalty There are different rules for when a player calls "snap" in error:
a) the player gives one card from his face-down pile to each of the other players;
b) the player's own face-up

pile is put into a central pool to be won like an ordinary snap pool.

End The game ends when only one player has any cards.

EASY SNAP

This version is particularly suitable for very young children. Instead of having individual face-up piles, each player plays his cards onto a central face-up pile. Players shout "snap" when the top two cards are of the same value.

SPEED SNAP

In this faster version of snap, players still turn their cards up one at a time but all players do so together.

Snap!

MENAGERIE

This hilarious and noisy game is similar to snap. It is sometimes called "animals."

Players It can be played by two players but is better with three or more.

Cards One or two decks of standard playing cards are used.

Objective Players aim to win all the cards.

Choosing the animals Players first choose the name of an animal with a long and tongue-twisting name. After checking that everyone has chosen a different animal, each player is given a small piece of paper on which he must write his animal's name. (An older person can help anyone who hasn't learned to write.)

All the pieces of paper are folded and then shaken together in a bag or hat. Each player then takes one piece of paper—and the name on that paper is his animal for the game.

Players should then learn the animal names of all the persons playing.

Deal The cards are dealt as for snap.

Play is the same as for snap, except that animal names are used instead of calling "snap." Whenever the top card on any two player's face-up piles are the same (eg two 7s), each of these two players must call out the other player's animal name three times.

The first player to do so, wins the other player's face-up pile and adds these cards to the bottom of his own face-down pile.

Penalty If a player wrongly calls out a name, he must give all his face-up cards to the player whose animal name he called.

ANIMAL NOISES

This game is played in the same way as menagerie, except that:
a) players choose animals that make distinctive noises (eg dog, cat, or duck);
b) players imitate their opponents' animal noises instead of repeating their animal names.

SLAPJACK

This is an exciting game that needs no skill. It can be enjoyed by the very young as the only requirement is that players can recognize a jack.

Players Two or more can play.

Cards Standard playing cards are used. If there are more than three players it is a good idea to mix two decks together. It does not matter if a few cards are missing.

Objective Players aim to win all the cards.

Deal One player deals out all the cards in a clockwise direction—one at a time and face down. It does not matter if some players have one card more than others.
Each player puts his cards into a neat pile face down in front of him.
Players are not allowed to look at their cards.

Play The player to the dealer's left turns over the top card of his pile and places it face up in the center.
Turns then pass around to the left, with each player placing his card on top of the previous player's card.

Slapping a jack When a jack is turned up, each player tries to be the first to put his hand on the card—ie to "slap the jack."
The successful player wins the central pile of cards and shuffles them with his own cards to form his new face-down pile.
The player to the winner's left starts the next round, placing a card face up in the center.
If more than one player puts his hand on the jack, the winner is the player whose hand is underneath.
If possible it is a good idea to appoint a referee to settle arguments.
If a player loses all his cards he can stay in the game if he is first to slap the next jack.
If he fails to slap the next jack he must retire from the game.

Penalty If a player slaps a card that is not a jack, he must give his top card to the player whose card he slapped in error.

End The winner of the game is either:
a) the first person to collect all the cards; or
b) the player with the most cards at the end of a time limit set at the start of the game.

Slapping a jack

WAR

An easy game, war is a good way of introducing young children to card playing.

Players This game is for two people.

Cards A complete deck of standard playing cards is used.

Objective Each player aims to win all the cards.

Deal One player deals all the cards.
Each player puts his cards into a neat pile face down in front of him.
Players are not allowed to look at their cards.

Play Both players turn over the top card of their piles, and place them face up, side by side, in the center.
The player who has played the higher card, regardless of suit, wins both cards and places them face down at the bottom of his pile.
Aces are the highest cards, followed by kings, queens, jacks, and so on down from the 10s to the 2s.

The "war" If the two cards turned up have the same value, the war is on.
Each player puts one card face down on top of his first card in the center. He then puts another card face up on top of this.

The two new face-up cards are compared, and the highest card wins all six cards in the center.
If the face-up cards match again, the war continues.
Each player puts out another face-down card with a face-up card on top.
Play continues in this way until someone plays a card higher than the other.

End The winner of the game is either:
a) the first player to win all the cards; or
b) the player with the most cards at the end of a time limit set at the start of the game.

WAR FOR THREE PLAYERS

This version of war is for three players.

Deal The cards are dealt out as in war for two, except that the last card is not dealt out. (In this way, all three players begin with the same number of cards.)

Play is the same as in war for two, except that:
a) when two cards of the same value are turned up, all three players engage in war;
b) when three cards of the same value are turned up, the players engage in double war.
In double war each player puts out two cards face down and then one card face up. If the cards still match, the three players then continue with single war.

PERSIAN PASHA

Persian pasha, also called pisha pasha, is a similar game to war.

Players It is a game for two players.

Cards A complete deck of standard playing cards is used.

Objective Each player aims to win all the cards.

Deal Cards are dealt as for war.

Play Each player turns over his top card and places it on a face-up pile next to his face-down pile.
Players continue turning over cards until their top face-up cards are of the same suit.
The player with the higher card then takes all the other player's face-up pile and puts these cards at the bottom of his face-down pile.

Rank of cards

War

MEMORY

This card game for any number of players is also called pelmanism or concentration. It is easy to play and is an excellent test of memory and observation.

Cards One or two standard decks of playing cards are used, depending on the number of players.

The cards should be clean and reasonably new, so that when they are lying face down they cannot be identified by creases, marks, or torn corners!

The playing area must be flat and as large as possible—the floor or a big table is best.

The deal One player shuffles the cards and lays them face down on the table—in all directions and so that no card is touching another.

Objective Each player tries to collect as many cards as possible by turning up pairs with the same rank (number or picture).

First player The player to the left of the dealer starts the game. He turns over two cards at random and allows the other players to see them.

If the rank of the two cards is the same, for example two aces or two kings, he takes them and may turn over two more cards. He continues in this way until he turns over two cards that do not match. If the cards that are turned over do not match, the player must put them face down in their original positions. His turn then ends.

Second player The person to the first player's left now turns over any two cards.

If the first card matches one that has already been turned over he must try to remember where that card is. If he is successful he takes the pair. He continues his turn until he fails to turn over a matching pair.

Successive players Play continues with the players taking their turns in a clockwise direction, until all the cards have been collected.

The winner is the player with most cards at the end of the game.

OTHER CARD-MATCHING GAMES

Memory and other card-matching games may be played with special cards. These can be smaller than standard playing cards and any number of pairs may be used, depending on the number of players.

The cards are printed with colored pictures, patterns, or symbols, and are particularly popular with young children. Rules for these games are like those for memory, with players trying to get matching pairs of, for example, pineapples, eskimoes, or boats.

To make play simpler for very young children, the cards may be laid out at the start of the game in rows, and fewer pairs may be used.

BEGGAR MY NEIGHBOR

Beggar my neighbor is an easy and exciting game. No skill is required as the outcome is wholly decided by the luck of the deal.

Players There may be two to six players.

Cards Any deck of standard playing cards may be used, and it need not be complete. For more than three players it is a good idea to mix two decks together.

The objective is to win all the cards. But, as the game may go on for a very long time, the winner may be the player who has the most cards at the end of an agreed length of time.

Deal One player deals out all the cards in a clockwise direction—one at a time and face down. It does not matter if some players have one card more than the others.

Each player puts his cards into a neat pile face down in front of him.

Players are not allowed to look at their cards.

Play The player to the dealer's left turns up the top card in his pile and places it in the center of the playing area.

Each player in turn, in a clockwise direction, then places the top card from his pile face up on the central pile. This continues until one player turns up an ace or a court card (a jack, queen, or king).

Payment of cards The player next to him then has to "pay" him by placing a certain number of cards on the central pile:

four cards for an ace;

three cards for a king;
two cards for a queen;
one card for a jack.

If, however, one of the payment cards is an ace or a court card, the payer stops turning over his cards and the player next to him has to pay the correct number of cards. This goes on until a player paying out cards turns over the correct number of cards with no aces or court cards.

When this happens, the last player to have turned over an ace or a court card may take the central pile and place it face down at the bottom of his own pile.

The payer then starts a new round by playing his next card face up in the center of the playing area.

As soon as a player has no more cards, he is out.

DONKEY

Donkey is a fast and noisy card game in which players are penalized with letters from the game's name.

Players Three or more can play.

Cards Special cards can be bought but donkey is usually played with sets of cards taken from an old deck of standard playing cards.

Each set consists of four cards with the same picture or number. The number of sets used is the same as the number of people playing. For example if there are five players, the aces, kings, queens, jacks, and 10s might be used.

Spoons, buttons, or some other unbreakable objects should be placed in the center of the table at the start of each round. There must be one object fewer than the number of players.

The objective is to collect a set of four cards and at the same time to avoid being the "donkey" (ie the first player to lose six rounds of the game). A player is penalized with one letter from the word donkey each time that he fails to pick up an object at the end of a round.

Play Keeping his cards hidden from the other players, each player chooses one card that he does not want and places it face down on the table. All the players then pass their unwanted card to the player to their left.

Each player than looks at his new card and again chooses a card to pass to his neighbor.

He may pass the new card if he wishes.

The game continues in this way, as quickly as possible, until one player has a set of four cards of the same value. When a player has a set of cards, for example four 10s, he should quietly put them face up on the table and pick up an object from the table.

As soon as any player does this, the other players must reach for an object whether they have a set of four cards or not.

The player who fails to pick up an object loses the round and is penalized with a letter.

Donkey The first player to be penalized with all the letters of the word donkey loses the game and must "hee-haw" three times.

PIG

Pig is a similar game to donkey. The number of players and the cards used are the same as for donkey, but in pig there is no need for any unbreakable objects.

The objective is to collect a set of four cards of the same value while also avoiding becoming the "prize pig."

Play is the same as for donkey, except that when a player has a set of cards he puts his finger to his nose. The last player to do so is pig for the round.

Prize pig The game is lost when one player becomes prize pig after losing ten rounds. As a forfeit, the prize pig must say "oink-oink" three times.

PIT

Pit is a very lively trading game played with special cards. It is trademarked and copyrighted by Parker Brothers of Salem, Mass.

Players attempt to collect sets of cards representing commodities traded on the American Corn Exchange: wheat, barley, corn, rye, oats, flax, and hay.

The game is made more exciting by the inclusion of bonus and penalty cards: a bull and a bear.

Cards are exchanged by any two players wishing to trade the same number of cards, and as all players are trying to trade at once the game often develops into a happy free for all.

MY SHIP SAILS

An easy game for beginners, my ship sails is also great fun when played at speed by those familiar with it.

Players Four to seven people may play.

Cards A standard deck of playing cards is used.

Objective Each player aims to be the first to collect seven cards of the same suit, for example seven spades.

Deal Each player cuts the cards and the one with the highest card (ace high) is the dealer.

He deals out the cards in a clockwise direction, one at a time and face down, until each player has seven cards. The remaining cards are not used.

Play Each player sorts his cards into suits in his hand and decides which suit he will try to collect. This will probably be the suit for which he has most cards at the start of a round, but he may change his mind during the course of play.

Exchange of cards Each player takes one card that he does not want and puts it face down on the table. When all the players are ready, they pass these cards to the next person to the right.

The players pick up their new cards, decide on another card to discard, and then pass it in the same way.

End Players continue to exchange cards until one person collects seven cards of the same suit. He then calls "my ship sails," and wins the game. If two players call together, the first to start calling is the winner.

My ship sails!

HAPPY FAMILIES

Happy families is a peaceful game much loved by children.

Players Three or more can play.

Cards Special cards are normally used, each illustrated with one of four members of a family.

Usually there are 10–13 families—often shown as different animals. Each family has a father, mother, son, and daughter. For example one family might be Mr Lion, Mrs Lion, Master Lion, and Miss Lion—each represented on a separate card.

(The game may also be played with standard playing cards— see "authors.")

Objective Each player tries to collect as many complete families as possible.

Deal One of the players deals out all the cards. If more than one round is played, the players can take it in turns to deal.

It does not matter if some players have one card more than others.

Play Each player looks at his cards and sorts them into families.

It is important that players keep their cards hidden from each other. (With young children it is a good idea if they can lay out their cards out of view of the other players.)

When all the players are ready, the person to the dealer's left asks any player, by name, for a particular card (eg Master Lion). He must already possess at least one member of the same family (eg Mrs Lion). If the person asked has the card, he gives it to the first player, who may again ask anybody for a card of any family as long as he already has one card belonging to that family.

He continues to do this until he fails to obtain a card.

If the person asked does not have the card requested, it is his turn to ask for cards.

When a player collects all four cards of the same family, he puts them into a pile face down in front of him.

End Play continues until all the families have been completed.

The person who collects most families is the winner.

OLD MAID

Old maid is a simple card game that is a great favorite with young children. It can be played with special cards, or with standard playing cards.

Players Old maid is a game for three or more players.

Cards Special decks of old maid cards consist of a single card with a picture of the "old maid" and pairs of cards showing other colorful characters.

If standard playing cards are used, one of the queens is is removed to leave the deck with an odd queen—the "old maid."

A pair of butchers

AUTHORS

This game is essentially the same as happy families. In some countries it is possible to buy special cards showing famous authors and the names of four of their works.

The name authors is, however, probably more commonly used for the variation of happy families played with standard playing cards.

To use standard playing cards, the ranks of the cards become the family names or "author," while the suits become the members of the families or the "books." For example, a player with the 8s of spades, clubs, and diamonds would ask for the 8 of hearts to complete his "family of 8s."

A family of 8s

Authors

FISH

This game is similar to happy families but the element of luck in winning is greater.

Unlike happy families it can be played by only two people—although it is better with more.

Cards Fish is usually played with standard playing cards but young players may prefer to use happy families cards.

Deal All the cards are dealt out as for happy families but a spare hand is also dealt—ie if there are four players, five hands are dealt.

The spare hand is placed face down in the center of the table and called the "fish pile."

Play This is the same as in happy families except that when a player is asked for a card he does not have, he says "fish."

Then the player who asked him takes the top card from the fish pile.

Play continues with the player who said "fish" asking for cards.

End The winner is the first player to have no cards other than his completed families. If two players finish at the same time, the one with the most completed families is the winner.

Fish

Deal One player deals all the cards face down, one at a time, to all players. It does not matter if some players have one card more than the others.

Objective Each player aims to get rid of all his cards by discarding pairs of equal value. The player who is left with the old maid card when play ends is the loser. There are no winners in this game.

Play Each player looks at his cards, making sure that none of the other players can see them.

If he has any pairs—two matching character cards or two playing cards with the same value, eg two 9s or two kings—he lays them face down on the table.

A player with three cards of the same value may only put down two of them and must keep the third, but a player with four cards of the same value may put down all four as two pairs.

The player to the dealer's left fans out his cards, keeping their faces toward him, and offers them to the player to his left.

The player who is offered the cards must take any one of them. He then looks to see

whether the new card pairs up with any of the cards already in his hand. If it does, he lays the pair face down on the table. If not, he adds the new card to the cards in his hand. He then fans out his cards and offers them to the player to his left.

Play continues in this way until all cards but the "old maid" have been played. The player holding the "old maid" is the loser, and all the other players call him "old maid" before a new game is started.

Variation To make the game last longer, cards may be considered as pairs only if their color matches as well as their number, for example two red 7s or two black aces.

LE VIEUX GARCON

This French game is similar to old maid.

It is played with a standard deck of playing cards, with the jacks of hearts, diamonds, and clubs removed.

The game is lost by the player left with the jack of spades—called "le vieux garçon" or "old boy."

BLACK PETER

This game is very popular in Germany. It is usually played with special cards, but standard playing cards can be substituted as for other games of this type.

Special decks of cards consist of a single "Black Peter" card, often showing a fierce black cat wearing boots and a hat, and pairs of other cards showing different animal characters.

It is played in the same way as old maid, and the loser is the player left with the "Black Peter" card.

A pair of 9s

A pair of red 7s

Animal pairs

Stealing bundles

STEALING BUNDLES

As soon as a player can spot that two cards have the same rank (face value), he is old enough to play stealing bundles. Other names for this game are old man's bundle and stealing the old man's bundle.

Players Two or four people can play.

Cards A standard deck of playing cards is used.

Objective Each player tries to collect as many cards as possible.

Deal One person is chosen as dealer. He deals the cards in a clockwise direction, one at a time and face down, until each player has four cards.

The dealer then places four cards face up in a row in the center.

Play The player to the left of the dealer begins.

If he has a card of the same rank as one of the cards in the center, he captures that card.

He places the captured card and his matching card face up in a pile in front of him. This is the beginning of his "bundle."

If two or three center cards have the same rank as one of the player's cards he may capture them all in the same turn.

If none of the player's cards matches a center card, he must place one of his own cards face up in the center. This is called "trailing."

Each player then plays one card in turn. In place of or in addition to capturing cards from the center, he may steal another player's bundle if his card matches the top card of that bundle.

Every time a player captures cards he places them in his bundle with the matching card face up.

If none of his cards matches any face-up card he must "trail" one of his cards.

Extra deals When all the players have played each of the four cards in their hands, the dealer deals out four more cards to each player. No cards are dealt to the center. Play then continues as before.

End The game ends when all the cards have been dealt and played.

The winner is the player with most cards in his bundle when play ends.

I DOUBT IT

Also known as cheat, this game is great fun for those who like taking risks and calling people's bluffs.

Players A minimum of three people are needed to play, but the more the better.

Cards One or two decks of playing cards are used.

Objective Each player aims to be the first to get rid of all his cards.

Deal One player deals out all the cards. Some players may have one extra card.

Play Players look at their cards. The player to the left of the dealer places one to four cards of the "same" rank (eg all 7s) face down in a pile in the center. He calls their rank as he does so. (In fact, the cards need not be what he claims—see cheating.) Subsequent players must then play—or claim that they are playing—one to four cards of the rank one higher than those played by the preceding player.

Cheating There are at least two ways of cheating.
a) Instead of putting down cards of the correct rank, a player can put down any other cards, as long as he pretends that they are all the same, and of the next highest value to those just played.

If a player does not have cards of the required value, he has no alternative but to do this. It is important that a player should avoid giving the others reason to doubt him.
b) A player may put down more cards than he states. Again, he should avoid

drawing people's attention to this.

Calling a player's bluff If a player suspects another of cheating, he can challenge him by calling "I doubt it" or "Cheat" before the suspect's cards are covered by those of the next player.

The challenged player must then turn over his cards for inspection.

If the player who called "I doubt it" is correct, the person who cheated picks up all the cards in the central pile and adds them to his hand.

If the player did not cheat, the challenger must pick up the central pile of cards.

The player who picks up the cards from the center starts the next round.

End The winner is the first person to succeed in playing his last card—ie either:
a) he withstands a challenge from another player; or
b) his cards are covered by the next player's before anyone has challenged him.

UP AND DOWN CHEAT

The only difference between this game and ordinary i doubt it or cheat is in the rank of the cards that can be played. Instead of only claiming to play cards in ascending rank, a player may also claim that he is playing cards that are either of the same rank or one rank lower than the last player's cards.

© DIAGRAM

GO BOOM

Go boom is a straightforward game for two or more players, which can be played by quite young children.

Cards A standard deck of playing cards is used.

Objective Each player aims to be the first to get rid of all his cards.

Deal The players cut for deal; the one with the highest card (ace ranks high) deals out the cards in a clockwise direction, one at a time and face down, until each player has seven cards. Spare cards are placed face down in a neat pile in the center.

Play Each player looks at his cards and sorts them in his hand. Turns pass clockwise around the players, starting with the player to the dealer's left.

The first player chooses a card from his hand and places it face up in the center. Each of the other players in turn, making a central face-up pile, plays a card that is either:
a) of the same suit, or
b) of the same rank (number or picture) as the card put down by the person before him.

If a player cannot follow suit or rank, he takes cards one at a time from the top of the central face-down pile until he has a card that he can play onto the central face-up pile. If all the cards have been taken, the player says "pass" and play moves on to the next player.

When each player has played a card or "passed," the cards are compared for the highest card (ace ranks high) and the player of the highest card starts the next round.

If two or more players tie for the highest card, the first one to play his card starts the next round.

End The winner is the first player to get rid of all his cards and shout "boom."

SCORING GO BOOM

This is a variation of go boom that is made more interesting by the introduction of a scoring system.

It is played in the same way as basic go boom, except that several rounds are played and points are scored for going boom.

When a player goes boom, he scores points for all the unplayed cards still in the other players' hands. Points are scored as follows:
a) 10 points for each king, queen, or jack;
b) one point for each ace;
c) the numerical face value of all other cards.

A game is won by the first player to score an agreed number of points (usually 250).

CRAZY EIGHTS

Crazy eights is the same basic game as go boom except that the 8s are wild.

A player may play any 8 after any card, and then decides what suit should follow.

As in scoring go boom, the first player to play all his cards scores points for the unplayed cards still in the other players' hands.

Points are scored as follows:
a) 50 points for an 8;
b) 10 points for each king, queen, or jack;
c) one point for each ace;
d) the numerical face value of all other cards.

If the face-down pile of cards is exhausted before any player plays all his cards, the game is blocked and the player with the lowest count in his remaining cards scores the difference in count between his own hand and the other players' hands.

SNIP-SNAP-SNOREM

A game with funny words to say, snip-snap-snorem is noisy, fast-moving, and fun to play.

Players It is a game for three or more players.

Cards A standard deck of playing cards is used.

Objective Each player aims to be the first to get rid of all his cards.

Deal Each player cuts the cards and the one with the highest card (ace high) is the dealer.

He deals out all the cards in a clockwise direction, one at a time, and face down.

It does not matter if some players have one card more than the others.

Play Each player looks at his cards without letting any other player see them, and sorts them in his hand.

Turns pass clockwise around the players, starting with the player to the dealer's left.

The first player places any one of his cards face up in the center (**a**).

If the next player has a card of the same rank (eg another queen if the first player played a queen), he places this face up in the center of the table and shouts "snip" as he plays it (**b**).

If he has another card of the same rank he keeps it until his next turn.

If he does not have a card of the same rank, he says "pass" and play moves on around the players.

The next player with a card of of the same rank (**c**) shouts "snap" when he plays it, and the player of the fourth card (**d**) shouts "snorem!"

The player of the fourth card starts the next round.

End The winner is the first player to play all his cards.

Variation If a player has more than one card of the same rank, he must play them all in the same turn, saying the appropriate words.

JIG

This is played exactly like snip-snap-snorem except that instead of playing four cards of the same rank, a sequence of four cards is played.

For example, if the first player puts down a 5, this is followed by a 6, then a 7, and finally an 8.

The cards can be from different suits.

Players call out "jiggety, joggety, jig" when playing the cards.

Go boom

Snip

Snap

Snorem!

a

b

c

d

Crazy eights

a   b   c

Play or pay

PLAY OR PAY

This easy game, sometimes called round the corner, is fun for players learning about the rank and sequence of playing cards.

Players Three or more can play.

Cards A standard deck of playing cards is used.

Counters Each player starts with 20 counters. (Beans or matchsticks could be used.)

Objective Each player aims to be first to get rid of all his cards.

Deal One player is chosen as dealer. He deals out all the cards in a clockwise direction, one at a time and face down. It does not matter if some players have one card more than others.

Play The player to the left of the dealer chooses any one of his cards and places it face up in the center.

The next player to his left then looks at his cards to see if he has the next card "in sequence."

A card is in sequence if it belongs to the same suit as the last card that was played and follows the order a, 2, 3, 4, 5, 6, 7, 8, 9, 10, j, q, k. If the last card was a king, the next card in sequence for this game is the ace of the same suit. This

is called a "round the corner" sequence.)

If the player has the next card in sequence he plays it face up onto the card in the center.

If he does not have this card, he must pay one counter into the center.

Play continues with each player in turn either playing the next card in sequence or paying a counter.

When all the cards of a suit have been played, the player who put down the last card has an extra turn and may play any card that he chooses.

End The first player to get rid of all his cards is the winner of the round and takes all the counters from the center. Each loser must also pay him one counter for every card left in his hand.

The winner of the game is the player with most counters after an agreed number of rounds.

SEQUENCE

This game is easily learned but calls for a little skill in choosing which card to play when starting a sequence.

Players Two or more can play sequence but it is best with four or five players.

Cards A standard deck of playing cards is used.

Objective Each player aims to be first to get rid of all his cards.

Deal One player is chosen as dealer. He deals out all the cards in a clockwise direction, one at a time and face down. It does not matter if some players have one card more than others.

Play The player to the left of the dealer starts by putting his lowest card of any suit face up in the center. (2s count as the lowest cards and aces as the highest.)

The player with the next card in sequence then plays it face up onto the card in the center. A card is in sequence if it is of the same suit as the last card that was played and follows the order 2, 3, 4, 5, 6, 7, 8, 9, 10, j, q, k, a.

Play continues in this way until the ace is played and the sequence ends.

A player who ends a sequence starts another by playing any card from his hand.

When part of a suit has already been played, a sequence ends with the highest card yet to play. The following sequence is then started by the player who played this highest card.

End The first player to get rid of all his cards is the winner.

Scoring If more than one round is to be played, players may each start with 10 counters or beans.

At the end of every round each loser pays the winner one bean for every card still in his hand. The winner is the player with most counters or beans after an agreed number of rounds.

CARD DOMINOES

This game of luck and skill is also called sevens, parliament, and fan tan. A player can increase his chances of winning by carefully choosing the order in which he plays his cards.

Players The game is for two or more players.

Cards One complete deck of standard playing cards is used.

Objective Each player aims to be first to play his cards onto a central pattern of cards in sequence.

Deal One player deals all the cards in a clockwise direction, one at a time and face down.

Play Each player looks at his cards and sorts them in his hand according to suit and sequence.

The player with the 7 of diamonds starts the game by putting it face up in the center. The player to his left must then try to put down either the 6 or 8 of diamonds or another 7. If he plays the 6 or 8 of diamonds he puts it respectively below or above the 7. If he plays another 7 he puts it next to the 7 of diamonds.

If, however, he does not hold any of these cards he "passes" and the play then goes to the next player to the left.

Play continues in this way, with each player in turn adding a card to one of the sequences, putting down a 7, or passing. The sequences are built up from 7 through 8, 9, 10, jack, and queen to king, and down from 6 to ace.

End The game is won by the first player to put down all his cards, but play usually continues until every card has been played and there are four complete suit sequences.

Card dominoes

ROLLING STONE

This popular game is highly unpredictable in its outcome. Just as a player is on the verge of winning he can get a new handful of cards to play. It is also known as enflay or schwellen.

Players Four, five, or six people can play.

Cards A standard deck of playing cards is used, but with cards removed so that there are eight cards per player.

The following cards should be removed before play:
a) for four players, the 2s, 3s, 4s, 5s, and 6s;
b) for five players, the 2s, 3s, and 4s;
c) for six players, the 2s.

Objective Each player aims to be the first to get rid of all his cards.

Deal Each player cuts the cards and the one with the highest card (ace high) is the dealer. He deals out all the cards in a clockwise direction, one at a time and face down.

Play Each player looks at his cards and sorts them into suits in his hand.

The player to the dealer's left starts play by choosing a card from his hand and placing it, face up, in the center.

The other players, in turn, then try to play one card of the same suit.

If all the players are able to "follow suit," these cards (called a "trick") are put to one side and are out of play for the rest of the game. The player who played the highest card (with ace high) then starts the next trick by playing another card into the center.

If any player is unable to follow suit, he must pick up the cards already played for that trick and add them to his own hand. He then plays the first card of the next trick, but must not use any of the cards that he has just picked up.

End The winner is the first person to play all his cards.

A trick, five players

LINGER LONGER

Linger longer is an ideal introduction to the principles of trump play that form the basis of many more complicated card games.

Players Three or more people can play. Four to six is best.

Cards A standard deck of playing cards is used.

Objective Each player tries to be the last person with cards in his hand. Players obtain new cards by winning tricks.

A trick comprises one card from each player played into the center.

Except when a trump has been played a trick is won by the highest card belonging to the suit that was led—ie to the same suit as the first card played in that trick.

A trump is a card belonging to the trump suit. The trump suit is determined before each game is played. A trump card beats any card belonging to the suit led.

Deal One player deals out the cards in a clockwise direction, face down and one at a time, until each player has the same number of cards as there are players. For example if there are five players, each one of them receives five cards.

The remaining cards are placed in the center in a face-down pile called the stock.

The last card dealt to the dealer is shown to all the players. The suit of this card is the trump suit for the game.

Play The player to the left of the dealer plays any card he likes face up into the center. Each player in turn then plays one card into the center. (These cards together form a trick.) If possible, players must play a card of the same suit as the first card—this is called "following suit." If a player is unable to follow suit, he may play a trump card or any other card.

A trick is won by the player who played the highest trump card or, if no trump was played, by the player who played the highest card of the suit led. Ace ranks high for this game.

A player who wins a trick places these cards face down in front of him. He then draws the top card from the stock and adds it to the cards in his hand (no other player draws). This player plays the first card of the next trick.

Players continue playing tricks in this way as long as they have any cards in their hand—ignoring the cards in any tricks that they have won. A player with no cards in his hand must drop out of the game.

End The last player left in the game wins.

KNOCKOUT WHIST

Knockout whist is another easy game with trumps. The players are eliminated until only one remains.

Objective Each player aims to win all the tricks of a hand.

Players Two to seven people can play this game.

Cards A standard deck of playing cards is used.

Deal One player deals out the cards face down, one at a time, and in a clockwise direction until each player has seven cards.

The remaining cards are put face down in a pile in the center.

Each time the cards are dealt, the number dealt to each player is decreased by one.

Play The top card of the center pile is turned over and this determines the trump suit for the first hand.

The player to the dealer's left then starts the first trick by playing any card he chooses. Each player in turn then plays a card, following suit if he can.

The trick is won as in linger longer and the winner starts the next trick.

When all seven tricks have been played anyone who has not won a trick drops out of the game.

The dealer collects all the cards, shuffles them, and deals six cards to each remaining player.

The winner of the most tricks in the first round chooses the trump suit and plays the first card in the second hand.

Play continues in this way—with players without tricks dropping out at the end of each hand.

End The first player to win all the tricks in a single hand is the overall winner.

If play continues to the seventh hand, each player will have only one card and there will be only one trick to win.

A trick, four players

Trumping a trick

Trumps ♦

Racing demon

Play to center

Play on
face-up cards

RACING DEMON

Racing demon is a fast and noisy game.

Players Any number can play.

Cards One complete deck of standard playing cards is needed for each player. Old decks with different backs are recommended.

Playing area This game requires a lot of space.

Deal Each player shuffles and deals his own deck.

After shuffling, each player first deals out 13 cards, face down, in a pile in front of him. This pile is then turned over so that only the top card is visible.

He then deals four cards face up, in a row alongside his pile of 13 cards.

His spare cards should be held face down in one hand.

Objective Each player aims:
a) to get rid of his pile of 13 cards;
b) to play as many cards as possible into the center.

Start of play One of the players is chosen to be the starter. When all the players have dealt out their cards, he starts play by shouting "Go!"

Play All the players play at the same time: there is no waiting to play in turn. Players may either play cards into the center or onto their own face-up cards.

Playing into the center If a player has an ace among his face-up cards, he should place it face up in the center. Once an ace has been played into the center, anyone with a face-up 2 of the same suit can play this onto the ace. A face-up 3 of the same suit can then be added by any player, and so on through to the 10, jack, queen, and king.

Playing on face-up cards As well as building up the piles in the center, a player can build piles of cards on the four cards alongside his original pile of 13.

Cards added to these piles must be in descending order and alternatively black and red (for example a black 6 can be added to a red 7 and then a red 5 added to the black 6).

Cards added to these piles may be:
a) the top card from the player's original pile of 13;
b) a card, or a correct sequence of cards, from one of the player's other face-up piles.

Any space left by the removal of one of the four face-up piles should be filled with the top card from the player's original pile of 13.

Spare cards If a player is unable either to play a face-up card into the center or to move any of his face-up cards, he turns to the cards that were spare after he first dealt out his cards.

These spare cards are turned over, three at a time, onto a separate pile, until one of them can be played into the center or onto a face-up pile.

When all the spare cards have been turned over, the player picks up the pile, turns it face down, and continues play.

End As soon as any player uses up all his cards from his original pile of 13, he shouts "Out!" and play ends.

Scoring The cards in the center are sorted into their separate decks.

A player's final score is the difference between the number of his cards in the center and the number of cards left in his original face-up piles.

The winner is the player with the highest score.

SPIT

Spit is an excellent game that calls for alertness and speed.

Players Two persons can play.

Cards A complete deck of standard cards is used.

Deal All the cards are dealt out equally between the two players.

Before play starts, each player lays out a row of cards in front of him, as follows:
1) starting from the left, he places three cards face down followed by a fourth card face up;
2) he places a second face-down card on each of the first two face-down cards and a face-up card on the third;
3) he places a face-down card on the first pile and a face-up card on the second;
4) he places a face-up card on the first pile.

Each player then places the rest of his cards face down in a pile to the left of his row.

Objective Each player aims to be the first to get rid of all his cards.

Start of play When both players are ready, either one of them calls "Spit!"

Immediately both players take the top card from their piles of spare cards and place them face up, side by side, in the center.

Playing into the center Each player then quickly plays as many cards as possible from his row of face-up cards onto either of the face-up cards in the center of the table.

A card may be played into the center if it has a numerical value either one higher or one lower than a central face-up card. (For example, a 9 or a jack can be played onto a 10. Either a king or a 2 can be played onto an ace.)

If playing a face-up card into the center exposes a face-down card in a player's row, this card should be turned face up.

Players continue to play cards onto the central piles in this manner until neither player can put out any more of his cards.

Spit If neither player can play any card from his row of face-up cards, one of the players shouts "Spit!"
Both players then take the top card from their piles of spare cards and place them face up on their central piles.
If possible, players then resume playing cards into the center from their face-up piles.
If players still cannot add any cards from their face-up rows, the other player calls "Spit!" and both players again play the top card of their spare piles. They continue in this way until either player can play a card from his row.
If a player wishes to call "Spit!" and the players' spare piles have been used up, each player takes his own central pile and turns it face down to form a new spare pile. The player then calls "Spit!" and play continues as before.

End of a round When a player has played all the cards from his face-up row into the center, he shouts "Out!" and wins the round. He then picks up his spare pile.
The other player then collects both central face-up piles, picks up the cards left in his row, and adds all these cards to the bottom of his spare pile.

Starting a new round
Players lay out their cards as for the first round.
New rounds are played in the same way as the first round, except that if one player does not have enough cards for a spare pile he does without and both players play onto a single central pile.

End of game A game is won by the first player to get rid of all his cards.

Spit

GIVE AWAY
Give away is a simple game that requires players to stay alert. The faster it is played the better.
Objective Each player aims to be first to get rid of all his cards.
Players Two or more can play this game.
Cards A standard deck of playing cards is used.
Deal One player deals out all the cards in a clockwise direction—face down and one at a time. It does not matter if some players have one card more than others. Players do not look at their cards but put them in a neat face-down pile in front of them.

Play The player to the left of the dealer turns over the top card of his face-down pile.
If it is not an ace, he places it face up by his face-down pile and ends his turn.
If it is an ace, he puts it face up in the center of the table and turns over another card. His turn continues until he turns over a card that he is unable to play to the center—a card may be played to the center if it is an ace or if it can be built in rank order (a, 2, 3, 4, 5, 6, 7, 8, 9, 10, j, q, k) onto a center card of the same suit. When he turns over a card that cannot be played to the center he places it face up by his face-down pile and ends his turn.
Each player then plays in turn. As well as playing to the center a player may play a card onto another player's face-up pile—provided that it is one higher or lower in rank than the top card of that pile. When a player plays his last face-down card onto his face-up pile, he waits until his next turn before turning over his face-up pile to start again. If he plays his last face-down card into the center or onto another player's pile, he turns over his face-up pile immediately and continues his turn.

End The first player to get rid of all his cards wins the game.

Give away

Play to center

Play on face-up cards

GAMES FOR VARYING NUMBERS OF PLAYERS

For any small group of two players or more (up to seven or eight)
Board games Hyena chase 14, Nyout 15, Game of goose 16, Alleyway 18, Snakes and ladders 18, Horseshoe 19, many contemporary board games 20-21.
Tile games Sap tim pun 75. **General card games** Napoleon 88, Purchase nap 88, Seven-card nap 88, Forty-five (even numbers only) 89, Spoil five 89, Auction pitch 96, Auction pitch with joker 96. **Target games** Marbles games 124-126, Coin throwing games 128-129, Fivestones and Jacks 130-132, Jackstraws 133, Spellicans 133, Tiddlywinks games 134-135, Ball games 136-137, Darts games 138-140, Ring target games 141. **Dice games** Most dice games 162-177. **Gambling card games** Brag (seven-card, nine-card) 235, Stop the bus 235, Card put-and-take 238, Lansquenet 240, Slippery Sam 240, Polish red dog 241, Hoggenheimer 242, Chinese fan-tan 243, Banker and broker 244, Monte bank (private) 244, Injun 246, Red dog 247, Six-spot red dog 248, Thirty-five 248, Yablon 250.
Word and picture games Many games 254-267. **Games of chance** Spoof 270, Fan-tan 272, Dollar poker 272, Put-and-take top 273. **Children's card games** Snap 304, Slapjack 305, Beggar my neighbor 306, Crazy eights 311, Go boom 311, Scoring go boom 311, Card dominoes 312, Sequence 312, Knockout whist 313, Racing demon 314, Give away 315.

For any small group of three players or more (up to seven or eight)
General card games Loo (three-card, five card) 88, Irish loo 88, Hearts games 94, Pope Joan 98, Michigan 100. **Gambling card games** Blackjack and variants 216-223, Poker games 224-233, Brag (three-card) 234, Horse race 239, Blücher 242, Thirty-one 248, Bango 250, Kentucky derby 251. **Word and picture games** Most games 254-267. **Games of chance** Bingo 274, Lotto 274, Picture lotto 275, Roulette 276, Boule 279. **Children's party games** Most games 282-299.
Children's card games Donkey 307, Pig 307, Pit 307, Happy families 308, Old maid 308, Authors 309, Black Peter 309, Le vieux garçon 309, I doubt it 310, Up and down cheat 310, Jig 311, Snip-snap-snorem 311, Play or pay 312, Linger longer 313.

Games that can be played by large groups of nine or more
Tile games Sebastopol 64, Tiddle-a-wink 64. **General card games** Oh hell 84.
Gambling card games Blackjack 216-223, Poker games 224-233, Brag (three-card) 234, Polish red dog 241, Injun 246, Red dog 247, Six-spot red dog 248, Thirty-one 248. **Word and picture games** Most games 254-267. **Games of chance** Spoof 270, Dollar poker 272, Fan-tan 272, Put-and-take top 273, Bingo 274, Lotto 274, Picture lotto 275, Roulette 276, Boule 279. **Children's party games** Most games 282-299.

GAMES FOR A SPECIFIC NUMBER OF PLAYERS

For one player
Board games Halma solitaire 42, Solitaire board games 58-59. **Card games**
Solitaire (Patience) card games 144-157. **Target games** Fivestones and Jacks 130-132.
Children's games Cup and ball 136.

For two players
Board games Ashta-kashte 12, Ludo 12, Pachisi 12, Contemporary board games 20-21,
Backgammon and variants 22-25, Nine men's morris and variants 28-29,
Fox and geese 30, Chinese rebels 31, Fighting serpents 32, Mancala games 33,
Queen's guard 34, Ringo 34, Checkers (Draughts) games 36-39, Lasca 40, Reversi 40,
Conquest 41, Salta 41, Halma 42, Chinese checkers 43, Brax (for two players) 45,
Chess 46, Shogi 50, Go (Wei-ch'i) 54, Go-moku 56, Hasami shogi 56, Hex 57.
Tile games Many domino games 62-67, K'ap t'ai shap 68, Tiu'u 68.
General card games Euchre (two-handed) 86, Five hundred (two-handed) 87,
Ecarté 87, Hearts (two-handed) 94, All fives 96, California Jack 96, Seven up 96,
Casino 97, Draw casino 97, Royal casino 97, Spade casino 97, Bezique 101,
Rubicon bezique 102, Piquet 104, Auction piquet 105, Imperial 105, Pinochle 106,
Auction pinochle 106, Kalabriasz 107, Rummy 110, Gin rummy 110, Cribbage 112.
Target games Conkers 127, Conquerors 127, Soldiers 127. **Double solitaire games**
Russian bank 158, Spite and malice 158. **Table games** Shove ha'penny 180,
Shovelboard 181, Shove football 182, Bagatelle 184, Burmese caroms 184,
English billiards 186, Carom billiards 188, Snooker 190, Pool 193, Eight-ball pool 197,
Table tennis 198. **Gambling card games** Fifteen 223. **Games of chance** Scissors,
paper, stone 270, Spoof 270, Mora 271, Shoot 271. **Children's party games**
Arm wrestling 293, Cock fighting 293, Stork fighting 293. **Children's card games**
Persian pasha 305, War 305, Memory 306, Fish 309, Stealing bundles 310.

For three players
Board games Ashta-kashte 12, Ludo 12, Pachisi 12, Brax (for three players) 45.
Tile games Blind Hughie 64, Block dominoes 64, Domino pool 64, Doubles 64,
Draw dominoes 64, All fives 65, All threes 65, Bergen 65, Fives and threes 65,
Matador 65, Picture dominoes 67, Mah jongg 70. **General card games** Preference 85,
Euchre (three-handed) 86, Five hundred 86, Knaves 95, All fives 96, California Jack 96,
Seven up 96, Casino 97, Calabrasella 100, Bezique (three-handed) 102,
Auction pinochle 106, Skat 108, Cribbage (three-handed) 113, Austrian tarock 114,
Tarocco 116, Japanese flower card games 118. **Children's party games**
Triangular tug of war 293. **Children's card games** Menagerie 304, Animal noises 305,
War for three players 305.

For four players
Board games Ashta-kashte 12, Ludo 12, Pachisi 12, Brax (for four players) 45.
Tile games Blind hughie 64, Block dominoes 64, Partnership block dominoes 64,
Domino pool 64, Doubles 64, Draw dominoes 64, Fortress 64,
Latin American match dominoes 64, All fives 65, All threes 65, Bergen 65,
Fives and threes 65, Matador 65, Forty-two 65, Picture dominoes 67, K'ap t'ai shap 68,
Tien kow 69, Mah jongg 70, Mah jongg (American) 76. **General card games** Whist 82,
Solo whist 83, Boston 84, Vint 85, Euchre (four-handed) 86, Call-ace euchre 86,
Railroad euchre 86, Five hundred (four-handed) 87, Auction forty-five 89,
Contract bridge 90, Auction bridge 93, Duplicate bridge 93, Grand 95, Polignac 95,
California Jack 96, Seven up (four-handed) 96, Casino 97, Bezique (four-handed) 103,
Auction pinochle 106, Partnership kalabriasz 107, Partnership gin rummy 110,
Canasta 111, Cribbage (four-handed) 113. **Table games** Shove ha'penny 180,
Burmese caroms 184, Table tennis 198. **Children's card games** Menagerie 304,
Animal noises 305, My ship sails 307, Stealing bundles 310, Rolling stone 313.

For five players
Tile games Blind Hughie 64, Sebastopol 64, Matador 65. **General card games**
Call-ace euchre 86, Polignac 95. **Children's card games** My ship sails 307,
Rolling stone 313.

For six players
General card games Call-ace euchre 86, Auction forty-five 89, Polignac 95,
Partnership gin rummy 110. **Children's card games** My ship sails 307, Rolling stone 313.

Which page is it on?

Picture credits